**PLACE IN RETURN BOX** to remove this checkout from your record.
**TO AVOID FINES** return on or before date due.

| DATE DUE | DATE DUE | DATE DUE |
|---|---|---|
| SEP 0 4 2000 | | |
| | | |
| | | MICHIGAN STATE UNIVERSITY LIBRARY JUN 28 |
| | | WITHDRAWN |
| | | |
| | | |
| | | |

MSU Is An Affirmative Action/Equal Opportunity Institution

c:\circ\datedue.pm3-p.1

# JAPAN AND AFRICA

# JAPAN AND AFRICA

## The evolution and nature of political, economic and human bonds, 1543-1993

Prof. Themba Sono

*Director*
*Institute of African Studies*
*University of Bophuthatswana*

HSRC Publishers
Pretoria
1993

ISBN 0-7969-1525-3

Electronic data capture: Tina Dicker
Cover Design: Glenn Basson

DT
38.9
.J3
Sww
1993

Published by:
HSRC Publishers
134 Pretorius Street
0001 Pretoria
South Africa

Printed by:
Sigma Press (Pty), Ltd
Pretoria

TO

Ms Midori Fujita
and
Chris and Wondy

# Acknowledgements

I am indebted to many individuals, but limited space compels me to cite only a handful whose contribution to the completion of this study is immeasurable. To Prof. Yukio Cho, President of Tokyo Gaikokugo Daigaku/Tokyo University of Foreign Areas Studies, for his enlightening brief on the role of his institution in foreign areas studies particularly in African cultures; Prof. Hiroyuki Umeda and his staff at the Institute for the Study of Languages and Cultures of Asia and Africa (ILCAA), of the same University, for providing me with a sizeable number of ILCAA's books and monographs, and for his stimulating recapitulation of ILCAA's contribution to Afro-Asian cultures; Prof. Eisei Kurimoto was helpful in introducing me to other Japanese scholars engaged in similar work as mine. Prof. Tsuneo Morino's insights into contacts between Japan and East Africa (Tanzania especially) were invaluable. Prof. Shigeki Kaji was also helpful through his expertise on the African civilisation in Central and Southern Africa.

Prof. Toshio Yamakazi, Director of the Institute of Oriental Culture, University of Tokyo, was resourceful at a critical juncture in my research. I cherish especially his introducing me to the archives of his university's library. To the NEC African Division executives at the Yokohama Plant (Messrs Kohei Muraoka, Tadao Furakawa, Mikio Yamada, and Suzumu Tanaka) who were so generous with their time in detailing NEC's C & C's contribution to their "world of tomorrow", and especially as concerned NEC's activities in Africa. Mr. Muraoka was indispensable in providing sources of the history of some prefectures in Kyushu, whose residents interacted with Africans in the early period of Japan-Africa contacts.

Many other corporate executives were also generous with their time and information concerning their company's activities in Africa: From Marubeni Corporation, S. Jibiki and H. Ogawa, and from Nippon Koei Co., Yusako Toya and Akikazu Tokumasu were unstinting in their response to my endless enquiries. Other executive officials from such institutions as the Japan Foundation, managing director Junpei Kato; Africa Society of Japan, managing director Eiji Fukunaga; Kobe City Museum, ethnologist Ms Akiko Kunikita, and director Hiroshi Yasuda; Osaka National Museum of Ethnology, general supervisor Takeshi Imori; JETRO (Masaaki Sasaki), all deserve special mention. Their contribution is irreplaceable, as my work clearly testifies.

To my translators and interpreters I am more than grateful: Ms Yumiko Ito, Ms Hiroko Watabe, Ms Miwa Irie, Shinichi Kunii, Kazuhiro Iwasawa, Ms Masahiko Umekita, and Ms Chiyono Sata. To Akika Shigemitsu, former Japanese ambassador to the USSR and Nigeria, for unselfishly sharing his experiences and understanding of the Japan-Africa relations. To the many African diplomatic, student and business personnel in Japan, especially Ambassadors Boniface Zulu of Zambia and Dr N.H. Katedza of Zimbabwe, as well as Ms Prisca Molotsi from the RSA/Zambia/UK/US my thanks for their contributions. To the many African youths in West, North and East Africa, for helping me to construct the African perspective in international affairs. To my students at UDC for providing a stimulating environment and retaining a positively inquisitive bent of mind. To Prof. Mohamed El-Khawas of UDC for his encouragement. Prof. William R. Jones of Florida State University, who never wavered in his encouragement of my research effort: To him I extend special gratitude. Prof. Philip Avillo, Jr of York College remained a pillar of consistency in his encouragement of my research pursuits for the past dozen years.

Two exceptional scholars I am particularly thankful to are Ms Midori Fujita, a doctoral candidate at the University of Tokyo, for her untiring efforts in both her research and publications on the early contacts between Africans and Japanese; for providing me with her published works in Japanese especially about early Africans in Japan, and for graciously translating some of this work herself for my purpose; and for her dedication to working for the development of this new field of Afro-Japanese studies. Last, but not least, to Prof. D. William Perdue for his selfless, untiring advice, and above all, for his warm friendship; for having read some earlier chapters of this work, and for providing invaluable suggestions.

I wish, lastly, to thank the HSRC Publishers for their professional and meticulous editing, particularly on verifying the accuracy of the many tables and graphs in this work. Special mention goes to Mr A.K. Welman.

Whether I have wisely integrated the advice and contributions of all the abovenamed is perhaps not for me to judge. If the reader finds merit in this work, let him/her bear in mind the contributions of the abovenamed. Any shortcomings are mine alone. I remain, nevertheless, solely responsible for researching, analysing, interpreting, and presenting this work.

*Prof. Themba Sono*
*Director*
*Institute of African Studies*
*University of Bophuthatswana*
*March 1993*

# CONTENTS

# PART III: THE DEVELOPMENTAL/AID QUESTION

# PART IV: THE HUMAN EXCHANGE ISSUE

# PART V: THE COMMERCIAL/TRADE IMPERATIVE

# PART VI: APPENDICES, NOTES, BIBLIOGRAPHY

# LIST OF TABLES

# LIST OF MAPS, DIAGRAMS AND CHARTS

*Page*

## Maps

## Diagrams

## Charts

# INTRODUCTION

This book examines the nature of African-Japanese contacts from the 1500s to the early 1990s. The work owes its existence to the profound gaps in historical research and political analysis re Africa-Japan ties. It seeks to house under one roof the welter of material, much of which is little known regarding the evolution and dynamics of the Africa and Japan contacts and relations. There is much information concerning this subject, yet its accessibility is hampered by the fact that the material is scattered and remote, and laborious to retrieve. A major reason for this work's existence is the obvious one that no book exists in the English-speaking world, at least, which has brought together vast material on the Japanese and African interactions and provided the kind of analysis that my work has presented. I have attempted to provide a broader basis for understanding the growing interrelations between Japan and Africa. Consequently, I have sought to weld the political, historical, economic, diplomatic and cultural factors involved in the processes of Afro-Japanese relations.

The continent of Africa and the island of Japan are a mass of paradoxes. Africa is a vast area of 30 million square km inhabited by about 600 million people; Japan is only a tiny island, 372 thousand square kilometres in area with a population of 120 million. Africa has almost all the known natural resources, and yet constitutes one of the poorest regions on earth. Japan, on the other hand, has virtually no major natural resources, and yet constitutes the second largest economy in the world. With all its vast natural resources, Africa accounts for only 3,3 % of world exports, less than 2 % of world industrial production, and 3,4 % of world trade. On the other hand, the island of Japan accounts for 9 % of world output, 9,04 % of world industrial production, and more than 10 % of world trade.

Since the main purpose of this work is thus to draw upon the stock of neglected material and to view the Japan-Africa ties from new and long-forgotten angles, it therefore needs no justification. Yet why do I justify it? Especially since there are endless books on Africa on the one hand, and on Japan on the other, particularly since the Meiji Restoration (1868) and the Berlin Partition of Africa (1884-1885)? Nearly all of these works, however, have one major defect: they cover virtually all aspects of Africa and the continent's ties with American, European, Russian, Indian and Chinese nations, and yet totally ignore the Africa-Japan ties. Similarly, there are hundreds, perhaps thousands, of books on Japan — including her relations with the rest of world, except Africa. Nary a work (save the aft-mentioned few) deal exclusively with Japan and Africa. Even some of the best works on Japan make elaborate attempts to dismiss the Japan-Africa connection, for example Professor Jean-Pierre Lehmann's otherwise excellent work, *The Roots of Modern Japan* (1982), dismisses the Japan-Africa ties in a cavalier manner:

> Japan's absorption into the modern world was not limited to the West. For the purposes of the period under review here (i.e. the Meiji Era), Africa, Latin America and the Middle East need not figure prominently. Africa, in fact, can be totally ignored (p. 168).

This uncritical assumption (whose preordained conclusion) should not be, but is nevertheless surprising considering that Meiji Japan, especially between 1885 and 1912, was actively involved in East Africa in the search for African markets and raw materials. Meiji Japan also used Africa extensively during the emigration of her nationals to Brazil from 1908 onwards. Indeed both Chapters 2 and 10 of my work are a *de facto* rebuttal of the Lehmann thesis. Many studies on Japan and the rest of the world adopt the Lehmann approach without necessarily repeating the naiveté expressed in this otherwise scholarly work, *The Roots of Modern Japan.* These, nevertheless, remain the specialist blinders which have shut out from their vision much of the world except that which is of interest to them. One major study that has sought to give clarity and coherence to the Japan-Africa ties is by Professors Joanne Moss and John Ravenhill, *Emerging Economic Influence of Japan in Africa*, (1985). But as is evident from both the title and subtitle, their work is narrowly focused and thus could only appeal to a narrower specialist audience. Moreover, the Moss and Ravenhill study treats Japan's involvement in Africa in terms of reference to US "interests" in Africa, as the authors themselves say. Clearly then, their work seeks not to illuminate the Japan-Africa economic connections as entities in their own right, but rather in terms of their trade ties as a tributary of the "national security interests" of the US. To subject the Africa-Japan ties to an Americocentric approach would truly be provincial and unlightening. To contend the value of such an approach is, of course, not to suggest that the US is irrelevant in the Japan-Africa issues. After all, US Commodore Mathew Perry (1794-1858), a proponent of Manifest Destiny imperialism, employed Africans (blacks) to defeat Japanese *sakoku* (national isolationism) in 1854; and *SCAP* Commander, Gen. Douglas MacArthur (1880-1964), with the help of African-Americans, brought an end to Japanese expansionism in 1945, and indirectly ushered in *kokusaki* (internationalisation). Secondly, Moss and Ravenhill are confined, in terms of time, space and focus, to what nearly all current journals, if at all, cover regarding Japan *and* Africa: the emerging economic influence of Japan over Africa. Moss and Ravenhill are limited, in any event, to the post-war period of African independence (1957-1984) and Japan's re-independence (1952-1984).

On the other hand, Arnold Rubin's pioneering booklet, *Black Nambans: Africans in Japan in the 16th Century*, (1974), again as the title suggests, is restricted to the near-beginning of the Japanese-African contacts. Rubin's work, nonetheless, deals with what no other book in English has tackled as a theme: Africans in Japan from the latter part of the 16th century. These black nambans have left a cultural legacy which is yet to be fully examined. Disregarding the several but scattered references and considerations by C.R. Boxer on earlier Afro-Japanese ties, there is no other work that remotely tackles this theme in English. (In Japanese a few excellent efforts have been undertaken and some are currently being researched.)

In between Rubin's and Moss-Ravenhill's studies are a few books that attempt to fill, unsuccessfully, this void which covers a wide period. One study by the Japanese Africanist, Eiji Fukanaga, *Japan's Position Toward Africa: Documentary Compilation on Recent Moves*, (1975, Tokyo), is however, yet another post-war effort to recast the Japanese perspective of Africa and highlight Japan's increasing role in Africa, especially in the early 1970s. The Nigerian scholar, Sunday O. Agbi in his work, *Japan's Attitudes and Policies Towards African Issues Since 1945: A Historical Perspective*, (1982, Tokyo) is, once again, only dealing with an examination of the post-war period. Moreover, the work is restricted to *Japanese*, while silent on African attitudes. Where, then, do we look to for the study of the Japan and Africa contacts during the interwar period? Or of African initiatives in Afro-Japanese relations? The closest study that partially answers this question is that of the Nigerian scholar, Gabriel O. Ogunremi, *Nigeria-Japan Trade Relations 1914-1979)* (1980, Tokyo). But this study, too, merely touches on a small area as can be seen from the title. In the work of Mahmood Mamdani, *Politics and Class Formation in Uganda*, (1976), we only come across a small section that is devoted to Japan and *East Africa*. But otherwise, there is no major work that gives us a sense of continuity in the ties between Japanese and Africans that Rubin's work introduced and the Moss and Ravenhill's work rounded up with, albeit the two works are not in the least comparable in subject matter or theme.

Let the reader reflect then that not only did an African join Shogun Oda's household, but also that Africans confronted Japanese Imperial Army soldiers in battles during World War II on the Burma Front, 321 years after they had first clashed in China. If the reader continues reflecting upon the anomaly that in both instances neither the Japanese nor the African had any cause to duel against each other — since in both cases Africans were merely playing the role of Western puppets — he/she will be struck by the fact that the Japan-Africa ties remain largely an untapped fertile

4

ground for scholars. *Africans* first arrived in Japan nearly 500 years ago (i.e. even earlier than they did in the US) while *Japanese* first landed in East Africa just before 1600 and stayed in Mozambique for six months before sailing for Rome.

May the reader consider this furthermore: while Africans were turned into chattel slaves in the Americas, in Japan, they were being encouraged by their Portuguese masters to own Japanese slaves! When this is contrasted with the fact that the Japanese are the only known major culture to have deliberately refused to enslave Africans when they had the opportunity, the Japan-Africa ties begin to assume, if not significant, then certainly interesting dimensions. In any event, between the 16th and 20th centuries are three centuries that have been largely unaccounted for regarding this subject. Neither has my work, despite its breadth and depth, covered all the neglected aspects. Yet it is a work that begins from a period much earlier than Professor Rubin's study, and details data ignored by Professor Lehmann's, and goes beyond Professors Moss' and Ravenhill's work, while in the process it details a mass of ground inconceivable to many previous studies. Even considering the Japan-Africa ties in the 1980s many aspects (e.g. human exchanges, cultural ties, etc.) are simply not dealt with even by the many specialized journals — let alone books — in the West.

But lest the reader think that in this book I am merely retracing the early historical steps between Japanese and Africans to the modern days, let me quickly disabuse of him/her of that notion. This is not an historical study *per se* as the reader will discover. It merely places historical analysis at the centre of a wide-ranging review of the manifold interconnections of this theme. Most of the few specific issues and events I have so far referred to are only a small part of Part I of this work. Only for clarity's sake have Parts I and V been treated somewhat chronologically and schematically. I contend, in any event, that the future direction, whether of Japanese or African culture, of Afro-Japanese relations, of Japanese influence in Africa, etc., will never be totally understood without a proper grasp of past interconnections between the island people in the Far East and the "emerging" people in the Far Continent. Was Japan,

5

for example, a procolonial power in Africa during the Meiji, Taisho and Showa Eras, as the eminent Japanese scholar, Professor Jun Morikawa, seriously but erroneously, I think, argues?

This book is divided into six parts; each part, except the last, is further divided into two chapters. Part I — the *Historical Factor* — ties down the story of contacts between Japanese and Africans from the earliest times known to the author to the end of the colonial era in Africa. Thus Part I deals with Africans in Japan *and* Japanese in Africa — their cultural and commercial interconnections. That is, Chapter 1 deals with the earliest ties, and Chapter 2 with the Colonial Period. Africans in Japan, called *Kurobo* by the Japanese, then attracted much attention from the citizens of Kyushu, who travelled long distances to see the dark-skinned visitors from the Far Continent. But Chapter 1 also deals with Tokugawa Japanese in Africa who were curious about Africa and Africans even as they were in transit to Europe. Only in Chapter 2 does it focus on Meiji Japanese in Africa and the commercial links between the two.

In Part II — the *Diplomatic Dimension* — I focus on Japanese Diplomacy Toward Africa (Chapter 3), and African Diplomacy Toward Japan (Chapter 4). Although this section is necessarily concerned with independent Africa and re-independent Japan (i.e. essentially from 1960 for the former, and 1952 for the latter) a serious attempt has been made to look at all diplomatic angles even before most of Africa became independent. Part II is perhaps the most comprehensive account of the Japan-Africa diplomatic linkages available in the English language. It deals also with the highly successful diplomatic strategy of Japan in Africa. Further-more, African diplomacy towards Japan is virtually unchartered ground, and is examined not only in the context of the conventional notions of African dependency and ideology, but also in the dynamism — or lack thereof — of shuttle diplomacy to Tokyo by the highest-ranking African leaders. How genuine is an African government's involvement in external relations in the context of great power influence in Africa? Since the internal and external policies of African governments are largely dominated by their respective country's relations with and position *vis-a-vis* Euro-

America, can African leaders who periodically troop to Tokyo, carve an independent policy towards Japan? Is there such a thing as *African* foreign policy diplomacy? What, in any event, are African concerns and expectations of Japan?

While many of the journal articles and book chapters that examine the Japan-Africa question invariably deal with Japanese Aid towards Africa, many such works (e.g. Oda and Aoki, White, Ravenhill, etc.) tend to be rather predictable: episodic, schematic, and conventional in their analyses. Many simply argue the "economic animalism" logic, and postulate it as an explanatory paradigm for virtually every move Japan makes in Africa. They tend to mostly recycle (Rix, Brooks and Orr somewhat expected) the conventional notion of the "miserly" and "selfish" nature of Japanese aid to Africa. My study is not so much a direct rebuttal of these arguments as it is to detail the comprehensive nature of Japanese aid.

Indeed, in Part III — the *Developmental/Aid Question* — I review the entirety of the Japanese aid efforts in Africa; much of the magnitude of Japanese involvement in Africa is little-known outside Japan. In Chapter 5 I deal with the rationale (political, philosophical, historical) of Japanese official development assistance to Africa. The principles, policies, priorities and programmes of JODA are examined. Budgetary allocations as well as the nature of Japan's role are reviewed — from tied to untied aid, from sporadic and tentative beginnings to the massive activism of the 1980s, from huge show-piece projects to small ones. In Chapter 6 I deal with a specific aspect of Japanese aid to Africa — the so-called Green Revolution. The focus here is on agricultural and food, fisheries, forestry and "desertification" efforts. African responsibility for the massive environmental bankruptcy of the continent is assessed, and Japanese contributions — cultural, financial, and technical — are examined. In short what is the solution for (what I have termed) *"Afrigulture"* and its relentless problems? What are Japanese proposals towards solving these *"Afrigultural" problems?*

Part IV — the *Human Exchange Issue* deals with the most complex of all: the exchange of human resources. Once again, this is a study that has not been given much attention in Africa or the West. That is, "Peace Corpsism" Japanese-style attains new and complex dimensions. In fact, Japanese commitment to the regeneration of the African environment and infrastructural, cultural, and agricultural condition is clearly elaborated in this section of my work. For it provides new material in assessing the role and impact of Japanese technicians, volunteers, and experts in Africa (Chapter 7), and African technical, vocational, and scientific trainees in Japan (Chapter 8). The latter chapter examines not only what I have called *Africulture*, but also common cultural values between Japan and Black Africa. Through *kokusaka*, (internationalisation) it even became possible to discover Japanese *Haiku* values in some African cultures, such as in Senegal for example.

Part V — the *Commercial/Trade Imperative* — develops fully the angle introduced in Chapter 2: i.e. trade linkages between Africa and Japan. In Chapter 9 I focus on economic and trade relations in 1961-1987, between Japan and Africa — South Africa excepted since she is treated separately elsewhere. Moss and Ravenhill's work (mentioned earlier) has dealt extensively with this aspect. My Chapter 9, however, is not limited to Black Africa as the Moss-Ravenhill work is, nor does it treat this subject as an extension of US-Japanese global competition. It adopts a unique and no less enlightening mode. In any event, this work obviously goes beyond 1984/5, at which point their work naturally stops. Chapter 10 deals with the problematic issue of the Japan-South Africa commercial connection. Japan is not only the largest trading partner of South Africa, South Africa is also the largest African trading partner of Japan. Japan depends heavily on South African rare and mineral resources; South Africa hungers for the Japanese consumer goods and market as well as the political benefits of stemming the isolationism which her *apartheid* policies brought upon her. The massive trade that goes on between Japan and South Africa has been dealt with by others (e.g. Morikawa, Payne, Ravenhill, Kitazawa, *et al.*) but I have updated the data and analysis. That is, Chapter 10 deals with the Japan-South Africa ties from 1910 till March 1993. The issue of *apartheid* politics and economy *vis-a-vis*

Japan is reviewed. It deals also with the question of African trading with South Africa. While Japan plays the *seikei bunri* with South Africa, so does Africa relative to the then *apartheid* regime in the RSA. This is a new field hardly treated by previous works. It probes the implications of South Africa-African trade (since nearly all African states traded with the *apartheid* regime even as they denounced it), and wonders about the legitimacy of African concerns regarding Japanese trade with South Africa. Could Africa have influenced Japanese economic policy towards South Africa while *African* trading with the *apartheid* economy clearly limited the scope and impact of that influence?

The last section, Part VI — *Appendix, Notes, Bibliography* —is the epilogue. Appendix, Notes, and the Select Bibliography are designed to serve as an aid to further research. Because of the extensive documentation of this work, and given the detailed nature of the notes, this part has been elevated to the level of the previous five parts of the book. To a certain extent, Part VI supersedes the rest of the work; for researchers who may seek to do a study on any aspect of Japan and Africa this section of my work may be found to be indispensable. Indeed, this book has been intended to be the irreplaceable companion of student and researcher alike. It is to be hoped that because of its minute approach in some sections, this work would become a standard reference on the Japan-Africa ties.

My book has depended heavily on Japanese sources — documents, published works, interviews. I have given pre-eminence to Japanese documents, literature, and interviews — not because of the famous complaint of Ms Fumiko Mori Halloran (10 July 1986) that books published in the West on or about Japan rarely consult Japanese publications or incorporate Japanese perspectives and views — but because, pro and con, there is an extensive body of knowledge and opinion about Africa in Japan that finds little currency and circulation outside Japan. Japan has recently "rediscovered" Africa and there is therefore much that Japan is accumulating in terms of African experience. Moreover, Japanese perspectives on Africa are the more fresh and interesting relative to those of the West. On the other hand, African (especially

9

governmental) perspectives on Japan are problematic, because they are virtually non-existent. (There are very few *White Papers* in Africa, or the few current government gazettes that do indeed review African diplomacy, especially towards Japan, that are particularly enlightening). These perspectives are also problematic because the African diplomatic voice is still so much attached to the West (think of Francophone Africa for example, or Liberia, etc.) But my work has sought to marshall as many of African perspectives as possible and attempted to give coherence to an otherwise undeveloped "international relations" arena. Although a lot of ground is yet to be uncovered, and despite the fact that this is only a small attempt in that direction, I have, nevertheless, chartered a new and important course in Afro-Japanese studies which, ultimately, will further attempt to break down the barriers of misunderstanding between the two cultures.

# 第一部
## 歴史的要因

# PART I
## THE HISTORICAL FACTOR

# CHAPTER 1

# EAST ASIA AND AFRICA — FIRST CONTACTS

---

*... They (the Japanese) like seeing black people, especially Africans, and they will come 15 leagues just to see them and entertain them for three or four days ...*

Jorge Alvares (1547)

Nagasaki, Japan

*... The streets (of this African city) are broad and the houses crowded together; but the customs of the people are extremely stupid; they are ... very lazy in the business of life, and therefore, the place is going to ruin ...*

Tokugawa Japanese in Africa (1862)

13

The initial point in history at which Africans and East Asians, particularly Japanese, first met, is not clear. It is the purpose of this introductory chapter to shed as much light on this neglected history as possible. Common mythology is that Africans and Japanese have discovered each other only in the last one hundred years. In this work I take the reader to the very early contacts, first between Africans and Indians and Chinese, and secondly, between Africans and Japanese, before proceeding to the present. The major periods during which Africans and Japanese interacted are (i) the latter part of the Ashikaga Era (1335-1573); (ii) the entire period of the Azuchi-Momoyama Era (1573-1603); (iii) the so-called Edo Period (i.e. Tokugawa Era (1603-1867); (iv) Meiji Restoration (1868-1912), (v) the Taisho Era (1912-1926) and, of course, (vi) the Showa Era (1926 - 1990). We look here at the footsteps of history across medieval times to the present. I seek to delineate the thesis that the Japan-African cultural and historical intercourse is a unique phenomenon, evolving, at least from the 1500s, not only in a nonconformist pattern, but resembling to a remarkable degree many cultural aspects. The absence of conflict in the history of contacts between Japanese and Africans is itself salutary if not exceptional, given the history of violence by Japan as well as the history of violent abuse of Africa by European imperial powers. Between 1547 and 1885 Japanese and Africans were experiencing contacts of unusual dimensions. Between 1885 and 1960 Japan had become active in Africa, seeking export markets and raw materials, but Japan was *not* formally involved in the search for African colonies. Yet the Japanese search for commercial markets in African colonies often meant Japanese acquiescence to European colonial hegemony in Africa, which hegemony is one of the historical factors which had impeded Japanese expansion in Africa, and retarded free and broader association with Africans.

There exists a great informational void in the area of Japan-African relations and contacts generally, particularly in the centuries earlier than the 17th, but also in the first four decades of this century. For instance it is not commonly known that three

14

African governments (prompted by their Euro-American suzerains), formally "declared" war against Japan during World War II (and fought a war on behalf of Euro-America while having no compelling reasons to do so). This was *not* an African war against Japan, it was more to further Euro-American interests in Asia than to advance African freedom in Africa. These World War II African battles against the Japanese Imperial Army in the Burma Front were more fierce than those of Canton when the Portuguese black slaves and Indian lascars army defeated the Dutch and Japanese-Malay army in 1622. During World War II, Africans were used by Europe to fight against Japan, just as they were used three hundred years earlier by one European group to fight against another European group and the Japanese in China; as well as against the Japanese shoguns whenever the Portuguese became entangled in some mischief against the Japanese. Much of this history is yet to be told. This void is so pervasive that even some prominent African and Japanese government officials frequently are oblivious of the early historical contacts that have contributed to shaping mutual images of their respective cultures and peoples. The point of departure for most Japanese scholars and government leaders in relation to Japan-Africa issues is the Meiji Restoration, when Japan *re-opened* her doors to European influence, after a two hundred and fifty year shut-door policy of the Tokugawa Shogunate. This view clearly lacks legitimacy for us here. A few African scholars tend to pay closer attention to Japanese-African contacts prior to World War II, but even for this group early 20th century Europe's colonization of Africa is their focal point of departure, and they thus conveniently ignore Japanese activities in Africa occurring, say, between 1884 to 1899. The majority simply focus on post-world war period of African independence, during which Japan changed her interwar commercial policies towards Africa from benign neglect to that of a complex web of trade, aid, cultural diplomacy, closer political ties, and the so-called "heart-to-heart interchanges".

The Japanese nevertheless have recently begun to rectify this omission and apparent indifference. Their publications[1] on the theme of Japan and Africa have begun to find their way into the African continent, and they reflect an avid desire to understand the totality of Africa. Africans too are beginning to identify with Japanese people and culture, just as Japanese youth, as I shall detail, have taken to interacting with Africans in diverse ways. Not only have numerous Japanese volunteers served in Africa but works in the Japanese language have been written dealing with the history, geography, culture and arts of Africa. Yet even in this Japanese effort and initiative — outside of which virtually no Western or African scholarly effort of significant magnitude to narrow the psychological gulf between Japan and Africa exists — the early history between the Japanese and Africans is just about non-existent. The exception is perhaps the University of Tokyo doctoral candidate, Ms Midori Fujita, who, like this author, has sought to bring the Afro-Japanese early contacts to a wider and broader scholarly circle.[2] Japanese scholarship on Africa virtually ignores two critical areas of the Japan-Africa contacts: when Africans first arrived in Japan, and when Japanese first arrived in Africa, though a recent crop of critical Japanese scholars has emerged to challenge this historical patina and inject a critical review of Japan and Africa relations.[3]

What this chapter seeks to accomplish is to erase this sinification of omission and introduce the study of Japan and African contacts and relations from as early a period and in as broad a range as possible. The objective is clearly to lay a historical background, as an introductory basis, of the broader latter-day cooperation, especially in development assistance terms, between Japan and the African continent. A historical perspective is essential because the gap between "then" and "now" is so great that today's Afro-Japanese relations cannot be placed in context without examining the past; for example, Africans first met Japanese in India and China on a smaller scale before arriving in Japan, mainly as slaves of the Portuguese. Japanese government officials often cite the claim that Japan came late to interact with Africa because Africa was, and remains, the Far Continent, in addition to it long being the preserve of Europe and the West, and that, at any rate, Japan was introduced to Africa by Europe. It is true that Europe introduced *Africans* to Japan — and this position shall hold till further research is done on the ancient African seafarers who crossed the Indian Ocean to the Far East — but it is not correct that this occurred in the Meiji Period (1868-1912). The period during the reigns of Oda Nobunaga and Toyotomi Hideyoshi to the Tokugawa Shogunate is the more accurate date of first contacts. What I additionally propose to show here is not merely that the first contacts between Japanese and Africans came in circumstances that showed intense Japanese interest in their black visitors, but that the Japanese were resentful of Portuguese trading in Japanese slaves, particularly when the Portuguese employed their *African slaves* to engage in trading in *Japanese slaves*. Such then is an aspect of the Asian and African contacts this chapter seeks to probe ...

In an address delivered before an American audience in 1880 on Africa's service to the world, the greatest black savant of the nineteenth century, the West African, Dr Edward W. Blyden, made the observation that : "... The Negro is found in all parts of the world. He has gone across Arabia, Persia, and India to China ... He is everywhere a familiar object, and he is everywhere out of Africa, the servant of others ... Africa (ns are) distinguished as having *served* and *suffered*".[4] Blyden's sentence should certainly have added "Japan", especially in the island of Kyushu at the port of Nagasaki, since this is where the Japanese and the Africans first met on a broader scale after their earlier encounter in Macao and Canton in China. From Nagasaki, Tanegashima, etc., Africans moved with their Portuguese masters to such other areas as Kyoto (Mikado), Sakai, Osaka, Uraga, Shizuoka, and even Yedo, the capital of the shoguns.

**EARLY CONTACTS**

Contacts between Asia and Africa go back at least nearly two millenia; between *East* Asia and Africa historical contacts are at least eight hundred and fifty years old. Many Asian merchant vessels plied the seas between India and the African coast, trading in silk, beads, ivory, spice and — occasionally — African slaves vendored by Arab traders. In the last couple of centuries some of these Asians settled down with their families and made Africa their home ... Others went to the interior, while the majority remained on the coast. Some even provided European explorers with maps and charts, and actively participated in the colonization of Africa.[5] Before Japanese ships visited the coast of Africa — in the sixth decade of the 19th century — on their way to Europe, or several centuries before Africans first arrived at the Japanese port of Nagasaki, Malay sailing ships visited the east coast of Africa and, in the 4th century A.D., some crewmen immigrated with East Africans to the uninhabited island of Madagascar. The Malays learned from the Africans how to cultivate millet, breed cattle, build storage-houses for cereals, wood-carving, as well as the use of spears and round-shields. The Malays in turn taught Africans how too grow coconut palms, yam, rice, and sugar cane. Indonesian mariners also arrived on the coasts of East Africa and brought with them the Asian banana which quickly took root in Africa and thrived far better than the African banana. These Indonesians came by way of Southern India, and together with the Malays and East Africans, colonized Madagascar island during the early centuries of the Christian era. In 1412, and again in 1416, a fleet of ships from China under the Ming Dynasty visited East Africa and returned with ivory ware and giraffes. Chinese money of that period has been discovered in different parts of East Africa. Africans, however, had also long reached China by a different route and method. African mariners as well as African slaves returned the Asian compliment by reaching East Asia early in the Christian era.

Ship traffic across the Indian Ocean before the Portuguese seafarers made it famous was not only a to-and-fro stream by Asians between East Asia and the East African coast. Seafaring Africans, including slaves belonging to Arab traders, travelled to the Far East as far back as the T'ang Dynasty (A.D. 618-907). There is some basis to assert that even earlier than that, going back to the fourth century, seafaring Africans reached the South China coast.

Before Africans touched Macao, Malacca, and Sinkiang, they sojourned in India; but the number of Africans who immigrated to India in medieval and early modern times is unknown. It would seem, however that the figures were considerable, if we may hazard estimates from the chronicles of the 14th century African Muslim scholar, Ibn Battuta, who visited Sri Lanka (*neé* Ceylon) in the mid-14th century — he also visited India, China, and Indonesia — and noted that the *wazir* of Kalanbu (modern Colombo) employed approximately "five hundred Abyssinians".[6] (During these times Africans, whether Ethiopians or not, were generally referred to as Abyssinians.) After the Muslim sultanate of Bengal was founded in 1352, its rulers adopted the practice of importing foreign slaves to act as government functionaries and palace guards. Bengal had extensive maritime links with the Red Sea, and therefore it was convenient to employ Arab intermediaries and slave traders to obtain the slaves they needed from Africa. By the time of the reign of Barbak Shah (1486-1494), himself an African, there were at least 8 000 African slaves in the kingdom.[7] Precisely three hundred and sixty-eight years later, the first official Japanese mission to reach Africa stopped at Colombo and was intrigued at the "blackness" of the natives of Ceylon, just as the shoguns three hundred years earlier were especially fascinated by the African slaves who reached Japan.

Not all Africans who toiled for their masters in India disappeared in the anonymity of slavery however. Some rose to prominence, like the slave, Jamal al-Din Yakut, "Master of the Stables" to Queen Radiyya of Delhi in the 13th century. Queen Radiyya ascended the throne of Delhi in the year 1236 and, in royal fashion, dispensed with female garments, discarded the veil, donned the tunic and, in a Joan of Arc style, assumed the headdress of man and led the cavalry in person, charging against her enemies like the ancient mariner. While Radiyya's brave black slave, Yakut, perished in the ensuing battle, the Queen herself was captured, deposed and later put to death.[8] Yet the most prominent case of Africans in India is the seven years' rule of the Habshi Sultans of Bengal. In India, from medieval times to the present, persons of African origin have been known as

19

"Habshi" or "Sidis". By the 19th century the two terms became somewhat synonymous. Between the 15th and 18th centuries writers used the term "Sidi" to refer to Africans belonging to the seafaring communities of the west coast, while "Habshi" was the preferred term for Africans living in the kingdoms of the interior. In Arabic, and thus the usage of Muslim India, a *Habashi* (plural Habshi) referred to an inhabitant of Abyssinia (Ethiopia). Although most Africans who went to India before the 19th century were of Ethiopian origin, the term came to signify Africans generally. Immigrants from Nubia, Ethiopia, Somalia, East Africa, Mozambique, and Madagascar were collectively referred to as Habshi.[9] In a harsh attack on the Indian government and the Brahmin ruling class, an Indian black published a booklet, *Apartheid in India*, in which he expounds on the "plight of India's Blacks who are not only untouchables but are unapproachables, unseeables and unthinkables".[10] These Indian blacks are the descendants of the Bengalese Habshi, who, as we have just noted, came from Africa in the first instance. Till today they remain the ignored Africans of the Indian subcontinent.

The Habshi of Bengal, swelling in ranks and feeling the heat of repression from Sultan Fath Shah, rebelled and assassinated him in 1486. The Habshi commander of the palace guard and leader of the rebels, Sultan Shahzada, ascended the throne as Barbak Shah? until he, in turn, was murdered by his fellow African, Andil Khan, seven years later. There were also Habshi in other parts of India such as those in the Bahmani Kingdom of the Deccan; but of all the Africans who played a great role in the history of India, the most famous was Malik Ambar, ruler of the State of Ahmadnagar from 1607 to 1626.[11]

Before Malik Ambar ruled this part of India, a procession of other Africans passed India aboard Portuguese ships on their way to China, and later Japan. It is this Portuguese plying of the eastern oceans which, amongst others, testifies to the fact that the "African presence in Asia",[12] like the Asian presence in Africa, was not confined to one area, but rather covered a wide geographical space spanning various nations. Yet for reasons that lay in both European and Japanese hands, the African presence in Asia is less known than the Asian presence in Africa. On the other hand, the first Japanese to touch Africa are well-known down to their middle names, while their African counterparts in Japan remain shrouded in darkness even though, thanks to the Japanese, we know the name of one of the first Africans to arrive in Japan. We know who the first three Europeans to reach Japan *were*, as well as the circumstances under which they arrived, but, on the whole, we know next to nothing about the arrival of the first Africans in Japan except that they were a mixed bag of slaves and free men.

In Portuguese involvement in the trans-Atlantic trade, African-bonded labourers were the main item of commercial intercourse. In the Portuguese trans-Indian Ocean trade African boatmen, stevedores, porters, sailors, interpreters, security guards, and simply do-it-all slaves featured prominently. This suggests that the European story in Japan is not complete without its African concomitant. Sailing down the west coast of Africa on the Atlantic Ocean, round the Cape of Good Hope and up the African east coast, they passed Mozambique, Mombasa, Malindi, and across the Indian Ocean towards Goa, Calcutta and Cochin, in India, and later proceeded to Macao and Canton in China, and still later to Nagasaki in Japan. As in the Atlantic littoral, the basis of the African presence in Asia was largely through involuntary servitude. At the risk of repetition, the Portuguese were often short of skilled deep-sea sailors in their East Indies ventures. This shortage was especially acute in the long voyages between Lisbon and Mozambique, Goa, Malacca, Macao and Nagasaki.[13] In the history of Africa and Asia as well as of African slavery in general, this issue is often ignored or glossed over as if it was of little consequence.

These voyages were hazardous ventures with a very high attrition of cargoes and manpower: for example between 1528 and 1558 over 30 000 Portuguese men died in Mozambique, primarily from malaria and bilious illnesses. Yet sailors often succumbed, not only to the frequent shipwrecks which resulted in heavy casualties, but also to the depredations of the English, the Dutch and other pirates on the high seas. The Portuguese often turned to local recruits to help in the navigation and their apprehension of African slaves as well as in conducting other chores. Non-European dockhands — Arabs, Indians (mostly Gujaratis), Malays, and Africans — soon came to make up the majority of crews, to the extent that in the Portuguese ships plying the Indian Ocean interport trade, the captain or master was sometimes the only white man on board.[14] But the Portuguese also brought Africans with them from Lisbon in their journeys to the Far East. Bartolomeu Dias, for example, left in three ships in August 1487 carrying a number of blacks who were to go inland with samples of spices and precious metals and ask the way to the legendary African Christian, Prester John, and India.[15] The Portuguese explorer in West Africa between 1445 and 1455, Cadamosto, was frequently accompanied by Africans who had been secured from the Senegambia region. They were first taught Spanish and/or Portuguese in Europe, and they could now act as interpreters for the Portuguese in many of their journeys. (Interestingly, the first chartered company in the world was established by the Portuguese to exploit their African discoveries around 1487). It is this same company that took Africans to Japan.

In July 1497 Vasco da Gama left Lisbon with four ships. In early 1498 his voyage obtained at least one black pilot in Mozambique and continued plying the seas till he reached Calcutta, India, on 17 May 1498. Those African sailors accompanying the Portuguese sea voyagers to the East, some of whom were not picked up from the African coast before heading into the Indian Ocean, were mostly skilful in a variety of duties such as mining, interpreting languages, navigation, artistry, soldiery, boat rigging, etc. The Portuguese also brought along black residents from Lisbon, some of whom were long domiciled in one part or another of Europe. A few of these African residents in Europe found themselves integrated in the maritime activities of the Iberian seafarers to the Far East. Enough negro hands were available in Europe for these sea voyages.[16] Often in the 15th century, Abyssinian (Ethiopian) missions came to Europe; one was in Lisbon in 1452.[17] A number of Bakongo noble youths were sent to Portugal for their education, where most of them studied at the College of Santo Eloi. In 1518, two scions of the Congolese royal house headed an embassy to the Pope and one of them even was baptized (as Dom Henrique), and was later consecrated Bishop of Utica at the insistence of King Manuel of Portugal.[18] Members from similar groups were found by the Portuguese to be dependable hands for their adventures, as the reader will learn momentarily. They played a crucial role as security guards or military support to the Portuguese commercial enterprise and its sailors in Asia, contrary to the plantation labouring role their trans-Atlantic counterparts played. The classic case of the black slaves of Macao, China, when the Dutch were severely routed, is a case in point. These slaves played a decisive role in the successful defence of that city against the Dutch attack.[19] In June 1622 the Dutch, with 17 vessels, had assailed Macao with a landing party of 2 000 men — 900 Hollanders and 1 100 Japanese and Malays. The Dutch contingent suffered a major defeat against the Portuguese, Africans, and Indians. Nearly half the Dutch were killed or taken prisoner. The Hollanders unabashedly stated that their defeat was due to the fighting ability of the Negro slaves, "for our people saw very few Portuguese", wrote the lone surviving Dutch Captain Jan Pieterszoon Coen.

The Portuguese reluctantly confessed that their Negro slaves refused to give any quarter. They also claimed that these black slaves busied themselves in relentlessly beheading the wounded heretics by way of celebrating the feast of John the Baptist. The Dutch captain however claimed otherwise: "Many Portuguese slaves, Kaffirs (i.e. Africans) and the like, having been made drunk, charged so fearlessly against our muskets, that it was a wondrous thing to behold ..." A year later, Captain Coen was still harping on the same theme: "The slaves of the Portuguese at Macao served them so well and faithfully, that it was they who defeated and drove away our people there last year". Captain Coen was, consequently, so chastened and impressed by the prowess of the blacks routing a European force,[20] that in 1623 he advocated the employment of slaves in preference to Dutch soldiers: "The Portuguese beat us off from Macao with their slaves; it was not done with any (Portuguese) soldiers, for there are none in Macao ... See how the enemy thus holds his possessions so cheaply whilst we squander ourselves". The simplest interpretation is: it is better to expend the lives of blacks, you fools, than to sacrifice those of whites in this European imperial adventure.

Euro-American history rarely gives credit to black people for anything that demonstrates remarkable capabilities, especially in relation to whites. The Dutch defeat here is one of the very few exceptions in history when "Europe" conceded its inferiority to African blacks. Whilst the Portuguese would like to take the entire credit for defeating the Dutch, even their Jesuit missionary, Father Queroz, however, was constrained to make special mention of the African black woman (soldier) who wielded a halberd with such deadly ferocity and effect, that she was admiringly compared with a medieval Portuguese heroine, the legendary baker's wench of Aljubarrota who slew seven Spaniards with a shovel.

The most striking testimony to the services rendered by these African slaves on this occasion was given by *Haitao* of Canton, who on being informed of the courage and loyalty they had shown, sent a gift of 200 piculs of rice for distribution among them. Subsequent to this victory, many of the European victors promptly liberated their African slaves in view of the signal courage shown. A precedent was set, since the victors in the only battle ever fought between Europeans on a Chinese soil owed much of their success to persons of different colour — black slaves. Twelve years earlier in Japan, when the Portuguese maritime entrepreneur, trading from Macao, Andre Pessoa, was menaced by the *samurai* at Fukabori on 3 January 1610, he was supported by his motley crew of African blacks and Indian lascars.[21] This was merely one instance among many when black slaves were used as palace guards or security personnel in the Portuguese Far East maritime enterprises. It would be misleading, however, to leave the impression that all of the

Portuguese traders felt constrained to grant liberty to their black slaves. The majority of them simply clung to their slaves because dispensing with this source of free labour would have clearly gone against the grain of mercantile entrepreneurship.

The essentiality and integrality of blacks to the operation of the Portuguese commercial establishment in the Far East is one of the great unheralded stories of the African experience. Their role showed that the real basis of the Portuguese imperial power, outside its commercial activities, was the army of these slaves. In this far-flung Portuguese empire the slaves clearly demonstrated that an imperial organization exists so long as it retains its superior capacity to intimidate and coerce. Once the Japanese rose to the occasion and, in a sense, drove a psychological wedge between them and their slaves, the Portuguese became defenceless as I shall show momentarily. The core of Portuguese strength in India and China lay in their Africans since the spearhead of their palace army was this negro guard. Its specialized role in time became indispensable to Portuguese activities in Asia. In a sense we could say the Portuguese were playing their African card. In the event of conflict, especially in China, the African guards were the first on the frontline: Not only the merchants, but the missionaries in time came to depend on their services. The Africans who arrived with the Portuguese in China, though a not too small a number, were preceded by an even larger number of their fellow blacks during the T'ang Dynasty (A.D. 618-907).

For a thousand years from about the fourth to the fourteenth centuries, African slaves were imported to China.[22] Most of them belonged to professional Arab traders who even found it essential to establish a distributing centre at Canton in the year 300 A.D. While the majority of the African slaves came to China directly by sea from the Middle East and the East African coast, some, however, came via mainland Southeast Asia and the islands; for example in 1382, over a hundred "male and female Negroes", probably transported from Africa to Indonesia at some earlier period, were sent to an emperor of the Ming Dynasty as tribute to Java.[23] Others came overland through the caravan route. The actual number of Africans enslaved in China is impossible to estimate because of the absence of records or statistics.

Neither the name Africa nor the phrase "Negro slave" was known in China during the period of the T'ang Dynasty, but from the individual works of the *Ts'ung-shu*, that is, "Collections of Reprints," has come also the term *K'un-lun-nu* which describes a black-skinned person.[24] Since both the literature of the T'ang (618-907) and Sung (960-1279) dynasties contains *many* references to black slaves, the physical appearance of Africans was well-known to Chinese even at this early period. In the work of Chu Yu, *P'ing Chiu K'o T'an* ("Notes on P'ing Chiu"), a vivid depiction of Africans is given:

> Many wealthy people of Canton keep *Keuei-nu* ('devil slaves'). These are endowed with prodigious strength and can carry burdens weighing several catties. Their language and tastes differ from ours, but they are docile and do not run away. They are also spoken of as *yeh-jen* ('savages'). *Their skin is inky black, their lips red, their teeth white, and their hair is woolly and tawny. They are of both sexes.*[25]

The Chinese image of blacks seems to have coincided very much with that of Medieval Europe's view of blacks, if the views of Marco Polo in his *Travels* may be regarded as representative.[26] Marco Polo certainly influenced many Chinese to view blacks consciously in this unattractive light. Chinese writers of the same period often wrote about blacks (*K'un-lun* people) in similar fashion. Europeans, Arabs, Persians, and Asians viewed Africa's blacks with a jaundiced eye — a view that went a long way to perpetuate rationalisations about the continued enslavement of black people. Africans who found themselves in China in this early period did not fare much better than those who found themselves in European hands — at least with regard to the contempt they received.

As already stated, Africans in China came as Arab slaves. The Arab trade in African slavery lasted for nearly one and a half millenia, and straddled two continents from the east coast of Africa to the east coast of China. In justifying their exploitation of Africans, these slave traffickers rationalised that the black African was a *pagan* and, as such, enslaving him was permissible under the laws of their religion; secondly, arguing like Christian slavers, these Arab merchants further argued that once a person was a member of a Muslim society, even though a slave, he had the opportunity to learn the precepts of the true religion and attain heavenly salvation. Through the slave route, these traders claimed, lay redemption for blacks. The Portuguese Catholics used similar language in justifying their engagement in Japanese and African slavery in both China and Japan, as well, of course, as in India. More utilitarian an Arab rationalisation, however, was that presented by Arab writers who portrayed black Africa as so savage a land filled with such wretchedness that it was preferable for an African to be a slave in the "civilized" world, rather than free in such a miserable place. As they continued trading in African slaves to the Far East, they once again found themselves having a common mission with Portuguese traders. It was a sort of communion of the "holy" men especially of Basra (Iraq) and Christian Lusitania, the common denominator being the paganism or blackness of Africans. It was perhaps due to this Portuguese perception of blacks that even the *Jesuit missionaries* in Japan during the 16th century kept African slaves in their mission residences.

There is sufficient evidence showing that blacks who reached China in the 7th century A.D., especially during the T'ang dynasty, were imported by Arabs, particularly those wealthy Arabs of Basra who employed African slaves in the exploitation of the neighbouring salt mines. They travelled through Arabia, Persia, Afghanistan, Pakistan and India to China along the caravan route. Sometimes they went to East Asia purely on commercial missions; at other times on diplomatic ones. Even during the latter missions however they still were accompanied by their African slaves. In 977 A.D., the official history of the *Sung Shih*, ("Dynastic History of Sung") notes that Arab ambassadors arrived at the Chinese imperial court:

> In the second year of T'aip'ing Hsing Kuo (i.e. A.D. 977) Arabia sent the ambassador P'usze-na, the vice-ambassador

Mo-ho-mo ('Mahmud'?), and the judge P'u-lo, with the products of their country as presents. Their attendants had *sunken eyes* and black skin and they were called *K'un-lun-nu.*[27]

Yet some Africans in China escaped their imposed anonymity by subterfuge, wit, luck, etc. One African slave who rose to prominence in China, and became a legend in popular Chinese works, is Moleh.[28] Mo-leh's chivalry, bravery, effrontery, cunning, and marketing qualities need no further elaboration here. As already noted there are not many instances in ancient or medieval history when black people, however exceptional their feats, are mentioned by name. Mo-leh is one of the few exceptions. If they are mentioned by name their blackness is often "Egyptized", and their Africanness simply glossed over and thus expunged from historical consciousness, like some useless relic of an era gone by.

These Africans came from an area that Marco Polo referred to as the "Region of the Blacks". In his *Travels* Polo referred to the blacks of Zenj.[29] The Chinese writer, Chao Ju-K'uo, in his description of *K'un-lun Ts'eng-Chi*[30] agrees with Marco Polo's Zanghi, Zanzi, etc. Since both the Chinese and Western descriptions of blacks mutually corroborate each other, we are now certain that the *K'un-lun* slaves were Africans. All doubt has now been dispelled that black slaves were once sent to the T'ang court in 724 A.D. via the kingdom of Palembang, and that they were African negroes imported to Palembang from Sumatra.[31, 32] Concerning the period of Mongol domination in China we read from the Japanese research documents some interesting passages regarding Korean female servants and African slaves:

All great officers and rich men deemed it to be unworthy of their dignity if they did not keep Korean maidservants and *K'un-lun* slaves. Ye Tzu-Ch'i in the latter part of the fourteenth century says: "With the northerners (men living in the North), maid servants were without fail Kao-li girls, man-servants were *negroes*. Otherwise they were said not to be perfect gentlemen".[33]

In China, the intermingling of entrepreneurs of various stripes as well as roving adventurers also *resulted in African slaves meeting for the first time the Japanese*, including those who also were slaves of the Portuguese. The Japanese, in China as well as in Japan, showed a curious lack of interest in enslaving Africans. *Instead*, it is the African slaves who ended having Japanese slaves! Thanks to Portuguese perfidy.

Though the Portuguese never exercised political power or control in the Far East through their trade, religion, and slaves, they exercised considerable influence in many parts of Asia outside India. In Malaya, Indochina and Indonesia their influence, while strong, was weaker than in their African or Indian suzerains even as their trade prospered. Their commercial prosperity in the China Sea during the period 1543-1640 was due mainly to the Chinese emperors of the Ming dynasty, because the latter proscribed all trade and intercourse between their vassals and the Japanese. Often there was friction at Macao among the Chinese, Japanese and Portuguese. In 1613, for instance, the Chinese viceroy, Ming-hang, issued a stern reprimand to the Portuguese:

> You must not harbor Japanese. Since you are Westerners, why do you employ Japanese when you have *Negro* slaves to serve you? In this way they multiply. The Law ordains that when they are to be found anywhere, they are to be killed out of hand; yet you persist in harboring these people, which is like rearing tigers ... When you go thither (to Japan) to trade, you must not bring back any ... and whosoever does so will be punished according to Chinese law by having his head cut off.[34]

The lot of the Japanese, residing in or passing through Macao, was sometimes even worse off than that of African slaves. In 1597 at Macao, a special law was decreed to curb the Japanese. The latter were forbidden to carry a sword of any kind, even in the case of a slave escorting his Portuguese master. The penalty for breaking this law was a life sentence in the galleys for slaves, and a ten years' stretch in the same for freemen.[35] A decade before this decree was passed, a viceregal fiat forbade slaves from being armed, save when accompanying their owners. The streets of the Portuguese colonies of Goa, Malacca, and Macao were rendered unsafe because of bands of roving armed slaves who frequently set upon and robbed passers-by. The 1586 decree enacted that any slave knifing a Portuguese should be sentenced to 10 years as a galley slave and have his right arm amputated. In March 1595 Mathias de Albuquerque promulgated a preamble to a decree that stated that the Chinese had made many grievous complaints against the Portuguese of Macao for being in the habit of kidnapping or buying Chinese, both for use as domestic servants as well as for export as slaves. The Viceroy in Council, with the High Court of Justice in concurrence, henceforth decreed that the purchase or sale of any male or female slave of Chinese nationality would be forbidden on pain of a fine of 1 000 *cruzados*, in addition to two years in prison. A number of decades earlier, an African Kongo King, Nzinga Mbemba, baptized soon after 1500 as King Affonso I, had made similar complaints against the Portuguese. After welcoming them when they came with promises of trade and useful knowledge, their appetite for African slaves however soon outweighed their usefulness. Portuguese agents disregarded Affonso's authority, rode roughshod over everybody, carried and kidnapped anyone they could lay their hands on, including members of the King's own family. King Affonso bitterly complained in a letter to Lisbon in 1526 of Portuguese "corruption and licentiousness" and noted that "our country is being completely depopulated".[36] Having succeeded in Africa with the enslavement of blacks, the Portuguese now transferred their success to India and to China and finally to Japan — where they met their Waterloo in the form of Japanese *shoguns* and *daimyos* and *samurais*. Even their African slaves and servants could not save them in Japan, as they had done in China against the Dutch and the Japanese.

# FIRST JAPANESE-AFRICAN CONTACTS

The Portuguese quest for spices, silk, sugar, slaves, and souls had by now obligated its maritime enterprise to venture to nearly all corners of the Oriental world — India, Indo-China, Indonesia, Solor, Timor, Flores, Ende, Malaya, Manila, China and Japan. Of course the Japanese were not idle either. The existence of human creatures across the seas, more distant than the Koreans or the Chinese, was vaguely known to them from as early a period as the 6th century, and frequently reported by the pirates from the 12th century. A hundred years before Magellan laid claim to the Philippines for Spain (in 1521), Japanese seafarers had been serving and colonizing in the Sulu sultanate of Mindanao in the southern Philippines. After 1510, the Japanese adventurers who were already scouring such places as Batavia, Java, Sumatra, etc., began to rub shoulders with the Portuguese at Goa. Goa is where the Japanese met not only the Portuguese, but Indians, Arabs and Africans as well — bond and free. The entire period of the Middle Ages saw the whole Indian Ocean seaboard interlocked by trading ports in all its maritime countries. One prominent scholar of the African scene cites the case of the Portuguese trader, Tome Pires, who found in Malacca, where he lived between 1512 and 1515, East Africans as well as Indians and West Asians (Arabs). Tom Pires mentions, among others, "people from ... Kilwa, Malindi, Mogadishu and Mombasa" (all African). Maritime links between East Africa and South-East Asia, in the words of Davidson, were many and of great antiquity.[37]

In 1529 Japanese buccaneers sent home some Indians to be inspected and interrogated at Kyoto. They sent word also of the existence of Africans who, obviously owing to their skin colour, were increasingly becoming objects of benign curiosity to the Japanese. The curious lack of Japanese interest in trading in African slavery has already been mentioned, and this was in complete contrast to Western appetite for African slaves.[38] In India, China and Japan there is no record of either massive and frequent African slave revolts or frequent escape attempts, as is the case in the West.

31

In America as well as in the English, Spanish, Portuguese, French, Danish and Dutch colonies these African slaves were, instead, given a new conception of themselves according to the different lights of their captors. Trans-Atlantic slaves underwent the "breaking-in" process which was unknown in the Trans-Indian slavery. A mental reprocessing took form to the degree that a black man was given a new conception, not only of himself, but of the world also.

The Portuguese introduced these slaves to every port they berthed at in Asia. The stations of Macao and Canton in China were particularly important. From here the Portuguese established a triangular trade among the cities of Canton, Macao and Nagasaki. The port of Nagasaki became the main centre of Portuguese commercial and proselytisation activities in the 16th century. It was a question of time before these were soon followed in turn by others, such as missionaries. In 1542, a Junco with three Portuguese sailors on board (Antonio de Mota, Francisco Zeimoto, and Antonio Peixoto), on its way from Macao to Siam, was blown off course and reached the Japanese island of Tanegashima. The fugitives stayed long enough to teach the Japanese the use of firearms. Soon thereafter two others, Fernando Mendez Pinto with his two companions, Christopher Borcalho and Diego Zeimoto, arrived in the service of a pirate who had taken them aboard his ship when they had lost their own. Pinto is the man to whom credit for the "discovery" of Japan is usually given, despite his mendacious tendencies.

**BLACK NAMBANS: KUROBO IN KYUSHU**

The Jesuit missionary from Spain, Francis Xavier, soon thereafter reached Japan (August 1549), landing at Kagoshima, and immediately began the Jesuit Mission in Japan whose missionisation saw, 30 years later, the number of Japanese Christians rise to 150 000. But it was Captain Jorge Alvarez who in 1547 first brought Africans to Japan — called *"Kurobo"* by the Japanese, and according to the Japanese scholar, Midori Fujita, the total number of Kurobo at one time in that period in Japan would have reached several hundred.[39] Indeed, Fujita points out that the first Japanese reference to the African negroes was documented in the work of Ota Gyuichi (1527-161?), *Shincho Koki*. The *Kurobo* in Japan were slaves in transit, sailors, valets and bodyguards — all serving their European masters.

In 1581 the Portuguese Captain, Major Bartolomeu Vaz Landeiro, greatly impressed his Japanese hosts with his flamboyance, as he strutted across the streets "everywhere attended by a suite of richly clad Portuguese and by a bodyguard of eighty Muslim and Negro slaves, armed with halberds and shields."[40] It was at this juncture that the Japanese, seeing large numbers of blacks on a regular basis, became fascinated by the sight and sought to entertain and engage these African visitors. On the other hand, across the Atlantic Ocean, black slaves were being herded *en masse* to auction blocks and generally brutalised, especially when their economic value declined. The Japanese remained curious about blacks. They wondered about the docility of these negro slaves, but their physical attributes intrigued them the most. Perhaps their curiosity about blacks was contributory to the Japanese often sparing the lives of Africans during the expulsion orders, while their Portuguese masters' necks often were severed by the *samurai* swords.

Following the creation of the Jesuit Mission of Japan, a delegation of (7) young Christian nobles from Kyushu island travelled to Rome in 1582, on a tour arranged by the Italian Jesuit Visitor, Alessandra Valignano, *there* to advertise and promote the achievements of the Jesuit Japan Mission on the one hand, and to provide the Japanese with first-hand witnesses to the power, glory and splendour of Europe on the other. They were on their way to pay homage to Pope Gregory XIII, only to arrive in 1586 to see the coronation of Gregory's successor, Pope Sixtus V. It was these youngsters that are the first known group of Japanese to set foot on Africa — in Mozambique specifically. They were late to reach Rome because they stopped in Mozambique for six months after their arrival in 1586. Learning from their European tutors they too concluded that Africans were lazy, incompetent and uncivilized. When Visitor Valignaro travelled to Kyoto in 1591 accompanied by the returning Kyushu ambassadors to present his credentials as Ambassador of the Portuguese Viceroy of India, he was so concerned with outshining the Korean delegation that in his procession he included not only magnificent steeds "each attended by an Indian groom attired in gorgeous costume and carrying a gigantic parasol", but also by the African slaves dressed in velvet, with collars and chains of gold, and walking alongside the Arab horse which was a gift from the Portuguese Governor-General of Goa to Shogun Hideyoshi.[41]

Letters of Luis Frois (1532-1597), the Portuguese Jesuit in Japan, reflect the faithful scribe who, in guarded moments, wrote of the "Portuguese and the pages" when describing Valignano's meeting with Hideyoshi, because these slaves (called "pages" by Father Frois) were actually young strong men skilled in a variety of functions performing all the essential chores that their Portuguese masters demanded of them. The ambiguity arising out of Portuguese enslavement of Africans raises a set of questions: since these Africans were often skilful even in undertaking repairs of merchant vessels as they remained anchored at the Japanese harbours, what degree of professionalism was expected — or demanded — of these slaves prior to being taken abroad? Had the special expertise of African slaves with prior maritime experience, especially of the long-distance variety been recognised and exploited by the Portuguese? If so could this, perhaps, have also been the reason accounting for the ambiguous status of the African slaves in the Portuguese empire? Whatever the answers, it is clear that Japanese paintings of the Portuguese and their vassals — bond and free — depict them carrying the large parasols, flags, palanquins, folding chairs, and wearing richly detailed costumes (which costumes were similar to regalia of Ghanaian — West African — chieftains, especially of the Akan peoples). This may, perhaps, suggest that these African slaves were extracted from a political, military and social elite of the village communities, rather than exclusively from the lower peasant groups.

The Japanese remained intrigued by this black entourage of the European maritime traders. They would often come from long distances, some "thirty or forty miles to see them, and entertain them honourably for three or four days at a time".[42] Today young Japanese volunteers are annually dispatched to Africa and their fascination with Africa remains high (see Chapters 6 and 7). In another work by Fujita we read:

> During the Edo Period (1603-1867) with Japan under a national isolation policy, black Africans, albeit small in number, continued to come and stay in Nagasaki. They were depicted in the diaries and essays of Japanese who visited there. For instance Shiba Kokan (1747-1818), well-known scientist and painter, witnessed a handful of kurobo working as servants in a small Dutch settlement in Nagasaki, and sketched two of them in his diary: One of them was apparently from Monomotapa, the country now known as Zimbabwe ... In mid-Edo, these dark-skinned people certainly aroused interest among Japanese as part of a trend toward exoticism.[43]

The fact that in the Momoyama and Edo Eras Africans were slaves of the Portuguese was not a motivating factor of Japanese curiosity on seeing black people. The fact of their enslavement was inconsequential; what was of interest was their colour. For example Sebastian Vizcaino remarked that when he was in Japan in the 1500s, the village as well as urban people were "much amazed" at his black African drummer. As a result Vizcaino saw visions of financial gain if he were to put his negro on show. We shall refrain from speculating what Vizcaino's black drummer was doing with him in Japan, so many thousands of miles away from home. Nor can we be certain that Vizcaino did in fact refrain from putting his drummer on stage to perform for the Japanese audience and thus attain part of his vision of financial gain. Interestingly, during the Edo Period Japanese kabuki actors performed some dramas wherein a major character was a kurobo. In any event the names of the kurobo (a name that originally meant black Africans, but came to signify dark-skinned) people in the Edo Period began to appear in criminal chronicles.

On 14 April 1581 the inquisitive populace of Miyako (i.e. Kyoto) broke down the Jesuit residence in their eagerness to inspect an African slave. The brawl that ensued as a consequence led to a number of fractured limbs. Shogun Oda Nobunaga was so curiously aroused by the commotion that he ordered the black man to appear before him. So intrigued was he by this African that he made him strip to the waist to satisfy himself that his black skin was authentic. The shogun promptly called his children to witness this extraordinary spectacle, and one of the ruler's nephews even gave the black man a sum of money. This African is the same legendary Yasuke, so named by the Japanese, who was "'offered' to Oda Nobunaga in 1581 as a tribute by the Italian Jesuit, Alexandro Valignano, who was attempting to avert Buddhist opposition and cultural collision, among other troubles".[44] Shogun Oda liked Yasuke, who in turn worked for the shogun until his death two years later. It should thus come as no surprise that the *Kurombojin* or blackamoor is frequently depicted in popular Japanese glyptics and applied art *(inro, netsuke')*, produced during the years between 1590 and 1614 as one can see at the Kobe City Museum (incorporating the museum of Namban Art), and also at the Idemitsu Museum in Tokyo, as I shall explain shortly. The Japanese however were not congenial to Portuguese slavery, though Japanese culture was accustomed to slavery — for it existed during the Kamakura Bakufu (1200-1333), the Ashikaga Shogunate (1335-1573), and during parts of the Tokugawa Shogunate (1603-1867). Such forms of slavery, however, were far inconsequential compared with those in the Americas, across the Atlantic. The Jesuits' locking up of their slaves in cells had also aroused Japanese curiosity.

Be that as it may, in the early 16th century when the Portuguese began to arrive in Japan from China on a regular basis for commercial activities they, in turn, triggered an increasing challenge to their monopoly on trade with Japan from other Europeans — Spanish, Dutch and English. A much stronger reaction was that of the Japanese. The issue of Japanese hostility concerned mainly two issues: Portuguese slave trade and Christian proselytisation. With regard to the latter, the Japanese correctly saw it as a prelude to Portuguese imperial colonisation of Japan. Although the Goa-Macao-Nagasaki route was crewed mostly by Asians and black slaves, supervised by the generally fewer than two dozen Portuguese officers, soldiers and gunners, the Portuguese officers still left many of their hosts uneasy, especially when Japanese saw the nature of Portuguese slavery. Slavery, as I noted, was not entirely foreign to Japanese society by the time the Portuguese arrived. Trade in slaves was common in Japan, and visiting Europeans often took advantage of the situation and purchased girls at will. Numbers of slaves were also transported abroad. Yet its Japanese forms were rare, not like the slave systems and forms that existed in the Christian world. The endless Tokugawa Shogunate depredations that were ravaging *Dai Nippon* then, together with the previous violent activities of the *Wako* in the China Sea, created an army of hungry waifs, strays, tramps and vagabonds (like the *muitsai* in China) — too poor to maintain themselves or their children, and who were prepared to sell either or both into bondage in order to gain their daily bread. Hence a flourishing traffic in human flesh grew up in the ports of Kyushu, the majority of the victims being unwanted girls sold by their indigent parents, although debtors, malefactors and Chinese or Koreans captured by warlords or pirates were often part of this human traffic.[45] African slavery showed remarkable similarities to the Japanese form, though the former was even more benign than the latter. The institution of slavery *per se* remained, nevertheless, repugnant to the Japanese as a nation. For example between 1624 and 1734 no fewer than *eight* enactments were issued declaring the sale or purchase of human beings punishable with death, imprisonment or confiscation of property, and forbidding that servants, male or female, should be bound for longer than 10 years. Nowhere in Europe, Arabia, or the Americas at this time in history is there the equivalent of these eight enactments.

More than anything else the Japanese people strongly resented Portuguese forms of chattel slavery. The Portuguese transference of this practice to Japan was bad in itself; but it was exacerbated when they violated a cardinal taboo: the Japanese held the belief that no Japanese person may be enslaved by foreigners, let alone by *foreign slaves*. Alien enslavement of the Japanese — tolerable in China and India by *those* regimes — was unquestionably repugnant to the people of the Land of the Rising Sun. The Ashikaga and Tokugawa shoguns had coupled their antislavery pronouncements with their anti-Christianity moves, and ordered the expulsion of foreign barbarians precisely because of the new values introduced by the Portuguese in Japanese society. Having reached the Kyushu islands dragging along their bad baggage of regarding foreign natives as expendable commodities, the Portuguese were, in turn, judged by those same values. As we have just seen what particularly angered the Japanese shoguns in Portuguese slave trade was this dual practice of engaging in Japanese slavery and permitting their own negro servants or slaves to enslave Japanese peasants. This was adding insult to injury. They put up strong resistance to Portuguese activities in Japan because they "fiercely resented the purchase of their countrymen (if not countrywomen) by the very Negro slaves and Indian lascars in the service of the Portuguese".[46] The fact that some of these traders were themselves black surely rankled these shoguns and *daimyos*, but in Japanese eyes paramount was that the laws of nature — at least of that nature expressed by those fertility cultists of the sun goddess in Kyushu — were violated when a foreign bond was himself granted privileges of freedom by an imperial factor to transcend the customs, traditions, and rights of the citizenry of a higher civilisation.

Their logic was: how could Japan remain Dai Nippon (i.e. Great Japan), with the great spirit of Yamato reigning, when prisoners of barbarians were themselves given a higher status in the land that Amaterasu (i.e. Goddess of the Sun) and her grandson, Ninigi, welding the 4 223 islands of the archipelago, bequeathed to the progeny of Izanagi and Izanami? Since the Japanese were (so they claimed then) of a divine race, how could inferior barbarians (*ebisu, namban-jin*) be allowed to befoul such a pure civilisation? The Tokugawa Shogunate responded to her own question by seeking isolation and self-containment, scouring for no alien lands or foreign trade, content with her rustic simplicity and Oriental introspection, adding thus to the legendary "Asian inscrutability".

An additional factor of resentment against the Portuguese was that the practice of slavery, then rampant in the world, certainly encouraged Lusitanian concupiscence on a large scale, since the Portuguese women were the most secluded in Europe at the time. A 17th century Portuguese writer was fond of boasting that a virtuous Portuguese woman left her home only for her christening, her marriage, and her funeral. A similar Japanese proverb that a woman has three successive lords during her lifetime — her father when she is a child, her husband when she is married, and her son if she becomes a widow — further made inevitable future conflict between Japanese and Portuguese men regarding Japanese women. The seclusion of the Portuguese women had helped accustom the Portuguese men to the harem — and Zenana-like seclusion imposed on women in most countries of the Asian East.[47] Many of the Portuguese merchants doing business in Japan for lengthy periods were, however, married to Japanese women, rather than merely living with them as concubines. Still, the Japanese remained unmollified by this partial concession to *their* custom. So convinced were they of foreign pollution that they expelled not only the Portuguese and their attendants but also their Japanese wives, concubines, and what offspring they had with these women. All were banished to Macao, which they called Namban. Even today some Japanese writers still see the pre-eminent hand and role of foreigners in their sexual revolution — or, as some now call it, their sex industry.[48]

What is not clear from the record, however, is the sexual relationship, if any, between the African slaves — or free black men — and Japanese women. The "popularity" with which Africans were viewed by Japanese, and especially the curiosity of their women folk, would suggest that these blacks were no more than exotica. Africans were so "popular" — or rather so compassionately regarded — in Japan then that even when the daimyos slaughtered an entire group of Portuguese traders, they were the only ones spared. By the time the Japanese joined the European commercial exploitation of the African colonies after the Meiji Restoration, their view of Africans had hardened somewhat to see them as no more than mere markets for Japanese textile products, or as a source of raw materials (see Chapter 2). The Japanese men were perhaps particularly fearful — if not of the reality, then of the possibility — of liaisons, matrimonial or sexual, developing between black men and yellow women. After all blacks were slaves and servants — thus inferior — to the Portuguese; and to the Japanese the black skins of Africans must have denoted inferiority to the white Nambans. Because the African black skins were an unusual sight to the Japanese, the latter's curiosity was tinged not only with contempt, but with compassion also.

What additionally aggravated matters between visiting European merchants and their hosts was the pervasive cheating habits of the Portuguese traders who used one set of measuring scales when buying from the Japanese, and a different set when selling to them. So unreliable and corrupt were the Portuguese that not even the friars were trusted by the shoguns and daimyos.

The Jesuits became fearful that the Portuguese slave traders were jeopardizing the missionary activities of the Roman Catholic Church. Consequently they joined the Japanese daimyos in protesting the secular slaving activities of their brethen, but the Jesuits conveniently ignored the fact that *they themselves* kept African slaves at their Japanese missions, similarly as the American Founding Fathers denounced King George's "enslaving" of the American colonies while conveniently neglecting to condemn their own enslavement of African negroes. This protest, coupled with passionate Japanese hostility towards Portuguese enslavement of their countrymen, nevertheless led to the publication of a decree by King Sebastian in March 1571, whereby the purchase or acquisition of Japanese of either sex as slaves was strictly forbidden, on pain of confiscation of the property of all offenders. Yet the decree lacked the temerity to order a cessation of trading in African slaves belonging to the Portuguese in Japan. So much for the much touted absence of racism either by the Lusitanian adventurers or the Jesuit holy men. Portuguese clergy and laity found themselves in opposite camps with regard to slavery.

The City Solons of Goa addressed a letter to King Philip of Spain and Portugal, in December 1603, remonstrating against the action of Viceroy Aires de Saldanha in belatedly enforcing the 1571 decree which was requested — allegedly — by the Jesuits in Japan. The Councillors rehashed the familiar but tedious claim that it was "good" for the souls of these slaves to be in bondage to the Portuguese, since the majority would, in time, be converted to Christianity, and would be released after several years; or else they would fall into the clutches of Hindus and Moslems, argued the Christian Catholics, which would have been tantamount to perpetual perdition. We have already seen how Arab Muslim slave traders used similar logic in arguing that the slaves were assured of a better fate with them, than they would otherwise have had either with the Christians or if left to their "pagan" selves. The Goa councillors once again recapitulated to The Royal, a few years later, not only their previous arguments concerning maintaining slavery, but invented new ones, namely, that to free these slaves was contrary to "elementary justice", since the slaves were bought in good faith, and liberating them would constitute "injustice" to their owners. They went on to state:

> And so much capital has been invested in these slaves, that some individuals would lose as much as a thousand or two thousand ducats therein. Your majesty orders that henceforth we should buy none of them. But these people are accustomed to sell their own children, and to sell them to other infidels like themselves. And since they sell them to heathen, surely it is lawful for Christians to buy them, since all those who are bought become Christians and are now so. Moreover the sales which were made hitherto, were made with the written consent of the Bishop of Japan, and with a

specified limit to the years' servitude, on the completion of which they are freed and become Your Majesty's vassals. There are many of these in this state, who are a very martial race and useful in war, as was clearly shown in the recent blockade by the Hollanders when many a citizen sallied forth with seven or eight of these lads with their muskets and lances, for these are the only slaves in India ... fit to bear arms, and a large city like this will frequently lack the garrison necessary for the defence of its walls.[49]

But more than the moral suasion and protests of the holy fathers of the Catholic Mission in Japan, it was the intense pressure brought to bear by the Japanese Napoleon, Toyotomi Hideyoshi, and the Tokugawa Shogun, Ieyasu (1542-1616), which was more effective in suppressing Portuguese slave trade in Japan.[50] These shoguns were not simple Abolitionists, they were at times very ruthless in some of their methods of proscribing foreign slave traders. They were of course not abolishing slavery *per se*, but rather the enslavement of Japanese peasants by foreigners as well as the namban spread of a "diabolic" Occidental value-system designed to alter the Japanese order.

Hideyoshi, who completed the unification of Japan, and who fought the Chinese in Korea (1592-1598) to a bloody stalemate in one of the costliest wars in human history, compelled all the clan lords to come to Kyoto and renew their vows to the Throne. His sixteen years' administration (1582-1598) was one period of Japanese history up to 1945 in which the real rule of the nation would be delegated to a man outside the wide pool of imperial blood.[51] After the disembarkation at Nagasaki in July 1590 of the Jesuit Visitor, Valignano, with his entourage of black slaves dressed in velvet liveries and chains of gold, Hideyoshi gave the envoy a solemn audience at his palace of Juraku at Kyoto on 3 March 1591, whereas Tokugawa Ieyasu, the icy, unlovable, cold-blooded but blue-blood royal lord, went on to make himself and his heirs the new shoguns of Japan. He sought a way to drive out the twin threats of white supremacy and militant Christianity from Japan's door. In 1587 Hideyoshi enacted an edict, reading, in part:

> Having learned from our faithful councillors that foreign *religieux* (i.e. members of religious orders) have come into our realm, where they preach a law countrary to that of Japan, and that they even had the audacity to destroy temples dedicated to our (native gods) Kami and Hotoke; although this outrage merits the severest punishment, wishing nevertheless to show them mercy, we order them under pain of death to quit Japan within twenty days. During that time no harm or hurt will come to them. But at the expiration of that term, we order that if any of them be found in our State, they shall be seized and punished as the greatest criminals.[52]

Although African slaves were not Christians, at least in the formal sense, they too, nevertheless, were subjected to the expulsion orders of the shoguns since they came along as Portuguese baggage. Militant Christianity could not have been accommodated in a country with such a long, proud and settled custom and civilisation. Having been also compromised on slavery issues Jesuits became, additionally, *persona non grata* in Tokugawa Japan.

After Emperor Go-Yozei had abdicated, Ieyasu issued an edict ordering the deportation of foreign priests, the demolition of churches, and the renunciation of faith by all those Christians who seek "to change the government of the country and obtain possession of the land".[53] He ordered the expulsion of Africans along with their masters. On 23 June 1636 the Shogun's Cabinet issued a harsh edict:

> No Japanese vessel was to be allowed to proceed abroad; Japanese trying to go abroad secretly were to be punished with death, the vessel and her crew seized 'to await our pleasure'. Any Japanese resident abroad was to be executed if he returned to Japan ... The descendants of Namban

(Portuguese) people shall not be allowed to remain ...
Whoever remains shall be punished with death, and his (or
her) relatives punished, their children, and those who may
have adopted them shall be delivered to Namban (Macao),
though death is due them all. So if any of them return to
Japan, or sends correspondence to Japan, he shall of course
be killed ...

By 1638 the shogun's police were rounding up the last Portuguese
priests and deporting them. One or two Catholic priests who were
smuggled in were hunted down and executed. This was of course not
new: a Jesuit Provincial, Spinola, was captured at Kuchinotsu (17
December 1625). He had been deported in 1614, but had returned in
1615 with others disguised as a merchant. He had been provincial
from 1622-1626 when on 20 June he was sent to the stake at
Nagasaki and died without recanting his Christianity. This
Dominican friar together with his Franciscan colleague was
beheaded with a number of his followers, including women. All
ships from Catholic countries were turned away at gunpoint. But
Ieyasu had already died, in 1616, the same year as William
Shakespeare. The Macao-based trader from Portugal, Andre
Pessoa, when confronted by the samurai on 3 January 1610 at
Fukabori, survived the confrontation, and once again like his fellow
traders before and after him, fell back on his motley crew of mainly
blacks and lascars for protection. What gratitude, if any, to his
black slaves for saving his neck from certain samurai swords, the
record is unclear. Whether Pessoa granted manumission to his
African slaves is a matter for speculation.

The Japanese were determined to eliminate most foreign
influence, sometimes brutally so. For instance when a Portuguese
vessel called in 1640 to plead the cause of commerce, it was refused
entry and sent back home with the grisly message to the outside
world in the form of sixty-one corpses of its crewmen who had been
beheaded. The four prominent ambassadors aboard (with rich
presents for the Japanese local daimyo and the shogun) when it

arrived at Nagasaki on 6 July also suffered the same fate. Before it was sent back the vessel was surrounded by Japanese guard-boats. The rudder and sails, and later the guns and ammunition, removed, and the envoys including Pacheco and all the ship's company, except the blacks aboard, were placed in a ward at the tiny Deshima/Dejima. On 3 August 1640 the four ambassadors with 57 of their companions were beheaded after having been read a final harangue. The only ones to survive intact as a group were the Africans. At the very least, this could be interpreted as evidence of absence of malice on the part of the Japanese towards Africans and probably the Indian lascars too. Nowhere in the world, at this time in history, were Africans as safe, while in the hands of foreigners, as they were in Japan. While it is true that the Shogun Cabinets were certainly sympathetic to those whom they called "the lowest among the crew," clearly the fact that they consistently spared the lives of Africans while others had their heads chopped off, is a significant pointer of early Japanese positive attitude towards the black nambans.

The era of Japanese contacts with the Western world had actually ended in the 1630s when in 1639 the Shogunate had established this national isolation policy in order to exclude Christianity from the Japanese islands. That decree, myopic or sagacious, depending on one's perspective, delayed Japanese international action for 250 years. The shogun's slogans *Sonno-joi* ("Revere the Emperor!" "Drive out the Barbarians!") in effect were an order sealing the nation from foreign influences. Needless to say, expulsions of Portuguese ended also this nascent cultural connection between Japanese and Africans. It expelled also the issue of Portuguese (and possibly African) men with Japanese women. These Tokugawa "philosopher-kings" administered Japan between 1638 and 1853 with such sterile, ruthless, and autocratic efficiency that in 200 years the population increased only from 26 million to 33 million. The birth and death rates almost cancelled each other.

The barbarians were driven out, but the *nanban byobu* retained the representatives of this foreign presence in Japan in the form of

45

Japanese artistic depiction of exotica. These artists were commissioned by feudal lords or wealthy merchants of Nagasaki. The namban screen paintings by artists of the Kano, Tosa and Sumiyoshi schools at Kyoto and Sakai, between 1590 and 1614, constitute an aspect of Japanese painting which cover a period well over a millennium. Most of these fine paintings that have survived fires, earthquakes, shogunate extirpations, injury in the flow of time, loss, theft, etc., remain in private collections in Japanese households.[54] It is some of these surviving screens which depict, among others, harbour scenes featuring the great Portuguese *nao*, its crew, missionaries, Japanese, and Portuguese merchants and other issues that were part of the Japan-Europe contacts of this period. Portuguese companions, most of whom exhibit pigmentation ranging from grey to various shades of yellow and brown to black, show exaggerated and animated facial expressions almost verging on the grotesque. The black figures — clearly representing Africans in Japan and perhaps Indian lascars too — are visible in terms of the subordinate status relative to other Portuguese. These are shown as deckhands on the ships, rowing or steering lighters, loading freight and carrying cargo. The representations also show these blacks supporting the enormous parasols which would seem to have been the prerogatives of the Portuguese merchants and captains. At several museums in Tokyo and Kobe, the Namban screens clearly depict interesting dimensions of early contacts between Japanese and foreigners, especially Africans. The details of Japanese artistry on the Namban screens reflect and express a curious vitality of the Japanese regarding, especially, their darker visitors. These namban (nanban) screens show Africans and Indians (as well as Portuguese of course) in various modes of active pose. Japanese artists (such as Naizen Kano) depicted the appearance and activities of foreigners as they perceived them. The 151,4 x 325,8 cm namban screens at the Tokyo Idemitsu Museum (these screens have also been woven into 2,2 m x 4,7 m tapestries at Kobe City Museum), portray fourteen or so Africans and Indians. The tapestry of Namban screens show black Africans barefooted, carrying parasols and umbrellas. A black here is leading a horse, two blacks there are holding a horse, some are carrying tropical animals.

Representations that clearly refer to Africans also show them in various ranges — from the brisk servile demeanour of black boatmen, porters, and stevedores to the acrobatics performed by the black sailors in the riggings of the *nao*. Some are carrying tigers. The Christian church procession shows Portuguese with their servants and valets. These namban screens portray costumes that resemble West African — especially Ghanaian — regalia of chieftains, and thus attain a certain premium of historical validity, if only we may recall that the Portuguese had a major slave fort at Elmina in modern-day Ghana. In the namban screens the Portuguese are flashily dressed in black robes, others in colourful dresses, with "ballooning" pants unlike those of the Africans.

## JAPAN REOPENS

How Japan resumed contact with Africans after the shogun expulsions of foreigners in the early Edo Era is our immediate concern here. A slight digression to show the extent to and thoroughness with which Japan became integrated into the market economy, scientific and technological innovation of the West is worthwhile, for it helps explain the degree to which Japan participated in the economies of Africa alongside European colonial rulers. To fully grasp the entirety of the Japan-Africa historical interaction it is appropriate to look, however briefly, at the Euro-Japanese contacts which led to increased Japanese knowledge of Africa, since Japan participated fully in the economic, rather than diplomatic, scramble for Africa. Such understanding would be facilitated by looking first at the re-opening of Japan to the West. Since the Japanese were forbidden at the beginning of 1636 from travelling abroad, those who were abroad by the time the decree was enacted were equally forbidden to return. The isolation and insulation of the Japanese from foreign influences was nearly complete.

In Nagasaki Bay, five hundred miles from the *de facto* capital of Edo (present day Tokyo), a small man-made island (only 300 paces long) called Dejima, was built for Dutch merchants and traders to station, provided they ceased from proselytisation, and its staff had to pay a high price for their profits. In order to prove their religious neutrality, the Dutch even had to provide the ships and cannon-fire which helped level the Shimabara Christian fortress during the Shimabara revolt. The Dutch traders were also annually expected to walk to Edo and kiss the feet of the shogun, perform some scientific tricks, and provide him with intelligence about events in the distant lands of the West. Dejima practically remained Japan's only window to the outside world until 1853, though the period 1643-1863 may properly be regarded as the re-opening of the sealed Japan. Dejima also briefly housed Africans who, unlike their Portuguese masters, had escaped the samurai swords.

It was only the Dutch and the Chinese who were permitted to trade at Nagasaki — Portugal and Britain having been banned. Many Japanese aspired to study the so-called "Dutch learning" during the Tokugawa period by going to Nagasaki.[55] In 1844 the King of The Netherlands, William II, had attempted to outflank the British by sending a diplomatic mission urging the bakufu to "open" the country, but bakufu rulers refused. Slowly the Tokugawa shogunate authority and credibility were crumbling, mainly from internal decay. The foreign arrival merely accelerated the speed of political collapse of the shogunate authority. Rarely does the demise of a civilisation come from without. The farmers, for example, were so well-taxed and policed that they exposed and abandoned all infants who could not be fitted into the national budget. The shoguns were so punctilious in their management of the Japanese society that the arts of peace, cultivated with an impressive sedulousness, relegated the arts of war to an antiquarian sport. By the time the "black ships" arrived the Japanese gunsmiths were producing only 200 firearms annually, compared with the previous high of 5 000 annually.

Visits by foreign ships began to increase. In 1844, 1845, and 1846, British and French warships stopped at Ryukyu Islands and

Nagasaki, ostensibly to request commercial relations, but in reality to intimidate the shogunate. The entry of US naval (the so-called black) ships into Japanese waters was in violation of the 1825 law of Japan, which decreed that foreign vessels approaching within range of the coastal batteries were to be fired on. Among these foreign countries, the United States nevertheless was rumoured to be contemplating sending an expeditionary fleet to Japan. In 1846 Commodore James Biddle of the American East India fleet with two warships in Uraga harbour forced his way to Tokyo to demand that the shogun sign the treaty which would grant American castaways good treatment and consular representation. The Tokugawa Shogun rejected the American demand and instructed his coastal guard to surround Biddle's men-of-war, cut their anchors, attached lines to their sprits and stays, and towed them willy-nilly to sea. Biddle's failure was a loss of face for the United States. Emperor Komei ascended the throne, demanded that Japan's defences be impregnable, and ordered the government to retain the policy of keeping foreigners out. In 1851 the Baltimore clipper, *Sarah Boyd*, arrived at Okinawa with a Japanese fisherman who was returning to his motherland, in the face of the death-law against returning citizens, after a seven years' stay in the US. Manjiro, it was his name, had learned English, basic navigation and mathematics while in the US. In Nagasaki, the shogun made good use of him, placing him in charge of American intelligence for the government.

The shoguns were highly conscious of how threatening some Western values were to Eastern societies. They were also fearful of the West's military power. In 1842 the shoguns had seen how Britain had fought and won a war on the China coast for British traders' right to sell opium to the Chinese masses after the Dutch had introduced the poppy to China. When the Japanese samurai conquered Taiwan in 1895 they found 14 per cent of the Taiwanese natives addicted to opium. The ruthlessly efficient efforts of the Japanese police had, by 1935, reduced addiction to less than one half of one per cent of the population. The Hong Kong colony is the result of the English opium war in China. Japanese concern at Western intrusion increased when they heard that the American,

Commodore Mathew Calbraith Perry, with his fleet of two warships and two side-wheelers with a total man-power of 560, was about to land at the harbour in July 1853. When Perry finally arrived with a note from US President Millard Fillmore addressed to "the Emperor", he demanded the "opening" of Japan to "normal" civilised commercial intercourse. Receiving no reply from Shogun Iyeyoshi, he departed empty-handed, only to return eight months later, fortified by a larger squadron and armed with a persuasive array of expensive gifts for the Emperor and his royal household.

Perry was an arrogant, imperious, exponent of Manifest Destiny imperialism. The new shogun during Perry's return, Iyesada, neglected to transfer these gifts to the Emperor, but signed the Treaty of Kanagawa, which conceded virtually all the American demands. This and later treaties opened major Japanese ports to foreign commerce. They specified and limited tariffs. Japan was compelled to concede to unreasonable demands, among which were that Americans and Europeans accused of crime in the islands be tried by their own consular courts. Americans further stipulated, and Japan agreed, that all persecution of Christianity would henceforth cease in the island empire. The US further offered to sell to Japan such arms and battleships as she might need, and to lend it officers and skilled personnel for the instruction of this warrior nation in the arts of war.[56] These were clearly humiliating treaties, and Japanese memory did not easily erase these extraterritoriality treaties until after World War II.

Even as Perry was seeking atonement from the shoguns for past Japanese miscreancy, a huge black population in the US enjoyed none of the rights that Perry's mission was demanding from the Japanese on behalf of Euro-American nationals, too lofty to be subjected to Japanese sovereignty and judicial system. Interestingly enough, Takahashi Korekiyo (1854-1936) who was born in the year Perry left Japan for the last time, and who rose to serve six terms as Minister of Finance of Japan, was once sold in San Francisco (1867) by his host family into slavery. He was freed by his friends at the age of 14 and returned home just after the Tokugawa Shogunate was overthrown. It is possible, at any rate, that of the hundreds of

Perry's sailors and crew that arrived in Japan to impose treaty conditions, perhaps a handful were black slaves labouring on deck. The prominence with which Americans displayed their negro servants on the appointed day when Commodore Perry met with the shogun indicates the charade that Americans were willing to engage their blacks in "taming" the Japanese. Wrote Perry's confidante, Rev. Francis L. Hawke, who was requested and supervised by Perry himself to compile and edit the voluminous notes of the US naval squadron's visit to Japan:

> On either side of the Commodore marched a tall, well-formed negro, who, armed to the teeth, acted as his personal guard. These blacks, selected for the occasion, were two of the best-looking fellows of their colour that the squadron could furnish. All this parade was but for effect.[57]

While all this parading of blacks was only but for effect, it also reflected, simultaneously, on the nature of American society at this time in history — in 1853 and 1854 slavery was still very much alive in the south of the United States. The next time the Japanese were to see black soldiers was a hundred years later in the Asian battlefields during the Second World War, when African soldiers, in a totally misguided mission, confronted the Japanese Imperial Army in Burma. (Africans were fighting not to avenge their defeat at the hands of Europeans at the battles of Burmi, Omdurman, Segu, Tabora, Ijebu, Umgungudlovu, Kumasi, Arochukwu, Maji-Maji, Mashonaland, Matabeleland, etc. They were fighting to consolidate the power of their erstwhile colonisers, conquerors and one-time enslavers, white European and American imperial powers.) Three years after Perry left Japan, the US Supreme Court held, in **Dred Scott v. Sanford** (19 Howard 393), that African slaves and their descendants, whether emancipated or not, were considered an inferior class of beings, "unfit to associate with the white race ... and so far inferior that they had no rights which the white man was bound to respect". In parading his set of black "inferior beings" with him, Perry was clearly emulating Portuguese Jesuits and merchants who paraded their black slaves when they first arrived in Japan and had audience with the shoguns. Since it created a fascinating spectacle with the Japanese then, so must the trick be repeated now, Perry must have reasoned. Moreover, Perry had known that the Japanese were somehow intrigued by blacks, otherwise other than for "effect" there was no need to bring black slaves to Japan. Perry, however, was not new to dealing with blacks. In 1843 he had policed the settlement in Liberia, by the American Colonization Society. Not only Perry was a good student of the comings and goings of the Portuguese in Japan, so were the Japanese good students; they were learning the art of dealing skilfully with Africans in commercial relations.

**TOKUGAWA JAPANESE IN AFRICA**

As the European and American powers increased their traffic to Japan, the Tokugawa Shogunate realized that the old Japan was about to expire, and there was nothing the Japanese could do, but to come to a systematic understanding with the Western powers. It was in this context that the Tokugawa Shogunate agreed to exchange envoys with Britain.

In December 1860 the shogunate dispatched an embassy to Great Britain. Along the way aboard the British H.M.S. *Odin*, the Tokugawa envoys stopped in Africa. The three principal envoys — Takenouchi Shimotsuke-no-Kami, Matsudaira Iwami-no-Kami, and Kiogoku Noto-no-Kami — together with 34 of their followers consisting of secretaries, interpreters, doctors, barbers and cooks arrived on the African coast of Suez. At Suez they disembarked and travelled overland by train to Alexandria in Egypt before they continued by another ship. In Africa they saw spectacular wonders, among which were the trains and railway — or, as they called the latter, a "steam-carriage road". Envoy Matsudaira's diarist, Ichikawa, with the meticulousness of a termite, recorded everything of importance that the Japanese saw and experienced, not only in Africa, but at all the stops between Kobe and London.

The Japanese today manufacture the world's fastest trains, but of the train they saw, in Northeast Africa in 1862, the Japanese recorder not only observed some things through hyperbolic lenses, but noted the details even of the surroundings through which the train passed:

> The steam-power of the carriage at the head of it can run like lightning 1 000 or 10 000 miles, with a train of carriages three hundred yards long behind it. At the side of the road, at every twenty yards, are planted posts about 18 feet high, on which are hung in small or great numbers the lightning-news-long-wires (telegraph). If there be a river in the road, an iron or stone bridge is thrown across, if they meet with a hill, they pierce its belly and make a tube-like road through it.[58]

The Japanese contingent was wonder-struck, not only by the train and telegraph wires, but also by the pyramids they saw in Egypt.

Of the local Africans and Arabs in Cairo and Alexandria — like the curly-haired black natives they saw in Colombo (Sri Lanka) — the Japanese were not impressed:

> This Alexandria was formerly a great and splendid place; the streets are broad and the houses crowded together; but the customs of the people are extremely stupid; they are, moreover, very lazy in the business of life, and therefore, the place is going to ruin which is also the state of Cairo.

Little did the Japanese know that this "stupid" nation would be one of the three African states to declare war on Japan during World War II; nor did they expect that the trade between Japan and Egypt would increase tremendously in the interwar period, and that Japan would be projected to surpass the United States as Egypt's largest aid donor by the year 1990. After seeing their first train in Africa, the Japanese diarist looked at the spectacular sights and lazy locals, and mused poetically: "To adopt what is proper, and to reject that which is bad, how fine a thing this is". The Tokugawa officials were

53

not actually the first Japanese to touch Africa in the 1860s. Approximately a year before the Matsudaira mission arrived in Egypt, another Japanese mission that had gone to the United States was returning via Africa and stopped in Angola and St Vincent Island only there to meet an African who had once lived in Japan and could speak Japanese;[59] suggesting, of course, that cultural and human intercourse between the Japanese and Africans had continued since the mid-16th century.

Despite their opening to Great Britain the shogunate, in any event, had lost credibility by now. The massive military presence of the western foreigners had not precipitated the fall of the Tokugawa Shogunate however. It had merely impressed upon the Japanese the foreigners' technological skills and capabilities as well as their military power and prowess. The civil wars that were raging on in Japan picked up steam after 1864, almost simultaneously as the American Civil War in 1860-1865. The Japanese Imperial Army fought to overthrow the shoguns. In January 1867, Emperor Komei died, either from smallpox or from poisoning — his death remained unannounced for four days, his funeral took place on the 33rd day after death, almost, but not quite, a record however, since Emperor Go-Tsuchi-Mikado, in 1500, holds the record, remaining unburied for forty-four days. Shogun Keiki surrendered, and Shogun Tokugawa Yoshinobu with his military retinue of 30 000 men fell to the Imperial forces outside Kyoto. On 1 January 1868 the new "Era of Meiji" officially began when the fifteen-year-old Emperor Meiji Tenno (Matsuhito), 1852-1912, son of Emperor Komei, and Emperor Hirohito's grandfather, ascended the throne, and became the 122nd Emperor of the Empire of the Rising Sun. The next year, in 1869, the Suez Canal was opened, and thus the distance between Europe and Japan was cut short drastically and, consequently, a new and more convenient African stop was established by the Japanese, from where Japanese trading companies were to launch their commercial ventures to the African colonies. With the Meiji modernizers Africa ceased to be the Far Continent. Between 1885 and 1960 Africa became for Japan not a mere half-way station anymore, but a full-time destination.

## MEIJI JAPAN ENTERS AFRICA

Meiji (i.e. Enlightened Rule) was indeed an enlightened ruler for Japan, since the dramatic technological and economic changes that are in Japan today have their roots in the Meiji Reign. It was this reign that had expanded the Tokugawa Shogunate reconnection of Africans and Japanese. Accounts of the rise of modern Japan and the Meiji role focus only on the impact of the West. Hardly a word is said about the role of Africa in the industrialisation of Japan. The Meiji young rulers supplanted the shogunate slogan (*sonno-joi* = "drive out the Barbarians! Revere the Emperor") with the new one *fukoka kyohei* ("a wealthy and strongly armed nation"). Japan had to grow strong before she could expand overseas. So unnerved was Japan by the imperial bullying tactics of the Western Perrys that she resolved to catch-up fast. To do so meant that she had to open herself to foreign expertise, experience and economic trade. Thus Emperor Meiji declared Tokyo open to all foreigners. Armed with this new westernising authority, the modernisers undertook a rapid transformation of their country. Englishmen supervised the construction of railways, erection of telegraphs and construction of a navy. Americans were busy establishing a universal school system; Germany organized medicine and public health systems. Frenchmen recast laws and trained the army. Italians, too, forgiven for Roman Catholic intrusions of earlier centuries, were brought in to instruct the Japanese in sculpture and painting.[60] Yet Japan, as the Edo Era clearly shows, had a much more sophisticated technological potential and socio-economic capacities to be a mere imitator of the West.

Hirobumi Ito and Kaoru Inouye, two of the legion of Meiji modernisers, braved their way through a variety of obstacles to Europe to study its industries and institutions and to inspect its railroads, steamships, telegraphs and battleships. (The Japanese diarist had by now disseminated the knowledge he acquired during his trip.) Emperor Meiji himself sent all but two of the fifteen sons and nephews of his father's advisor, Prince Asahiro, away to Europe to study not only the suitability of Occidental industry for Oriental society, but also to learn the western arts of war, some of them even went to witness European wars in Africa. At Sandhurst, St Cyr, Brest, Dartmouth, the Polytechnique and Gottingen, these sons and nephews learned military physics and gathered together groups of poorer Japanese students to brave the loneliness of European and American societies. In 1871, after fiefs had been abolished, Iwakura Tomomi took a mission abroad to explore the possibilities of treaty revision. In Washington the group which included Okubo Toshimichi, Kido Koin, Ito Hirobumi as well as Iwakura was lectured on the inadvisability of such treaty changes. The mission became then more concerned with the acquisition of knowledge than with diplomatic negotiations. In London Ito inspected factories; in Berlin Iwakura listened to the virtues of *real-politik* from the German Chancellor, Otto von Bismarck, even as the latter was plotting the partition of Africa. In Germany the Japanese fell in love with the German political system — even with its African colonies, after 1885. When these emissaries and half-westernised Oriental princes returned home they became part of the Imperial council of advisors.

It became a patriotic duty to absorb the material strength of the West without losing the spiritual integrity of Japanism. The century following the Meiji Restoration was truly an era in which Japan welcomed industrial transfers with open arms: she relied on the importation of technology, goods, know-how, capital and management methods. Foreign experts (*oyatoi gaiko kujin*) in science and technology came in numbers. One such expert was Edmund Morel (1841-1871) who arrived from Britain in 1870. He immersed himself in his engineering work with such fervour that he soon fell victim to tuberculosis and died one year after he arrived in Japan — just like a Japanese medical scientist, Hideyo Noguchi, was to die in West Africa one year after he arrived in Ghana in 1928. The Meiji leaders understood that knowledge was to be sought in the West, whose goodwill was essential if the unequal treaties were to be revised, or, in the event of war, whose secret of technological skills and military power was to be conquered. More than 130 foreign teachers and engineers were employed every year from 1871 to 1879 by the Meiji

Government,[61] but it was not enough merely to hire foreign teachers, the Japanese had to learn the science themselves by undertaking study missions abroad. These missions were mainly undertaken through the activities of the specialised trading companies during the Meiji period, some of which were to later play a crucial commercial role in Egypt, Kenya, Uganda, and Tanganyika. The already mentioned 1871 Tomoni Mission in search of the Western magic wand[62] reflected the anxieties that Japan felt at the factor of Western intrusion in their society. Japan's modernisation process was such that in 1870 the British legation in Tokyo formally complained to the Japanese government that Japanese brewers were even copying the labels on British beer bottles.[63] The Japanese looked mostly to Europe rather than to the US because the period 1846-1876 was a time when American science was just beginning, and was mediocre in comparison as well as unpromising.[64]

The point here is that it was during these visits to Europe, which were undertaken by ship since it was the sole means of travel overseas, that Japanese came in contact with Africans once again. Yet these visits were usually restricted to the duration of the ship's taking on of supplies during their African stops. Naturally, the knowledge of Africa gained from these contacts remained peripheral since these contacts concerned only such things as historic spots and sights in the vicinity of such cities as Cairo, Cape Town, Mombasa, Luanda and Leopoldville (now Kinshasa). Only those parts of Africa lying along major shipping routes became of interest to the Europe-bound Japanese westernisers. It was in this sense that the Japanese Foreign Minister, Toshio Kimura, in addressing a group of African diplomats in Tokyo stated that

> Japan's first but very slight contact with Africa was made about a century ago, from the socalled Meiji Restoration of 1868 when Japan opened its door to foreign countries in an effort to modernize itself — Japan's contact with Africa up to the termination of World War II had been considerably limited. In those days Japanese, in order to seek knowledge

on modern technology, crossed the seas to Europe. Some of them stopped at African ports on the way to replenish their fuel and supplies.[65]

We have seen of course that the Tokugawa Japanese earlier re-opened the Africa-Japan contacts through Egypt, through which the Meiji Japanese mainly entered Africa. Even Cape Town declined in significance after 1869 because the Suez Canal further cut the distance between Japan and Western Europe. But both Cairo and Cape Town and East Africa were to later develop into strong markets for Japanese salesmen. In fact as I show in the next chapter, Japan's involvement with Africa was not slight at all. The Meiji Europe-bound Japanese discovered something in Africa that was more than a mere historic sight-stop. It was to permanently cement the ties that have bound Japan and Africa since, even as the Meiji Japanese tended to exhibit a condescending attitude towards blacks as the Japanese scholar Terutaro Nishino observed: "Africa was introduced to the Japanese after the re-opening of the country as an undeveloped dark continent in which cannibal savage people lived."[66] But on the whole the Japanese traders widened the window of familiarity with Africa, albeit through the route of colonial markets.

## CHAPTER 2

# JAPAN AND COLONIAL AFRICA: 1885-1960

---

*During the period Africa was a colony of Western Europe, Africa was, for Japan, nothing but an export market for consumer goods which centered mainly on textile products* ... Japanese Ministry of Foreign Affairs.

1961 Diplomatic Blue Book

*If the Japanese are to facilitate the* authentic *development of Africa, they must be made to meet Africans on an African plane. This means the Japanese must understand the history of colonial exploitation* ...

Professor William D. Perdue[67]

*...(I)t is a historical fact that Japan participated in the colonial exploitation of Africa. Japan's relationship with Africa was not noncolonial, peaceful, or reciprocal, but rather imperialistic · and colonial in nature.*

Professor Jun Morikawa[68]

*... In her commercial relations with Africa, Japan was never a colonial factor, never a political force nor a military presence, never an imperialist predator, only a pro-Japanese search for export-import markets.*

Author

Doi Shigenori, a Japanese scholar, has noted that there is no appropriate historical point from which to begin a study of Japanese-African relations. In his (Japanese language) study of the history of relations between Japan and East Africa, Shigenori arbitrarily begins with and dwells on the 1944-1945 Japanese-African battles in the Burma Front.[69] Although he does note that Japanese prostitutes around 1900 were plying their wares in Zanzibar, Shigenori however confines his study to the King's African Rifles against the Japanese Imperial Army. As the reader is already aware, despite facing the same dilemma as Shigenori, this study is burdened by no such difficulties in deciding the point of departure for the study of Japanese-Africans relations.

In this work I make a distinction between *European colonial rule* and *Japanese commercial role in Africa*. Some Japanese scholars (e.g. Morikawa) confuse this Japanese commercial presence with the precolonial role of a collaborator. Granted that there were one or two Japanese scholars in 1918 who advocated that since Germany was at war with Japan, the latter should seize German colonies in Africa;[70] granted also that Japan begged to no avail to be admitted to the European Club of Colonizers of Africa. Yet Japan never played a colonial role in Africa, however extensive her commercial activities, in spite of Meiji Japan's expansionism. This is precisely what the Japanese Ministry of Foreign Affairs has repeatedly attempted to explain, yet without making its case clear enough to dispel the fog about the nature of Japanese involvement in Africa, at least for the first sixty years of this century. Rarely have the numerous studies on Japan and her economic, military and political engagements world-wide treated the phenomenon of her role in Africa. Many studies betray a peculiar unawareness of the long existence of a relationship between Japan and Africa. Moreover, Japan's role in this scramble has been obscured by a number of factors, not the least among which are Japanese unstudied statements. As recently as February 1986 a Japanese Ministry of Foreign Affairs official, Noboru Nakahira, laconically although correctly stated: "Japan is geographically distant from Africa, and has no history of colonialism there ..."[71] Even some Japanese scholars have taken to echoing this line of thought dutifully without emendation or significant reflection, arguing that the Japan-Africa relations are unencumbered by the shadow of a colonial past,[72] and thus failed to substantiate these assertions, and hence unwittingly perpetuated the colonial analogy by default. Sufficient statistical data and other historical information clearly show that Japan was *not* a colonial force in Africa, merely a trading participant in the economy.

Concomitant with this colonial absence is, in the Japan-African contacts, the absence of the stigma of racism that has governed European-African contacts. It is rare to find Africans who regard the Japanese as racist, as they would most likely respond regarding white-black, European-African ties. Even the most bitter African prisoners of war of the Japanese in Burma never considered the Japanese as colonial masters in Africa; at best they considered them merely as fellow-travellers out to cut a commercial deal at the expense, largely, of European colonial overlords. Western, and some Japanese, scholars have made the claim that Japanese attitudes towards blacks are as racist as, if not worse than, those of the West. In turn, some Japanese scholars, and political figures, had argued, rather unconvincingly, about the Japanese "clean-hands" role in Africa.

Yet the Japanese "clean hands" theory should not be dismissed for two reasons: one, in comparison with, say, Japan's relations with contemporary Korea or Formosa, which are heavily marked by a colonial past, her relations with Africa are testimony to the "purity" of Japan's role in the African colonies; two, in comparison with the European imperial powers in Africa, Japan's role is unblemished, since Japan had not a single formal political colony in Africa, and thus on the *diplomatic* level, her African role between 1885 and 1960 is unimpeachable. But we cannot say that Japan's "clean hands" role in Africa is thus equatable to, say, that of Ireland, Canada, Poland, Rumania, Sweden, Finland, Iceland, Norway, etc. These nations also had *no* formal political colonies in Africa. They had not even an informal commercial presence in Africa, a factor which cannot be cited regarding Japan. Clearly then, comparing Japan and

Sweden, or Poland and Japan, with regard to the African colonial question is like comparing night and day in terms of the presence of sunlight, for the simple reason that the European scramble for African colonies was first and foremost an economic process that was buttressed by a politically violent subjugation of the locals. It would be sheer casuistry to mount as a consequence a theory of Japanese imperial aggression against Africans which was nearly analogous to the European variety. In fact it was Egypt rather than Japan which sought to imperially colonise, militarily subdue, and politically control another African people, with short but nasty and disastrous consequences.

This is to say that Japan's *non-colonial role* in Africa is no more than that, a commercial role of immense magnitude. *In Africa, Japan neither ran with the colonised hares nor chased with the colonising hounds*; all she did was merely to look after her interests with the (reluctant) help of both the African locals and the imperial powers of Europe. Like Germany before 1914, Japan certainly benefited a good deal more from gaining access to the markets and materials of African colonies (especially of the British Empire), without having to shoulder the political responsibility and financial burden of "developing" and administering them. Of course Japan's absent diplomatic role in colonial Africa was neither for lack of will nor for want of desire. It was fortuitous. It was due mainly to two reasons: one, opportunity. Japan came relatively late to the African scene — that is, in comparison to Europe — for reasons I have already adduced in the previous chapter (including the insignificant but infamous nautical-geographical distance between her and Africa),[73] and for the reasons of her preoccupation, internally, with her industrialisation (1869-1900), as well as her engagements with the external question of the newly acquired Eastern responsibilities: her own empire-building in China and Russia after defeating those countries. Between 1875 and 1920 Japan had added some 112 000 square miles to her home territory, thus certifying her empire building.

Secondly, and perhaps more importantly, the 1858 unequal treaties were only terminated in 1899 when the new treaties ended extraterritorial privileges for foreigners in Japan. While these treaties were in operation, it is hardly likely Japan would have had the audacity to venture through predatory imperialism into the African colonies, which clearly were the preserve of Europe. Moreover, in the 1894-1895 Sino-Japanese War, Japan had acquired a new prestige — the victory over China in 1895 led to her war with Russia (1904-1905), and the decade 1895-1905 found Japan firmly committed to the consolidation of her imperial gains. In 1910 she formally annexed Korea and subsequently crushed all military resistance. By the end of the Meiji Period two years later, the "Celestial Empire" had achieved some equality with the West, and was clearly the strongest military and imperialist power in Asia. Yet the Japanese Empire was too weak to undertake (even if she had wished) a long-distance imperial adventure to the African colonies which, as already stated, had been securely locked in the hegemonic sphere of influence of Western Europe. Considering this relative weakness *vis-a-vis* European imperial powers already entrenched in the African colonies, Japan's entry to the African colonial economy of necessity had to come under the umbrella of European imperial powers. The memory of the bombardments of Shimonoseki and Kagoshima by the United States and British warships in 1862-1863 had been a grim reminder of Japan's weakness in facing the West. Industrialisation thus became a major concern of state policy in the Meiji Restoration, sometimes called the Revolution or Renovation. The entrepreneurial responsibility fell upon the state in Japan's economic development.

After Japan became a colonial power, following her victories in China and Russia, she shifted her attention to Africa in search of models of colonial administration, as well as scouring for raw materials for her continuing industrial expansion. By 1889 Japan had adopted German methods of administration, of military organisation and of economic control. So it was in the tradition of her faddish copying of things Western (particularly German) that she looked to the African colonies to learn and study how to micromanage her own colonial natives in Formosa, Manchuria and later Korea. In this regard the so-called German East Africa (i.e.

Tanganyika including Rwanda and Burundi) became of interest to the Japanese — and together with Kenya, Uganda, as well as with Egypt, Mozambique, Ethiopia, Sudan, and South Africa, Tanganyika played a crucial role in feeding the Japanese — especially the textile — industries in need of raw materials. But in East Africa Japan became interested instead in cotton markets rather than in acquiring colonies. The so-called British East Africa, German East Africa, Lower Congo, Upper Congo Basin, and even Zanzibar became the new focus of activity. Already active in ivory and rubber exports, these areas had acted like a magnet to draw the international rivalries of their respective metropolitan government, and became devices to advance the cause of Empire and European control over interior markets. In mercantilist doctrines imperialism meant the *acquisition* and *use* of colonies as a base of supplies needed by the mother country, as a source of raw materials that could be worked up into manufactures for export, and as a market for the products of the metropolitan society. In practice this meant the simultaneous political control of the destiny of the natives. It is through the reluctant tutelage of European powers that Japan was introduced to African commerce, specifically by the Congo Basin Treaties.

## THE CONGO BASIN TREATIES

After the industrial revolution, with its incessant demand for raw materials and markets, had gained momentum in Western Europe, European powers, talking mysteriously about the geo-political "vacuum" of Africa, saw African colonisation, exploitation and settlement as the necessary counterweight. In the 1880s the world was witnessing two concurrent major social phenomena: the rapid expansion and culmination of the Industrial Revolution in Western Europe on the one hand, and, on the other, Meiji Japan's feverish campaign to industrialise, in order to catch up with the West in everything from beer brewery to ginnery, gunnery, telegraphy, photography, painting, etc. — and thus proving that industrialisation was not a western monopoly.[74] The two phenomena, intricably interlocked, found Africa the apotheosis of their need gratification for raw materials, cheap labour and new markets. At the same time, the European scramble for Africa brought the African economic productive capacities to the needs and demands of European industrial economies by converting African colonies into European satellite economies, (Table 2.1) with the consequent flood of European settlers in Africa.

Africa's external commerce expanded greatly with the penetration of colonial investments in such infrastructural projects as agriculture, transport, extractive industries, distributive systems and export-import services.

### TABLE 2.1
### REGIONAL DISTRIBUTION OF WORLD TRADE 1876-1960

|  | Trade as % of Total World Trade | | % change |
|---|---|---|---|
|  | 1876-1880 | 1960 | 1876-1960 |
| World | 100,0 | 100,0 | — |
| Europe | 66,9 | 51,4 | - 23,1 |
| N. America | 9,5 | 18,4 | + 93,6 |
| C. and S. America | 5,4 | 7,6 | + 40,7 |
| Asia | 12,9 | 14,3 | + 10,8 |
| Africa | 1,9 | 5,5 | + 189,4 |
| Oceania | 3,4 | 2,4 | - 29,4 |

Sources: A.G. Kenwood and A.L. Lougheed, *The Growth of the International Economy, 1820-1960 (1971), p. 93; U.N. Yearbook of International Trade Statistics (1966).*

In fact as Table 2.1 shows, between 1880 and 1960, Africa's share of world trade grew by 189 per cent. Japan, as we shall see, played an important role also. East Africa became the opportunists' "sphere of influence": Anglo-French, Anglo-Portuguese, Anglo-German, etc., rivalries were rampant. Tensions were sometimes connived by entrepreneurial opportunists such as Carl Peters of the German

Society of Colonization and his German East Africa Company, William MacKinnon and his Imperial British East Africa Company, as well as by the king of all these imperialist opportunists, King Leopold II of Belgium. All major — and several minor — European states wanted new imperial possessions from which they could draw raw materials to feed their industrial revolutions. They were inspired also by a desire to establish new markets to carve out new strategic interests as well as to respond to the "divine" mission to "civilise" Africa. The political subjugation of Africans became the necessary prop in this quest.

In 1884 a veritable scramble for African territories began and culminated in the partitioning of the African continent into a bewildering mosaic of European colonial possessions. (See 1885 and 1895 maps.) This wave of colony grabbing in the 1880s continued right down to the outbreak of the First World War. The resultant European rivalries caused the imperial powers to position and manoeuvre for special rights and territories in the various parts of Africa. Hence the convening of the Berlin Conference of 14 nations on African Affairs organised by the German Chancellor, Otto Von Bismarck, and the French Premier, Jules Ferry in 1884-1885. The purpose of this conference was to agree upon the orderly partitioning of Africa in general, and to decide the future of that vast territory of the Congo in particular — thus the Congo Basin Treaties. Rivalry between French, English, and German trading companies began in and around the basin of the Niger River, which lies at the base of the West African bulge. The conference itself had developed out of the abortive Anglo-Portuguese Treaty of 1884 concerning sovereignty over the Congo Basin. Of the many decisions taken at the conference the establishment of the Congo Free State under King Leopold II of Belgium as his personal possession is not our immediate concern here. The Congo Free State began, however, as the International Association of the Congo which was transformed in 1885 as the Congo Free State. In 1908 after a period of brutal methods of exploitation of Africans were used in the rubber, ivory, and slave trades, it was taken over by Belgium. Idiosyncratic and oxymoronic contradictions implicit in a

"Free State" being the personal possession of an absentee landlord should not detain us, since it is the logical outcome of imperialism's gerrymandering. At any rate, being anachronistic, Leopold, like a 17th century monarch, identified the interests of his dynasty with those of the national economy. It is for this that he was prepared to invest the fortune of his family in the colonial enterprise of the International Association of the Congo. Colonial rivalry and conflict of financial interests were the characteristics of the convening imperialism in Berlin that November 1884 to February 1885.

Of immediate concern to us is that the agreement which was legally codified as the Berlin Act, 1885, whose Article 35 recognised, among others, freedom of trade and of transit as well as the establishment of authority in regions occupied by the signatory powers, became the gambit by which Japan entered Africa however antagonistic European powers were towards her. Article 1 of this treaty stated that the "trade of all nations shall enjoy complete freedom."[75] Two provisions of the act laid down the procedures to be followed by imperial and would-be imperial powers: Acquisitions of territories would henceforth have to be formally announced, and would not be internationally recognised unless the claiming power could demonstrate *de facto* physical occupation of the colony. This put Japan at both an advantage and a disadvantage: by having no political power to impose her wish all she could do was beg for admission to the Club of Colonizers, which admission could not, and was not, granted, since she was a non-white power. At the same time, the military, financial and political motives of the Meiji westernisers after 1873 had consciously included the desire to create new exports.[76] But Japan was not a signatory power at Berlin in 1884, merely a beneficiary power as the rest of this chapter will amply demonstrate.

The Berlin Treaty was the first of a series of the Congo Basin Treaties — others were signed and ratified in 1886, 1887, 1890, 1891 and 1894. The last of these treaties was the Convention of St Germaine-en-Laye in 1919 by Britain, Belgium, Portugal and Japan. Both the US and Italy signed but did not ratify. Japan ratified in April 1922.

# MAP 2.1
# AFRICA in 1830

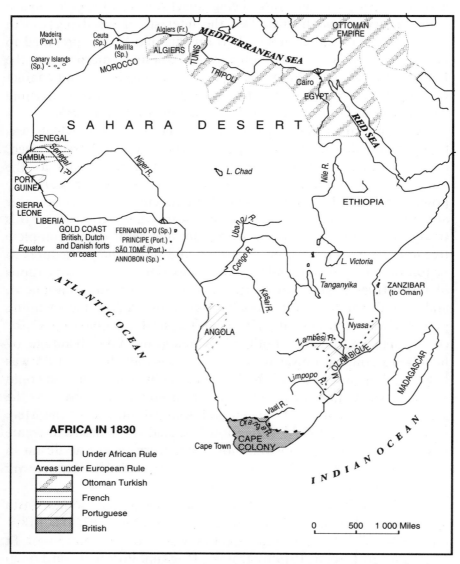

AFRICA IN 1830

☐ Under African Rule

Areas under European Rule

▨ Ottoman Turkish

⋯ French

▧ Portuguese

▨ British

0    500    1 000 Miles

Source:    *The Columbia History of the World*. New York: Harper & Row,
1972.

# MAP 2.2
# AFRICA in 1880

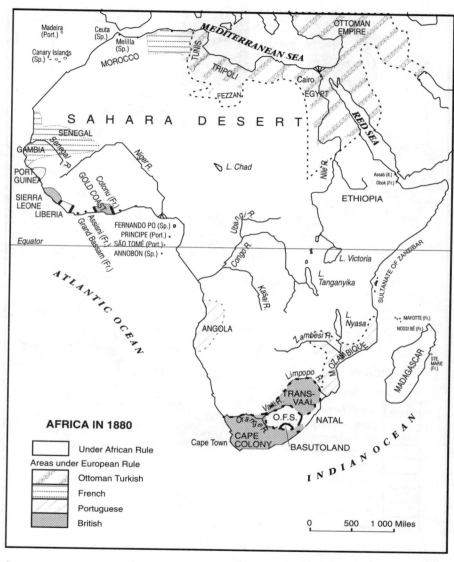

AFRICA IN 1880

☐ Under African Rule

Areas under European Rule

▤ Ottoman Turkish

▦ French

▨ Portuguese

▩ British

0    500    1 000 Miles

Source: *The Columbia History of the World.* New York: Harper & Row, 1972.

# MAP 2.3
# AFRICA in 1885

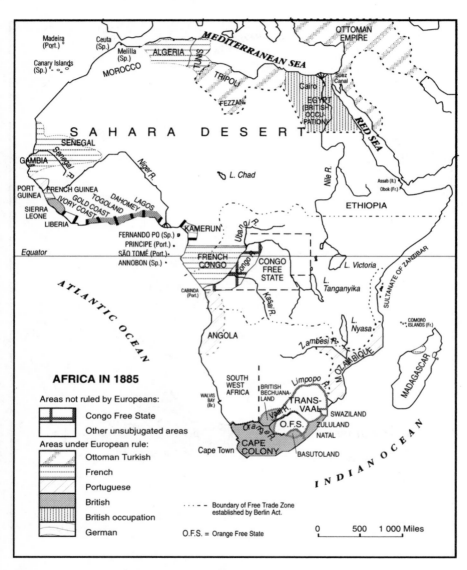

Source: *The Columbia History of the World.* New York: Harper & Row, 1972.

# MAP 2.4
# AFRICA in 1895

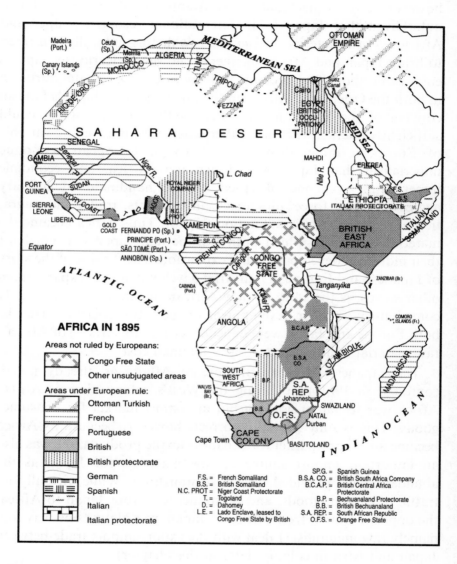

Source: *The Columbia History of the World.* New York: Harper & Row, 1972.

All these agreements theoretically guaranteed equality of access to the markets of the whole region of the participants. In reality, however, devious machinations constantly sought to elbow Japan out. Given that Japan is an international resource pauper and Africa is a raw materials *taikun*, the two factors naturally conspired to bring Japan and Africa together — however vicariously Japan's entry came about. But because of the nature of Occidental intrusion in both the Orient and Africa on the one hand, and Japan's faddish copying of the West on the other, neither of the factors could sufficiently interact with each other outside the intervening variable of European imperialism. It is through European economic imperialism that Japan was drawn into Africa, and economic imperialism, someone observed, is the handmaid of military aggression since force, diplomacy, investments, trade, and migration are employed in combination thereof. Thus Africa became the material base from which both Europe and Japan depended for their industrial development and expansion. The flipside of the story of Japanese and European industrial development and expansion, in other words, is the story of how African material base was highly contributory to other development of these two societies. That is, both Europe and Japan were dependencies — of sorts — of Africa's raw material wealth extracted at a minimal cost.

The Japanese Ministry of Foreign Affairs as already noted, confessed in 1961 that during the West's colonisation of Africa, Africa was to Japan nothing but an export market for consumer goods. This is only partially correct, however, because as Africa became an export market for Japanese textile products, she was also an important import source of raw materials for Japan as the abundant data provided clearly demonstrate. While virtually all traffic of capital, goods, and personnel was from Japan to Africa, the opposite traffic, from Africa to Japan, was almost one-way too, namely raw materials. (I deal with the export-import trade between Japan and African colonies later in this chapter).

This dual traffic was facilitated by the Congo Basin Treaties, for on the political-diplomatic level they provided the European powers with the legitimation of their hegemony over Africa. The European colonial administration militarily "pacified" the native resistance. In order to show this European colonial cushion for Japan in Africa, let us first recall that by 1889 Japan was such an admirer of Germany that she did not only adopt the German constitution for her parliamentary system, she also adapted German methods of political administration, military organisation and economic control. Secondly, if we look at how Germany "pacified" African resistance and made African peasantry amenable to Japanese commercial trade with these colonies, understanding of the Japanese role will be greatly facilitated.

By the 1890s Imperial Germany had established colonies not only in Tanganyika (then including Rwanda and Burundi) but as far south as Ovambo-, Herero- and Namaland (what became known as German Southwest Africa, and is today known as Namibia). Tricks, evasions, and brute force were employed by the Germans. It was the Rhenish missionaries who persuaded the Nama chief, Joseph Fredericks, to sign two initial treaties with the German business-man Luderitz, and these "treaties" gave over a coastal strip of land about 200 miles long. In the second of these treaties the coastal strip was defined as being "twenty miles in breadth". *But what was 20 miles to the African chief was not 20 miles to the German thief.* The Nama chief thought that 20 miles meant the only kind they knew of — 20 *English* miles; while the Germans were resolved to make it mean 20 *German* miles, and one German mile equals 4 $^5/_8$ English miles. The German wrote a letter home to his imperial masters to the effect that the African chief should be left to keep thinking for the time being "that we mean English miles". Later on, Imperial Commissioner Goering (father of the Nazi leader, Herman Goering) reported to Berlin that the African group "heard with horror that according to the text of the treaty they had sold almost their whole country", which, of course, did not prevent Commissioner Goering from trying to make the "treaty" stick.[77]

Similarly, the Herero chiefs just to the north of the Namas suffered the same fate when they "sold" away huge tracts of land to the German settlers and companies. Through similar scams, fraudulent treaties, etc. the Hereros also lost virtually their entire stock. Before the arrival of the Germans in 1883, the Hereros grazed over 100 000 head of cattle, but by 1902 their livestock had been whittled down to 46 000 head, while about one hundred to two hundred German settlers who arrived empty-handed 10 years earlier, were now the proud owners of about 45 000 head of cattle. Driven to despair by the systematic looting, confiscation of their livestock, lands, and rights to the benefit of the Germans, the Herero declared outright war on the German Army on 12 January 1904. When General von Trotha finally subdued them a year later, only a small number of them had survived. When the Nama finally joined them — too late to have much impact — they too suffered a similar fate. By 1911 only 15 130 Herero out of a former total of about 80 000, and only 9 781 Nama out of about 20 000 survived. Even African groups which did not join in the fight against the Imperial German Army, such as the Bergdama, lost almost a third of their population, the Germans being unable to distinguish between them and the Herero.[78] In other parts of Africa, other African groups — for instance Ovimbundu in Angola, Mashona and Matebele in Zimbabwe in the 1890s, and the He-He in Tanganyika, etc. — suffered a similar fate.

In Tanganyika, which, as we have seen, included Rwanda and Burundi, and where (together with Uganda, Kenya, Ethiopia, Mozambique, Egypt and South Africa), Japan was to play an increasing commercial role, the Maji Maji War against the Germans in 1905-7 is yet proof enough — that European imperialism in Africa was achieved as a violent act of aggression against Africans. Beginning in the 1890s the defeated Africans adopted the *Africa-for-Africans* slogan; but Japan, naturally, clung, for reasons of expediency, to the *Africa-without-Africans* approach of the imperial powers who, of course, did not recognise the rights of Africans. While Japan was invited to play the role of an innocuous imperial factor she was not accorded the political accountability for these colonies. It is due to the absence of this political responsibility for the colonies that made the Japanese remain restricted to trade — unlike the Europeans who found, also, plenty of African men and boys who were drafted into their armies during both World War I and II.

The Japanese acquired their colonial image of Africans through imperial Europe at this juncture. The view so well described by a Japanese Africa correspondent for *Mainichi Shimbun*, a Tokyo-based newspaper, has much of its origin in colonial times:

> The average Japanese almost automatically thinks of wild animals, savage human beings acting like animals and undeveloped landscape when asked about Africa ... During my career as staff-writer on African affairs, I have actually come across a diplomatist who started to count the remaining days of his assignment immediately upon his arrival (in Africa) and quite a few diplomatists who did their job reluctantly, depending on the information by American diplomats, many businessmen who never minded calling their African employees 'nigger' and several journalists who made complaints about not being appointed a Washington correspondent, and who collected their information from American and European newspapers and magazines rather than digging it for themselves.[79]

Some Japanese scholars who made a close examination of Japanese prejudice on racial issues, found an unfavourable Japanese view of black people. In fact some western Japanalysts now contend that Japanese "attitudes towards blacks are seldom better than the views of whites and frequently worse".[80] There is more than sufficient documentation to rebut and refute the superficial analyses by these Japanese and western writers.[81] Japanese and African people have no known history of racial bigotry, conflict, or prejudice against each other outside the battles already cited. It is simply *not* an African perception that the Japanese are antiblack, despite the perception rendered by the disparaging remarks about blacks and Hispanics of the Japanese former premier, Yasuhiro Nakasone. It is in fact in this vein that the celebrated African scholar, Chinweizu, in that fascinating work *The West and The Rest of US* writes:

> The temporary defeat suffered by France, Britain and Holland in South Asia at the hands of Japan cracked the myth of white supremacy. Ah, our conquerors, who pretended to rule by the divine sanction of their white skins, could be beaten by nonwhites! An encouraging observation indeed. Besides, African troops fighting for the Allied imperialists were told they were fighting for freedom and democracy.[82]

Chinweizu's work reflects African attitudes towards the Japanese, similar to that of the Swahili author of *Graveyard Without A Cross*, who wrote of his experiences on the Burma battlefields. As the Japanese East African scholar, Professor Tsuneo Morino, who spent two years in Tanzania, recounted to me: whenever he met Africans who had fought in Burma, they would often hug him and exclaim "Oh! my brother enemy! How fierce a fighter you Japanese are!" (see also Chapter 7).

In order to justify their involvement in Africa, Europeans had distorted a still highly inaccurate Eurocentric presentation of colonial societies in Africa. They viewed these societies as no more than a

> collection of warring states and savage tribes between whom and with whom trade was impossible before colonial 'pacification'. The colonial powers, moreover, did not remove all institutional barriers to commercial intercourse — they merely replaced them with their own. Customs and exercise duties, commercial codes, currency and labor legislation, administrative structures and transport systems, all tended to operate against intercolony transactions while advancing both intracolony exchange and commerce between the colony and its European metropolis.[83]

Since imperialism was not a philanthropic charity the colonies were expected to pay for themselves. The smallness of the African purchasing power made it imperative for the imperial regimes to augment their coffers by direct taxation. Hut and poll taxes compelled many of the Africans to work for wages or to grow cash crops to earn tax money. Those without money to pay taxes were compelled to give their labour instead. Conscripted workers were forced to build railroads, work plantations, collect jungle products, and had their lands permanently expropriated. It is into such a colonial system as described above that the Japanese formally arrived in 1898 on a larger commercial scale. Japan arrived three years *after* the second partition of Africa commenced (in 1895) during which time the extension of European control met increasingly bitter African resistance. European powers, paradoxically, pre-empted Japan's military or political role in the African colonies, while facilitating her commercial role in the same colonies. It is from such an historical arrangement that I seek to show in detail that the revolution in Japanese industrial development was firmly wedded to inter-Afro-Japanese ties in commercial activities. By the end of 1897 all the leading powers of Europe had signed treaties with Japan on a footing of equality, meaning that Japan's role in African commercial trade could not formally be discriminated against as the European imperial powers had wished.

## JAPANESE TRADE WITH AFRICAN COLONIES: 1898-1941

As the Berlin Partition of Africa was going on in 1884-1885, the Japanese Government was sponsoring the formation of two formidable shipping companies — the *Nippon Yusen Kaisha* and the *Osaka Shosen Kaisha* also established 1884-1885. The Yokohama Specie Bank was founded in 1880 to serve as monetary organ for traders engaged in foreign trade. An interesting point to observe in the formation of Nihon Yusen Kaisha is that the young Tosa *samurai*, Iwasaki Yataro, who founded the Mitsubishi group, got his real start with 13 ships the Meiji Government gave him to ferry troops for the Formosan imperial expedition in 1874. After a series of mergers and further government subsidies, the original 13 multiplied into the Nihon Yusen Kaisha which today remains Japan's premier shipping line. Both shipping lines were to play a critical role in the interwar years in transporting materials and men between Japan and East Africa. The legendary geographic distance between Japan and Africa was compressed into a *monthly* run of ships between Kobe/Osaka and East Africa (Mombasa and Dar-es-Salaam especially).

Yet strangely enough, some Japanese officials in the 1980s would still argue about the prohibitive nature of the geographical distance between Africa and Japan, and thus perpetuate the logic that "Japanese relations with the countries of Africa were necessarily very sparse and limited before the war in that Africa is geographically distant from Japan and Africa was under colonial domination by the West European powers".[84] In fact the very distance between Japan and Africa is something that augurs so well for Japan's relations with Africa. That is, *despite* the distance, Japan *did* forge some relations with Africans however limited the colonial commerce between them. Japanese contacts with Africans were indeed limited *precisely* because the buffer zone, European colonial governments, were the interlocutor between the Japanese and the Africans. The decade of the 1890s had marked a turning point in the development of the Japanese economy. The navigation law, promulgated in 1896, accelerated the inauguration of overseas navigation by Japanese shipping companies. In 1897 Japan became a gold standard country. Until 1887, about 87 per cent of Japan's export trade and 88 per cent of her import trade was handled by foreign merchants. In 1900, the foreigners' transactions in exports were 63 per cent and Japanese transactions 37 per cent, the former's import transactions had decreased 61 per cent and the Japanese transactions increased 39 per cent. The more the Japanese controlled their trade the faster Japanese-African trade was consolidated.

In 1896-1897 the Japanese Government established the Yawatu Iron and Steel Works which began production in 1901. Although it was established largely for military purposes, the Yawatu in time came to play a significant commercial role in Africa. This concern was a pre-eminent state-operated enterprise to the degree that it dominated the steel industry for many years. Until 1933 it churned out 60 per cent of all the pig iron produced in Japan Proper and almost half the steel.[85] Preparing for the "Chinese incident" of 1937 the government in 1934 extended even further its control by the merger of Yawatu with six *zaibatsu* firms to form the Japan Iron Manufacturing Company. Two years after the establishment of the Yawatu Iron Works, trade between Africa and Japan began in earnest, and continued to increase during the remaining part of the Meiji Period (Table 2.2).

In 1900 the Japanese exports to Africa were a middling 278 000 yen, while her imports, as we can see from Table 2.2, had risen 5,28 times.

## TABLE 2.2
## MEIJI JAPAN TRADE WITH AFRICA 1898-1912[a]
### *(Unit = 1 000 yen)*

| Year | Exports | Imports |
|------|---------|---------|
| 1898 | 116 | 356 |
| 1899 | 661 | 939 |
| 1900 | 278 | 1 468 |
| 1901 | 308 | 1 890 |
| 1902 | 449 | 2 418 |
| 1903 | 323 | 2 402 |
| 1904 | 419 | 2 476 |
| 1905 | 284 | 2 999 |
| 1906 | 379 | 1 670 |
| 1907 | 386 | 3 457 |
| 1908 | 616 | 5 073 |
| 1909 | 841 | 5 464 |
| 1910 | 807 | 4 192 |
| 1911 | 688 | 5 502 |
| 1912[b] | 1 338 | 6 391 |

[a]  South Africa is treated separately. Her data are not included here.
[b]  The end of the Meiji period and the beginning of the Taisho period as well as the beginning of trade with South Africa.

Source:   EPA, *Economic Statistics of Japan* in Morikawa (1985).

The first decade of this century saw Japanese imports from Africa rise 26,8 per cent, while her exports to Africa for the same period rose 33 per cent. From the beginning of her trade with Africa, Japan's exports were mainly textiles — especially silk and silk tissues, cotton fabrics — but in time, it evolved to such diversified products as buttons, matches, potteries and porcelains. Included in this variety of exports were also such commodities as shoes, toys, cement, and soap. Her imports also began moderately with such raw essentials as cotton, cotton seed, wool, etc. but by 1930 the imports included such items as caustic soda and soda ash. For five months in 1927-1928 a Japanese government economic fact-finding mission to East Africa — i.e. Uganda, Tanganyika, Kenya, Zanzibar, Mozambique, Ethiopia and Madagascar — was undertaken, and this is yet one more proof of the fallacy that Japan's contact with Africa was virtually non-existent prior to 1960 because Africa was a European preserve. The years between 1897 and 1913 saw the phenomenal doubling of the value of Tropical Africa's external trade — from 71 000 000 pound sterling to 188 000 000. This was in keeping with the pace of total world trade which grew from $1 274 billion in 1899 to $2 769 billion in 1913. Japan featured prominently in African commercial ties, especially in its cotton trade, without earning the colonial stigma attached to westerners whose role in Africa was very much resented.

**East African-Japan cotton trade**

Actually, silk dominated the export trade of Japan from the early Meiji years. Between 1868 and 1893 silk and silk manufactures alone accounted for as much as 42 per cent of total exports abroad, and as late as 1930 silk exports continued to be the main source of foreign exchange to finance Japan's industrialisation.[86] Raw silk trade was extensive to the degree that it financed no less than 40 per cent of Japan's entire imports of both foreign machinery and raw materials utilized, domestically, over a period of 60 years.[87] Although silk textiles began first, cotton production quickly followed.

The cotton mill industry in Japan achieved its first sustained growth after 1890 with its spinning industry continuing expansion through the 1900s. From 1880 to 1913 cotton spindles increased from 13 000 to 2 287 000 or 176 times. By 1913 the Japanese export of cotton yarn and thread was worth twice that of Germany and 40 per cent of that of the United Kingdom (UK). As we know already, the role of the colonies in the world market was to supply not only cheap labour, but raw materials — minerals, plants and animals — to the industrialising countries. Thus in the relatively proximate area of East Africa, what particularly attracted Japan was the fast-growing cotton production, especially in Uganda as shown in Table 2.3.

TABLE 2.3

UGANDA'S COTTON PRODUCTION

| Year | Number of bales |
|------|-----------------|
| 1906 | 500 |
| 1910 | 12 000 |
| 1920 | 81 000 |
| 1928 | 204 000 |
| 1938 | 418 000 |
| 1965 | 445 200 |

A complementarity of factors was playing the critical role of attracting the Japanese and East African commercial activities to each other. Here was a perfect marriage: the rapidly expanding cotton spinning industry in Japan depended on a constant feeding of a stable raw material — amply produced in Uganda, Tanganyika and later Kenya. From 1929 to the late 30s Egypt began to export raw cotton to Japan in larger quantities. The yen value of raw cotton exported from Egypt to Japan increased from the 1930 figure of 12 592 million to 39 787 000 in 1934. Japan's import of Egyptian raw cotton and ginned cotton declined from the 1935 amount of 51 304 million yen to 37 093 million in 1939. But it was Uganda that supplied not only Japan but India too which in turn exported to Japan. The Japanese statistics often reflect India as the exporting country, whereas much of the "India" cotton is actually from East

Africa, especially from Uganda. For example Japan imported from British India raw cotton in these values: 1930 (147 688 000 yen), 1932 (91 746 000 yen), and 1934 (252 434 000 yen). Yet the dozen or so Indian ginning companies in Tanganyika and Uganda were exporting huge quantities of East African cotton to British India. In fact it was *Indian* companies that were giving British traders much stiffer competition than the Japanese companies. Indian companies (with capital based in India), and Indian-Ugandan companies (with Indian capital based in India) had a total of 54 ginneries in Uganda alone. Of the 114 ginneries in Uganda in 1925, 100 were owned by Indians. In 1937 East Africa recorded exports of cotton and ginned cotton to the value of 21 529 000 yen. In 1939 this figure declined slightly to 19 144 million yen. But the overall export figures to Japan were much higher, since Indian companies fronting for Japan in Uganda exported an even higher quantity to Bombay, before it was transshipped to Kobe and Osaka. For East Africa Uganda remained the pivotal player in this cotton export.

As Table 2.3 shows, in the first four years cotton production in Uganda jumped 24 times, and a decade later in 1920 it had jumped 6,75 times from the 1910 figures. In Uganda, cotton made up from 55 to 85 per cent of the country's exports between the 1910s and the 1950s, by which time coffee was beginning to play a major role. Total export earnings rose in Uganda from 1 500 000 pound sterling in 1921 to 47 400 000 in 1951. Japanese cotton spindles meanwhile had reached nearly 2 million by 1910. From the 1900 to 1913 spinning mill output rose 150 % — from 268 to 672 million pounds. After 1913 a growing share of Japanese exports began to take the form of cotton cloth. Uganda — and to a lesser extent Tanganyika — played an important role in the Japanese import-export trade in cotton and cotton textiles. The Japan-Africa trade rapidly improved to the extent that Africa's share of Japan's total overseas trade moved from 0,3 % of exports in 1913 to 4,2 % in 1940; and from 1,0 % of imports to 2,7 % for the same period as shown in Table 2.4.

To facilitate this trade three Japanese trading companies opened branches in Uganda: *Nihon Menka Kabushiki Kaisha* (1919) — (i.e.

Japanese Cotton Trading Co., Ltd.), *Toyo Menka Kabushiki Kaisha* (1926) and *Gosho Kabushiki Kaisha* (1926).

## TABLE 2.4
## AFRICA'S SHARE OF JAPAN'S TOTAL OVERSEAS TRADE
### (including North Africa)

| Year | % of Exports | % of Imports |
|------|--------------|--------------|
| 1913 | 0,3 | 1,0 |
| 1918 | 2,6 | 2,5 |
| 1920 | 2,2 | 3,9 |
| 1925 | 2,0 | 1,1 |
| 1930 | 4,2 | 1,7 |
| 1934 | 9,7 | 3,5 |
| 1937 | 8,7 | 5,5 |
| 1940 | 4,2 | 2,7 |
| 1942 | 0,0 | 0,0 |

Source:   Economic Planning Agency *figures in Morikawa* (1985).

The *Nichimen Company* extended its cotton ginning activities to owning a ginnery in Tanganyika as well as in Uganda. Like the Gosho, Nichimen also rented others in Uganda. But even before these companies opened their branches in Uganda, trade was facilitated by a number of Indian companies which fronted for Japan. For example the Indian companies of Ramdas Khimsi and Iserdas Bhogilal, both financed by the *Gosho Kabushiki Kaisha* of Japan, played a dual role of simultaneously supplying India and Japan with Ugandan cotton. Both of these companies had a total of six ginneries, and when other Japanese companies' ginneries are included, the total ginneries were well over a dozen. It is from these ginneries that ginned cotton exports to Japan were to keep increasing till the outbreak of the Second World War. Around 1917 when the Japanese Nichimen Company began to purchase Ugandan cotton it procured as its agents the Indian-owned

Narandas Rajaram and Company.[88] Nichimen also purchased a ginnery in Tanganyika. The Ugandan Commercial Company which was financed by the Homi Mehta group of industries in India was later partly financed by Toyo Menka of Japan.[89] The "big three" importers of raw East African cotton into Japan handled some 80 per cent of total imports.

With the Japanese Government's annual 40 000 pounds sterling subsidy to the *Osaka Shoresen Kaisha*, which ran a *monthly* shipping service to the East Coast of Africa, the Japanese began to give the British companies — such as British Cotton Corporation (BCC) — stiff competition, to the dismay of the Colonial Office and British traders. Because of the dominance of the Indian traders and the entry of the Japanese, the British East Africa Corporation was forced to withdraw from the ginning industry altogether — and thus precipitated a rivalry similar to the one that reigned in the early 1880s to 1885. In order to circumvent the stiff Indian and Japanese competition, the BCC proposed that all ginneries in Uganda be nationalised by the government, that compensation be paid by the British treasury, and that the BCC be appointed as government agents responsible for the management of the ginning side of the industry. The BCC was alarmed at the rate at which the industry was "rapidly passing out of British control" into Japanese hands, who were becoming "a real and serious menace ... in Uganda".[90] A Col. Franklin, the British Government's Trade Commissioner in East Africa, wrote a letter on 15 April 1927 to the Colonial Office, and bitterly complained of the "very distressing news" of the Japanese takeover. He observed that "during the past year the Japanese have come into the open and acquired quite a number of ginneries in Uganda and if they continue at this rate, they will largely control the industry before we know where we are".[91] Despite the British Government's commitment to buy British, the Japanese competition in cheap manufactures, especially after the Depression of the 1920s, grew by leaps and bounds throughout the colonial Empire. The Japanese production was particularly strong because it was aimed at the bottom end of the market and sold at prices which gave opportunities to consumers which British manufacturers previously were unable to reach.[92] This expansion of Japanese sales in East Africa coincided with a rapid decrease in British exports (Table 2.5).

TABLE 2.5

BRITISH AND JAPANESE COTTON TEXTILE EXPORTS TO EASTERN AFRICA 1929-1936

| | Quantity (million yards) | | | Distribution (%) | | |
|---|---|---|---|---|---|---|
| Year | Britain | Japan | Total | Britain | Japan | Others |
| 1929 | 23,6 | 32,6 | 109,4 | 21,6 | 29,8 | 48,6 |
| 1931 | 13,0 | 50,5 | 96,5 | 14,1 | 52,4 | 33,5 |
| 1933 | 11,7 | 78,2 | 104,0 | 11,3 | 75,2 | 13,5 |
| 1935 | 13,1 | 110,0 | 130,4 | 10,1 | 84,6 | 5,3 |
| 1936 | 10,5 | 122,4 | 140,1 | 7,5 | 87,3 | 5,2 |

Source: Hubbard in Brett, *Colonialism and Underdevelopment in East Africa (1973)*. Including Kenya, Uganda, Tanganyika, Nyasaland, and Zanzibar.

To contend with this onslaught of Japanese competition, there was not much the BCC or the Colonial Office could do, since the Congo Basin Treaties (the Berlin Act of 1885 and the Brussels Act of 1890) prohibited any discriminatory act against any of the signatories. Although Japan was not a signatory to these treaties, she was a signatory to the Convention of St Germaine-en-Laye which contained the same antidiscriminatory clause as contained in the earlier Congo Basin Treaties. To the dismay of many British businessmen these international obligations, as the Colonial Office noted, prevented any formal discrimination against Japan. The British, however, devised new schemes to limit Japanese trading activities. For example after May 1934, following the breakdown of Anglo-Japanese trade talks, quotas were imposed on Japanese imports into West Africa, which severely curtailed them there. Still new and dubious schemes were devised to constrain Japanese exports, such as precluding colonial populations from purchasing cheap Japanese products, all to no avail however, since the Japanese had created new markets which high-cost British producers found very difficult to maintain. The East African Treaty situation continued to create a delicate situation particularly since in the mid- to late 1930s the international situation had become brittle because of the German, Italian and *Japanese* demands for colonies in order to give them access to free supplies of raw materials and export markets.[93] Here, again, Japan demanded, but she could demand all she wanted — she was turned down because she was *not* a colonial power in Africa, let alone a European one. She had no legitimate claim to the African colonies, only *European* imperial powers had such "legal" rights. Ah! what a neat game these European colonisers were playing. By November 1936 Japan and Germany were allies of sorts — they had signed the Anti-Comintern Pact; but it would not be long before Germany broke the pact and unjustifiably accused Japan of reneging.

The Japanese were a beneficiary in their African trade in three ways: firstly, the capitalist countries' legal clauses in the African partition treaties prevented *formal* discrimination against a fellow capitalist, however "negative" a role he may have been seen playing. Only colonial powers played a "positive" role in Africa, and Japan's was "not". Secondly, European colonial administration had made the African peasantry amenable to labouring in cotton fields for low wages, a natural condition for a fastidious capitalist power playing the "catchup" game. Thirdly, and similarly, Japanese colonial administrative experience and its tough quality control policy secured for the home industry high grade cotton at low wages. Japan was equally experienced in imposing harsh labour conditions in its home cotton industries, which were heavily dependent on low-wage *female* labour. For example in early 20th century in the weaving sheds and silk filatures, largely rural industries, nine out of 10 workers were women. Even in the cotton spinning mills, over 80 per cent of the operatives were female:

One out of four was under sixteen years of age. These girls were recruited on contract from peasant homes, often reluctantly. They were housed and fed in company dormitories which blended the factory system of the West with paternalism and strict discipline of traditional Japan. Wages were low ...[94]

In African colonies, on the other hand, poor uneducated and politically unrepresented peasants bore the brunt of cotton production for their European masters, similarly at low exploitative wages. We may, of course, infer that *African male cotton producers were the equivalent of Japanese female cotton workers.* Cotton in East Africa was produced by hundreds of thousands of small peasant producers,[95] though they were less vulnerable to falling prices than estate producers were. The Japanese-Africa cotton trade had such a good beginning that, today, Japan *imports* 40 per cent of Africa's cotton.[96]

**Africa-Japan export-import trade: 1929-1940**

The 1930s were a hectic decade for Japan in Africa. It was a period during which Japanese exports to Africa increased not only in volume, but also in diversity as well as in the number of different African colonial markets targeted by Japan. Between 1929 and 1935 the bulk of these exports were textiles (knitted goods, silk tissues, cotton tissues, silk kerchiefs, etc.) and mostly were exported to the major African extremities of Egypt, East Africa, the Union of South Africa and the so-called French Morocco (Tables 2.6, 2.7 and 2.8). During the entire period of 1913-1938 Japanese gross national product grew at the annual rate of 4,4 per cent. The yen had drastically depreciated and thus facilitated the expansion of exports.

Japan exported even matches to African countries: In 1930 the value of matches exported to Africa was 26 000 yen. This figure kept rising till it reached 90 000 yen in 1934. In 1928 the Japanese had tried, and failed, to establish a match factory in Tanganyika. As the British official remarked about the incident:

## TABLE 2.6
## VALUE OF MERCHANDISE EXPORTED TO AFRICA
### *(Yen 1 000)*

| Country | 1929 | 1930 | 1931 | 1932 | 1933 | 1934 | 1935 |
|---|---|---|---|---|---|---|---|
| East Africa | 13 123 | 10 663 | 10 867 | 15 760 | 23 174 | 37 454 | 53 800 |
| Egypt | 31 352 | 28 997 | 22 829 | 41 876 | 55 607 | 72 988 | |
| French Morocco | — | — | — | — | — | 19 076 | 18 813 |
| Union of South Africa[a] | 13 179 | 14 196 | 19 282 | 16 418 | 26 740 | 29 534 | 32 769 |

a   South Africa is included here and in the rest of the tables in this chapter, but I treat it separately elsewhere in this work.

Source:   *The Japan Year Book* 1936.

## TABLE 2.7
## JAPANESE EXPORTS TO SELECTED AFRICAN MARKETS
### IN 1938 AND 1939 *(Yen 1 000)*

| African market | 1938 | 1939 |
|---|---|---|
| Anglo-Egyptian Sudan | 11 895 | 8 923 |
| Angola | 1 027 | 1 060 |
| Belgian Congo | 6 927 | 8 593 |
| Cameroons | 1 637 | 2 837 |
| Egypt | 13 997 | 15 666 |
| Eritrea | 920 | 1 177 |
| French Africa | 1 387 | 1 619 |
| French Morocco | 18 727 | 20 593 |
| Gold Coast | 2 121 | 2 026 |
| Kenya, Tanganyika, Uganda | 22 504 | 22 874 |
| Mozambique | 9 830 | 10 665 |
| Nigeria | 4 084 | 2 955 |
| Rhodesia | 641 | 994 |
| South Africa | 35 291 | 46 802 |

Source:   Compiled from *The Japan Year Book* 1946-1948.

## TABLE 2.8
## VALUE OF CHIEF COMMODITIES EXPORTED TO AFRICA FROM JAPAN PROPER AND KARAFUTO *(Yen 1 000)*

| Commodity and country | 1934 | 1935 | 1936 |
|---|---|---|---|
| **Cotton tissues** | 492 351 | 496 097 | 483 591 |
| Anglo-Egyptian Sudan | 7 293 | 9 671 | 9 004 |
| Kenya, Uganda and Tanganyika | 15 601 | 15 956 | 18 724 |
| Union of South Africa | 4 458 | 6 341 | 7 358 |
| Mozambique | 2 333 | 3 509 | 2 290 |
| Nigeria | 1 176 | 1 095 | 1 011 |
| **Raw silk** | 286 794 | 387 032 | 392 809 |
| **Rayon tissues** | 113 484 | 128 260 | 149 170 |
| Union of South Africa | 6 250 | 5 149 | 5 838 |
| Egypt | 8 076 | 5 449 | 2 941 |
| Kenya, Uganda and Tanganyika | 607 | 765 | 851 |
| Mozambique | 876 | 622 | 795 |
| **Silk tissues** | 77 488 | 77 444 | 68 027 |
| Union of South Africa | 4 651 | 4 008 | 4 005 |
| Egypt | 3 601 | 2 559 | 2 333 |
| **Knitted goods** | 47 618 | 50 266 | 49 988 |
| Union of South Africa | 1 884 | 1 701 | 2 711 |
| Egypt | 3 030 | 1 698 | 3 030 |
| Kenya, Uganda and Tanganyika | 585 | 1 011 | 906 |
| Mozambique | 756 | 1 123 | 892 |
| **Woollen tissues** | 29 849 | 32 401 | 45 956 |
| Egypt | 2 835 | 2 278 | 4 051 |
| **Porcelains** | 41 877 | 42 735 | 43 192 |
| Union of S.A. | 904 | 849 | 1 144 |
| **Iron manufactures** | 35 277 | 37 504 | 40 302 |
| Union of S.A. | 628 | 614 | 697 |
| Kenya, Uganda and Tanganyika | 404 | 562 | 544 |
| Mozambique | 367 | 375 | 468 |
| **Toys** | 30 386 | 33 852 | 36 459 |
| Union of S.A. | 866 | 645 | 891 |
| Egypt | 349 | 449 | 644 |
| **Glass and manufactures** | 19 454 | 23 337 | 25 627 |
| Union of S.A. | 757 | 785 | 831 |

## TABLE 2.8 *(continued)*

| Commodity and country | 1934 | 1935 | 1936 |
|---|---|---|---|
| **Timber** | 23 915 | 23 182 | 24 703 |
| Union of S.A. | 757 | 785 | 831 |
| **Hats and caps** | 1 084 | 16 284 | 19 736 |
| Union of S.A. | 217 | 533 | 913 |
| **Cotton blankets** | 5 380 | 7 452 | 6 908 |
| Kenya, Uganda and Tanganyika | 200 | 179 | 552 |
| **Cotton towels** | 7 216 | 6 477 | 6 830 |
| Union of S.A. | 315 | 437 | 644 |

Information had been received that Japanese interests were establishing a factory for the manufacture of matches in the Tanga district, which might result in the diminution of the public revenues of Uganda, Kenya and Tanganyika of 30 000 derived from existing import duties ...[97]

The British were clearly determined to prevent Japan from commercially running rampant in (British) West Africa, as she did in (British) East Africa to the chagrin of the British. In the same year (1934), they were successful in frustrating Japanese efforts to extend its efforts to Nigeria, Gold Coast, etc. With skilful industriousness and diligence the Osaka Shosen Kaisha opened, nevertheless, a West African maritime route in 1933. From 1934 to 1940 Japan had, consequently, opened new African export markets in no less than 20 African colonies and between 1938 and 1939 these colonies were fully operational in consuming Japanese products. (Table 2.7)

Thus Table 2.8 shows that Japanese exports to colonial Africa varied, commodity-wise, from cotton blankets, cotton tissues, silk and silk tissues, rayon tissues, to woollen tissues, toys, potteries and porcelains as well as iron, glass, timber and hats. Similarly, beginning with 1934 and continuing to 1939, Japan had opened up new export markets ranging from the condominium of Anglo-

Egyptian Sudan to Mozambique and Nigeria in West Africa as shown in Tables 2.7, 2.8 and 2.9. In Tanganyika alone Japanese exports as a percentage of Tanganyika's imports rose from the 1925 figure of 7,2 % to the high of 23,8 % in 1937 before declining to 17,2 % in 1938. This figure, however, was still 10 percentage points above the 1925 percentage figure.

While Africa was also busy consuming Japanese products in ever larger quantities, the African producers were also supplying Japan with raw materials. Japanese imports fluctuated in the period between 1935 and 1939. Around 1935, as already noted, Japan was demanding from her fellow European imperial powers that they share access to African colonies with her. European powers had begun to look for subtle and devious ways to exclude Japan from

TABLE 2.9

AMOUNTS OF IMPORTS FROM AFRICAN COUNTRIES
1935-1939 *(Yen 1 000)*

| Country | 1935 | 1936 | 1937 | 1938 | 1939 |
|---|---|---|---|---|---|
| Egypt | 51 304 | 45 737 | 74 118 | 36 315 | 50 312 |
| Kenya, Uganda and Tanganyika | 2 955 | 29 865 | 24 155 | 6 020 | 19 699 |
| Union of South Africa | 4 762 | 22 561 | 88 852 | 7 807 | 8 249 |
| Eritrea | — | — | 1 879 | 2 270 | 3 995 |
| Anglo-Egyptian Sudan | — | — | 5 858 | 435 | 2 780 |
| Italian Somaliland | 2 357 | 2 879 | 2 608 | 3 216 | 2 341 |
| Denmark[a] | — | — | 1 449 | 1 232 | 2 339 |
| Greece[a] | — | — | 603 | 1 096 | 2 106 |

[a]  Included only for comparison

Source:   *The Japan Year Book* 1946-1948 (Tokyo).

African markets, as we have just seen. As the Second World War approached, African exports to Japan began to taper off (Table 2.9), no doubt the result of European export restrictions to Japan.

91

Japan was also busily exploring Francophone African markets, which were slow to open up to Japan because of the influence of

## TABLE 2.10
## CHIEF ARTICLES OF TRADE BETWEEN JAPAN AND
## TWO AFRICAN AREAS 1931-1935
*(Yen 1 000)*

| EGYPT | | | | | |
|---|---|---|---|---|---|
| | 1931 | 1932 | 1933 | 1934 | 1935 |
| **From Japan** | | | | | |
| Cotton yarns, silk and | 43 | 325 | 259 | — | — |
| rayon tissues | 3 954 | 9 182 | 7 704 | 8 076 | 8 006 |
| Cotton tissues | 14 957 | 27 068 | 38 351 | 46 833 | 31 683 |
| Knitted goods | 1 305 | 1 818 | 3 370 | 3 029 | 1 698 |
| Cotton towels | — | 408 | 438 | 627 | — |
| Potteries | — | 195 | 451 | 516 | — |
| Others and total | 22 829 | 41 876 | 55 607 | 72 988 | 53 800 |
| **To Japan** | | | | | |
| Sulphate of ammo; crude | 1 390 | 3 664 | 5 960 | 4 787 | — |
| seed cotton and ginned cotton | 11 619 | 15 300 | 19 084 | 39 787 | 43 009 |
| Others and total | 13 567 | 19 787 | 26 455 | 46 259 | 51 304 |
| EAST AFRICA | | | | | |
| **From Japan** | | | | | |
| Total | 10 867 | 15 760 | 23 174 | 37 454 | 25 083 |
| **To Japan** | | | | | |
| Caustic soda, etc. | 1 627 | 1 155 | 229 | 1 261 | 1 207 |
| Others and total | 2 263 | 3 414 | 14 356 | 21 305 | 2 945 |

Source:    *The Japan Year Book* 1936, p. 428.

France which was reluctant to allow Japanese competition in Francophone Africa.

The nature of the bilateral trade between Japan and two African regions is illustrated in Table 2.10. In 1934 Japanese exports to

Africa totalled 182 397 000 yen. The ratio to total exports was 8,4 per cent, making Africa the fourth largest consuming continent of Japanese products (after Asia 53 %, North America 18,8 %, Europe 10,5 %).

This ratio was one full percentage point above that of the previous year's ratio to total exports. Thus in continental terms, Africa was consuming more Japanese products than the continents of South America, Australia, and Oceania. As Table 2.9 shows many African colonies were also exporting more to Japan than, say, Denmark or Greece in Europe were.

The role of Egypt and East Africa in helping foster the growth of the Japanese economy is clearly not an insignificant one. It should be recalled that when the Tokugawa Japanese first touched Africa (in Egypt) in 1862, they remarked on the laziness of Egyptian Africans and Arabs. But since then however, with only temporary intermissions of a couple of years, Japan and Egypt have embarked upon a number of cooperative economic ventures that have spiralled bilateral economic relations tremendously. By 1990 Japan had surpassed the US as Egypt's aid donor. Egypt, like other African countries such as Ghana, Kenya, Nigeria, Niger, Senegal, etc. as we shall see in Chapter 4, plays an important role in today's Japanese-African trade.

Interwar Japan embarked upon a vast programme of commodity acquisition — especially raw commodities in order to fuel her industrial expansion. Thus prewar Japan, in the words of Japanese scholars, plundered the wealth of weaker nations and wrested lands from foreign countries in order to alleviate the burden of her huge population through a national policy of spoliation and folly backed by military strength.[98] For Japan colonisation and commercial trade worked hand-in-glove in Asia. For example the post-World War II Nissan automobile industry is an offshoot of the company founded by Aikawa in the 1930s to help in the colonisation of Manchuria. Many trading companies from Japan played this complementary role with the government to benefit from abundant commercial opportunities of the African colonial markets. The trading companies already mentioned — such as Nichimen, Gosho, Toyo, etc. — played, in both the interwar period and the postwar era, a critical role of a commercial intercourse with African colonies. Not a single African's blood was shed either protesting or defending Japanese interests in Africa while thousands of African lives were lost in World Wars I and II defending European interests. Just as the industrialisation and administrative bureaucratisation of Japan was facilitated by the increasing role of foreigners — between 1876 and 1895 nearly 4 000 foreigners were brought by the government to work in Japan — so the African peasants had been incorporated by Europeans in the Japanese commercial activities, especially between 1913 and 1940, in East Africa. During the 1929-1940 period, African rural workers in these plantations exposed to European colonial control were often exploited with relatively little bargaining power. Compared with the industrialised countries, peasants' opportunities in the African colonial plantation were drastically reduced. The differences between such rural sectors and workers of the industrialised countries were well pronounced.

> The backward peoples have to contend with three types of monopolistic forces: in their role as unskilled labour they have to face the big foreign mining and plantation concerns who are monopolistic buyers of their labour; in their role as peasant producers they have to face a small group of exporting and processing firms who are monopolistic buyers of their crop; and in their role as consumers of imported commodities they have to face the same group of firms who are monopolistic sellers or distributors of these commodities.[99]

It is in this context that most of the foreign firms and their front companies played a role in East and West Africa during the entire interwar period.

### Colonial era ends: 1945-1960 trade

At the end of the war in 1945 colonial powers — all over the African continent — regarded African independence as a thing of the distant future. The French Government had made this clear when it declared at the 1944 Brazzaville Conference: "The establishment one day of self-governments in the colonies, even a day far off, is to be eliminated from any consideration". In June 1945 the British Report of the Commission on Higher Education in West Africa was similarly complacent about the foreseeable emergence of an African state, unrealistically claiming that it will arise "within a century". The Japanese, however, were content simply to reconstruct their war-damaged economy upon the material base of African resources. Although much of the Japanese trade with European colonies in Africa between 1940 and 1945 was disrupted by war, Japan showed no appreciable change in her trade policies with colonial Africa from the interwar period to the first postwar period: precisely because in the African scene the Japanese role began and continued as a commercial role till the 1960s when African colonies achieved nominal political independence. For example, Japanese exports to and imports from East Africa for the interwar period of 1934-1936 on the one hand, and her export-import figures with the same region in the postwar period 1957-1959 on the other, clearly reflect this continuity of policies as is evident in Table 2.11.

## TABLE 2.11
## EXPORT-IMPORT TRADE WITH EAST AFRICA
## 1934-1936 AND 1957-1959

| Exports[a] | | | | | | Imports[b] | | | | | |
|------|------|------|------|------|------|------|------|------|------|------|------|
| 1934 | 1935 | 1936 | 1957 | 1958 | 1959 | 1934 | 1935 | 1936 | 1957 | 1958 | 1959 |
| 22 329 | 25 083 | 30 602 | 33 934 | 28 451 | 28 900 | 15 188 | 2 955 | 29 865 | 18 306 | 21 189 | 27 017 |

[a]  The 1934-1936 figures are in yen values; (1 000 yen)
[b]  The 1957-1959 figures are in dollar values; (1 000 dollars)

What these figures show, besides the big jumps from the interwar low yen value of trade to the postwar large dollar value of trade is, to repeat, the continuity of Japanese trade policies during the two colonial periods in Africa. They reflect the same relative continuity for Africa as is reflected in, say, New Zealand-Japan trade. In 1930 Japan exported to New Zealand to the value of 3 226 million yen and, nearly 30 years later (1959), she exported to the value of nearly 30 million dollars. The continuity of Japan's policies to Africa in both the interwar and postwar periods is made even more remarkable by the fact that interwar Japanese governments were *militarist* oriented, while postwar governments are *pacifist*. All the postwar Japanese prime ministers have made a number of invariably similar statements about Japanese commitments to pacifism,[100] but, owing to Japan's dependence on many of her raw materials from Africa, it was not possible for the country to distance herself from the European colonial programmes and policies in Africa for that would have clearly shut off one of the most vital pipelines of her survival. In fact a case can be made that Japan increased her commercial activities in Africa even as some European colonial powers had announced their dubious "decolonization" programmes.[101] This increase was of course clearly not designed to supplant European colonialism in Africa, but rather to increase her influence with the emerging authentic African leadership in order to continue her beneficial commercial ties to Africa.

Between 1894 and 1945 Japan was governed by a pugnacious militarism, whereas postwar Japan is a haven of passive pacifism[102] thanks not only to the Japanese Peace Constitution but also to the vigorous peace movement in Japan.[103] World War I gave the greatest impetus to the Japanese economy — both qualitatively and quantitatively. Her exports, which totalled only 600 million yen in 1914, jumped to 1,1 billion yen in 1916, to 2 098 billion yen in 1919. Her imports, similarly, in 1919 were less than 600 million yen, but three years later had increased to one billion yen, and finally reached 2 336 billion yen in 1920.[104] Between 1916 and 1918 Japan had witnessed a great surge of exports. The combined export excess for the period totalled 1,408 billion yen. This trade prosperity had naturally influenced, as we have seen, the shipping business which greatly facilitated the Japanese export-import trade with Africa, as the various tables in this chapter amply indicate. What is of interest to us in this paragraph is that war and rumour of war greatly influenced Japan's industrial and commercial expansion — from the Sino-Japanese War, to the Russo-Japanese War to World War I, and finally to World War II. (In Africa, too, since the outbreak of World War II, a considerable expansion of trade between Japan and African nations took place. Between 1938 and 1960 total exports increased in value nearly 13 times).

But if militarism had been a great spur, pacifism, having freed Japan from the burdens of military expenditures, has equally propelled an unparalleled economic growth and expansion. Common to both militarist and pacifist governments were Japanese commercial policies. We have already seen how militarist Japan had sought to ingratiate herself with European colonial powers between 1885 and 1940. We now see how *pacifist* Japan dallied with the same (albeit de-imperialised) European powers in Africa during colonialism's dying moments (1945-1960) to the same extent as its interwar *militarist* predecessor had done. It is in this context that the "clean hands" theory of Japan's involvement in Africa becomes tenable. Of the European powers which were in Africa, not a single one *in African eyes*, merits such an accolade as Japan's.

Between 1940 and 1945, as just stated, much of the Japanese trade with African colonies was naturally disrupted by war, though a large expansion of African exports to European countries took place as a result of the increase in the demand for primary commodities during World War II and in the immediate postwar reconstruction period. In 1955 Japan's exports to Africa increased by some 50 %.

In 1956 Liberia became Japan's second-most important export market, the result of exports of ships to companies operating under the Liberian flag. Ships became Japan's second most important export in 1956, exceeded only by cotton textiles.[105] Except for ship exports to Liberia, Japan's trade with colonial Africa continued to increase markedly since 1955, three years after Japan had regained her sovereignty from the American-imposed Occupation Administration. During the eight-year period between 1954 and 1962 Japanese exports to Africa increased by 2,4 times, and imports by

4,3 times. The export expansion centred mainly on British colonies such as those constituting East and West Africa (Table 2.12).

## TABLE 2.12
## JAPAN-AFRICA SELECTED EXPORTS-IMPORTS
## 1957-1959
### *(1 000 dollars)*

| Country | Exports | | | Imports | | |
|---|---|---|---|---|---|---|
| | 1957 | 1958 | 1959 | 1957 | 1958 | 1959 |
| British East Africa | 33 934 | 28 451 | 28 900 | 18 306 | 21 189 | 27 017 |
| British West Africa | 54 652 | 54 854 | 53 626 | 819 | 3 337 | 7 096 |
| Egypt[a] | 22 513 | 681 | 12 289 | 32 158 | 30 020 | 16 600 |
| Liberia[a] | 273 119 | 236 731 | 209 456 | 969 | 208 | 2 306 |
| Ghana[a] | 24 488 | 16 910 | 22 516 | 872 | 739 | 2 228 |
| Union of South Africa[b] | 38 997 | 51 762 | 34 096 | 15 964 | 34 507 | |
| Australia[c] | 42 126 | 62 549 | 78 344 | 362 800 | 225 561 | 292- - - |
| France[c] | 17 952 | 8 823 | 11 960 | 28 652 | 20 744 | 24 928 |
| Malaya[c] | 14 357 | 13 120 | 19 348 | 154 164 | 114 380 | 166 298 |
| Iran[c] | 29 393 | 47 647 | 49 746 | 30 205 | 27 503 | 29 859 |

[a]  Independent African States — Egypt since 1922, Liberia (1847), Ghana (1957)

[b]  South Africa is discussed elsewhere in this book

[c]  Included only for comparison

Source:  Ministry of Finance (Tokyo) figures in *Japan Economic Year Book* 1960.

Export-import returns for Japan and North African countries in 1945-1947 were mainly in cotton fabrics and phosphate and salt as reflected in Table 2.13. But by the mid- to late 50s goods ranged from food (fish), fruits and vegetables, raw materials, tea, beverages, tobacco, textile yarns and fabrics, non-metallic mineral products, transportation equipment, camera, electric machines, mineral fuels, wood, etc. North Africa was increasingly shipping such items as Alexandria salt, Port Said salt and phosphate.

TABLE 2.13

EXPORT AND IMPORT RETURNS 1945-1947 (NORTH AFRICA)

| Exports | | | |
|---|---|---|---|
| Country | Description | Quantity | Unit |
| Egypt | Cotton fabric | Yard | 3 251 760 |
| East Algeria | Cotton fabric | Yard | 2 889 760 |
| Anglo-Egyptian Sudan | Cotton fabric | 2 944 560 | |
| Former Tripolitania | Cotton fabric | 600 000 | |
| Former Italian Eritrea | Cotton fabric | 1 250 400 | |
| Cyrenaica | Cotton fabric | | 150 400 |
| Imports | | | |
| North Africa | Alexandria salt | M/T | 167 493 |
| North Africa | Port Said salt | M/T | 8 863 |
| North Africa | Phosphate | M/T | 115 810 |

Source:    *The Japan Year Book* 1946-1948.

During the war years Britain set public investment in her African colonies through such legislations as the Colonial Development and Welfare Acts of 1940 and 1945. The French operated through the *Fonds d'Investissement pour le Developpement Economique et Social* (Investment Fund for Economic and Social Development — known as FIDES) which originated from a law passed in April 1946.

During the decade 1947-1957 FIDES invested more capital in Francophone West Africa than the total estimated investment from both public and private sources in the period 1903-1946.[106] Thus while increased investment by Britain and France in the economic infrastructure of their respective colonies was taking place, between 1945 and 1960 Japan was making no similar investments in these colonies since the latter were obviously the hegemonic responsibility of imperial Europe. The bulk of the trade was therefore with the particular European power to which the colony "belonged", yet Japan, naturally, stood to benefit from the African colonial structure laid down by Europe. For example, by 1958 in the field of cotton fabrics, Japan was still maintaining her prewar position as the world's top exporter. Japan continued the expedient *Africa-without-Africans* policies until independence of African states; she was deterred from expanding her commercial ties with West Africa, primarily in the Francophone part of West Africa, by French trade and tariff restrictions, more than by the so-called Far Continent theory.[107] The ground she may have lost was however quickly won over, especially in the decade 1974-1984, when Japan showed her multidimensional diplomacy towards the African continent.

# 第二部

## 外交の特質

# PART II

## THE DIPLOMATIC DIMENSION

## CHAPTER 3

# JAPAN'S DIPLOMACY TOWARDS AFRICA

*... Japanese diplomacy is all things to all people.*

John Ravenhill (1982); K.G. van Wolferen (1986)

*Most Japanese used to see Africa as a very remote part of the world and one of little immediate interest. However with the increased role the African nations have come to play in the international political arena, and the importance this region has taken on with regard to global peace and prosperity, Africa has grown immensely in its significance, not only to Japan ...*

Shintaro Abe, Foreign Minister
Creative Diplomacy (1985, MOFA), p. 26

*... Our Ministry (of Foreign Affairs) is working hard for Japan to extend what I may call "diplomatic infrastructure" in Africa. Japan is stepping up diplomatic contacts in Africa. We are increasing Japanese embassies in Africa.*

Kunio Shimizu, Director, First Africa Division, Ministry of Foreign Affairs: "Interview", 26 November 1987: Tokyo

*The Japanese government hopes to extend and deepen relations with Black Africa. The future of Africa lies with Africans. Japan has embarked upon policies of extending contacts with Africans on a broad scale.*

Ryoichi Horie, Deputy Director, Second Africa Division Ministry of Foreign Affairs: "Interview", 27 November 1987: Tokyo

In the postwar period Japan's principal diplomatic goals have been to promote her prosperity, to insure her security, to foster global pacifism as a leading (economic) world power. This leads to the question: what are Japanese concerns regarding Africa? What do the Japanese think about African relations? To answer this question one needs to probe the deeper recesses of Japan's diplomatic policy — its philosophy, its evolution and history, its economism, its priorities and principles. Japan's creative qualities and unique characteristics in the diplomatic sphere (as elsewhere) are immense, as this chapter shall detail. Her Africa diplomacy in the late 80s demonstrates enterprising and multifaceted quality. Yet for an economic super power Japan was slow to project a more human (as distinct from purely trade and commercial) face in her diplomacy, especially in Africa where she has been active for at least the past 90 years, as we have already seen. Since Africa is a continent most of whose countries are seriously beset with economic difficulties such as accumulated external debts, slower (even negative) economic growth, depressed commodity prices, and many other structural adjustment problems, Japanese diplomacy has therefore come to be viewed by many critics through the narrow prism of a predatory economism. To arrive at the quality of Japan's diplomacy in Africa we may have to go via the route of the quantity of its activities. While these activities are primarily economic I shall, however, provide the *political* content to the "economy-first" principle; that is, outline its moral and historical parameters.

Since the turn of the century to the mid-1970s, Japanese foreign policies towards Africa have largely been commercially oriented, while African policies towards Japan have greatly been constrained by ideology and the dependency complex, and thus remained firmly wedded to the developmentally expectant framework. Cases such as Zaire, Somalia, Ethiopia, Niger, Uganda, Rwanda, Egypt, Ghana, etc. illustrate this syndrome of development dependency. In Part II of this study I focus on the two interactive and mutually inclusive factors of the "aid-oriented" Japanese diplomacy towards Black Africa especially, and African diplomacy towards Japan. Part III's focus is on the technical aspects, as well as philosophical imperatives of Japanese Official Development Assistance (JODA) to Africa. (See Chapters 5 and 6.)

In this chapter I concern myself with the value packages and realm of Japanese diplomacy towards Africa. In the process I consider the evolution of this diplomacy from a historical angle and a moral dimension as well. Only in Chapter 4 do I turn my attention to "African diplomacy towards Japan", if there is indeed such a phenomenon. Japanese diplomacy in Africa is at best not well understood; and of the diplomacies of the major economic or political powers in the world, Japan's is neither well articulated even by the Tokyo government, nor is it much discussed outside the "commercial imperative" framework that both Western and Japanese scholars are fond of ritually operating within. Yet, despite the fact that this diplomacy has historically been all things to all nations which sold her raw materials and bought her products, it is one of the few consistently creative, coherent, and rational public diplomacies. That controversies occasionally arise, as when Japan sometimes uses her economic super power status to sway some African countries injudiciously, should be attributed more to that perennial Japanese quest for security as well as to the learning experience of Africa. In the past, especially in the 1960s and 1970s, Japan tended to adopt the myopic traditional stance of urging African nations to be more trusting of their former colonial masters.

Diplomatic myopia is not entirely alien even for a nation with one of the best long-term views of world developments. Still, considering some of the "quietly" rhetorical atmospherics in which it is sometimes articulated, her diplomacy is over-all positive. This does not negate the fact that on the whole Japan has failed to present her Africa policy clearly, at least until very recently. The task of Japan's diplomacy toward Africa is doubly burdened. Not only must it search for the accommodation of the "normal" differences among states, but it must also search for a viable relationship with a group of states operating from a very different set of premises. A review of the (annual) *Diplomatic BlueBook*, at least the 1961 to at least the 1980 editions, reveals a paucity of explanation, elaboration, and analysis, suggesting that it is more the product of preordained committee bureaucracy than that of visionary flexible policy planners. Frequently, the presentation lacks colour or depth. It is only in the latter part of the 80s that there is a marked improvement in the Japanese Government's articulation and formalisation of this diplomacy.

Given the role played by the Ministry of Foreign Affairs (MOFA) bureaucrats who are not only in charge of the day-to-day micromanaging of African affairs, but who bring with them a combined and broad African experience (such as Naoto Amaki, Kunio Shimizu, Ryoichi Horie, Hidetoshi Ukita, Makito Takahishi, Takahisa Tsugawa, etc.), Japan's diplomatic activism in Africa would seem destined to no longer run like a stray dog, proceeding without proper international attention. The episodic and peripheral role that Africa played in Japanese policy-makers is fast giving way to changing perceptions, especially in political terms as well as in human understanding. The MOFA and MITI (Ministry of International Trade and Industry) bureaucrats have historically been inflexible regarding issues that would lead to genuine shifts in policy, but with regard to Africa the MOFA envoys now reflect a balanced and serious Japanese desire to move towards a more broadly based constructive diplomacy to Africa. A review of the values and norms of this diplomacy on the one hand, and an analysis of its implementation, history, and future direction on the other, is long overdue. This chapter is an attempt to formalise that review and analysis.

The Japanese Government documents regarding its diplomatic objectives and philosophy often restate positions that outline shared socio-economic values, political systems, and those that transcend ideological differences and systems. That is to say postwar Japan has embarked, first, upon a path of strengthening cooperation with those countries with whom she shares political ideals and economic and social systems. Secondly, she has embarked on carrying out wide-ranging diplomatic activities which transcend differences in political systems and positions.[108] Regarding Africa, Japan believes that the "most effective way to promote Japan's relations is to expand and strengthen diplomatic channels".[109] By this yardstick however Japan's diplomacy would seem to be somewhat less than successful, since she maintains diplomatic embassies in less than half of the continent's nations. But such a conclusion would clearly not only be erroneous, since Japan has, in effect, diplomatically "covered" all the countries belonging to the Organization of African Unity — OAU. It would also be ignoring the essence of what the Director of the First African Division in MOFA, Kunio Shimizu, in remarks to the author in November 1987, indicated are strategic priorities: Japan is — so to speak — preoccupied with first clearing the "diplomatic infrastructure" in Africa — creating congenial working conditions for Japanese diplomats such as providing medical, communications, security, electrical, etc., infrastructure and equipment, given the difficulties of life in Africa for those not used to the conditions. At any rate, argued Shimizu, Japan has diplomatic relations with *all* African countries. Indeed, since 1952 when Japan herself regained her independence, her *diplomatic recognition of the African states has risen in proportion to the independence of these states*, despite some such aberrations as the failure to recognise Ethiopia and Liberia much earlier. It is correct, still, to assert that the chronology of the birth of new African nations coincides with the diplomatic recognition by Japan of most of these states. In many cases Japan extended diplomatic recognition on the very day they gained flag independence, even if diplomatic relations in certain cases still awaited several years, while in others they have yet to be consummated. Being an economic super power, more is increasingly expected of Japan especially by the developing nations, inarguably by African states.

By the end of 1973 Japanese diplomatic missions in Africa had increased slightly to include the following nation states: Algeria, Egypt, Ethiopia, Gabon, Ghana, Ivory Coast, Kenya, Liberia, Libya, Madagascar, Morocco, Nigeria, Senegal, the Sudan, Tanzania, Tunisia, Zaire and Zambia. (See Appendix A.) Prior to 1973 permanent diplomatic missions of Japan in Africa were 4 (1957), 5 (1960), 15 (1970) and in 1975 the figure was 18, and 1978 it was 22. To some critics the diplomatic recognition — that is diplomatic history — is not a very useful barometer of the depth of mutual bilateral relations. Indeed they even cite the fact that Japan has more intense "real" relations with South Africa than say with Rwanda, even though she has "diplomatic relations" with the latter while she had "none" with South Africa till 1992. Indeed, among the Japanese the Morikawa School of Thought attaches very little significance to diplomatic relations since the real process of interaction is economism and thus, consequently, South Africa ranks first among African trading partners of Japan.

Japanese diplomacy was formally declared by the Foreign Office when in 1957 it published its first *Blue Paper (later called the Diplomatic BlueBook)* in which the Tokyo Government declared its basic principles of diplomacy :

(i) Adherence to the principles of the United Nations.

(ii) Close co-operation with the Western countries (especially the US).

(iii) Solidarity with the Afro-Asian nations.

These principles became the core values of Japan's universal diplomatic pacifism and international co-operation. I shall deal more with these basic principles in the course of this chapter.

While Japan's basic diplomacy towards Africa has, over time, remained essentially unchanged, her operational motives for the broadening of political relations have varied in terms of priorities and emphasis: but

(i) economic/commercial motivation,

(ii) security and strategic considerations,

(iii) increased recognition of global interdependence,

(iv) an awareness of her position as a world economic power,

(v) and the question of humanitarian and development aid goals have all conspired to frame a more coherent and rational diplomacy towards the so-called "Far Continent".

The notion of the "Far Continent" should, of course, be obsolete especially for the Japanese, given that Africa in today's Japan has really been transformed almost into the "Near Continent" considering the extent of Japan's diplomatic, trade, aid, and cultural connections with African countries. Besides, not even a relatively "backward" nation as China uses such obsolete references as the "Far Continent" given the villagisation of our global world today.

Although this chapter seeks to focus on Japan's "new" Africa diplomacy — especially as articulated in the pronouncements of the foreign service Africanists — a historical and theoretical review of Japan's diplomacy in the first 73 years of this century is imperative if a coherent and holistic frame of reference of the Japan-Africa ties is to be presented. Given Japan's diplomatic and pacific activism in Africa, and Africa's newly acquired "aggressive" diplomacy in seeking to bridge the Tokyo-Africa gaps, it would seem that by the turn of the 21st century Japan would by far be the major economic and political influence in Africa despite her current near-zero political influence. (In Ghana alone "affection" — or what passes as such — for Japan today just about surpasses that of any other Western country). By 1990 Japan had overtaken the US as Egypt's largest aid donor, as she also has surpassed the rest of the Western donors in Ghana. Even in Francophone Africa (a historically problematic area for Japan), states such as Mali, Niger, Senegal, Ivory Coast, etc. are slowly but unmistakably shifting their focus and expectations to Japan, rather than to their traditional suzerain, France). Or, as Takashi Yuki of the Long-Term Credit Bank of Japan once pointed out: "In Francophone Africa there is a high degree of interest in Japan." But what he clearly meant was interest in Japanese manufactured products not in human relations. Here we deal, instead, with diplomatic products, human policies. The paradox of Japan's diplomacy is that she has been very successful in penetrating the African economies without accruing much political influence, or increasing negative image that was once injected by France among the Africans since colonial times. This is that Japan's singular failure in Africa so far has been her continued inability to play an overt significant role in the continent's political affairs. Her political role is not discernible; her influence lies more in economic, developmental, and cultural manifestations. Ironically, her policy of separating politics from economics when she deals with Africa is responsible for this non-discernible political clout. The continued success of this strategy is in doubt though, but Japan has already recognised its limits, and she has consequently shifted up to a higher gear in her dynamic Africa diplomacy. Indeed Japan's diplomacy in Africa is considerable — it is subtle, sophisticated, and successful, thanks to the suave MOFA, unlike the unidimensional MITI.

## A THEORETICAL REVIEW NOTE

In the interwar (1918-1940) and postwar (1952-1960) periods of Japan's *benign diplomacy* towards African colonies and two or three free African nations, during which Japan was compelled by reasons of expediency and European hegemony to adopt the *Africa-without-Africans* approach, commercial and trade emphasis with Africa, especially in the securing of African markets for Japanese finished goods and African raw materials for Japanese industries, dominated the "relations" with colonial Africa as I have already demonstrated in the last chapter. From 1960 to 1973 Japan's benign diplomacy was undergoing a steady but imperceptible transformation when she was suddenly jolted by the reality of her oil dependency upon fragile foreign sources. Regarding United Nations resolutions on South African, Portuguese and Rhodesian colonialisms, Japan generally abstained at first, arguing that genuine solutions, especially to the South African problem, did not lie in political sanctions. Japan's indifference to the African orchestrated UN resolutions infuriated many African nations (especially Liberia, Ethiopia, Egypt, Libya, etc. which had supported Japan's admission to the UN in 1956 over the Soviet Union's objections). Despite this stance Japan, a past master of the long-term view, was inexorably inching closer to Africa, because the reality of African "independence" (see Chapter 4) could not be ignored. Africa's initial jitteriness about Japan's cosiness to the former colonial masters of the Black Continent was systematically but quietly overcome even as Japan accumulated a mound of lack of political influence. Implicit within this diplomacy was the systematic search for mineral resources and raw materials and export markets. The already cited MOFA Africanist (Shimizu) sees Japan's Africa diplomacy in three stages:

1. The 1960s: Introduction of Africa to Japan.

2. The 1970s, especially from 1974: Resource Diplomacy.

3. The 1980s: Humanitarian / Aid Diplomacy.

These schemata, particularly with regard to the first item, will not do for us for two reasons: one, Africa was (at least her products were) introduced to Japan in the interwar period, even though via a distorted Eurocentric prism; two, one could indeed cite the ironic fact that a more genuine introduction of Africa to the Japanese is currently under way under the stewardship of the same Africanists, Shimizu and his counterparts, Amaki and Horie. These particular bureaucrats have extensive first-hand experience in Africa, and if their Africa experience is factored in the raising of Japanese awareness of Africa, the Shimizu thesis (at least) in reference to the first item), appears deficient. A consideration of this notion has already been undertaken in Chapter 2. On the other hand, this thesis has validity only in terms of the fact that as a *human factor* the African continent did not receive any appreciable consideration at the governmental level by Japan, since Japan first transformed her military-oriented bravery (of the interwar period) to an economy-oriented toughness (of the postwar period). There was no room for the kind of humanness of her Africa diplomacy of the 1980s. This indifference continued until Japan was rudely awakened by the unpleasant reality of the oil crisis. Thus *benign diplomacy* — during which the *Africa-without-Africans* approach reigned supreme — was followed by the activist *resource diplomacy* of the post — oil crisis period following the Arab-Israeli War of October 1973.

It was during this period of *resource diplomacy* (1974-1984) that Japan realized that in constructing a broadly based national security

111

policy she would have to shift to a more pronounced *Africa-for-Africans* approach, because the previous approach could not foster more friendly and closer ties with Africa. Historical precision demands however that it be noted that Japan actually began the *Africa-for-Africans* approach at the outset of African independence in the 60s, which meant that it was a continuation of the interwar policies of the search for raw materials, but her efforts and activism during 1960-1973 were so low-key that even Africa failed to recognise this as positive diplomacy; Japan was instead severely criticized for her "unfair" trading practices. Having learned the lessons of cartel politics from the Organization of Petroleum Exporting Countries (OPEC), and fearing that resource-rich Africa might follow OPEC in cartelling off many of her raw commodities, Japan began a systematic search to secure for herself a more favourable position, especially with those African countries rich in mineral and energy resources. Indeed, in February 1986 four African oil producers — Nigeria, Algeria, Gabon, and Libya — formed the African Hydrocarbon Association by which the four OPEC countries were determined to carry out concerted and appropriate action to restore the stability of the market. Prior to this Japan had paid little attention to Africa as a source of energy. In the 1974-1984 decade Nigeria, Gabon, Niger, Algeria, Zambia, Zaire, etc., now attained a new image in Japanese eyes. The Middle East and Africa North of the Sahara had previously been the main focus of Japan's diplomacy, since much of Japan's oil energy originated from these two regions. Even as of this writing the MOFA Second Africa Division includes the Middle East Bureau, reflecting the schizophrenia-like US State Department perspective of Africa: North of the Sahara is handled as if it belongs to a distinct region and continent apart from South of the Sahara.

This schizophrenic perspective began with Foggy Bottom in the 1950s, even while SCAP was reigning supreme in Tokyo, and inculcating among the Japanese the values of "good" Americanism. In his maiden policy speech to the 111th extraordinary session of the Diet on 27 November 1987, Japan's Prime Minister, Noboru Takeshita, reiterated the tedious Japanese refrain: "Relations with the United States are the cornerstone of Japanese foreign policy" even as he was pronouncing the equally obligatory accompaniment: "Japan's existence and development are premised on world peace and prosperity". Like most Japanese prime ministers on such occasions Takeshita made no reference to Africa. (Despite these prime ministerial ritual homages to America, Japan is of course quietly moving ahead to supplant the US in every economic and technological sphere outside the military complex. This is not to say that Japan is not operating within the American orbit of political influence and military hegemony, after all beginning in 1990 Japan doubled her $150 million financial contribution to US armed forces based in Japan. Since she relies so much on American markets much of her foreign policy (even in Africa) is mortgaged to US priorities. But Japan is looking to a future without American hegemony when she will no longer be needing American protection.)

In any event the period of *resource diplomacy* (which as we have seen in Chapter 2 has operated since the turn of the 20th century during colonial days when Japan, being an international resource pauper, was foraging and scavenging for raw materials and new markets to feed her relentless and continuous war effort) — this resource diplomacy meant in the 1970s that Japan toned down her image of excessive commercialisation with African countries. A new framework of Japanese Africa diplomacy was reordered in the 70s. With the *new* resource diplomacy phase — especially of the decade 1974-1984 — this meant that this diplomatic activism would be accompanied not only by seeking to balance trade with African countries, but also by elevating her *humanitarian* assistance face — the ODA phase — (see Part III of this work). The old indifference was scuttled because Japan suddenly realised that her dependence on distant and uncontrollable sources of energy and raw materials would lead nowhere without constructing a more *human* factor in the hitherto impersonal relations between the Celestial Empire and the Far Continent. In the previous 73 years that Japanese commercial personnel crisscrossed Africa, they failed to generate the human contact with Africans that has now become common in the short period of 1974-1990. Nevertheless the postwar pacific globalisation of the Japanese economy was aided by the dynamic character of her resource diplomacy.

Prior to the maturation of the enlightened resource diplomacy phase, the Japanese "economic animals",[110] having never known the use of the *samurai* swords in Africa, had dominated the Japan-Africa relations with their one-dimensional pursuit of things commercial. Political contacts between Africans and Japanese of any significance outside trade were virtually non-existent, and these non-contacts were exacerbated of course by the European colonial walls, some of which remained indissoluble, indivisible, and invisible despite their alleged tumbling in 1960. As already mentioned Japan increased her expansive contacts with Africa, and her diplomatic policies in the *resource diplomacy* phase were thus designed to attain the twin goals — unattainable during the *benign* phase: of maintaining the flow of resources from Africa and, through official development aid programmes and policies, of helping to *rebuild* the infrastructural integrity of African economies and create new cultural and interpersonal ties, the so-called heart-to-heart inter-changes.

All these interactive factors mean, however, that Japanese foreign policy towards Africa operates within a narrowly circum-scribed set of options, which simultaneously point to Japan's considerable dexterity in diplomatic manoeuvres considering the breadth and range of her ties to and engagements with Africa. In the final analysis the basic features of Japanese foreign policy towards Africa have remained remarkably stable over the postwar decades. It is necessary to delve deeper into the dimensions of Japan's diplomacy in Africa for obvious reasons. To do so means we must first cast a broad canvass of this diplomacy — warts and all — on a longitudinal evolutionary scale. Only then would we return to her diplomacy of the 1980s and the 1990s, and expound its basic values and moral parameters as well as the empirical components of its "economicentrism", an economy-oriented world view.

## EVOLUTION OF JAPANESE AFRICA DIPLOMACY

Before World War II only Egypt, Ethiopia and Liberia were independent in Africa.[111] At a theoretical maximum Japan could have maintained diplomatic ties with three African countries. In reality, however, the situation was different. All Japanese embassies in African countries were established after Japan regained her independence in 1952, although in 1922 Japan had recognised Egypt when the latter became independent. Liberia which had been independent since 1847, and Ethiopia, independent since time immemorial, were only recognised on 29 December 1952 and 1955 respectively. Yet, Japan only established its embassy in Liberia in 1973. This was unusual considering that since 1956 Liberia had been Japan's second most important export destination as a result of Japanese export of ships to companies under the Liberian flag. But Japan is aware, of course, that Liberia has been nominally independent since 1847, when she was planted by America on African soil and has since remained a client of Washington to this day completely without independent industrial capability. It is always preferable to negotiate, not with the clowns, but rather with the owner of the circus. Liberia did not seem much different from a 51st state of the US. Such may have been Japanese reasoning regarding Liberia (before 1973) since the latter was (and still is) merely hiring her name and flag to the highest bidder, and she was not the one either paying the bills or consuming the ships. Hers was merely a flag of convenience and because of the close US-Japan ties Japan naturally and correctly took Liberia for granted.

For five months in 1927-1928 the Japanese Ministry of Foreign Affairs dispatched a diplomatic and economic mission headed by Dr Ujiro Oyama to East Africa. The Oyama Mission was the second ever to tour Africa from Japan. Mention has already been made that in 1926, one year before the Oyama Mission, the Japanese Government inaugurated the *Osaka Shosen Kaisha* maritime route linking Kobe, Japan, and Mombasa, Kenya, in East Africa. In 1932 a Japanese consulate in Mombasa followed, 14 years after the Cape Town consulate was opened in South Africa. Meanwhile, during

115

this period (1920s-1930s) Japan was actively engaged in a kindred "imperial" court diplomacy with the Empire of Ethiopia. This occurred a year after the regency of Ras Tafari (later Emperor Haile Selassie) began in Ethiopia, i.e. after the end of the Taisho Era and the beginning of the Showa period of Emperor Hirohito of Japan. On 21 June 1927 Japan and Ethiopia had signed a Treaty of Friendship and Commerce. The Treaty was repeated on 15 November 1930, thirteen days after Ras Tafari was crowned Emperor of Ethiopia under the name of Haile Selassie I.

Japan's nascent African diplomacy (in Ethiopia) fell victim to imperial intrigues, even before the Japanese legation in Addis Ababa — a legation established by the 1930 Treaty of Friendship — was emplaced on 1 January 1936. Out to avenge the humiliating defeat that the Ethiopian Imperial Army of Emperor Menelik II (1844-1913) had inflicted on the invading Italian army in 1896 at the Battle of Adowa, Mussolini's Fascist Italy invaded Ethiopia on 2 October 1935 with the blessing of the Vatican. Actually, Benito Mussolini's invasion and occupation of Ethiopia ruptured not only the fledgling Japanese diplomacy in Ethiopia, but divided the conservative militarist-civilian leadership of Japan. For example, some of the ultra-conservative Japanese nationalists strongly denounced Fascist Italy and rallied to the side of Ethiopia.

Uchida Ryohei and Mitsura Toyoma and their rightwing secret Black Dragon Society or the Kokuvyukái for instance had promptly called a mass demonstration in Tokyo to express solidarity with "our fellow coloured people" of Ethiopia.[112] When the Ethiopian Emperor, Menelek, heard of Japan's victory over Czarist Russia he congratulated the Japanese Imperial Forces for a splendid performance. Emperor Haile Selassie who strenuously sought Ethiopia's modernisation — made an impassioned plea before the League of Nations, and Japan, perhaps in a desire not to be associated with this annexation by Italian Fascists, closed its legation in Addis Ababa on 3 December. In a move that certainly exposed her to the critical hounds, Japan failed to extend recognition to the Ethiopian government-in-exile, despite the plaintive pleas of the diminutive Lion of Judah, the King of

Kings, Emperor Haile Selassie I. As already noted Japan only recognised Ethiopia in 1955, and opened her embassy in Addis Ababa in April 1958. Still, Emperor Haile Selassie was the first African head of state to make an official tour of Japan and to confer with Emperor Hirohito in 1956 and in 1970.

Italy could, in a way, have claimed that it was Japan that had set a precedent for Fascist Italy's invasion of Ethiopia — since on 1 March 1932 Japan had proclaimed the establishment of Manchu-kuo in China, and exactly a year later, withdrew from the League of Nations. Ethiopia on the other hand had remained a member of the League even after the Italian invasion. Thus if a policy of imperial aggression and defiance of an international legal body could succeed in Asia, Fascist Italy must have reasoned, why should it not succeed in "Dark" Africa? Thus inspired, Mussolini's Fascists decided that they could emulate Japan and have their own African Manchu-kuo.[113] Even the British Foreign Secretary, Sir Samuel Hoare, and the French Premier, Pierre Laval, were resigned to the establishment of an Italian "protectorate" over Ethiopia (cf. the Hoare-Laval division plans).

In September 1940 Japan concluded the Tripartite Pact with Germany and Italy. By the end of 1940 — after the establishment of the "New Order" in Western Europe — Germany was proposing that the four powers: Russia, Germany, Italy and Japan define their "spheres of interest" — in a "southerly" direction. For herself Germany would be seeking additional *Lebensraum* in (of all places) Central Africa! Japan had already turned "South" in Asia, Italy had also turned South in Northeast Africa, the Soviet Union expressed no significant interest. A short while later three African nations were compelled by the United States and European imperial powers to "declare" war on Japan, beginning with the Ethiopian government-in-exile on 14 December 1942. Liberia followed on 27 January 1944, and Egypt on 26 February 1945. African soldiers, especially of the 81st West Africa Division, the 82nd West Africa Division, and the 11th East Africa Division, confronted the Imperial Army of the Empire of the Rising Sun in the punishing jungle battles of Burma.[114, 115] Africans should, of course, have turned

117

their military weapons and fury not against Japan, but rather against those nations that had colonised and/or conscripted them to fight in foreign wars that had virtually nothing to do with African freedom and sovereignty. To some African critics the US should have been fair game too, for her role was far from being salutary in Africa. Germany, Britain, Belgium, Italy, Spain, France, Holland and Portugal should have been the chief culprits nevertheless: Africans could not have forgotten those battles during which thousands of their compatriots fell at the might of imperial forces at Burmi, Omdurman, Kumasi, Segu, Arochukwu, Tabora, Ijebu, Isandlwana, and numerous others battle spots. When Italy invaded Ethiopia no European power organised Europeans or *its* colonial Africans to declare war against Italy. Even a regime, South Africa, whose repression of Africans was legendary, declared war against Japan, and yet with impunity from African rage. Not a single African state, group or individual, was encouraged by European suzerains to declare war on South Africa despite her having subjugated many Africans in the numerous wars of dispossessions that have taken place since 1652. The fact nonetheless is that Africans had no material differences with Japan. Japan's interwar failure to offer material support to Ethiopia during her travails caused by the Italians has however left a legacy of distrust of Japanese role in Africa, a legacy only erased in the closing years of the 70s.

As of 15 June 1939 there was only *one* African state with an embassy in Tokyo, and that was Egypt, whose diplomatic representative, Abdel Wahab Daoud Bey, held the rank of Minister. Egypt also had a consulate in Kobe, that great Japanese port that has seen much of the trade traffic between Japan and Africa. Egypt remained the sole African bridge in the Japan-Africa link that was informally established by the Tokugawa Japanese when they had landed on African soil in 1862. Egypt was joined by other African states only in the 50s after Japan had regained her sovereignty in 1952. The Japanese counterpart to the Egyptian envoy, Bey, was Masayuki Yokohama who was stationed in Cairo. He had replaced Tokuji Amagi, who had been the *Charge d'Affaires* at the Legation du Japon in 1936. The Japanese also had consulates in other parts of Egypt in 1936 — Port Said and Alexandria, in British East Africa (Mombasa) and also in South Africa (Cape Town). Although Japan had maintained for a while a consulate in what was known as Italian Oriental Africa — parts of Somalia were also under Italian control — in Addis Ababa, Japan withdrew this legation after a short while. By the end of 1937 African residents in Japan totalled only 26 — all from Egypt since the three others from South Africa were clearly not African. By August 1945 African residents in Japan had all but disappeared — only five remained. By the end of 1984, the number of these residents had risen from the 1937 figure to 1 063.[116] In 1937 their Japanese counterparts in Africa numbered nearly 200. By the end of World War II this number had been greatly reduced, for obvious reasons. The number of Japanese residents in Africa today is approximately 7 500.

## JAPAN'S DIPLOMACY AND AFRICAN INDEPENDENCE

The result of World War II was the decisive defeat of German, Italian, and Japanese imperialism, and the definite crippling of British, Belgian, French and Dutch imperialism — both of which experiences not only impaired the bonds of Empire, but subordinated also the rest of these imperialisms to the dominant imperialist hegemony of the United States. The Soviet Union emerged as the menacing superpower antidote to the United States. Beginning with her defeat of Czarist Russia in 1905 and her initial defeat of the Allied forces in Asia, Japan initiated, ultimately, the liberation of millions of colonised peoples from the burden of Western imperialism — despite, during the process, a large number of them having been subjected to an equally cruel Japanese imperialism. Japan's challenge to Western imperialism led, finally, to the destruction of a Western-imposed world order.

The weakening of imperial ties in turn ushered in a new tidal wave of nationalist challenge by the African and Asian peoples against their former colonial overlords. If Europe desires and deserves freedom and respite from Hitler's Nazism and Mussolini's Fascism surely Africa and Asia desire and deserve freedom and

119

respite from European colonialism and, in the of case Southeast and East Asia, from imperial Japanism. So went the argument of the African and Asian colonies. For example the Indonesians and the Indochinese (Vietnamese) were greatly encouraged by witnessing their colonial masters — the Dutch and French respectively — humiliated and severly defeated by the Japanese, and reduced to puppets. With the Japanese arming these colonial peoples the latter in turn grew stronger in direct proportion to the weakening of their colonial masters. Even Africans attained a high anti-colonial psychological boost, as the eloquent African scholar Chinweizu has shown in his work, *The West and The Rest of US*.

Ironically, as African demands and clamour for independence persisted, so did Afro-Japanese congruence develop on the exigencies of African liberation from colonialism. Japan gave *verbal* support not only to Asian colonies seeking independence, but to the African peoples as well. The birth of the Asian-African Conference in April 1955 at Bandung, Indonesia, was the culmination of this new spirit of Afro-Asian solidarity. Yet the liberation of Africa has historically not been of serious interest to the Japanese. Until recently priority was given to economic self-interest over and above the political aspirations of Africans. Yet at Bandung Japan's demeanour towards Afro-Asian solidarity was flawless.

The Asian-African Conference — Bandung I as distinct from Bandung II which took place from 24-25 April 1985 — had set out the principles by which nations should live together peacefully. The Bandung I communique formed the basis of the Nonaligned Movement six years later.[117] Bandung delegates were from the independent, nearly independent, and the non-independent nations. From Africa came Egypt, Ethiopia, Gold Coast, Liberia, Libya and the Sudan. Twenty-three others (including Japan) came from Asia. At Bandung Japan played the model role of a pacifist diplomat. Specifically, she strongly supported the Afro-Asian peoples to gain their freedom from colonialism. Still smarting from the irrational atomic bombings (at Hiroshima and Nagasaki) and from the humiliating extra-territoriality treaties of an era gone-by, imposed also by Western gun-boat diplomacy, there was nothing unusual about Japan's sympathetic attitude towards the colonised peoples of colour. Toyoma and Kingoro were actually a few of these new *Asia-for-Asians* messiahs — not unlike the trans-Atlantic *Africa-for-Africans* protagonists of similar period in both Africa and the US (e.g. Marcus Garvey).

Tatsunoke Takasaki, head of the Japanese delegation, embarking on the official pacifist policy adopted by the Japanese Government since 28 April 1952, addressed the conference to the effect that Japan was greatly interested in the success of the conference, since it was "necessary to recognize that the peoples of many countries who have history's pathfinders as their ancestors are lagging behind today in the adoption of modern scientific technologies and various economic systems, while possessing abundant manpower and material resources".[118] The Japanese delegate expressed confidence that once the African and Asian peoples were aware of such a situation they would endeavour through "self-reliance and mutual cooperation to carry out economic development and attain true independence and progress". In its *Final Communique*, in addition to adopting a number of Japanese arguments about emphasis on *economic development* and *world peace* (the dual cornerstones of Japanese diplomacy today), the Bandung Conference gave strong backing for Japan's admission to the United Nations. Japan was admitted to the UN in December 1956, and from 1960 (the "Year of Africa") Japan began to support some African resolutions in the United Nations even if she tended to abstain more often than she cast votes in support. Virtually all these resolutions were pacifist in nature and intent but they focussed on African criticism of Southern African apartheid, racism and colonialism. As African cohesion mounted Japan gradually and systematically began to vote with the Africans in the UN. Some critics dismiss this support as the cynical currying of favour by a resources-starved island-nation with an eye on Africa's resources. But such analysis is simplistic since it tends to ignore totally the pacifist (although idealistic) nature of Japan's postwar diplomacy and the philosophical implications of such pacifism. This is not to say that Japan's pragmatism was not also buttressed by a philosophical dimension to her diplomacy. Nor does this analysis recognise the logic and inevitability of Japan diversifying her diplomacy and foreign relations. Japanese pacifism remained susceptible to criticism nevertheless. Her pacifism was merely the constitutional outcome of her military defeat in World War II. It was not like the sincere Gandhian (Indian) tradition of non-violence and Jawaharlal Nehru's deep commitment to peaceful change. One was the *a posteriori* and belated recognition of the futility of war, another was the *a priori* rejection of all militarism and violence; but what the critics miss is that *Japan was not so much concerned with changing the international scene, as it was merely to adjust to it*. While Marx had pointed out that the cardinal rule is not to interpret the world, but to change it; for Japan, the rule was not to change it, but to join it.

In 1957 Japan was invited by the unofficial Afro-Asian bloc to be a member. Japan's responsibility to these nations was made apparent when her then Foreign Minister, Mamora Shigemetsu, in accepting his country's UN membership, admonished the Afro-Arab-Asian nations to beware of extremist nationalism. At Bandung though, Japan had strongly come out against colonialism not only in Africa and Asia, but "everywhere". This position was clarified during her support for a Turkish resolution condemning "all forms of colonialism". Again Japan at the UN was not like India when it came to African issues. The Indian delegates strove to identify themselves with African aspirations even before the majority of these states were independent. India won the friendship of Africans and found a forum for exercising leadership until the new Africans in th early 60s took over their own cause at the UN. So Japan's mutual support for the African-Asian nations at Bandung should not be interpreted as the convergence of policy or philosophical objectives between her and the African-Asian nations. If the words of the Japanese Prime Minister in 1946-1947, and 1949-1955, Shigeru Yoshida, could be regarded as a yardstick, Japan had actually begun distancing herself from the "backward" nations of Africa and Asia even before the Bandung resolutions were published.

Yoshida wrote in his *Memoirs:*

> According to some people, Japan too ... regained ... her independence in 1952 after nearly seven years of foreign Occupation, and, our plight being therefore much the same as those of other countries of Asia and Africa, we should throw in our lot with them in opposition to such 'colonial' Powers as the US, Great Britain and France. Such a view is (untenable) ... Japan is more Western than Asian (or African) ... Whereas many of the countries of Asia and Africa are still undeveloped or underdeveloped, industrially and economically and their peoples have still to attain the standards of living which modern civilization entitles them to aspire. In short, they are what we are forced to recognise as backward nations, which as yet have little to do with international economic relations.[119]

It is this same Yoshida, feeling the sting of American Occupation, who once described his people's plight as the "comic helplessness of being Japanese". Some Japanese scholars in time came to denounce this "comic helplessness" as the function of the tragic "philosophical incompetence" of Japanese leaders who had given Japanese pacifism the appearance of being "unprincipled, situational and unreliable". The critics conceded, however, not only that the basic problem confronting Japan was "powerlessness", but also that this Yoshida-like pacifism was the only appropriate survival technique.[120] Yoshida, in any event, argued that these Afro-Asian nations were still guided by a "negative neutrality" and "negative philosophy" and thus their policies could not be regarded with anything approaching significance in the international arena. Still Yoshida could conclude that Japan was well suited — geographically and economically — to understand Asia and Africa, since "racially speaking ... other Asian and African nations tend to feel a greater sense of kinship towards Japan than towards the peoples of the West". This parametrical Japanese view became the guiding light of Japanese diplomacy in Africa between 1952 and 1960. It was also this kind of governmental attitude towards Africa that contributed to Japan's historic lack of political influence in the Black Continent.

That is, Japan failed to contribute significant *material* (and perhaps even moral) support for the liberation of African peoples from European colonialism, especially since she tended to temporise with the colonialists when Africa and some Asians were denouncing colonialism in the southern cone of the Continent. For example unlike India whose colonisation under Britain was still so fresh her delegates tended to bring personal feelings of racial humiliations out of the colonial experience, during UN debates, the Japanese UN delegates on the other hand temporised with these former colonialists. It was a Pakistani delegate who accused the British and other colonial powers of having a "beautiful front and a very large and stinking backyard" covering the whole continent of Africa. Even after admission to the UN the Japanese delegates mimicked the tedious ambiguities of their pacifist leaders. The tenures of Japanese prime ministers[121] merely saw the entrenchment of a particular emphasis in each period of this basic Japanese diplomatic paradigm. Concomitant with this generic view of Africa was the slow and subtle diplomatic transformation which finally achieved authoritative coherence in the diplomatic formulations of foreign ministers Toshio Kimura, Sunao Sonoda and Shintaro Abe. After conferring with the leaders of Egypt, Ghana, Nigeria, Tanzania and Zaire (between 31 October 1974 and 9 November 1974) Foreign Minister Kimura, for instance, publicly restated that Japan should stand for anticolonialism, anti-apartheid, and support to the national liberation movements in Southern Africa. He added that Japan should deepen economic cooperation with Africa.

Shintaro Abe called for more aid to Africa, for expanded personal and cultural exchanges between Africans and the Japanese. But both these activisms came in the 1970s and 1980s and they reflected some of Japan's most forthright positions regarding some pet African issues. Even then Japanese government ministers visiting Africa are not as forthright and specific as Chinese visiting

Africa. For example in 1982-1983 the Chinese premier Zhao Ziyang with his huge entourage spent one month in Africa during his 11 African states tour. He was specific in addressing the Zaireans: "We are here to learn how to promote understanding, friendship, solidarity and cooperation with African peoples". And he promptly remitted payments of a $100 million credit to the kleptocratic regime of Mobutu. In Guinea he told President Sekou Toure that China reaffirmed her support for the South African People's struggle and that China would never have any political, economic or trade relations with South Africa. He criticised the US for its attempts to obstruct Namibia's independence by supporting South Africa's refusal to implement the UN Security Council resolution on Namibia. Chinese leaders however do not regularly visit Africa like Japanese government bureaucrats do. It is in this sense that Japan seems more advanced than China in their African probings, although China is really a latecomer to the African scene even as she has ideologically been far ahead in her championing of African liberation and freedom from colonialism.

In any event, due to the continued activism of the liberal wing of the then ruling *Jiyu-Minshitu* (Liberal-Democratic) Party — such as Utsonomiya Tokuma, Matsumura Kenzo, Fujiyama Aiichiro and other *Diet* members — there continued a strong undercurrent in the governing Liberal-Democratic Party (LDP) to improve pacific relations between Japan and Africa, as well as between Japan and Asia. This liberal wing eventually formed the Asia-Africa Problems Study Group in the LDP on 28 January 1962 to continue its lobby for improved relations between Japan and the African-Asian nations.[122] The Japanese *Africa-for-Africans* votaries — a much later species than its African counterpart — were eclipsed by those Japanese for whom the *Africa-without-Africans* approach still dominated their thinking, at least on issues concerning Japan and Africa. Many of them were still harking back to the colonised Africa of the 1920s whose eastern seaboard was much frequented by the Japanese in search of markets and raw materials. It was an approach that recognised the pre-eminence of European colonial *rule* in Africa. After African flag independence this approach turned to recognising the pre-eminence of European neo-colonial *role* (called Western "sphere of influence"). The *Africa-without-Africans* approach continued to undergo a cautious metamorphosis and debasement till, beginning in 1960, the year Japan called the "African Year", and beyond the oil-shock period of the 1970s, the *Africa-without-Africans'* Japanese finally scuttled their reactionary approach and embraced, instead, a policy which coincided with the diplomatically-orientated *resource diplomacy*. After her admission to the United Nations, Japan adhered to a foreign policy which gave priority to UN Charter principles. In tandem with this new position in the early 60s as we have already seen, when not abstaining, (reluctantly at first, but enthusiastically much later) Japan supported the anti-apartheid United Nations motions by African and Asian nations. Some of these nations remained leery of Japan's motives, and often doubted her enthusiasm in extending economic aid to these countries, even while they themselves had begun to import many Japanese products.

The second part (1960-1969) of this period in Japan was a period of rapid growth, a decade during which Japan sought to open her economy to foreign competition by liberalising trade and the flow of international capital. It became a new era which called forth a new diplomacy since the natives had wised up to the value of their resources. Japan had by now moved full circle: from the overwhelming militaristic Japanism of 1904-1945 to the disarming Japanese pacifism of the entire postwar period. In the words of a Japanese Foreign Minister in 1979:

> In light of the terrible experience Japan witnessed during World War II, our country has decided to carve out an honorable position in the international society by con- tributing to the maintenance of world peace without resort to military force.[123]

Japan's militarism had been interred with the bones of her defeat in 1945; and in its wake, like the Phoenician Sphinx, emerged a new pacifism that, once again, taught the world a lesson in the arts of national discipline: national power was marshalled to the ends of a pacifist, albeit opportunistic economic, diplomacy. Pacifism permeated and governed all Japanese international behaviour. Japan is for instance a conscientious member of the United Nations, yet she had declined (until 1992) to participate in any peace-keeping role by contributing a detachment or even observers to the United Nations "peace keeping" forces, notably in Lebanon, although on numerous occasions, as the MOFA Yearbook (*Diplomatic BlueBook*) states,

> Japan has made it clear that it is prepared to cooperate in *civil* administration should a United Nations Transition Assistance Group (UNTAG) be sent to facilitate Namibian independence.[124]

The Japanese people seem now to have developed a negative attitude towards militarisation of any form, and because of this most Japanese are committed pacifists who have no wish to get involved in military affairs of other states.[125] Abhorrence of war and opposition to the militarist tendencies of the interwar period have now come to dominate the postwar national temper. This new pacifism became the unreasoning desire for peace even if its diplomatic policies tended to encourage repression in other countries. On the contrary, because it was a deep-seated moral force, Ghandian (Indian) pacifism strenuously challenged and opposed injustice in other countries. Japan's past military role obviously hampered a judgmental diplomatic approach in her relations with kleptocratic, despotic, pigmentocratic, etc. regimes in Africa and elsewhere.

In the Africa-Japan diplomatic ties one historical weakness has been the absence between Tokyo and Africa of a broad framework within which to conduct relations. We leave the question of whether Japan and Africa could develop shared interests that might eventually lead to the establishment of a genuine Afro-Japanese nexus to later sections of this work. Suffice here to note that Japan was slow to realise the significance of her ties with Africa because she saw not enough of a *quid pro quo* involvement. In her *White Papers* and annual *Diplomatic Bluebook* the Japanese government formulates this *quid pro quo* insufficiency as follows:

> Japanese relations with the countries of Africa were necessarily very sparse and limited before the war in that Africa is geographically distant from Japan and most of Africa was under colonial administration by the West European powers.[126]

Even while lamenting this distance, Japan sought ways and means to redress the historically "sparse" relations, since, in the words of the MOFA,

> in view of the importance of Africa and its increasing role in the international community as well as Japan's international responsibilities in today's increasingly interdependent world, Japan has promoted personal exchanges with African countries to enhance mutual understanding.[127]

We shall see some of these "personal exchanges" later in the work.

During their tenure as Foreign Minister, Toshio Kumura (1974, and 1978), Sunao Sonoda (1979) and Shintaro Abe (1984) paid official visits to Africa. Following the oil crisis the Japanese Prime Minister, Masayoshi Ohira, saw the necessity to change Japan's view of Africa. During his tenure as Foreign Minister while speaking to a (1978) Tokyo conference of Japanese ambassadors stationed in Africa, Ohira noted that it was "widely recognized today that the African continent is rapidly gaining in importance in the international arena". He acknowledged that "Japan's existence and prosperity (could) no longer be viewed as something unrelated to the vast area that is Africa." Ohira remarked that given the altered circumstances, what was required was an "indepth assessment", and that the "problem of where to position Japan's relations with Africa in this country's diplomacy represents a task to be tackled from now on". This "in-depth assessment" tackled the task by compelling Ohira to dispatch his Foreign Minister to visit Africa.

In 1974 Kimura, the first Japanese Foreign Minister to visit Africa, made official visits to Ghana, Nigeria, Zaire, Tanzania and Egypt. As noted previously, following this visit, Kimura promised the Africans firm Japanese commitment for anti-apartheid, anti-colonialism, and national liberation movements in Southern Africa. Although the Kimura Mission pledged more Japanese trade with African countries and less dependence on South Africa, it simply promised more than it was able (or willing) to deliver. This has in the past been the problem with Japanese bureaucrats regarding Africa: the inability to deliver on promises made. In other cases however problems lay more with Africa than with Japan as when for instance, albeit for economic self-interest, Japan wanted to build (reluctantly by some accounts) a Trans-Sahara *Highway*, African nations concerned haggled instead over a Trans-Sahara *Railway*, the latter clearly a more expensive undertaking. The Trans-Sahara Highway is only part of the planned Trans-Africa Highway System which will eventually criss-cross the continent from Botswana to Tunisia, Morocco to Mozambique, Senegal to Somalia, Kenya to Ghana. Japan nevertheless had ushered in a diplomatic policy that was no longer centred on the great powers, but toward one which placed increased significance on the opinions of the developing countries. In July 1979 Foreign Minister Sunao Sonoda visited Nigeria, Ivory Coast, Sengal, Tanzania and Kenya. This 1979 Sonoda visit, like the 1974 Kimura visit, occurred just after the second and first, respectively, oil crises. Some Japanese and Western analysts concluded that the "principal cause" of these visits was the desire to secure raw materials because Japan was keen to move away from the dependence on Middle East oil and gas. Although "fuel diplomacy" was a phrase regularly on the lips of virtually every Japan watcher when Sonoda visited Africa, naturally he ventured into other areas of common interest during his 11 days' stay in Africa. According to the 1979 MOFA *Information Bulletin*, during his discussions with African leaders, Sonoda described Japan's relationship with African nations as "partnership in pursuit of peace". While in Nigeria, Sonoda pledged that Japan would not recognize the regime of "Zimbabwe-Rhodesia", as well as promising that Japan would scale down her trade with the regime of South Africa. He sweetened his political commitments with development loans of $16 million to Senegal, $215 million to Kenya (plus a grant of $9 million) and $29 million to Tanzania. Critics of Japan nevertheless maintained a negative view of Japan's relations with the developing world, especially with Africa.

Even Japanese embassies' public relations efforts, as well as the few friendship associations that existed in foreign capitals, were dismissed as "mainly used for commercial purposes".[128] They held that this was only a symptom of the theory of economic animalism on the march. Some Japanese analysts then concluded that this was proof positive that

> Japan has given priority to economic demands over political commitments. It can be said, therefore, that Japan's African diplomacy continues in the customary pattern, although it became more positive after the first oil crisis, both in the political and economical fields.[129]

Any unidimensional analysis would most likely miss the complexity of Japanese diplomacy towards Africa. The foregoing criticism falls in this category. Moreover, it denies the emergence of the notion of altruism among nations. It is *pari passu* another way of endorsing that avuncular notion of British premiers: we have no permanent friends, only permanent interests.

Nor does it take into consideration both the moral imperatives of and philosophical demands to Japan's Africa diplomacy. Without denying the role and influence of the fluctuations of the raw materials market I wish to say that there are undoubtedly other values in Japan's diplomacy towards Africa. The economic-animalist explanations are only one of the complex. How, for example, do we categorise that every year Japan buys maize from Zimbabwe and distributes it to other African countries? Or that since she buys rice from Thailand and sends it to Ethiopia the motive may be to gain economic benefit from a country with the dubious distinction of being the world's foremost bread-basket? Is it to curry favour, and for what purpose? MOFA's Ryochie Horie remarked to me that such an economic transaction has obviously no commercial profit motive behind it. He seems to believe that some other moral value is operational here. Obviously there has to be and I deal with these aspects below. Perhaps the Japanese counsellor in Ghana, Terufusa Ariga, was closer to the truth when he remarked: "It is partly for humanitarian reasons, partly for economic reasons". He could also have added: partly for national prestige, partly international interdependence.

## BASIC VALUES OF JAPAN'S AFRICA DIPLOMACY

On 9 October 1984 Japan announced that she would conduct "a positive diplomacy" for the preservation of world peace and the realisation of world prosperity as the second largest economy in the non-communist world.[130] At a Tokyo reception in November 1987 hosted by the Zimbabwe Ambassador to Japan, Dr N.H. Katedza, in honour of the new Japanese Ambassador to Zimbabwe, Ken Ikebe, the latter reiterated this point of view when he remarked that Japan was embarking on a "new positive diplomacy toward Africa". Ikebe's response to Katedza was, because of its brevity, extremely unlightening since he never bothered to expound on the meaning of this "new positive diplomacy". What this positive diplomacy purports to be, what its values and principles are, constitute this chapter. The assertion that this is a new policy is clearly without merit, for in 1988 it cannot obviously be new since we began seeing its "newness" at least from the early 1980s.

As we have already seen some critics harshly dismiss any non-commercial diplomacy Japan adopts towards Africa, and cynically lump it under the new bottle, old wine label of "economic animalism"; or as Ravenhill puts it:

> Japan's rapidly growing economic links with Africa attest to the success of the principle underlying Japanese foreign policy — *seikei bunri* (the separation of economics from

politics or, as its critics allege, the art of being all things to all people)[131]

That in effect is what Japan is, and for that matter, any successful diplomacy must be the art of all things to all people, especially if some of its guiding values are peace and non-aggression and world cooperation.

Japanese critics in the main also conclude that Japan's "interest (in Africa) seems to be confined to the fields of economic cooperation, trade, and investment ... (and thus) Africa's position in Japan's foreign relations is still relatively minor",[132] and which condition makes for a "fragile partnership". Importing more than 90 per cent of her crude oil from the Middle East and Africa, Tokyo clearly recognises that for a continent rich in commodities, it would not long be lost on the lessons of the OPEC — like cartelisation of commodity power. It therefore became an important principle of Japanese foreign policy not only to remain on good terms with the oil-producing African-Arab world, but also to cultivate a diversity of close ties with many other African countries — commodity rich or poor. Critics descended upon Japan on the basis of her obvious vulnerability to resources viability. They naively concluded that explanation of Japan's diplomacy should be consigned to the economic motive forces. If queried most of these critics would probably swear that they were not Marxist, even if the Marxian theory of economic determism of political life looms, indeed, so large in their analyses that it is the only explanation offered for Japan's international role. Forgotten too is the simple historical fact that Japan was a nation even before the concept had evolved in Europe ... These critics also tended to gloss over a paramount historical issue concerning Japanese diplomacy: the LDP elites had recognised the turmoil that *political activism* had brought to Japan in the Second World War. They then eschewed politics in favour of the *economics — first principle*. Trade was a safer route to influencing the world than political hegemony or military conquest. Before World War II Japanese diplomacy seems to have endorsed the view of General Karl Von Clausewitz who regarded war as "nothing else than the continuation of state policy by different means". Japan then saw no dichotomy between those international relations using violence (war) and all other international relations (diplomacy). In any event Japan's diplomacy has changed since then. She has in fact reversed course and principle ... although there are some critics who see tell-tale signs of Japanese reversion to *ante-bellum* policies.

Occasionally Japan played in her critics' hands nevertheless, as when she recognised Zambia at the time of the latter's independence (1964), only to have the Japanese embassy in Lusaka opened in 1970 just in time to coincide with the visit to Zambia of the huge Japanese economic mission headed by Fumihiko Kono, board chairman of Mitsubishi Heavy Industries and Vice President of the powerful *Keidanren* (Federation of Economic Organizations). Kono was accompanied by 26 business leaders and government officials. Mitsubishi's need for copper or the *Keidanren's* relish in commercial trade was not missed by the critics, nor the fact that *Keidanren* bankrolls the LDP at election time. Sometimes the *Keidanren* chairman is more powerful than the Japanese Prime Minister; that's how important these *Keidanren* missions are. The second Kono Mission visited Tanzania, Ivory Coast, Nigeria and Senegal in February 1978. Members of the Japanese Diet have actively visited Africa almost every year since. Every government, however, is first of all a finance-generating and an economic management entity. Social organisation and national cohesion are arranged around this primary premise. In the Japanese system, like in all other world systems, the government protects big companies, at least those producing large quantities of national revenue, manufactured goods, employment services, etc., no less than it does extend protection to its citizens. That is, institutions that organise financial strength, manage economic infrastructures, promote monetary solvency, maintain the efficiency of the supercompetitive export machine, and help endow the citizenry with the wherewithal to pursue life, liberty, and happiness, all these institutions will generally tend to go to bed with Caesar Augustus. Hence the collaboration between the Japanese Government and the home commercial companies, and this without much questioning from the Japanese public. These gentlemen who run the LDP (and thus the government) embody that complete fusion of commercial and bureaucratic experience, half public and half private, which makes competence in the Japanese system a *sine qua non*. Commercial management and government bureaucracy become the extremities of the pendulum between which these men swing.

Yet despite this criticism of Japanese diplomacy there is, perhaps, an equally important diplomatic principle involved here. Japan's foreign service ministry has been espousing and advocating this principle since the beginning of the 1980s:

> In order to fulfill its international responsibility in the present day world marked by deepening interdependence, Japan is stepping up the exchange of people with African nations to deepen mutual understanding, and at the same time, contributing to the economic and social development of African nations by extending maximum possible economic and technical cooperation in a broad range of fields.[133]

That is, there are moral principles which dictate Japanese diplomacy, besides economic considerations. Yet moral principles and economic considerations may be intertwined. Consider the Japanese policy of avoiding vulnerability (on account of her pauperism in mineral, energy and primary resources). Is it not a moral imperative for Japan to stabilise her economy in order to stave off starvation for her 120 million population? In other words, were Ethiopia to follow the same policy would this be considered "economic animalism" greatly lacking in moral principles? We may of course ignore the utterances of diplomats, since diplomats are supposed on the whole to be lying on behalf of their governments. (The three major functions of the diplomat remain of course the following — reporting, representation, and negotiation.). Yet one cannot ignore the apparent validity of diplomatic philosophy implicit in Japan's current policies toward Africa. This view was expressed during discussions between myself and the Africa-desk director, Kunio Shimizu, during which the latter stated:

(i) "Japan wants *good and friendly* relations with all of Africa (including even those countries from which Japan stood to gain absolutely nothing in economic returns)". Thus Japan "has no political difficulties with any African countries";

(ii) in some African countries "Japan has close *'emotional'* ties, for example Ethiopia";[134] the human, emotional interest is very strong here;

(iii) Japan seeks to "maintain stronger ties elsewhere in Africa because of the *geopolitical factor:* Zambia and Zimbabwe are two such examples;"

(iv) the "question of *economic* ties is only *one* of the factors that plays an important role in this diplomacy," e.g. Ivory Coast, Kenya, Nigeria, etc.

Shimizu conceded that with some countries Japan has "less intense ties" even though the resources factor is paramount in the equation of bilateralism, e.g. Niger and Chad.

The Shimizu thesis thus points out to a broadly based congeries of diplomatic principles that shape the Africa-Japan ties. During 1984 the image of Africa that was projected to the Japanese public, especially by the high-profile activism (e.g. in "Africa Month", "Blankets for Africa" programmes, etc.) of the then Foreign Minister, Shintaro Abe, was not only of high-minded Japanese humanitarianism, but was also one of famine, brokenness, drought, disease and *apartheid*. A Japanese scholar based in Canada, Toru Kotani, believes that the then (1985) African emphasis of Japan's diplomacy seems to owe much to the "idiosyncratic activism" of Abe. The pestilential persistence of these social pathologies is however undeniable, nor were they of course created by Shintaro Abe, whose shrewd public relations gambit — or the art of symbolism — to draw Japanese public awareness of Africa is of great intrinsic value, even if it may be viewed as an educational goal in itself.

## DIAGRAM 3.1
### Regions in which Japan should intensify her future economic cooperation

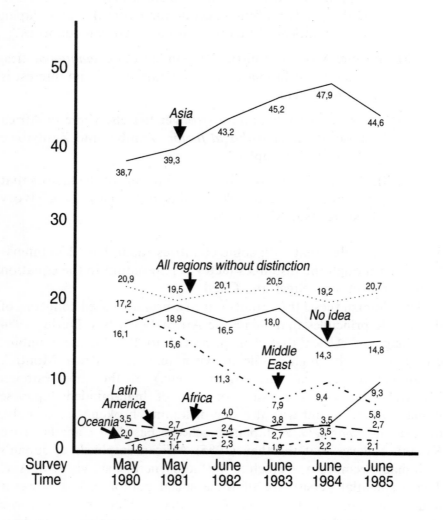

Source:    Public Opinion Survey: Prime Ministers' Office (1986).

It also happens that the highest rate of Japanese public interest in Africa, as is evident in the *Public Opinion Survey on Diplomacy* of the Prime Minister's Office (see Diagram 3.1) was registered at this time. Japan's official interest had perhaps peaked by the end of 1984. The continued inability of Africa to rise from her semi-permanent state of socio-economic paralysis is clearly a disincentive for continued Japanese diplomatic interest in Africa. Much of Africa today is caught up in the vicious grip of war, civil strife, famine, political conflict, constitutional confusion, and economic malaise.

We see from this diagram that there was a noticeable increase of those who mentioned Africa from the 1984 figure of 3,5 % to the 1985 figure of 9,3 %. But in terms of "degree of interest in foreign countries," the 1986 Japanese public opinion registered a decline for Africa from the 1985 figure of 17,4 % to the 11,3 % of 1986.[135] Yet this survey revealed that, in comparison with the previous one, those placing importance on ASEAN, African and East European regions gained slightly. In the 1986 *Public Opinion Survey on Diplomacy*, 39,3 % of the Japanese considered that "of these (i.e. ASEAN, Oceanic, Middle Eastern, African, East European, West European and Latin American) regions" Africa should come first. In the 1979 survey 38,0 % had thought so.

In previous (1979-1984) surveys when respondents were asked: "Do you consider relations with African countries important?" the percentage of those who considered this *"very important"* in 1979 (8,9 %) continued to fall through the years, till in 1984 it reached 5,9 %.

While those who thought this *"fairly important"* in 1979 were 29,1 %, in 1984 they had increased slightly to 32,4 %. (See Diagram 3.2.)

Yet the Japanese Government maintained a *diplomatic* course in terms of building bridges with Africa, with the emphasis placed on the new *humanitarianism*. It is only when we look at Table 3.1 however that some of the "mystery" of Japanese public interest in Africa begins to be removed.

# DIAGRAM 3.2
## Do you consider relations with African countries important ?

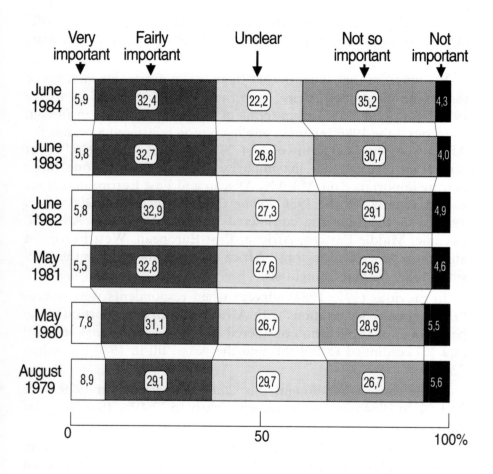

Source: Office of the Prime Minister: Public Opinion Survey On Diplomacy (1985).

## TABLE 3.1

## REASONS WHY JAPAN SHOULD BE FRIENDLY WITH A SPECIFIC COUNTRY

## SAMPLE: RESPONDENTS WHO NAMED A PARTICULAR COUNTRY

| Countries to be friendly with | | | Rich in resources such as petroleum | Large agricultural production | Important for security | Likeable people | Culture and tradition | Strong international voice | Promising country | Geographical proximity | Others, not clear | Total |
|---|---|---|---|---|---|---|---|---|---|---|---|---|
| | % | (persons) | % | % | % | % | % | % | % | % | % | % |
| USA | 43,3 | 1 029 | 7,6 | 7,4 | 45,1 | 3,8 | 3,0 | 22,8 | 4,8 | 0,4 | 5,2 | 100,0 |
| USSR | 3,0 | 71 | 7,0 | 1,4 | 36,6 | - | - | 29,6 | 7,0 | 8,5 | 9,9 | 100,0 |
| China | 19,5 | 462 | 6,9 | 4,3 | 3,5 | 6,3 | 9,3 | 0,4 | 30,3 | 37,0 | 1,9 | 100,0 |
| ROK | 0,6 | 15 | - | 6,7 | - | 6,7 | 6,7 | 6,7 | 6,7 | 53,3 | 13,3 | 100,0 |
| ASEAN nations | 0,3 | 7 | - | 14,3 | - | - | - | 57,1 | 57,1 | 28,6 | - | 100,0 |
| Oceanian nations | 0,6 | 15 | 26,7 | 33,3 | - | 13,3 | - | 26,7 | 26,7 | - | - | 100,0 |
| Middle East countries | 1,1 | 27 | 81,5 | - | 3,7 | - | - | 7,4 | 7,4 | 3,7 | 3,7 | 100,0 |
| African nations | 0,2 | 5 | 20,0 | - | - | - | - | 60,0 | 60,0 | - | - | 100,0 |
| East European countries | 0,0 | 1 | - | - | - | - | - | 100,0 | 100,0 | - | - | 100,0 |
| West European countries | 1,0 | 24 | 4,2 | 8,3 | - | 20,8 | 33,3 | 8,3 | 8,3 | - | 8,3 | 100,0 |
| Latin American nations | 0,3 | 7 | - | 14,3 | - | - | - | 28,6 | 28,6 | - | 42,9 | 100,0 |

Twenty (20) per cent of the respondents held that it was more important to befriend Africa because of its abundance of mineral *resources*. An equal number believed that African nations have a strong international voice. Hence three times that number (i.e. 60 %) believed that Africa is a promising region — a continent of the future and friendly relations with Africa were thus essential. But when the question was narrowed to: "Which regions do you think it

139

important for Japan to have relations with?" the Japanese respondents consistently voted Africa the least important. (See Diagram 3.3.)

The fact however that Africa was rated much lower than even the Oceanic countries was illustrative, even though, perhaps, this may have been due to a number of reasons, one of which is the proximity of Oceania to Japan, and thus there are more Japanese settlers in this region than in Africa. Japanese Africa diplomacy closely reflects Japanese public opinion of Africa, even though the MOFA is always a step ahead in charting closer ties with Africa.

In any event, although a highly principled diplomat, and one strongly interested in African regeneration as his trips to Africa have shown, Abe's pro-Africa activism failed to address some of the significant issues binding (or dividing) Japan and Africa.

These issues are delineated, for instance, by the Shimizu thesis. It was Shimizu who has stated in the already mentioned discussion that it was "difficult (for a Japanese diplomat) to live in Africa, not only because of tropical disease, poor electricity, security for our embassies, etc. but because Africa is 'psychologically' not known (in Japan)".[136] Still Shimizu remained appreciative of the Japanese public for giving the Japanese Government support, or at least non-opposition in her "positive" Africa diplomacy.

In his 1984 book, *Creative Diplomacy,* Abe's analysis of African diplomacy however merely confines itself to the traditional and rehashed themes of the MOFA *Yearbook.*[137] Because the sheer number of African countries gives them a certain degree of political visibility, if not clout — at least in the United Nations — the Japanese Government no doubt recognises the value and significance of maintaining cordial if not close relations with the African region. As Table 3.1 has already shown, at least 20 per cent of the surveyed Japanese public consider Africa's international voice to be strong enough to warrant closer Japanese ties with the region. When top Japanese diplomats based in Africa gathered in Tokyo in 1983 for their annual review of Japan-Africa relations and African realities, some of the perennial *political* questions which cropped up

## DIAGRAM 3.3
### Which regions do you think are important for Japan to have relations with ?

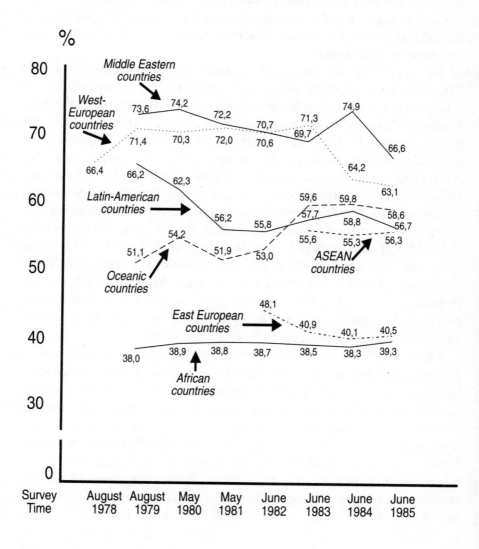

Source: Prime Minister's Office (1986).

were: How could Japan bolster its diplomatic capabilities? How should it steer future diplomacy on the question of Namibian independence and *apartheid*? During the meeting Japan's Africa envoys were also reminded by the then Foreign Minister, Shintaro Abe, that Japan must also pay heed to the *strategic* importance of the region where East-West confrontation would hold great sway for peace and stability.

To underline its political significance the Japanese Prime Minister, Yasuhiro Nakasone, was urged by the envoys to pay an official visit to the continent of Africa, thus becoming the first Japanese Prime Minister to do so. Yasu, like his friend Ron, never made the trip to the Far Continent. Were Japan's diplomacy to particular regions measured by prime ministerial regional visits, her Africa diplomacy would rank just about at the bottom. In January 1974 Prime Minister Kakuei Tanaka, responding to Southeast Asian countries' public hostility to Japanese economic penetration, visited five countries of the Association of Southeast Asian Nations (ASEAN). Tanaka tried to placate the ASEAN public with more economic cooperation packages and friendship between ASEAN and Japan. Tanaka and then Prime Minister Masayoshi Ohira have (separately) visited Latin America. As Chapter 4 will show, many more higher ranking African government officials have visited Japan than their counterparts have visited Africa.

From 16-21 November 1984 Abe paid official visits to Zambia, Ethiopia and Egypt. In Egypt, the Hosni Mubarak Government and Shintaro Abe consummated an agreement to cooperate in building schools in Egypt for seamen, nurses and other trainees from African countries. In his discussions with President Mubarak, Abe did not limit himself to Africa — he ventured into the treacherous Middle East problems, especially those concerning the Iran-Iraq war. When he reached Ethiopia, he announced that Japan would extend supplemental food and agricultural aid to Africa amounting to 11,7 billion yen ($50 million) in fiscal 1984, in addition to the 27,6 billion yen ($115 million) already pledged. He held discussions with the Ethiopian leader, Col. Mengistu Haile-Mariam, as well as with Foreign Minister, Goshu Wolde. He visited the drought-stricken region of Makelle in northern province of Tigre, thus becoming the first Foreign Minister from a Western bloc nation to observe conditions first-hand. In Zambia, Abe conferred with President Kaunda and his Foreign Minister, Lameck H.H. Goma, not only on strengthening Japan-Zambia relations, but also about the problem of South Africa in the region. A variety of Japanese officials have landed on the African shore with the hope of making a significant difference in terms of the growth of bilateral relations and the development of Africa. Other Foreign Ministry officials to visit Africa were Ishimatsu Kitagawa, parliamentary Vice-Minister for Foreign Affairs, who visited Zimbabwe, Malawi, Madagascar, Central African Republic, Somalia, Guinea, Senegal and Ethiopia in June and July of 1984. Parliamentary Vice-minister for Foreign Affairs, (Mrs) Mayumi Moriyama, visited Cameroon, Kenya, and Uganda in July 1985. Although there has been no Japanese Prime Minister to date to have visited Africa, Japanese official visits to Africa, like African official visits to Japan, have been varied in composition, scope, purpose and duration since the days when Crown Prince Akihito and Crown Princess Michiko visited Ethiopia in 1960. In March 1983 the Crown Prince and the Crown Princess visited Zambia, Tanzania and Kenya. Their second trip to Africa was designed to reciprocate on behalf of Emperor Hirohito the state visits to Japan by the Presidents of Zambia and Tanzania (1980 and 1981 respectively). The Kenyan President visited Japan a couple of weeks after the crown prince left. Akihito returned to Africa in February 1984 (i.e. to Senegal and Zaire). In Zambia the Crown Prince expressed his "sympathy" (sic) for the humanism philosophy of President Kenneth Kaunda. In Tanzania he "lauded" President Nyerere's nation-building efforts. In Kenya, Akihito expressed his "support" for the "Nyayo" spirit advocated by the Kenyan President, Daniel arap Moi, that sets forth "peace, love, and unity".

⟨ Beginning in 1974 Japan had initiated efforts to cultivate African goodwill by accelerating her low-key support for certain political stances such as recognising Guinea-Bissau, Mozambique, and Angola as well as support for certain "third world" positions in the United Nations. But Japan's ideological mission in Africa retained, as always, its mute character except that its political objectives continued to be mainly subservient to the West's (especially the United States). It is in the latter notion that the concept of Japanese *"security diplomacy"* in Africa was developed, for Japan is careful not to conflict with US *"strategic* and *security interests"* in Africa, and Japan fears most (for the moment) to be excluded by US decision-making process, especially during the tenure of the now expired Ron-Yasu phenomenon. Yet it is also true that except for the 1945-1952 Occupation period, Japan has never submitted to foreign dictation, the 1858 exclusion treaties notwithstanding. The Japanese have acted as free agents in all their modernisation or westernisation drives throughout Japan's history. Despite operating under American hegemony this is so, also, in its African diplomacy where Japan desires to achieve the status of a leading power without resort to military conquest or massive re-armament. Thus its political diplomacy is intertwined with its economic diplomacy. Foreign Minister Takeo Fukuda had put it this way:

> We wish to employ our economic strength to gain an increasing voice in the international community. The tradition once was that a nation used its economic power to become a military power, but that is not the case with us today.[138]

Thus in addition to political and economic diplomacy Fukuda adds *cultural diplomacy*, for he recognises that for Japan to maintain a status and prestige of a world economic power and influential leader, such power and prestige of a world economic power and influential leader, would not be achieved without the African world shifting its acquiescence and respect for the West to Japan. Not only in MOFA but also in such institutions as the Japan Foundation is there a broadly based pursuit of *cultural diplomacy*, as its managing director, Junpei Kato, explained to the writer in December 1987.

Most critics of Japan's alleged economic animalism miss precisely this interesting point: despite the fact that Japan is an economic superpower she has virtually no international influence. Her lack of political influence is manifested by her lack of foreign followers, with the possible exception of some ASEAN countries. For an economic giant whose FY 86 (ending 31 March 1987) had a trade *surplus of $101 billion (compared to the US trade deficit of* $167 billion, of which nearly $58 billion was with Japan), and whose 1992 surplus favouring her exceeded 133 billion US dollars Japan's lack of a significant foreign following certainly diminishes her status and national prestige. In 1987 and 1992 Japan was the world's largest creditor country, and remains so today (728 billion US dollars). The four largest banks in the world are Japanese. Today Japan ranks first in human development index, life expectancy in years (1991 figures) and GNP/capital (1990 figures). Yet if we measure the impact and influence of Japan in the international arena, it would not be surprising if we find it nearly non-existent. This absence of political influence would not be commensurate with her economic power. The *political principle* is beginning to assert itself in her foreign diplomacy however. It is thus incumbent upon Japan to seek friends in her own right, outside the tutelage of the US. In fact Japan is no longer dependent on the US, but it is the other way around, including even on the African question since "Japanese dependence on America has been replaced by US reliance on Japan to provide foreign aid to strategically placed countries around the world".[139] In 1985 Japan voted 66,3 % with the US in the UN and thus ranked 12th behind such countries as Canada, Grenada, Portugal, etc. In the 1990s however Japan will likely vote even more in favour of the United States, not because of US hegemony this time around, but because the weakened state of the US economy might lead to even more temperamental US behaviour as happened with the "Toshiba Syndrome" in the 1980s. It would thus be a deficient analysis to postulate that Japan would be doing such chores purely — and persistently — on behalf of the US, when it is clear that as the 20th century winds down, Pax Americana's sun is visibly setting while the Land of the Rising Sun is clearly overshadowing the American sphere of global economic hegemony. It is in Japan's interest of course to portray an image of *following* the US in all her diplomatic initiatives; but it is clear that Japan is carving for herself a niche of freedom of action, without American supervision. Hence with more international support that she could muster, Japan could easily smooth her path of moving from the number two spot to the number one. *To achieve that she needs a highly principled diplomatic philosophy*, which is what she is seeking to display in the developing world. Her role in Africa has this long-term objective. It is clearly a diplomatic strategy of immense value since it seeks to win the "hearts and minds" of one of the most abused humanity in the world: African victims of colonialism. The so-called *Maekawa Report* (that is the much discussed *1986 Report of the Economic Council's Special Committee on Economic Restructuring*), although severely denounced in some Japanese quarters such as MOFA, *Nihon Keizai Shimbun*, etc., recognises this *moral imperative* of Japanese diplomacy. In order to attain these objectives Japan would of course have first to resolve some of the glaring contradictions in her Africa diplomacy.

The summation of former Foreign Minister's, Shintaro Abe's understanding of the rationale for Japan's diplomacy and responsibilities, is appropriate:

> Japan can no longer maintain the passive attitude it has adopted in the past. At present, Japanese diplomacy is being called upon to continue and to accelerate the trend of the past several years, increasing Japan's awareness of itself as a nation charged with weighty responsibilities in serving the cause of world peace and prosperity and acting positively upon this awareness.[140]

The pacifist diplomacy of Japan is no longer willing to suffer dismissals by critics who argue about its idealistic attempt to be all things to all men.[141] Japan's pacifist diplomatic innovation merits an objective evaluation in its own right, even if it lacks the moral power and force of Gandhism. The pursuit of world peace and world prosperity according to the norms of Japan's foreign policy in relation to Africa is undergirded by the following value packages:

- Strengthening political cooperation and relations of solidarity with pro-West African nations.

- Loosening and prying Socialist/Marxist nations away from the then Eastern bloc through diplomatic dialogue, economic ties and development assistance in order to expand her arena of friends.

- Offering humanitarian assistance and development aid to those peoples and nations adversely affected by the ravages of nature and the mismanagement by their regimes.

- Creating security and strategic alliances through "security aid" and/or economic cooperation for the purpose of fostering "peace".

- Preserving and nurturing traditional and "emotional" friendships with some nations.

- Establishing interdependent relationships, not only because "African nations have increased their international role", but also because interdependence is a basic philosophical objective and pragmatic necessity of our time.

- Pursuing economic and commercial self-interest.

Despite this omnibus "categorical imperative" it should not be naively concluded that, at all times, Japanese diplomacy is largely morally high-minded in Africa. The "national interest" is (correctly) the guiding light in all areas of her diplomatic activities. Even without considering the Japan-South Africa connection which has irritated many Africans, Japan occasionally contrives, and has in the past precipitated, crises in Africa for economic reasons, such as when she attempted to change Seychelles' stance of total ban on whaling by using economic aid as a leverage. This action subsequently led to the seizure of the Japanese fishing boat "Sumi Maru" in angry retaliation.[142] There are areas other than the

Seychelles in which Japanese diplomacy has episodes of either failure or bungling — Zimbabwe, Zambia, Ivory Coast, South Africa, etc., are merely a few of them, though Japan's failure rate in Africa is relatively low if we discount her earlier problems especially with Francophone states on the issue of Article 35 of GATT (General Agreement on Trade and Tariffs). For many years since independence African states had applied Article 35 on Japanese commodities. Many Japanese diplomatic missions visited Africa to persuade these states to withdraw the GATT clause. Kenya became the last African country to withdraw the clause. Yet Japan's diplomacy is, on the main, considerably superior to that of (imperial) Europeans or Americans,[143] despite the fact that Japan had begun her positive Africa policy on a rather indifferent pace. The prospects for future Japan-Africa ties seem good, especially in the 1990s, if Japan's overtures to Africa were to continue on an incrementally balanced keel, and her diplomacy was not derailed by the formidable bureaucratic-entrepreneurial partnership that has brought Euro-American economies into a new reckoning with a disciplined national capitalist development system. At any rate Japan has successfully cultivated very close ties with Kenya, Tanzania, Egypt, Ethiopia, Nigeria, Senegal, Zambia, Zimbabwe and Zaire as well as Ghana.

For Japan to attain such giddy heights, nevertheless, she would have to contend not only with the blatant and subtle intervention of great powers, but also with a formidable European legacy in Africa which includes *slaving, conquest* and *colonisation*. In fact some Europeans (let alone some Francophone Africans) consider Africa to be *Eurafrica*. In the Ivory Coast for example not only 30 000 French today reside there (there are more French people today than there were during the colonial era), but the second most powerful man in Ivory Coast in the 1980s like the second most powerful man in Senegal and Central African Republic, was a Frenchman. (A corresponding African figure in France is yet to be born). The words of the assassinated Burkina Faso President, Capt. Thomas Sankara, directly thrown in the face of French President, Francois Mitterand, when he visited Oagadoogoo, on why he boycotted French-African summit meetings, put the hegemonic role of France and the vassal-like dependency of Africa in perspective: "African vassals bring their grievances to the French sovereign, only then to pay him their respect". On African military cooperation with France, the martyred revolutionary leader remarked: "There is not a Burkinabe who does not remember an uncle or a father who died so that France could be free".[144] Thus the road to *Nipponafrica* may not necessarily lie in Europe, but it will have to outmanoeuvre "Eurafrica", especially Francoafrica first, if the Nippon-Africa ties are to blossom.

Such route may lie in commercial ties with Africa as Japan seems to be succeeding in Francophone Africa. It may also lie in greater cultural and educational ties between Japan and Africa. In any event Japanese diplomatic relations with Africa developed through negotiations with Europeans and Americans in Paris and New York, long before they were initiated with Africans in the 1960s. Because of the unique way in which Japan has blended the authority of the state and the creative energy of the citizenry, she is more likely to succeed than either the modern (now defunct) socialist (i.e. USSR *et al.*) or old capitalist (USA *et al.*) economies. Her Africa diplomacy is rapidly reaching the bloom of maturity and sophistication as she has now developed a variety of diplomatic channels: cultural, educational, technical, scientific, etc. in addition to the traditional diplomatic modes. In a sense, quietly but efficiently, Japan is opening Africa in a more profound way than perhaps any other major economic power in the last 50 years. But her biggest challenge will remain the socio-economic detritus that litters the whole of Africa.

## CHAPTER 4

# AFRICAN DIPLOMACY TOWARDS JAPAN

*Japan is beginning to open up to Africa, and Zambia is reciprocating fully. Zambia wants friendly productive relations with Japan in all spheres. We prefer that Japan should greatly lower her presence and role in South Africa and increase it sharply in Black Africa, especially in southern Africa, Zambia particularly.*

Zambian Ambassador to Japan, Boniface S. Zulu[145]

*Zimbabwe's diplomatic policy is to increase technological, economic, commercial and human ties with Japan and to simultaneously discourage similar connections between Japan and the apartheid regime.*

Zimbabwe Ambassador to Japan, Dr N.H. Katedza[146]

*Tanzania is a non-aligned nation and as such we request Japan to join our efforts in persuading the NATO powers to close down their overseas military bases in compliance with the proclamation that the Indian Ocean would be a zone of peace ...*

Tanzanian President, Julius Nyerere (1981, Tokyo)[147]

Beyond the issue of whether there is such a genre as "African diplomacy," is the additional question of whether African governments have a coherent foreign diplomacy toward Japan, and what that diplomacy is. Defining such a task is the focus of this chapter, and it involves more than the mere restatement of that diplomacy because it is more important to know, for instance, why Rwanda favours closer ties with Japan than simply knowing that it prefers to do so. The task is daunting not only because there is a virtual absence of documents, data, and literature addressing this issue, but also because African governments are, in the main, notoriously incompetent in responding even to basic questionnaires about *their* public diplomacy towards Japan.[148] The difficulties are compounded by the absence of African public opinion in foreign policy decision-making. Because of the uncertainty in Africa's foreign policies, especially as regards East Asia, there is thus a tendency for African states to engage in flexible flirtations with various great powers in order to maximise benefits and increase freedom of action for themselves. Nonetheless, there is also the additional problem of whether weak, unstable states can have a foreign policy, an international diplomacy, worth analysing.

In the African case this dilemma is doubly so since Africa's Japan policy still lacks dynamism, and it is governed by a fuzziness that only dramatises the impecuniousness of inputs from the foreign service bureaucrats, political envoys, policy and academic analysts. That is to say, most African states are ineffectual in their design and implementation of policies. There is a poor fiscal base, a weak structure of central administration, limited expansion of the bureaucracy, and a virtual absence of a responsive political order that is structured upon a genuine participation of a large populace. The dearth of these vital inputs perpetuates the village-chief mentality and approach to foreign policy by many African regimes. This is what Professor Ali A. Mazrui once characterized as the monarchical tendency in African political culture.[149] Zaire, Tunisia, Malawi, Liberia, Gabon, Central African Republic, Sierra Leone, etc., are dramatic examples of this political culture. But we should not despair because, like Pliny some 2 000 years ago who discovered that *ex Africa semper aliquid novi* — out of Africa, always something new (comes) — we too may discover that African diplomacy affords at each turn a new lesson in the human character of social experiment.

The foreign policy behaviour of any given nation is naturally linked with the kind of political system that nation has. Moreover, whatever minimal role political envoys/policy makers play, the recognition of this relationship leads policy makers to shape their expectations of any country's foreign policy partly in terms of their conception of that country's political system. In the African realm too a nation's foreign policy is determined primarily by its form of government. But African foreign policy formulation and formalisation, elaboration and completion is still dependent upon coordination with Western donor countries. Donors of cash and commodities, aid and advice, ideas and ideologies, techniques and technologies, have perhaps a more critical influence in African policy decision making than the foreign service bureaucracy of these states. That influence remains critical especially when it comes from the West. The chronic weakness of the foreign service in African bureaucracies does not only hamper African governments' information gathering and representation; it maximises dependency on the West also. Especially unfortunate in the African setting is the common regard for ambassadors who, rather than seen as a source of primary information and as spokesmen for their country's foreign policy interests, are frequently regarded as the beneficiaries of patronage, cronyism, and nepotism; as the consumers of prestige and as children of friendship, rather than as diplomatic envoys fulfilling an important function in the national interest. To elucidate on these issues would require a brief review of the theoretical constraints within which African diplomacy operates in general.

## DEPENDENCY AND SELF-RELIANCE, IDEOLOGY AND PRAGMATISM

The landscape of the political economy of Africa is contoured with the topographical terrain of great power intervention precisely because Africa's weakness, needs, and dependency invite the intervention of non-African powers in African affairs.

The invitation to foreign intervention is inherent in a dependent, less developed, political economy. With great socio-economic inequities and enduring political iniquities Africa seems, at least for the foreseeable future, a region whose destiny will effectively remain in the hands of powerful foreigners rather than in those of powerless locals.[150] Even though much of Africa falls in the Western hegemonic camp, despite the prospective abating of Cold War tensions in the 90s, the Soviet Union's "friendship treaties" with Mozambique (1971), Angola (1976), Ethiopia (1978) and Congo (1981) remained a potential source of superpower rivalry as the American-led West sought to bring the entire continent under its sphere of influence, if not control. The Cold War rivalry in Africa to all intents and purposes was for a while matched by that between Israel and the Arab states, at least on the emotional, rhetorical level. Africa's vulnerability thus leads her to participate in "third" diplomacies, and in turn thus exposing these regimes to the pressures and dynamics of the external antagonists. The Arab-Israeli conflict is one such classic example. Japan however is probably the only major (economic) power with the least (political) contentiousness in Africa's external relations, despite the then potentially explosive issue of close Japanese-South Africa trade ties. (See Chapter 10.)

Considering the low level of socio-economic development and political instability of most African states north and south of the Sahara, *a development-oriented dependency* and a *self-reliant ideology* are the keystones of the foreign policy approaches of these states. As a consequence there seems to be a duality of wars in Africa: on the one hand there is the confrontation between dependence and self-reliance, and on the other, between ideology and pragmatism. While ideology may be both a response and a description of reality, it is inarguable however that were it to fall upon an African environment that was stable and prosperous, harmonious and self-justificatory, self-sufficient and predictable, it would be like a barren seed on sterile soil. Since economic priorities and political ideals find their locus in national demands, ideology in diplomatic intercourse has limited impact if survival issues compete for national attention. When ideological wants are superimposed upon practical necessities as national-interest needs, the whole tension between rhetoric and reality mounts and overflows to the extent that conflict between dependence and self-reliance intensifies. As a whole Africa has yet to resolve the problem of what the continent needs rather than what it wants and thus political instability and social precariousness is almost always on the surface. Much of Africa nevertheless uses the language of Nigeria's former head of State, Olusegun Obasanjo, who in his article "Africa's Needs", intoned that the US can assist Africa in developing its agricultural resources so that individual countries can once again feed themselves.[151] Precisely because African governments' authority lies more in their access to the means of control rather than in their access to the means of production, much of African foreign policy is a search for this Obasanjo-like semi-industrialisation with its enduring dependence, rather than a search for enduring self-reliance which calls for detachment.

The overwhelming majority of African regimes are preoccupied with domestic — and sometimes external — exigencies of political stability, regime survival, national legitimacy and economic solvency. Nigeria for example has a gross national product that is larger than that of South Africa and a population that accounts for approximately one in five Africans. Yet since independence in 1960 Nigeria has endured no less than six coups (and many coup attempts), three presidential assassinations, and has one of the shakiest political stabilities. In contrast, the last assassination of a Japanese prime minister was in 1932. Similarly, as three candidates in 1987 were holding hands and negotiating who should be Prime Minister of Japan, a bloodthirsty assistant was pumping a thousand rounds of bullets into his long-time "friend" and the national leader of Burkina Fasso. What a contrast in leadership succession! By 1984 half of Africa's 52 countries were ruled by military-dominated

155

governments. By the end of 1992 however, only a handful were so ruled. With a high degree of political instability African governments consequently reduce their long-term focus in policy formulation to the immediate or near-immediate. The leaders of most of these states generally revert to repeating platitudes about issues and ideologies of self-determination in the face of fast-receding self-determination in areas of vital importance: for example food production, primary commodities pricing, international security, etc.

In situations of critical national demands, ideology plays a relatively insignificant role, rhetorics to the contrary nothwithstanding, because the issues confronting the regime's survival and national recuperation simply transcend ideological prescriptions. In such instances what has occurred is that pragmatism often takes over where ideology fails because ideology gratifies not primary needs, but satisfies secondary wants. To a considerable extent Africa depends on the outside world for her socio-economic resources and the necessary skills to develop the economy and advance the industrial and agricultural infrastructure. This dependency ramifies into consumer and manufactured goods, finance capital, technical skills, acquisition of modern arms, maintenance of currency systems and the like. Where self-reliance has not fully developed and thus failed to stem the eruption of a national crisis, a condition of *de facto* dependency is in existence. The classic case is Ethiopia: regardless of the 1974 change from a modern imperial regime to a Marxist military government, the weak *dependent* character of the state has continued to force her leaders to advance their cause through military force or international diplomacy.[152] In the first decade of her existence as a Marxist state her leadership has harangued and excoriated the West for the latter's imperial role in Africa, especially in Ethiopia since Fascist Italy's invasion. Yet despite this ideological stance of self-reliance (or at least non-dependence on the West), when the great famine and drought of 1983-1985 occurred, Ethiopia quickly and understandably accepted Western aid. The Ethiopian regime was not impressed with the

West's response in dispatching hundreds of millions of dollars in food aid, presumably because she had long warned the international community of the impending tragedy.[153] Conversely, even as she was receiving aid from the West, Ethiopia continued denouncing her Western benefactors — especially Britain, France, USA, Israel, and West Germany, particularly when the issue related to South Africa.[154] While ideology remains wedded to *declaratory* policies, in *actual* programmes however, structural imperatives for regime/state survival override these hortatory declarations.[155] In virtually all of Africa it can be shown that pragmatic policies (including those of dependency) assume pre-eminence especially in times of national crises. Unfortunately, as I shall show in Chapter 5, "Japanese Aid To Africa", the latter has come to depend, pathologically, on foreign aid.

Ideology and pragmatics, just as dependence and self-reliance, are of course not always mutually exclusive; indeed in certain cases their mutual complementarity is visible even to the naked mind, while in other situations their cooperation is more subterranean. They engage in what one may call a "fugitive cooperation". In such instances the empirical components and extrinsic demands of foreign dependency always tend to supersede the constraints and strictures of ideology, as is evident in cases such as Ghana, Mozambique, Ethiopia, Angola, Mali, etc. But "dependent development" in Africa has clearly not led to *real* development since dependency in the "Third World" does not, and cannot, lead to self-reliance. Even during an era of interdependence, self-reliance means precisely what the term says — reliance on the self (national, regional, or continental). It clearly does not mean reliance on foreign capital financing, technology, skills, exchange, etc., because such dependency has a tendency to perpetuate indefinitely the state of non-developmental extrarelations between the dependent recipient and the independent donor. But real self-reliance is impossible without a basic structural transformation in Africa. Most African states remain weak, both politically and economically, and thus remain dependent upon external finance capital and markets abroad. As the African continent continues in its march to incorporation into the world capitalist system, the problem of dependence continues to be a vexed one.[156] Yet even before there can be a horizontal interpenetration among "Third World" countries (such as Egypt's and India's export of manpower, or Arab aid to African countries,) there has to be a sound structural base transcending the ideological prescriptions of whatever regime may be in power.[157]

Ideologically, African states can be classified into capitalist, socialist and Marxist-Leninist.[158] According to this (Aluko view) ideology affects the way these African states align themselves in global politics. The tempting simplicity of Aluko's assertion merits no more than a passing effort at rebuttal. The assertion is cited merely because of its commonness, and not for its validity. Suffice to employ Zartman's observation: "Africa is a nonaligned part of the Western World. Its background, values, dependencies, exchanges, and aspirations are primarily with the West, as it works out its own nature and concerns".[159]

The point being made here is that employing Aluko's ideological classification approach is not a useful or valid method of analysis. What would be achieved by classifying African foreign diplomacies into conservative, moderate, and radical, or into any other categories when African *behaviour* would just as promptly nullify those same typologies? Yet Zartman's thesis in effect means that imperialism still dominates Africa to the extent that making rigid but vain distinctions or typologies of ideologies such as Aluko's illuminates nothing. In fact with the possible exception of Ethiopia, no African country could have been regarded as firmly in the Soviet Union's ideological camp despite the aforementioned "friendship treaties". At any rate the "Aluko assertion" does concede that considerations of survival and economies, a well as historical legacies, remain the more powerful determinants of behaviour and diplomacy.

In Zaire dependency has been the keystone of the Zairean regimes since independence. The survival of the oligarchic elite rather than any ideological premise or projection of Zairean role in global or regional context has been the only consistent and predictable determinant of Zairean foreign policy.[160] The issue of kleptocracy in Mobutu's regime is yet another consistent factor concerning Zaire, a factor which in analysing the regime's diplomacy cannot be disregarded, because it recurs like a common vulgar fraction. This is not to debunk the usefulness of ideology (especially of self-reliance) since it has played and will continue to play a role in African "dependent development" in the extra-African relations, such as when African and Japanese diplomats discourse on Afro-Japanese relations and the factor of South Africa invariably cropped up. When the Burkinabe President, Capt Thomas Sankara, refused for instance to attend the annual Franco-African summits, he was in fact suggesting that ideological independence must continue to play a dominant role in diplomatic policy of the African states, a strategy which was adopted without success by Guinea's Ahmed Sekou Toure (1958-1984) when he struck out an independent path "outside" French hegemony. The very existence of Franco-African Summit (now known as the Summit of French and African Heads of State) is positive proof of the high profile France maintains in Africa, itself of heavy ideological valence.

As a consequence Francophone Africa has become diplomatically useless. The absence of authentic diplomatic policy owing to the overseeing role of France complicates our understanding of African foreign policy outside France's national interest. French economic and security interests in Africa, as well as the role of Africa in France's foreign policy, are so intertwined that it would be a contradiction in terms to speak of a free/independent Francophone Africa. Even after more than a quarter of a century of independence, France's influence over her former colonies has remained very strong.[161] Mauritius is for example officially non-aligned, and although she retains very strong cultural ties with France, India and Britain much of her foreign diplomacy reflects French expectations. A member of the Organization of African Unity (OAU), Mauritius has no diplomatic ties with apartheid South Africa, but she operates a trade mission in Johannesburg. Her

Prime Minister, Anerood Jugnauth, rejected apartheid as "inhuman and immoral" but could still aver:

> Mauritius ... has developed ties with South Africa for historical, geographic and economic reasons. We are working towards reducing our dependence on South Africa as far as tourism and our economy is concerned.[162]

French influence plays a crucial role in Mauritius' non-aligned foreign policy, similarly as it does in other areas of the French "Empire". The Gabonese economy and its state-owned enterprises are largely under French control and management. On the basis of GNP (which is $3,670 per capita, and the highest in black Africa) Gabon is the richest independent Sub-Sahara African country, and it is thus a fertile area for French presence. Even the Presidential Guard has for many years been commanded by French officers. Some units of the regular armed forces are also under French command. In key administrative positions of the government French officials are equipped with full powers. A French elite armed force is permanently stationed in Gabon, clearly protecting the regime of Omar Bongo.

In addition to Gabon, French armed forces are also stationed in the Central African Republic, Ivory Coast, Senegal, Zaire, Chad, and perhaps Djibouti. Even in states such as Ivory Coast where there is ostensible independence in diplomatic forays, French influence is strong. Ivory Coast has diplomatic relations with 70 nations. Ivorian diplomacy stresses principles which are characterized by respect for the sovereignty of each state, a desire to reinforce regional organisations while keeping Africa out of ideological conflicts, and finally, by the promotion of inter-African and international cooperation. Yet the role of France remains powerful even in the context of this seeming Ivorian autonomy. Despite the instability of African regimes in any event, the Ivorian authorities have succeeded in maintaining and increasing their relations by only recognising states rather than regimes.

Although less intensive the situation in Anglophone Africa has not been much different from Francophone Africa (except that in Southern Africa an exception could be made since the former colonial possessions of Britain which constitute the majority in the economic union, Southern African Development Coordinating Conference, SADCC, now known as SADC, i.e. Southern African Development Community, have strenuously sought to escape the brutal embrace of the apartheid regime of South Africa, i.e. to move away from dependency to self-reliance). In the most powerful (population-wise) African state, leadership and foreign policy in Nigeria require reconsideration in terms of her linkages especially with Western economic partners.[163] But the lack of a clear and coherent domestic policy leads to an incoherent foreign policy. During the oily days of booming development when Nigeria put her faith in oil she amassed $100 billion in 10 years, but today with the collapse of the oil-price she has mounted a foreign debt of at least $21 billion, and her urban population is dependent on foreign imports. Her agricultural and rural population is now incapable of feeding the 100 million citizens, let alone any other regional states devastated by drought in the Sahel. Nigeria's dependency on foreign support is not a result of the vicissitudes of nature, as is often the case in the Sahel or in some parts of Ethiopia. It is largely the result of governmental ineptitude and public mismanagement. Mention has already been made that an incoherent domestic policy cannot lead to a coherent foreign policy. Nigeria is a clear example. Despite the heavy presence of the Japanese role in Nigeria, the latter has no known articulate and formal policy towards Japan, just as her domestic policy is equally retarded. In Malawi, Kamuzu Hastings Banda's famous shrill slogan: "To Hell With (colonially-imposed) Federation" merely goes to magnify the dramatic ephemerality of ideology in the face of "dependent developmentism," since Banda's regime has moved away from the go-it-alone nationalist approach that she initially espoused, to a *de facto* incorporation into the South African economic zone, her membership in SADCC notwithstanding. She also depends to a great extent on Japanese aid.

In Luso-Africa a similar vogue in scuttling ideology for dependent development is apparent. For instance Angola, a former Marxist-Leninist State, has now moved away from the Soviet model of economic centralism to the so-called free-market system, as part of a general move to the West (or what the Angolans call diversifying). This is a radical move by a regime that only a few years ago tried to become the first African member of COMECON, the economic union of the Eastern bloc countries. In the autumn of 1987 President Jose dos Santos toured Western Europe — Lisbon, Paris, Rome, and Brussels. It was his second trip to France and his first as President of Angola. Angola, a SADCC member, has suffered immensely from the punishing aggressions and invasions by South Africa, just as her fellow Marxist Lusophone, Mozambique, has been subjected to similar incursions and destabilisations. Indeed just a few months before he died in a plane crash, Mozambique's founding president, Samora Machel, visited Japan and requested help from the Japanese in speeding up the development of his country (see below), in order to liberate her from dependency on South Africa. He was accompanied by his then Foreign Minister and now successor, Joaquim Chissano, who continued not only Machel's move to the West, but also reconfirmed the Japan-Mozambique ties even though neither country had an embassy in the other's capital. Equally interesting is Guinea-Bissau which for 13 years during her war for national liberation depended on the Soviet Union for military weapons' supply. In April 1975 she signed a 10-year fishing accord with the Soviet Union. Now Guinea-Bissau has joined such other West-oriented states as Equatorial Guinea, Liberia, Morocco, and Senegal in prohibiting Soviet fishing. The waters off the west coast of Africa which have long been the Soviet Union's largest overseas source of fish — with the latest action by Guinea-Bissau — have increasingly become off-limits to (the former) Soviet fishing boats.

What the foregoing paragraphs suggest is that the typical African state is a European artefact with virtually unchanged colonial jurisdictional and identity values. The foreign policies of most of these states towards Japan will ultimately reflect these interlinkages with Europe. It is precisely because of this that this analysis is at variance with Zartman's endorsement of the values of Euro-Africanism:

> Capitalising on its increased independence, Africa is able to exact a higher and higher price for a lessened European presence. Thus it can be seen that the dependency approach at best describes a static moment, while decolonisation theory accounts for changing relations ... From an evolutionary point of view, therefore, the Lome Conventions are a welcome development. Neither ... neocolonial association nor ... institutionalization of dependency.[164]

As a liberal internationalist, Zartman places not much stock in the dependency approach. Nor is he correct, of course, that there is a reduced European presence in Africa (except perhaps in places like Algeria, Mozambique, Angola and Zimbabwe). In several African states there are more Europeans now than during colonial times.

The dependency/self-reliance tensions and the ideology/pragmatism dichotomy play, in any event, a crucial role in the governance of extra-African relations — despite the tendencies of many African leaders to improvise and continually innovate their foreign policy approaches. Consider again for a moment, Ethiopia. As noted earlier she was (until recently) an avowed Marxist-Leninist state very much aligned with the then Soviet Union (USSR). Yet she was compelled by circumstances to accept Western charity (and concomitant pressures) during the great drought of 1983-1985, and in 1988 she finally acquiesced to Western demands that she change her agricultural policies. In 1984 she had received $534 million from abroad for famine and development aid, even though she had spent $449 million on military weapons, thanks to the longest insurrection in history. The highly ideological former regime of Mengistu Haile Mariam retained her policy towards Japan almost intact as inherited from the deposed Emperor, Haile Selassie. That Ethiopia could receive military aid from the bloc of Marx and food-emergency aid from the bloc of Adam Smith is neither contradictory nor unusual in African external relations — it is not only the result of the fusion of dependency and ideology, but also the function of the diplomacy of improvisation and innovation. Many other African states have engaged in similar contradictions. If we consider Mali, for instance, we note that the Malian regime once defined its foreign policy as one of "uncompromising and dynamic non-alignment". This could mean that Mali was prepared to accept aid from whoever offered it. The definition could *also* be accurate of course. In any event acceptance of aid irrespective of the ideological bloc from which it originates presupposes a degree of detachment from the various blocs. This circumstance naturally permits the military to be trained by the bloc of Marx while simultaneously accepting aid and food assistance from the bloc of Adam Smith.

The conclusion to be drawn from this, as I have noted earlier, is that there are few consistent and predictable determinants of foreign policy behaviour of African states outside the aforementioned complex. The fluidity of the situation thus generates a state of diplomatic flux, improvisation, and innovativeness. Hence much of African perceptions and formal diplomatic interactions with Japan all operate within this orbit. Outside the strategic doctrines and security interests of great powers, as well as outside the *ad hoc* principles of African states, formally inserting Africa in the international system without incapacitating the logic of dependency or ideology is nearly impossible. In the 1960s ideological diplomacy of African states was the essential operational norm during which ideological criteria were pronounced regarding racism, colonialism, apartheid, independence, development, and "non-alignment" etc. As the 60s gave way to the 70s, the limits of ideology in foreign policy, or external relations, became more visible, particularly when structural maladjustments began to manifest themselves more dramatically. During this period ideology in foreign policy took a back-seat to dependency. African economies began to unravel and political instabilities mounted. One scholar even argues that having "occupied an accepted place in cold-war relations for most of the past two decades ... (T)here is relatively little on Africa's place in the world,"[165] i.e. outside the strategic doctrine. In a previous study this scholar had argued that "Ideology cannot be an exclusive basis of foreign policy because its specific recommendations are limited and unclear".[166] Regarding ideology in African diplomacy towards Japan, my primary concern is with African states' attempts to isolate South Africa not only from Japan, but also from the West and to enlist the support of Japan in seeking a quick but peaceful change in South Africa and the then South Africa-occupied Namibia. But other ideological issues do protrude, and they included such factors as the East-West, North-South equation. In the protocols of international diplomacy Africa brings also non-ideological baggage, especially in her foreign policy dialogue with Japan, and this concerns the pressing problem of long-term economic structural readjustments, the debt problem, and the aid issue.

## DIPLOMACY BY INNOVATION AND IMPROVISATION

Analysing African diplomacy towards Japan (unlike in the case of African policies towards the USA, EEC or COMECON) is a paradox: because of the lack of formal White Papers or regular foreign policy pronouncements from African governments regarding African-Japanese relations, foreign policy analysis tends to be either speculative or retrospective. Much of this analysis is based especially on past conventional parameters of African relations with the West.[167] On the other hand, precisely because of this lack of diplomatic policy data, African diplomacy becomes relatively easy to analyse because diplomatic issues are easily anticipated on the basis of already established patterns, for example development, aid, debt, Southern Africa, colonialism, trade relations, etc.[168, 169, 170, 171] or else they are treated rather speculatively in terms of the dominant issues that *might* be relevant to African growth, development, and pacifism, as is clearly visible in President Nyerere's statement on the title page of this chapter.

African states' foreign policies towards Tokyo have, in large part, taken advantage of media interest in, and world attention on the structural problems, food, and drought crises in Africa, as well as the natural revulsion towards South Africa's apartheid and aggression against her neighbours to manipulate foreign policy symbols and generate new diplomatic initiatives. In turn, Japan has adjusted accordingly — i.e. she has herself influenced changes in her strategies and tactics; but not necessarily her policy goals. Quantitatively she increased aid to Africa as a consequence. Thus in analysing and depicting the diplomatic realities of African states one is confronted with a general state of fluidity, of transformation, a kind of *ad hoc* innovative or improvising approach, as suggested for example in Martin's study's subtitle: *pour une sociologie de l'innovation politique en Afrique noire.*[172]

Diplomatic innovation in Africa is not entirely foreign to current international conduct; it is almost as old as the majority of African independence. Hatch was in essence recognising diplomatic innovation when he wrote:

> The formation of the Organization of African Unity in Addis Ababa in 1963 created a form of continental association unknown to other continents. Europe had sought in vain for a central forum of interstate decision-making over a thousand years. The American had merely succeeded in establishing a continental association dominated by the United States. Asia has never seriously tried. Yet, within a few years of the start of the European withdrawal and even before many countries had attained full self-government, Africans succeeded in creating an organization to which every African government became affiliated.[173]

This diplomatic improvisation, in form and content, was particularly poignant at the United Nations and other international organisations. As Rivkin notes:

> The African presence in the United Nations has taken on massive proportions — numerically and substantively. One quarter of the membership (in 1963) is African, and starting in mid-1960 every session of the General Assembly and the

Security Council has been confronted with a major African issue.[174]

Rivkin further observed that this large African presence not only made the world conscious of the African presence but that, as well, this had basically altered the political balance of power in the world. This is one of the reasons the Japanese *Yearbooks* have repeatedly stated that Japan was in the process of developing closer relations with Africa because of the significant international role played by African "states". The Japanese public, as we saw in the last chapter, regarded Africa as important as a result of her resources as well as her influence in international forums.

But even without a clear-cut foreign policy towards Japan, the Africans have now launched a new diplomatic offensive, a strategy of official visits to Japan. Indeed, Japan has become a "regular part of the globe-trotting African Heads of State".[175] While the behaviour of African diplomats and government leaders is generally of little significance in studying diplomacy *per se*, their public pronouncements during their visits to Japan afford a rare opportunity for students of Japan-Africa relations to gain insight into official thinking regarding this diplomacy. As McKay once noted "African diplomacy operates in a milieu of internal stress and strain, compounded by a multitude of external pressures".[176] In the Japan-Africa relations these external pressures are less intense nonetheless. So it is essential to evaluate the role and significance of visits of African government elites to Tokyo within the context of their policy to the Japanese Government.

**DIPLOMACY BY OFFICIAL VISITS TO JAPAN**

*The success of most African leaders who go on international trips is judged by the variety and volume of new aid commitments they bring back home. (*New African, *London.)*

Beginning with Ethiopian Emperor Haile Selassie's conference in Japan with Emperor Hirohito barely a month before Japan was

167

admitted to the United Nations, through the 1979 conference between Senegal's President Leopold S. Senghor and the Japanese Emperor, to the late Mozambican president, Samora Machel's 1986 meeting with Japanese government officials and the Emperor, to the 1988 visit to Japan by the Zimbabwean President, Robert Mugabe, and the 1992 visit by President de Klerk, African official visits to Japan — like Japanese official visits to Africa — have increased not only in number but also in sophistication. In 1981 the number of African official visits to Tokyo by leading figures at ministerial level and higher, totalled thirty. (See Appendix B for Select African Official Visitors To Japan between 1984 and 1987). That is, diplomatic orality has its uses. For one, it makes for effective representation, either positive or negative.

These rising African diplomatic expectations of Japan are clearly reflected in this cross-section of government leaders: emperors, presidents, prime ministers, and simple dictators. Emperor Haile Selassie of Ethiopia (November 1956 and May 1970), General Mobutu Sese Seko of Zaire (April 1971), President Ahmad Ahidjo of Cameroon (April 1973 and 1978), Prime Minister D.K. Jawara of The Gambia (1978 and 1983), President Omar Bongo of Gabon (1978), President Leopold S. Senghor of Senegal (1979), President Kenneth Kaunda of Zambia (September 1980), Prime Minister Robert Mugabe of Zimbabwe (May 1981), President Julius Nyerere of Tanzania (March 1981), President Daniel arap Moi of Kenya (April 1982), President Hosni Mubarak of Egypt (April 1983), Prime Minister Mohamed Mzali of Tunisia (October 1984) and President Samora Moises Machel of Mozambique (May 1986). Lesser luminaries such as ministers of foreign affairs, cooperative development, industrial development and planning, youth and sports, commerce and trade, etc., have also tailed along their leaders, or else have visited Japan on separate occasions.

In 1986 when President Machel sought economic aid from Japan he toured a variety of places in his five-day stay. He held discussions not only with the Emperor and Prime Minister, Yasuhiro Nakasone, but also with other key Japanese figures such as MITI's

Minister Michio Wanatabe, and agriculture, forestry and fisheries Minister, Tsutomu Hata. Besides touring a Toyota automobile factory and visiting the old imperial palace in Kyoto, President Machel met with the LDP Vice President, Susuma Nikaido, on 28 May who hosted a reception for Machel and his party. The latter included Foreign Minister Joaquim Chissano and Minister of International Cooperation, Jalinto Veloso. On this occasion diplomacy was largely in the service of commerce and "development aid". A number of Diet men and representatives of Japanese companies doing business in Mozambique also attended. Nikaido remarked that Japan and Mozambique may be far apart geographically, but that they had managed to forge and maintain close ties. President Machel in turn expressed great interest in Japan and considered the country "the most important link in African-Asian economic relations". Machel restated that he had come to Japan to strengthen Mozambique-Japan relations and, pursuant to this end, he requested Japan's help in improving the industry and infrastructure of his country. He noted the destructive and destabilizing role of South Africa in Mozambique and other areas in Southern Africa. He urged Japan to take an active role in finding a solution to the political problems clouding the relations between Japan and Mozambique.[177] Neither the Japanese nor Mozambican dignitaries betrayed an awareness that a Mozambican/Monomotapan African, named Yasuke by the Japanese, had served as Shogun Oda Nobunaga's court hand nearly 400 years earlier, and thus was the father of the Japan-(Africa)-Mozambique ties. A few months later President Machel died in a plane crash just inside the South African border, and his Foreign Minister, Chissano, who had visited Japan two years earlier (14 March 1984), became President of Mozambique and continued the policy of bringing Mozambique closer to Japan, at least in diplomatic terms.

When African heads of state arrive in Tokyo they often bring a diplomatic bag loaded with a variety of issues. We have already seen for example in President Julius Nyerere's statement at the beginning of this chapter (note 146), that in his week-long discussions in

March 1981 with Japanese leaders, he expressed the "non-aligned" wish of seeing the Indian Ocean demilitarized, without foreign bases and permanently a "zone of peace". Nyerere also repeated the arguments of the so-called MSAC (most seriously affected countries) concerning the present commercial and trade systems under which the transfer of wealth from the poor to the rich countries proceeds inexorably. He asked for Japanese help in changing these systems.[178] At a meeting with Japanese Premier Zenko Suzuki, Nyerere obtained pledges of further economic aid from Japan. Suzuki responded by assuring Nyerere that the Japanese Government had earmarked another $23,3 million for a soft loan to Tanzania. Tokyo further promised to provide $10 million in commodity loans and to dispatch a survey team to Tanzania for the construction of a technical training school with a Japanese grant. When President Nyerere broached the problem of South Africa, Suzuki replied that the Government of Japan would play a greater role in resolving the Namibian question and promoting closer links with the African nations.[179] The Tanzanian Foreign Affairs Minister, Benjamin Mkapa, visited Japan in September 1987 to be briefed, among other things, on Japan's new non-project type of aid. Tanzania and Japan have a particularly close relationship, one coming close to rivalling the extremely close ties between China and Tanzania. Tanzania's importance to Japan has clearly not been explicable outside the world renown of President Nyerere whose influence in the UN, OAU, Common-wealth, and Non-Aligned Movement Japan could turn to good use. He had also a temporising influence on Africa's radical regimes.

Similarly, when Prime Minister Robert Mugabe of Zimbabwe arrived in Tokyo just a few weeks after Nyerere returned to Tanzania from Japan, economic, trade, and political issues dominated the talks between him and his Japanese counterpart. It is South Africa however, which featured prominently in these discussions.[180] At the time of Mugabe's arrival in Tokyo neither Japan nor Zimbabwe had an embassy in the other's capital city. In fact Japan had just suffered an embarrassing diplomatic trade *faux pas* in Zimbabwe, on which incident a Japanese journalist based in Africa was to base his caustic comments regarding the Japanese Government and business circles. Yutaka Shinoda chastised the "mentality of the Japanese firm and the government (which) was that 'money talks'"[181] The Zimbabwe embassy in Tokyo has since defined its policy towards Japan as a "desire for closer cooperation in the fields of trade, technological transfer, investments, human resources development, cultural exchanges and cooperation in the international forum".

The Zimbabwe ambassador, Dr Katedza, leaned heavily towards technological benefits as the logical consequence of Zimbabwe's overtures towards Japan. That President Mugabe returned to Japan in 1988 for an official visit, even before a Japanese Foreign Minister had yet to pay an official visit to Zimbabwe, indicates among other things, that the Harare Government had thawed its initial indifference or coolness towards Japan.

Mugabe, like other African leaders, reflecting Zimbabwe's closer ties with China, more than with Japan, had actually begun his tour in China before proceeding to Japan, India, and Pakistan. Before he arrived in Japan, the Chinese Government had offered Zimbabwe $1 billion in agricultural and other aid. Japan in turn agreed to $170 million in aid, and to supply equipment for rural development in Zimbabwe, while India had made trade arrangements as well as agreements to supply technical assistants and scholarships. Pakistan bottomed with a $2 million promise in training programmes and decided as well to send up to 50 railway technicians.[182] Nonetheless even as Mugabe was concluding his talks with Japanese leaders, his Minister of Information, Nathan Shamuyarira, was unveiling a new Zambian mass media complex which was being built by the Japanese. The Zimbabwe minister warned that Zambia and Zimbabwe (two countries that Japan regards as of geopolitical strategic significance) were to launch a joint venture to make anti-apartheid broadcasts to South Africa.[183]

In his September 1980 visit to Tokyo, during which discussions with Japanese Government and business leaders he covered much of

171

the area that the 1981 Nyerere and Mugabe visits were to deal with, the Zambian President, Kenneth Kaunda, explained to the Japanese not only his "humanism philosophy", but his abhorrence of South African apartheid. He solicited not only Japanese cooperation in development aid for Zambia, but also "peaceful aid" to be rid of the South African menace. The Tanzanian, Mozambican, Zambian, and Zimbabwe leaders indeed reflect a virtually identical diplomatic stance towards Japan, especially when it relates to Southern Africa problems. In my 1987 discussions with the Zambian and Zimbabwe ambassadors to Japan, Boniface Zulu and Dr N. Katedza, respectively, I detected a coterminity of views regarding their countries' policy towards Japan, especially when it related to trade, aid, and South African apartheid and aggression. Both ambassadors expressed strong reservations regarding Japan's policy towards South Africa. The Zambian ambassador was also particularly displeased with Japan's "slavish" following of the International Monetary Fund's (IMF) policies in Africa, especially in its lending rules which tend to demand the dismantling of "socialist programmes" as a condition for aid/loans. In December 1986 President Kaunda was forced to rescind an IMF-inspired 120 per cent increase in the price of maize meal, Zambia's staple food, after clashes between security forces and the rioters. The Secretary-General of the ruling United National Independence Party (UNIP), Grace Zulu, angrily commented that the "IMF has brought about untold misery and suffering in many a developing country, Zambia included".[184] Ambassador Boniface Zulu bitterly echoed Secretary-General Zulu's words. His remarks, that when Zambia suspended IMF programmes in December 1986 the $10 million that Japan had promised Zambia was abruptly diverted to Madagascar in 1987, were couched in a critical tone, however "diplomatic" his phrases. Still, he vowed that Zambia would not change her principles just to suit the IMF or Japan.[185]

Zambia and Japan have nevertheless close ties especially in commercial trade which in 1987 reached $400 in Zambian exports to Japan, according to a Zambian trade attache in Tokyo. These close ties are also reflected in international activism. Peter Dingiswayo Zuze who is not only Zambia's permanent representative to the United Nations, but also the President of the UN Council for Namibia, also visited Japan in 1987 to enlist Japan's "influence" to pressure South Africa to withdraw from Namibia. He urged the then Foreign Minister, Tadashi Kuranari, to let the Japanese public know about the plight of black people of Namibia who live under the illegal occupation in South Africa.[186] While Japan had repeatedly stated her opposition to South Africa's policies in Namibia, and has also on numerous occasions restated her readiness to assist the UN in effecting a transition to Nambibian rule, she lacked nonetheless the political clout that the Zambian official visiting Japan had hoped to enlist. But when the Zambian Prime Minister, K.S.K. Musokotwane arrived in Tokyo in September 1987 the Japanese Government was eager to explain the character and policy of her new non-project aid. Namibia, in any event, is free today, 1993, and sooner than later, its president, Sam Nujoma, will too be making his pilgrimage to Tokyo to ask for "aid".

In October 1984 a Cameroonian economic mission headed by a Vice-Minister for Planning and Development, Elizabeth Tankeu, arrived in Tokyo to receive a grant of 540 million yen for water supply equipment in Cameroon. Coinciding with her arrival in Japan was the Tunisian Government mission headed by Prime Minister Mohamed Mzali, whose official agenda with his Japanese counterpart included the proverbial need to "strengthen bilateral cooperation" between the two countries. Japan had agreed to contribute to the financing of development projects in infrastructure, industry, telecommunications and agricultural development in Tunisia. This was not only indicative that much of Africa's Japan policy outside trade and commerce is devoted to the aid question, but also that Japan is equally active in Africa North of the Sahara. Indeed, one of Japan's closest African friends is an Afro-Arab country, Egypt.

Leaving China on 3 April 1983 for Japan via North Korea the Egyptian President, Hosni Mubarak, arrived in Tokyo two days later. Before the end of Mubarak's visit to China, Egypt and China had signed the 1983 trade protocol under which the volume of trade between the two countries amounted to $140 million. Mubarak had conferred with the Chinese leader Deng Xiaoping, and Communist Party chief Yaobang on the first day of his visit. Interestingly the Japanese Government had announced, shortly before Mubarak arrived in Tokyo, a decision to allocate to Egypt $250 million in credit to buy machinery, ships, and planes. This credit line for fiscal 1983 and 1984 started from 1 April, four days before President Mubarak's arrival. The MITI minister, Sadanori Yamanaka, had informed the Egyptian Minister of Investment and International Cooperation, Wagih Shindi, that the Japanese Prime Minister, Yasuhiro Nakasone, would tell President Mubarak about the credit line, to which the Egyptian minister responded by hoping that Japan would increase her imports of Egyptian products to correct a trade imbalance in Japan's favour. In 1982 Japan's exports to Egypt had reached $661 million and its imports had totalled $167 million. Three Japanese companies had won a joint 23 billion yen ($96 million) order from Egypt's Alexandria National Steel Company for construction of part of an $800 million integrated mill. [187] Mubarak's 1983 visit was not only to cement old ties but also to open new avenues for bilateral cooperation, including the Middle East question.

Although many African government leaders' visits to Japan are generally undertaken at relatively short notice, some are the outcome of protracted negotiations haggling over a variety of bilateral issues such as trade and tariffs, economic and technical aid, cultural and educational exchanges, diplomatic protocols, etc. The Senegalese President's visit to Tokyo in April 1979 is one such example. On 4 November 1960 Japan had recognised the Republic of Senegal and established its Embassy in Dakar on 6 January 1962. Senegal, in turn, opened its Tokyo embassy *thirteen years* later (5 September 1975), and the first trade agreement between Japan and Senegal was signed in Tokyo on 2 November 1976, even then only after Senegal had withdrawn invocation of Article 35 of the GATT against Japan on 29 December 1975.[188] Actually, a couple of years before GATT restrictions were revoked, a group of eight Japanese city banks had extended a syndicate loan of $20 million for Senegal's economic plan. This loan was a cushion for the 1976 Trade Agreement which came into force on 9 August 1977, two years before President Leopold S. Senghor had held discussions with the Japanese Emperor as well as with government officials.

President Senghor's visit was however preceded by several Senegalese ministerial visits to Tokyo. The July 1972 visit of the Minister for Youth and Sports, Lamine Diack, was followed by the November 1976 visit of the Minister for Industrial Development and Environment, Louis Alexandrenne, whose specific mission was the signing of the Japan-Senegal Trade Agreement. The latter was actually an "event diplomacy", but it was also a preparatory mission since it helped diversify the range of areas of common interest which were to be explored by later higher level Senegalese officials. Ibrahima Caba, Director-General of Economic and Technological Affairs in the Ministry of Foreign Affairs was the last Senegalese official to visit Tokyo before Senghor arrived a year later. A variety of Japanese government officials on the other hand, i.e. members of the House of Representatives, House of Councillors and of JETRO, visited Senegal on *five* different occasions between 1977 and 1978. During this period 13 Senegalese technical trainees were dispatched to Japan and 7 Japanese experts arrived in Senegal. Today, there are 112 Japanese in Senegal — all in the city of Dakar, and 30 Senegalese currently reside in Japan.[189]

A couple of weeks after President Senghor returned home from Japan the African diplomatic corps in Tokyo, in cooperation with the Africa Committee of the powerful *Keidanren* (Federation of Economic Organizations), hosted a meeting and reception commemorating the 16th anniversary of the establishment of the Organization of African Unity. This anniversary was one of occasional gatherings during which African official visitors to Japan, like African diplomatic corps in Tokyo, enjoy opportunities of meeting with members of the Japanese foreign affairs service outside the regular bureaucratic formal settings, the complaints of the Rwandan ambassador to Japan, Alloys Uwinana, notwithstanding. Following a diplomatic reception in Tokyo held by the International Bureau of the LDP on 30 June 1987 for 67 foreign ambassadors and ministers representing 64 different countries, the Rwandan Ambassador complained that

> Prime Minister Nakasone talks about internationalization but there are few diplomatic receptions or other opportunities for us to meet Japanese working in foreign affairs. I look forward to more such receptions in the future.[190]

Yet when the future came Ambassador Uwinana was not only conspicuous by his absence from a "diplomatic reception or other opportunity" where he would have certainly met "Japanese working in foreign affairs". His failure to attend this same diplomatic occasion was significant because it was hosted by his colleague, the Zimbabwean Ambassador to Japan on 26 November 1987, at which occasion I counted no fewer than four "Japanese working (not only) in foreign affairs", but specifically in the Africa Divisions of the MOFA. Ambassador Uwinana's absence was further aggravated by his failure to "spare five minutes" on the telephone to "recapitulate in a sentence or two" his country's policy towards Japan outside the procurement of aid ritual.

On 21 May 1983 the completion of the largest Japanese aid project in Black Africa was celebrated at a ceremony in Matadi where a suspension bridge spanning the river was constructed. One of the world's 10 longest bridges, construction of the 722-metre long bridge was financed by a 34,5 billion yen loan extended by the Japanese Government in compliance with a request by the Zairean dictator, President Mobuto Sese Seko, when he visited Tokyo in April 1971. Actually Japan had begun feasibility studies for the bridge in September 1967 when a Japanese survey team visited Zaire. Construction began in February 1979, eight years after Mobuto had requested assistance. No sooner had the bridge been completed than Mobuto's corruption came to the fore: instead of the bridge named, say, the Japan-Zaire Friendship or the Matadi-Boma Bridge, on the day it was inaugurated Mobutu announced in the presence of a Japanese member of the House of Councillors, Atushi Ejima, that it would henceforth be called the Mobutu Sese Seko Bridge.[191] This was vintage Mobutu in the kleptocratic "authenticity" tradition that he is famous for.

Mention should be made at this juncture that not all high African government officials visiting Japan are on official business, nor are they state guests of the Japanese Government. Other heads of state (such as Presidents Ahidjo of Cameroon and Omar Bongo of Gabon) have visited Tokyo on an informal basis, though Bongo did make a state visit from 18-21 September 1984. Mention too should be made that significance should not be attached in the case of those African heads of state who have visited Japan as state guests, and yet whose visits have not been elaborated upon above (e.g. that of the President of Kenya, Daniel arap Moi). Indeed in the case of Kenya for instance, Japan has very close ties because Kenya is (or was) an American window of "democracy" in Africa. She also plays a critical role in US military strategy in the Indian Ocean. Illumination would not, however, thereby be served by further accumulation and detailing of minutiae. A framework of analysis however sketchy has already been provided, and Japan's successful strategy in Africa is now unfolding even more clearly. Africa's Japan diplomacy on the other hand is only now coming out of a self-induced miasma of political poverty. The quintessence of Africa's diplomacy could perhaps be summed up in the 1983 remarks by the President of ADB during his visit to Tokyo to address the Keidanren. In typical African remarks Willa Mung Omba said:

> In terms of aid, available information indicates that there has (sic) been commendable efforts made by the Government (of Japan) to increase official resource flows to Africa. While in 1980 Africa received 9 per cent of Japan's official development aid, the figure is now estimated to have risen to 13 per cent. And, if the reported intentions of the government are anything to go by, Africa's share should increase to 20 per cent soon.

This is probably the nature of African diplomacy when African leaders go to Japan.

As a concluding word, perhaps, should be added the observation that in African diplomacy too, as in all things political, relativity governs, formulae all suspect. It would thus not be possible to force the flow of African diplomacy *vis-a-vis* Japan or otherwise into a theoretical nicety and logical pattern. Such pattern and nicety would exist more in the abstraction than in the reality. It was perhaps partly in this sense that the French historian René Sedillot once remarked that history has no sense. But in the African context, sense or not, the diplomatic interpretation of political history is that pacific "development" is the final arbiter, constant social experimentation notwithstanding. I have shown in the foregoing that in Japan, African diplomacy seeks many different things, but chief of which are the instruments of human survival and national revival. Such instruments are perhaps clearly seen in the next two chapters.

# 第三部
## 開発・協力問題

# PART III
## THE DEVELOPMENTAL/ AID QUESTION

## CHAPTER 5

# JAPAN'S AID TO AFRICA

---

*The OECF, the largest official bilateral development lending agency, has extended concessionary loans to various governments in Sub-Sahara Africa. [It] has strong intentions to increase its lending activities in Sub-Sahara Africa, in line with commitments by the Japanese Government to expand ODA.*

Hiroaki Suzuki [192] (1986)

*Japanese aid was given in line with Japanese national interest rather than in response to the demands and situation of recipients, in spite of the expectations of African countries.*

Hideo Oda and Kazuyoshi Aoki[193] (1985)

*Japanese aid is allocated with little regard to the requirements of recipients. It is given on Japanese terms and in Japanese ways.*

John White[194] (1964)

*We never feel that Japanese aid is conditioned on us being good boys from their point of view ... Everyday it's a new agreement with the Japanese, I can't even count them.*

Dr. Obed Asamoah[195] (1987)
Ghana's Secretary for Foreign Affairs

The size of Japan's presence in Africa can be measured in various ways; chiefly by factors or figures of aid, trade, diplomatic personnel, financing, loans, investments, or technology transfer. In this chapter the focus is on the factor of bilateral aid, i.e. Japan's Official (termed, incorrectly by some, Overseas) Development Assistance (henceforth JODA). Aid (*enjo*) is clearly one of the three major indicators of Japanese presence in Africa; the other being commercial trade (Chapters 2, 9, and 10) and diplomacy (Chapter 3). In Chapter 6 the focus will be on a specific aspect of JODA: food/agricultural development, fisheries, and forestation/desertification efforts.

Japan's Africa aid (in the form of grants, technical assistance, and to a lesser extent, loans) has, by the end of 1990, become the primary link between Japan and (especially Black) Africa, extending over 49 African countries. By the end of 1992 Africa received 10 per cent of JODA; but by the beginning of 1993 Japan allocated 15 per cent of her ODA to Africa per annum amounting to 1,6 billion US dollars. Although this chapter is devoted to bilateral JODA, passing references will be made regarding Japanese multilateral contributions to African development. Japan is, after all, the second ranked contributor to both the African Development Bank (ADB) — which she joined in 1983 — and African Development Fund (ADF); she participates as well with other countries in the World Bank's Special Joint Financing Facility for Africa, e.g. beginning in FY 1985 for three fiscal years, Japan has contributed $310 million to the Africa Fund. The Japanese Government made a commitment in 1987 to allocate $10 billion, including a three billion Special Drawing Rights (SDR) loan to the IMF, and a 330 billion yen ($2,16 billion) Japan Special Fund to the World Bank, promised on the occasion of Prime Minister Nakasone's visit to the US in April 1987. Again at the June Economic Summit in Venice she promised to make an additional $20 billion in funds available to developing nations, including untied loans to be provided by the Export-Import Bank of Japan. She has an official policy goal of increasing her aid to multilateral organizations. Recently, Development Assistance Committee (DAC) countries such as the US, UK, etc., have reduced their contributions to multilateral agencies, while Japan has steadily increased hers.

In 1985 Japan gave $1,24 billion in ODA to multilateral agencies, the largest amount from a member nation. Multilateral agencies include the World Bank group (the International Bank for Reconstruction and Development — IBRD, the International Development Association — IDA, and the International Finance Corporation — IFC), the Asian Development Bank (AsDB), the African Development Bank (which finances socio-economic development of 50 African nations), and United Nations agencies. Japan is the second largest contributor to the UN ($240 million in 1985), and to the World Bank. She has also increased her IDA contributions — and IDA provides interest-free loans to the so-called MSAC (most seriously affected countries), most of which are in Africa. In the 1984-1986 budget period, Japan contributed 18,7 % of the $9 billion total. For 1987-1989, however, Japan decided to contribute 21 % or $2,6 billion of the $12,4 billion total. The IDA Special Facility for Black Africa, referred to earlier, covers the 1985-1988 period.

Secondly, this chapter does not deal with economic assistance from the private sector, which not only supersedes the entire global JODA in terms of capital volume, but also directly promotes the expansion of economic activities in the developing countries, according to MITI's 1987 *White Paper*.[196, 197] Private economic assistance, which is involved in providing human resources for development, is growing, as are the number of private sector organisations involved in this type of assistance. For example the Japan Overseas Development Corporation (JODC), a non-profit foundation established in February 1970, was formed between private organisations and the Japanese Government in order to promote and contribute to the industralisation and modernisation of developing countries. More specifically, JODC is active in

(i) the Japanese Expert Service Abroad (JESA) Program;

(ii) financing the overseas investment activities of Japanese corporations;

(iii)  import financing for primary and secondary processed products manufactured by a production sharing system or by joint ventures in developing countries.

Since the JESA Program was begun, JODC has dispatched over 650 consultants and experts to nearly 30 countries in Africa, ASEAN, Middle East, Central and South America. Lastly, reference has already been made (Chapter 4) to Japanese private banks that have extended a $20 million loan to Senegal.

Japan's aid to Africa is particularly significant at this juncture, not only because much of Africa is becoming environmentally bankrupt and bureacratically inept and thus "in need" of aid (financial, technical, and human); but also because, for Japan, it would constitute a timely and persuasive rejoinder to the long festering congeries of critics of her aid. Some of these critics have lashed at Japan's "dismal aid record" which was seen as a concomitant of Japan's "disdain towards African aspirations and sensitivities", and which attitude "in foreign aid (has led to her failure) to meet the political challenge of its new position in the world economy". Hence Japan's aid to Africa "continued to appear miserly in the context of the country's overall prosperity".[198] By the beginning of 1988, however, as opposed to 1985 (when John Ravenhill published this criticism), Japanese aid had undergone a qualitative and quantitative change. Today's JODA to Africa has rendered Ravenhill's criticism obsolete. Still other and more recent criticisms emerged, not only relating to alleged kick-backs paid by Japanese firms to the Ferdinand Marcos regime in the Philippines, but more significant was the accusation championed especially by the US, that Japanese foreign aid was heavily tied to trade. Indeed, the US chided Japan for allegedly using foreign aid for "predatory commercial purposes". Hence, the US and her European allies became interested in discounting about 40 % of what Japan now counts as aid, presumably because Japan's low interest rates made aid-giving cheaper. This was typical Western whining whenever confronted with veritable competition from Japan.

184

Nonetheless, in the past other critics (e.g. John White) have so peremptorily dismissed Japanese aid to Africa as "inadequate, wrongly motivated and administered, too narrowly and selectively applied, and out of line with the aid programmes of other donors",[199] that the fallout of this criticism is still doing the rounds in many areas, especially among other lending agencies and nations. The fact that Japanese aid in the late 1980s is radically different from what it was in the early 1960s sinks but slowly in the corridors of entrenched chauvinism. In any event, at the 1964 United Nations Conference on Trade and Development — UNCTAD I — representatives of developing nations roundly criticised Japan for her emphasis on the trade effects of aid. At that time Japan had published a 1961 MITI report (itself an outgrowth of the 1958 MITI *Economic Cooperation: Present Situation and Problems* report) which took the myopic position that Japan undertook economic cooperation not for political objectives arising from the Cold War, nor support for developmental objectives arising from decolonisation, but rather in order to develop her home industry.[200] This was clearly a blatant linkage of "aid" to the goals of Japanese trade promotion.

Hence, domestically, some critics were emboldened to wonder why Japan should provide assistance to a continent such as Africa given, especially, the absence of "compelling" historical, ethnic/racial, or geographic reasons. The moral "imperative" of a rich country's "responsibility" toward poorer countries was a specious argument in the critics' view. Neither the fact that since Japan was herself the recipient of enormous foreign assistance through the World Bank, the GARIOA and EROA programs, it would be in her interest to be involved in aid programmes such as she was involved in during the late 50s in Southeast Asia. Nor the fact that these loans made it possible for Japan's Shinkansen, steel mills, power plants, and large-scale agricultural water ways to be built made a convincing persuasion to the earlier opponents of Japanese aid to Africa. Japan is in fact the only industrialised country — including West Germany — which is both repaying foreign loans and providing foreign aid simultaneously. Japan is unique in that between 1870 and the 1960s she largely dispensed with foreign loans.

Further criticism of Japanese aid to Africa (which also, I believe, was equally overtaken by present-day realities) argued that interest on Japan's loans and her repayment schedules had generally been more stringent than those of other donors; but again, such criticism was really more sound than sense. According to the *Annual Report* for FY 1984 of the OECF, for example, the softest loans extended by OECF bear an annual interest rate of 1,25 per cent and have a repayment period of 30 years with a grace period of five years. On the other hand, the hardest loans bear a 5,75 per cent interest rate, and have a repayment period of 15 years with a grace period of five years. The economic condition of recipient countries and the specific nature of projects are taken into account when deciding the interest rates on loans to foreign governments. For the 1976-1985 period the average annual interest was 3,27 per cent with a repayment period of 27 years 5 months and a grace period of 8 years 1 month. Her other domestic critics also regretted Japanese policy of granting aid on a request-only basis.[201] It was in fact this requirement that was to pique some African countries, such as Zimbabwe which in 1981 declined Japanese aid under this "by-recipient-request-only" basis. In the request-only regime, development proposals could not originate in either a specific government ministry or an agency involved in aid policy. It had to originate with the recipient country. Of course the "by-request-only" basis had some merit, since the recipient's objectives were at least recognised and respected. The Japanese government was actually motivated by a "principle" of non-interference in the internal affairs of African countries; yet some of these states felt this principle was making them feel "beggarly". Some Japanese critics in fact felt that the requirement was also open to abuse since it permitted the Japanese corporations to lobby recipient governments for project requests. However, when Zimbabwe refused to comply with the "by request-only" basis Japan lost the deal to a consortium of British corporations.

The last but one criticism often heard internationally is that the proportion of Japan's GNP devoted to ODA is below the average for DAC. The fact that JODA is second in total value only to the US's was considered "meaningless" even by some Japanese critics. These critics noted that although JODA has almost quadrupled from $1,15 billion in 1975 to $4,32 billion in 1984, the 1984 figure amounted to only 0,35 per cent of GNP, making Japan only the eleventh (11th) highest among 18 DAC countries. However, when the President of the World Bank, Barber Conable, visited Japan in 1987, he was full of compliments regarding the Japanese Government's contribution to *his* organisation, further expressing satisfaction with JODA commitments to the LDCs. One final major criticism levelled at Japan was that of "tied" aid, which calls for a broader review as a preliminary statement to a deeper analysis of Japanese aid in Africa.

**TIED AID UNTIED**

But aid tying (e.g. reduction in real value of development and discrimination against recipient countries)[202] was not a Japan-only "sinful commission"; it was the standard practice in the European Economic Community (EEC) and the Organization for Economic Cooperation and Development (OECD), despite these organisations' countries' often repeated principle that aid should not be tied. The common rhetoric was that aid was not to be tied, but the reality was otherwise. In general, multilateral non-discriminatory world trade aims not to have long-term bilateral aid tied. On the average, between 1966 and 1967 for instance, as Jossleyn Hennessy observed, 50 per cent of all bilateral capital assistance from the OECD/DAC members was contractually tied (Table 5.1).

Aid untying is certainly one other indicator of the quality of ODA; and Japan adopted the policy of expanding untied loans in 1972, but it was only since 1974 when the "Memorandum of Understanding on Untying of Bilateral Development Loans in Favor of Procurement in Developing Countries" was concluded within the DAC that the Japanese government loans became LDC-untied *in principle*. The practice only emerged slowly as I indicate on the next page.

## TABLE 5.1
## OFFICIAL AID FLOWS TIED TO PROCUREMENT
## IN DONOR COUNTRIES[1]

| Country | Gross disbursements | Total official dev. assistance[2] | Bilateral capital aid[3] |
|---|---|---|---|
| | 1961-65 | 1966-67 | 1966-67 |
| | Per cent | | |
| Australia | 10-30 | 17,1 | 21,0 |
| Belgium | 0-10 | 4,5 | 12,5 |
| Denmark | 0-10 | 19,7 | 84,5 |
| Federal Republic of Germany | 30-50 | 35,0 | 47,3 |
| France | 10-30 | 17,2 | 34,5 |
| United Kingdom | 30-50 | 43,8 | 57,7 |
| Italy | 30-50 | 46,2 | 62,9 |
| Japan | 60-80 | 70,8 | 84,5 |
| Canada | 60-80 | 72,5 | 97,4 |
| Netherlands | 10-30 | 16,7 | 37,3 |
| Norway | 0-10 | 1,3 | 10,7 |
| Austria | 60-80 | 83,1 | 99,2 |
| Portugal | 0-10 | 0,1 | 0,2 |
| Sweden | 0-10 | 8,8 | 39,3 |
| United States | 60-80 | 77,9 | 95,6 |
| Unweighted average | 30 | 34,3 | 52,3 |
| Weighted average | 50 | 63,0 | 79,5 |

[1] Contractually tied project aid, contributions in kind, and official export credits. Official export credits in some cases play a decisive role in the Federal Republic of Germany, Italy, Japan, Canada, Austria, and the USA. If they are disregarded, tied aid's share of all public bilateral capital assistance for 1966-1967 on the average amounts to 30 per cent in the Federal Republic of Germany, 32 per cent in Italy, 73 per cent in Japan, 76 per cent in Canada, 20 per cent in Austria, and 82 per cent in the USA.

[2] Bilateral aid flows (incl. technical assistance and official export credits) plus flows to multilateral agencies.

[3] Total official development assistance minus multilateral and technical assistance.

Source:     Jossyleyn Hennessy/Eastern Economist 56:17.

Since tied aid reduces the real value of the assistance to the recipient countries (because it also means the dimunition of the "grant element" which is the real basis for measuring the level of genuine aid), this is yet one of the negative elements of aid; the others will be explored later in the next chapter.

The most pervasive aid-tying practices were those of the US, especially between 1959 and 1975. As the balance of payments deficits persisted, especially with the entry of Japan and Western Europe as competitor, American official bilateral capital assistance became tied to procurement in the US. The US, and later other Western European countries, saw their aid-tying as a "defensive" measure. This assertion freed them from the constraint of severely criticising Japan for "imitating" them, since their rationale was that Japan was essentially pursuing a market-capturing strategy with a large amount of aid-tying to procurement of Japanese goods. But the criticism was a case of the "pot calling the kettle black".

The Japanese rationale and methods nevertheless were perceived as restrictive since the Japanese EX-IM Bank's statute, again like most Western donors, stipulated that all credit extension was based on tying. Naturally, this opened Japan to a long-running chorus of criticism. However, of the Japanese aid-giving institutions, only the OECF was free of such statutes and stipulations. The ODA loan is provided through the OECF after consultation among three ministries and one agency — MOFA, MITI, MOF (Ministry of Finance) and Economic Planning Agency (EPA).

Still, at the beginning of the 1960s, all Japanese capital assistance was fully tied. It began to decrease *slightly* around the mid-60s, which period saw a lowered ratio of 85 per cent in the average of the two years 1966 and 1967. Since 1974 the percentage of OECF loans to some African and other governments from the less developed countries that were untied increased. When Japanese aid began to increase in earnest in 1980 (i.e. as the "grant element" began to increase), Japan initiated a basic policy of generally untying of government loans pledged since April 1978.[203] As Table 5.2 reflects, the share of generally untied aid in the JODA sharply increased from 53,2 per cent in 1981, 63,9 per cent in 1982, to 68,7 per cent in 1983, conversely as the share of tied aid decreased from 30,9 per cent in 1981, 20,7 per cent in 1982, to 15,6 per cent in 1983. By the end of 1987, as I shall show momentarily, Japan had improved her aid to Africa to the extent that it muted just about all earlier criticism. Untied loans to the less-developed countries allow these recipients to purchase materials, equipment, and services from Japan *or* from other developing countries, while general untied loans permit purchases from countries that belong to the DAC of the OECD, as well as from developing countries.

## TABLE 5.2
## TYING STATUS OF TOTAL JODA
### (Gross Disbursement) ($ million)

|  | 1980 |  | 1981 |  | 1982 |  | 1983 |  |
|---|---|---|---|---|---|---|---|---|
|  |  | % |  | % |  | % |  | % |
| Untied | 1 891,45 | 52,3 | 1 873,65 | 53,2 | 2 148,28 | 63,9 | 2 901,58 | 68,7 |
| Tied | 1 088,47 | 30,1 | 1 086,46 | 30,9 | 697,15 | 20,7 | 659,66 | 15,6 |
| Partially untied | 635,41 | 17,6 | 559,59 | 15,9 | 516,95 | 15,4 | 661,28 | 15,7 |
| Total | 3 614,33 | 100,0 | 3 519,70 | 100,0 | 3 362,70 | 100,0 | 4 222,52 | 100,0 |

Source: *Ministry of Foreign Affairs* (1984).

## REASONS FOR JODA's LATE ENTRY TO AFRICA

Aid is generally a post-world war phenomenon (the most famous being the Marshall Plan for Europe). Since the end of World War II an urgent need for international cooperation for the economic and social development of the developing countries was widely recognised. A number of international cooperation organisations, including the International Bank for Reconstruction and Development (World Bank) were established. Beginning with the 1950s, in addition to such multilateral assistance, bilateral assistance was extended by developed countries. JODA for Africa emerged only in the 1960s. The reasons were essentially of complex historical, economic, and philosophical origin. It was not a single overriding factor even though paramount was that Japan's *first* obligation was surely to rebuild her war-torn industries, and to accelerate her own economic growth, before venturing to distant places and regions.

Japan's economic development was supported mainly by Western industrial transfers and the introduction of science and technology from the West. So it became an article of faith that Japan should direct her attention to Western countries (Chapter 1).[204] Thus, Japan inexorably cast an useeing eye, at best a condescending glance, at the non-western world with the exception of Southeast Asia, because of geographical proximity and other political reasons. Some of the ASEAN countries signed war reparations' agreements with Japan. Before war reparations, Japan had given foreign aid in the form of technical assistance to the countries of Southeast Asia. Japan's technical aid had derived from her participation in international technical cooperation schemes, such as the United Nations Expanded Programme of Technical Assistance (UNEPTA) and the Colombo Plan. The war reparations and grants to Southeast Asia naturally increased Japan's geographical bias towards this region, which still holds true, though by the early 1990s Japan had begun to shift away from this "Asia-first" approach.[205] Having lost the Northeast Asian source of raw materials, Japan was encouraged by Japanese business to turn towards Southeast Asia (via the mode of war reparations) as a way of re-establishing trade relations. The Japanese Government had nonetheless preferred "grants" rather than war reparations. In any event, the bottom line is that Japan's aid was "Asia-centered" from the beginning, and continued this way for a considerable period. Because Japan's orientation was to rebuild her economy first, her economic cooperation with the Southeast Asian nations mainly took the form of export financing to Japanese exporters through the Export-Import Bank of Japan. But most of the economic activity revolved around the United States, given the nature of the US SCAP Occupation of Japan in 1945-1952.

That is, significant economic reason for JODA's late entry to Africa was that Japan reflexively focused her priorities upon the reconstruction of her war-torn economy by integrating her economic activities with those of her Asian neighbours, and with the EuroAmerican industrial societies. The travails of the "Far Continent" naturally occupied the lowest rung in Japan's hierarchy of priorities. Although this was tantamount to denying to the African world the use of the road she herself had travelled when she used foreign assistance, Japan was not yet ready to lend an aiding hand to Africa until 1966 — but when she finally did, she surpassed virtually all other aid donors in Africa as I shall show in this chapter and elsewhere.

Another obvious reason for her late entry is that most of Africa had become independent in 1960 (barely a decade after which Japan had *regained* her independence). The former colonial powers of Europe, especially France, had extended a jealous arm over their former colonial possessions (see Chapter 4), and were thus hostile to many Japanese encroachments upon *their* African fiefdoms or possessions; "neocolonies", in the words of the founding president of Ghana.[206] And since Japan was feverishly seeking to avoid isolation, she could not afford to be perceived as "aggressive" in her involvement in a "traditionally non-Japanese region" — i.e. a kind of unspecified Euroamerican Monroe Doctrine which precluded and restrained a free-winging Japanese role in Africa.

An additional reason to be considered is an amalgam of the Confucian ethic and the Japanese custom of *ninjo* (compassion). *Enjo* is not unrelated to *ninjo* which is an integral element in interpersonal relationships, and which develops with strong bonds of obligation in close *emotional* ties (cf. the Shimizu thesis in reference to the strong "emotional" bonds between Japan and Ethiopia, Chapter 3). In the context of aid obligations which arise out of the *ninjo* that ties two individuals, a development of some relationship generally occurs, leading to the exclusion of others. Because of the Confucian ethic — which is more deep-rooted in Japan than the "Protestant work ethic" is embedded in Europe/America — the Japanese would thus not attach much importance to the *noblesse oblige*. That is, since the "Japan miracle" was nothing but the result of "hard work" and sacrifice as much as it was a patient postponement of material gratification, why could Africa not follow in the same tradition? Why should she depend on alms? Such was the reasoning of some Japanese policy-makers in the early 1960s — a view not entirely without merit, as 1 argue elsewhere. This is one of the least discussed, but noble, Japanese cultural views regarding foreign aid. Between 1868 and the early 1900s Japan herself shunned foreign aid except the puny 5 million yen that she borrowed in 1870 to build the Tokyo-Yokohama railroad. Moreover Japan was not enamoured of borrowing foreign capital, having witnessed the unhappy experiences of Egypt and Turkey, who mismanaged foreign capital and thus invited the wrath of foreign intervention.

The last, and least noble reason was the blend of materialistic selfishness and the lack of confidence in Africans as shown by some Japanese government bureaucrats and business leaders. Africa was the "black hole" into which fortune could be sunk in perpetuity without visible returns or gratitude. Alan Rix puts it concisely thus:

> At a more materialistic level, they (the Japanese) perceived that trading benefits to Japan from aid to Africa were insufficient to warrant a shift in priorities. Africa was regarded as something like the 'dark continent' into which Japanese aid disappeared with no acknowledgement of its origins. Some multilateral aid officials saw the African Development Fund as offering Japanese multilateral assistance far less visibility than did, for example, the Asian Development Bank.[207]

These critics were thus rather more impressed by large-scale or show-piece projects of the 1960s and 1970s (such as the Matadi-Boma Bridge in Zaire) than by many small projects which may, in fact, have a better chance of success. All the above notwithstanding, Japanese aid to Africa has grown tremendously, as Table 5.3

reflects. (See also Table 5.7 for the countries' breakdown for the latest figures.)

## TABLE 5.3
## JAPAN'S ODA TO AFRICA
### (Bilateral net disbursement)

| Year | Unit = $ million |
|------|------------------|
|      | Amount |
| 1970 | 8,00 |
| 1975 | 116,11 |
| 1980 | 222,91 |
| 1985 | 278,04 |
| 1986 | 418,46 |

## POLICY OBJECTIVES AND AIM OF AID TO AFRICA

What then is Africa to Japan? It is

- a rich source of natural resources, and has been Japan's source for many raw materials for close to a century;

- a steadily growing market for Japanese exports with a great potential for Japan-Africa commercial trade growth;

- the political force of the world's largest bloc (and Japan is a veritable international state);

- the hungriest continent on earth, while Japan is one of the most well-fed nations in the world;

- the ancestral home of 30 million Americans who are part of the large American market that happens to consume one-fifth of Japan's annual production for export, and

- the home of 600 million other *human* souls.

In a sense, then, these six points sum up not only what Africa is, but also her potential, strength and problems, and it presents opportunities and challenges that no great power such as Japan could afford to ignore. Given this consideration Japan's aid philosophy may be summed up, first, by former Prime Minister Yasuhiro Nakasone's words: "There can be no peace and prosperity for Japan without peace and prosperity of the developing countries".[208] Secondly, this view may be specifically summarised in the composite words of a variety of government officials (in the Prime Minister's Office, MITI, MOFA, JETRO, JICA, JOCV, and Japan Foundation), academic figures (at Tokyo University, and Tokyo University of Foreign Area Studies), and corporate executives (at Nippon Koei, NEC, and Marubeni) with whom the author conferred:

> Africa should be assisted because it is the firm belief of Japan, a member of the free industrialized world, that it has a duty to the international community to undertake economic cooperation befitting Japan's economic capabilities; reflecting interdependence with developing countries. Therefore official development assistance overseas may properly be regarded as a moral obligation and an essential instrument of contributing to world peace and prosperity.[209]

This is as representative a view as can be found in the published philosophy and policy aim of JODA to Africa. Moreover it is a view consistent with the policy of Japanese diplomacy towards Africa as discussed earlier (see Chapter 3). It is a view without which, irrespective of earlier criticism of Japanese aid to Africa, Japan's current role cannot be understood. This does not in any way imply that Japan's need for Africa's raw materials (oil, iron, bauxite, uranium, copper, chromium, platinum, manganese, gold and diamond) is secondary; nor does it imply that Africa's needs (capital, investment, new technology, managerial skills, and markets to develop other products) are paramount. All that it implies is that over and beyond material considerations, there are human issues that compel Japan and Africa to elevate their relations to a higher premium.

It is Japan's firm principle that the political, economic, and social stability of African countries is indispensable to the preservation of a pacifist and stable international order, since economic disorder in the developing world may lead to the rise of political and social instability. The former Governor of the Prefecture of Hiroshima, Hiroshi Miyazawa, and now member of the *Diet* put it this way:

> Japan has two major missions to accomplish within the international community. One is to extend economic cooperation in order to provide world stability and improve the citizens' lives ... The evaluation of Japan in the international arena depends on how Japan uses her economic strength to achieve world prosperity in the years to come ... (Secondly) Japan must also contribute to the establishment of world peace.[210]

This Japanese aid policy is in fact a distillation of the views of Western leaders. Compare, for example, Yasuhiro Nakasone's statement above with that of the French President, Francois Mitterand in 1983 ("To help the third world is to help France"), or that of US President, Richard M. Nixon in 1969 ("The main purpose of American aid is not to help other nations but ourselves").

Although both Mitterand's and Nixon's views are not fundamentally at variance with those of Japan as reflected in official publications and pronouncements, I shall argue, nevertheless, that Japan is beginning to depart radically from this egoistic view, especially from the Nixonian ethic to a more altruistic world-view. Yet this remains the basic philosophy of aid of all donors, including the largest of them all, the World Bank. JODA is thus not only essential for the developing world, it is of strategic value and security benefit to the developed, industrialised world.[211]

Hence, given such a view it was not incongruous that Japan increased aid to those African areas she considered important for the maintenance of world peace and stability, as well as to those which would help in strengthening the Japanese economy. The corollary of this is that Japan does not extend military assistance. On the basis of the Japanese Constitution Japan neither has a draft system, nor is she permitted to send troops abroad or to export arms. Indeed, according to Resolutions of the Standing Committee on Foreign Affairs of the House of Representatives 5 April 1978 and 25 March 1981), these specifically preclude Japan from extending economic and technical cooperation

(i)  applicable to military purposes, or

(ii) in relation to warring countries capable of encouraging escalation of conflict.

However when in 1980 Prime Minister Masayoshi Ohira (the only Japanese Prime Minister to die in office since 1932) embraced "comprehensive national security" as national policy — in which consideration of military and non-military factors in security issues was made — he linked Japanese aid to Japan's long-term strategy for defence, energy, and food, though in a *non-military* fashion. Because policy was "comprehensive", aid was also designated for international security. Countries that fell in the "sphere of influence" of the "Western" alliance were included in this "security aid".

Thus, because of the expansion of Japan's global political, economic, and diplomatic role, the rationale for JODA programmes has naturally become more complex. As one analyst puts it: "The promotion of economic development abroad, commercial gain, strategic motivation, humanitarianism and global interdependence all play a part in determining the scope and direction of ODA outlays".[212] Two analysts, William L. Brooks and Robert M. Orr, have outlined four distinct stages of Japanese aid policy:

(a) 1950s-1965: Japan's aid was in the form of war reparations.

(b) Mid-1950s - early 1970s: Excessively tied aid was used primarily as a means of promoting exports, particularly in Southeast Asia.

(c) Mid-1970s: Aid concentrated on resource-rich countries and countries along shipping routes so as to achieve economic interdependence.

(d) Second oil crisis (1979): Aid policy emphasised basic human needs, poorer countries, and a sensitivity to the humanitarian needs of countries of strategic importance.[213]

To these four should perhaps be added the fifth:

(e) 1984-1987: From 1984 emergency aid (as in African food and famine crises, etc.) and from 1987 the Non-Project Type Grant aid to the so-called LDDCs whose criteria for selection include: structural adjustment efforts; debts arising from JODA loan; and bilateral relations with Japan.

The LDDCs' grant is a new scheme for the Japanese Government, which seeks to address African needs for external currencies needed for macroeconomic policy reform or structural improvement of specific sectors. Over the next three years from fiscal year 1987, Japan has allotted $500 million. For 1987 alone the amount was $150 million.

## NATURE OF BILATERAL JODA TO AFRICA

In her aid policy to Africa Japan has emphasised the following: agricultural and rural development, human resources development/technical assistance, emergency aid and crisis relief assistance. In her continuing aid programmes priority is given to the following sectors:

● Rural and agricultural development

● Energy resources development

● Human resources development

● Promotion of small and medium-sized enterprises

● Crisis relief

In recent years Japan has placed emphasis of her aid efforts to increasing the aid through capital grant assistance and technical assistance toward the basic living sectors, i.e. food, fisheries and forestry, and such human resources development as are undertaken by the Japan International Cooperation Agency (JICA) and by the Japan Overseas Cooperation Volunteers (JOCV): e.g. medical care and public health, etc., wherein the recipient populace has direct access to the benefit of such aid. This chapter focuses on bilateral ODA exclusive of agricultural/food, fisheries, and forestation efforts, which are treated in Chapter 6. >

The first Japanese government loan was made to Uganda in 1966 (refer to the long history, dating to the early 1920s, of the Japan-Uganda contacts fully treated in Chapter 2), followed by credits to Tanzania, Kenya and Nigeria in the same year. The country which received the greatest number of Japanese loans was Egypt, and Zaire in Sub-Saharan Africa. Japan had always shown interest in Egypt since 1862; after 1973 she renewed her interest, but private enterprise demonstrated interest barely four years after Japan regained her freedom. Private economic diplomacy — launched with the active participation of the Japanese Government in the postwar period, began in 1956 with Egypt, Ethiopia, and Sudan by Ito Takeo, chairman of the *OSK Line* (see Chapter 2 about *OSK Line*). Ito had the title of roving ambassador. In March 1960 Kagawa Hideshi, chairman of *Toyo Menka* (see Chapter 2), led a government-sponsored mission to Ghana and Nigeria. In 1961 JETRO led a government mission to Kenya, Uganda, and Tanganyika. Today Egypt, Ghana, Kenya, Tanzania, Ethiopia, Zambia, Zaire, Malawi, Senegal and to a certain extent, Nigeria and Sudan, are Japan's main aid recipients. After Egypt, Nigeria was the largest recipient of JODA in Africa. African loan recipients, according to Alan Rix, suddenly increased after 1973, especially following Toshio Kimura's 1974 trip to Africa.[214] In 1974 bilateral JODA to Africa amounted to $51,76 million which rose sharply to $116,11 million in 1975. But in 1976 the figure fell to $91,90 million, though Japan's total global ODA reached $1,424 billion. From 1976 to 1984 Africa's share of JODA was $239,61 million. The first Japanese OECF office in Kenya (and thus Africa) was established in Nairobi in 1976; by 1978 Japan was not only a major African donor, she was involved in a wide range of donoring activities ranging from the very large showpiece projects to small projects hardly noticeable outside their villages.

As the Ghanaian Foreign Secretary observed, Japanese aid projects (not only in Ghana, but all over Africa) are numerous and diverse. In the fifty African nations north and south of the Sahara, they range from fisheries in the Cameroon, food in Ethiopia, irrigation in Guinea, regional maritime academy in the Ivory Coast, debt relief for many African countries, television station for Liberia, water wells for Mali, power plant expansion for Niger, suspension bridge in, and farm machinery for, Zaire, satellite ground station for Rwanda, road building for Tanzania, to microwave, colour television broadcasting, and medical health facilities for Ghana, and to numerous other areas.

Regarding the latter areas there is, for example, Japan's participation in the Second International Conference on Assistance to Refugees in Africa (ICARA-II) which was convened by the UN Secretary-General and held in Geneva from 9-11 July 1984, with delegations representing 112 countries and such intergovernmental organisations as the United Nations High Commissioner for Refugees (UNHCR), United Nations Development Program (UNDP), and the OAU attending. Japan's parliamentary Vice-Minister for Foreign Affairs, Ishimatsu Kitagawa, explained Japan's humanitarian assistance for African refugees and announced to the ICARA-II delegates that Japan would contribute $6 million to the UNHCR's African refuge relief programme for FY 1984. During ICARA-I (1981) Japan had pledged $5 million to the UNHCR's African refugee relief programme. Kitagawa added to the ICARA-II delegates that Japan was concerned about the refugee problem not only for *humanitarian reasons, but also because she wished to promote friendly relations with African nations*. He noted that Japan's contribution and cooperation should be commensurate with her responsibility as a member of the international community of nations.

The refugee aid was merely a small amount of a larger picture. On a net disbursement basis the total volume of bilateral JODA to

45 SubSaharan countries in 1984 increased about 13-fold from 1973 ($186 million). Table 5.4 reflects JODA to selected African countries in 1984.

Percentage-wise, its share increased four-fold from 2,4 per cent to 9,9 per cent in the same period. During this period both the amount and share of JODA for Africa had become approximately equal to those of the Middle East and Central and South America. The significance of Japan's ODA contributions can be reflected by the fact that Japan was the ninth DAC donor country in terms of volume in 1981, the sixth in 1982, and in 1983 she occupied fourth place.

### TABLE 5.4
### JAPAN'S AID TO SELECTED AFRICAN COUNTRIES 1984
#### (in millions of dollars)

|  | Grants | Technical assistance | Loans | Total |
|---|---|---|---|---|
| Total | $ 133,69 | $ 39,93 | $ 37,20 | $ 210,83 |
| Burkina Faso | 4,50 | 0,07 | 0,00 | 4,57 |
| Burundi | 3,97 | 0,12 | — | 4,08 |
| Ethiopia | 2,01 | 1,60 | -1,14 | 2,47 |
| Gambia | 3,27 | 0,09 | — | 3,36 |
| Ghana | 6,34 | 2,94 | 3,39 | 12,67 |
| Guinea | 2,41 | 0,45 | -0,14 | 2,71 |
| Kenya | 10,64 | 11,40 | 7,97 | 30,01 |
| Liberia | 1,14 | 1,34 | 1,15 | 3,63 |
| Malagasy | 3,29 | 0,37 | 3,21 | 6,87 |
| Malawi | 2,78 | 2,51 | 1,11 | 6,40 |
| Mauritius | 3,73 | 0,16 | -0,20 | 3,69 |
| Mozambique | 6,27 | 0,03 | — | 6,30 |
| Niger | 4,79 | 0,33 | 1,61 | 3,51 |
| Rwanda | 2,21 | 0,87 | — | 3,07 |
| Senegal | 10,16 | 1,96 | 0,55 | 12,68 |
| Somalia | 2,63 | 0,18 | 0,40 | 3,22 |
| Tanzania | 12,87 | 5,41 | 7,78 | 26,06 |
| Togo | 2,59 | 0,04 | — | 2,63 |
| Uganda | 5,52 | 0,09 | -0,33 | 5,28 |
| Zaire | 3,31 | 1,45 | 0,14 | 4,91 |
| Zambia | 14,85 | 3,12 | 8,03 | 26,00 |
| Zimbabwe | 7,87 | 0,47 | 9,33 | 17,67 |

Source: MOFA

Overall, however, as a result of attempts to achieve the targets of the Medium-Term ODA expansion set up in 1977 and 1981, Japan's ODA (on net disbursement basis) in 1984 amounted to $4,32 billion which then placed her in second place among the 17 industrialised countries of the OECD moving ahead of France and behind only the US. Because the yen loans had since the 1960s become the mainstay of JODA, her share of grants overall hovered around 40-50 % — i.e. 43,6 % (1981), 39,6 % (1982), 55,2 % (1983) and 46,2 % (1984) — which compared unfavourably with the DAC averages for the same period: 75,2 % (1981), 76,1 % (1982) and 79,7 % (1983).

In 1985, however, Japan's economic aid budget (on net disbursements) ranked first among the DAC member countries for the first time. Her 1985 JODA ($3,8 billion) was 12,1 per cent down over the 1984 figure nonetheless. As we have already seen, Africa's 1985 JODA share was $278,04 million. Still, by 1986, Japan ranked 18th in the world on a vital aid element that mattered: *grant element*. Sweden, with 100 per cent grant element, was number one. In 1986 Japan still ranked second to the US in terms of the volume of ODA. The US with $9,784 billion was nearly twice ahead of Japan ($5,634 billion). However in terms of ODA/GNP ratio Japan ranked 14th, and was ahead of the US. (Norway ranked first, and Sweden fourth) in the African context, bilateral JODA for the decade 1976-1986 grew from 6,1 per cent to 11,7 per cent — i.e. $46 million (on net disbursements base) to $450 million on a similar base, respectively (Table 5.5).

While the JODA loan for Africa has increased between 1984 and 1986, so has her capital cash grant, as well as her technical cooperation grant (Table 5.6), reflecting her growing African role. In 1986 nearly all the Sub-Saharan countries received more outright grants than loans.

For example 39 African countries received a *capital cash grant* compared with 25 which received a JODA loan. An even larger number received technical cooperation grants than JODA loans for the same period. (See Table 5.7.) For the decade 1973-1983 Japan had expanded her grant assistance to Africa 15-fold, as I have already noted elsewhere, which was indicative of a continuous growing role of Japan in the Far Continent.

In the 1985 fiscal year budget, included was a 8 billion yen increase over the previous year, to 60 billion yen, and some 8 100 million in yen loans.

Official loans play a significant role in development assistance, but because of Africa's growing structural, economic and environmental problems, and thus poor ability to repay, Japanese bilateral aid is increasingly taking the form of capital grants.

### TABLE 5.5
### AFRICA'S SHARE IN TOTAL BILATERAL JODA

| Year | Japan's bilateral ODA to Africa ($ million) | Share in total bilateral ODA ( %) | Japan's bilateral ODA in total ($ million) |
|---|---|---|---|
| 1976 | 46,27 | 6,1 | 752,95 |
| - - - | - - - | - - - | - - - |
| 1984 | 239,62 | 9,9 | 2 427,39 |
| 1985 | 278,04 | 10,9 | 2 556,92 |
| 1986 | 451,18 | 11,7 | 3 846,21 |

### TABLE 5.6
### DISBURSEMENTS OF ECONOMIC AND TECHNICAL COOPERATION

| Fiscal year | JODA loan grant | Capital cash Cooperation | Technical |
|---|---|---|---|
| 1984 | 8,462 | 44,221 | 8,727 |
| 1985 | 9,540 | 51,754 | 10,345 |
| 1986 | 39,853 | 54,389 | 11,057 |

(ODA loan and capital cash grant — Exchange of notes base)
(Technical Cooperation — JICA outlays base)

Source:     Data supplied by MOFA (1987).

## TABLE 5.7
## JAPAN'S ODA TO BLACK AFRICA 1986
### (by countries and modalities of aid)

| Country | Capital cash grant | Technical Corp. | Total Grants | ($ million) ODA loan | Total ODA |
|---|---|---|---|---|---|
| Angola | — | 0,01 | 0,01 | 0,46 | 0,47 |
| Benin | 2,64 | 0,04 | 2,68 | — | 2,68 |
| Botswana | — | 0,04 | 0,04 | 1,19 | 1,23 |
| Burkina Faso | 4,12 | 0,16 | 4,28 | — | 4,28 |
| Burundi | 5,74 | 0,29 | 6,02 | — | 6,02 |
| Cameroon | 3,51 | 1,34 | 4,85 | — | 4,85 |
| Cape Verde | 1,36 | 0,43 | 1,80 | — | 1,80 |
| Central Africa | 6,97 | 0,38 | 7,34 | — | 7,34 |
| Chad | — | 0,00 | 0,00 | — | 0,00 |
| Comoros | 0,59 | 0,27 | 0,86 | — | 0,86 |
| Congo | 0,24 | 0,01 | 0,25 | — | 0,25 |
| Djibouti | 1,19 | 0,07 | 1,26 | — | 1,26 |
| Equatorial Guinea | 0,59 | 0,59 | — | 0,59 | — |
| Ethiopia | 4,58 | 2,69 | 7,27 | -1,94 | 5,33 |
| Gabon | 0,20 | 0,63 | 0,83 | -1,37 | -0,54 |
| Gambia | 1,19 | 0,40 | 1,59 | — | 1,59 |
| Ghana | 14,00 | 4,57 | 18,57 | 10,87 | 29,43 |
| Guinea | 3,25 | 0,40 | 3,65 | -0,15 | 3,49 |
| Ivory Coast | 1,48 | — | 1,48 | — | 1,48 |
| Kenya | 6,16 | 0,61 | 6,77 | 9,45 | 16,21 |
| Lesotho | 17,74 | 15,26 | 33,00 | 16,79 | 49,79 |
| Liberia | 0,58 | 0,05 | 0,63 | — | 0,63 |
| Madagascar | 4,30 | 1,73 | 6,03 | 1,17 | 7,20 |
| Malawi | 11,04 | 1,04 | 12,08 | 3,74 | 15,82 |
| Mali | 2,78 | 2,89 | 5,67 | 10,43 | 16,09 |
| Mauritania | 4,87 | 0,45 | 5,32 | — | 5,32 |
| Mauritius | 3,26 | 0,07 | 3,34 | 7,64 | 10,98 |
| Mozambique | 2,59 | 0,53 | 3,12 | 2,09 | 5,21 |
| Niger | 13,94 | 0,34 | 14,29 | 1,21 | 15,50 |
| Nigeria | 6,66 | 1,66 | 8,31 | -2,66 | 5,66 |
| Rwanda | — | 2,75 | 2,75 | 10,21 | 12,96 |
| Sao Tome and Principe | 8,24 | 1,34 | 9,58 | -0,32 | 9,26 |
| Senegal | 3,33 | 0,02 | 3,35 | — | 3,35 |
| Seychelles | 7,27 | 5,48 | 12,75 | — | 12,75 |
| Sierra Leone | 0,15 | 0,21 | 0,36 | — | 0,36 |
| Somalia | 2,01 | 0,38 | 2,38 | 1,53 | 3,91 |
| Swaziland | 11,87 | 0,46 | 12,33 | 17,93 | 30,26 |
| Tanzania | — | 0,51 | 0,51 | — | 0,51 |
| Togo | 21,67 | 8,69 | 30,35 | 4,65 | 35,00 |
| Uganda | 4,09 | 0,27 | 4,37 | 14,84 | 19,20 |
| Burkina Faso | 2,97 | 0,11 | 3,08 | -0,46 | 2,61 |
| Zaire | 7,76 | 2,70 | 10,46 | -0,45 | 10,01 |
| Zambia | 15,20 | 8,00 | 23,20 | 29,02 | 52,22 |
| Zimbabwe | 1,78 | 1,21 | 2,99 | 1,35 | 4,34 |
| Reunion | — | — | — | — | — |
| Unallocated | — | 0,88 | 0,88 | — | 0,88 |
| Sum | 211,90 | 69,35 | 281,26 | 137,20 | 418,46 |

Of bilateral financial assistances, capital grant assistance is financial assistance extended to a recipient country without requiring any repayment. On the other hand, technical assistance is involved in technical cooperation which is to develop human resources for the nation-building of the recipient country to support its self-reliant efforts for social and economic improvement. Japan has extended her technical cooperation to African countries in such areas as public works and utilities, mining and industry, and agriculture, forestry and fishery. Technical cooperation is an important component of development aid, because it promotes mutual understanding of peoples through direct contact among individuals, as well as the transfer of technology to the developing countries. (Details of this aspect are explored in this and the next chapter.) Because of the vast discrepancy in the level of economic development between Japan and Africa, "cooperation" will naturally be characterised by a strong colouring of support. Japanese development aid for Africa cooperatively covers nine sectors:

- (i) Civil engineering
- (ii) Human resources development
- (iii) Communications
- (iv) Transportation
- (v) Agriculture, fisheries and forestations
- (vi) Manufacturing
- (vii) Electric power and energy resources
- (viii) Medical and health
- (ix) Commodity loans.[215]

The technical cooperation programmes are implemented mainly by MOFA through the JICA in consultation with other ministries concerned. In terms of the geographical distribution of Japanese technical cooperation by expenditure, Africa at $41,7 million falls behind Asia ($238,67) million) US, USSR, Australia, etc. ($117,48 million) and Central and South America ($83,68 million). In Japan's technical cooperation programmes the dispatch of experts and the acceptance of trainees and students account for approximately 50 % of the total expenditure. The training programme accepts middle to higher level technicians, researchers and administrative officers from Africa (other developing areas) at the request of the governments concerned.

## TABLE 5.8
## COMPOSITION OF BILATERAL ODA FOR AFRICA
## COMPARED WITH BILATERAL ODA FOR OTHERS

|  | Capital grant assistance | Technical assistance | Grants | Loans |
|---|---|---|---|---|
| Asia | 20,4 | 15,4 | 35,8 | 64,2 |
| South Asia | 20,5 | 15,0 | 35,5 | 64,5 |
| Far East |  |  |  |  |
| Middle East | 17,2 | 29,6 | 46,8 | 53,2 |
| Africa | 44,2 | 14,9 | 59,1 | 40,9 |
| North Africa | 12,2 | 10,8 | 23,0 | 77,0 |
| Sub-Sahara Africa | 63,0 | 17,2 | 80,2 | 19,8 |
| Central and South America | 12,7 | 36,5 | 49,3 | 50,7 |
| Europe | 0,00 | 7,8 | 7,8 | 92,2 |
| Oceania | 45,9 | 33,3 | 79,2 | 20,8 |
| Total | 22,4 | 21,4 | 43,8 | 56,2 |

Source:   Ministry of Foreign Affairs (Tokyo)
          OECF commitments

As we have already seen from OECF staff and now working at the World Bank (see note 192) the OECF organisation, the largest official bilateral development lending agency, has further intentions of increasing its lending activities in Sub-Saharan Africa (SSA) in line with Japanese Government commitments. Before looking at the OECF extended concessionary loans to African governments, a brief outline of the OECF would shed some light on the process and priorities of the organisation's loan activities.

The so-called "three sisters" of bilateral ODA were originally

(i) the Export-Import Bank of Japan (established in 1950 as the Export Bank of Japan, the present name being in effect since 1952);

(ii) the Overseas Economic Cooperation Fund (OECF, established in 1961); and

(iii) the former Overseas Technical Cooperation Agency (OTCA, founded in 1962).

The OECF has been the implementing agency responsible for direct government loans as ODA since July 1975; in August 1974 the OTCA absorbed the Japan Emigration Service (JES) simultaneously as it took over some of the functions of the JODC and was reorganized as the JICA. With the revision of the Act in April 1978 the JICA was empowered with some of the bilateral financial aid responsibilities on a grant basis. Hence JODA's implementation has been bifurcated between the OECF as the main agency specialising in financial assistance on a loan basis, and the JICA as the principal agency specialising in technical assistance. That is, as the specialist agency for direct government loans, the OECF is supervised by the EPA, while the MOFA, MITI, and MOF are the consultative ministries.[216] More will be said regarding the JICA later.

The OECF was established on 16 March 1961, and its objective was to promote economic cooperation between Japan and the Southeast Asian developing countries and other regions. Since then, the OECF activities may be divided into three categories:

(i) loans to foreign governments, including local public corporations and local governments;

(ii)  loans to, and equity investments in Japanese corporations engaged in development projects overseas; and

(iii) contributions to buffer stocks under international commodity agreements.

Since 1966 the OECF has extended concessionary loans to governments and government agencies, including those of Africa. By 1984 these loans from the governmental institutional nucleus (i.e. OECF) accounted for almost half of JODA, as the OECF FY 1985 *Annual Report* shows.

Each year, the OECF loans have ranged from 40-50 per cent of JODA. In fiscal 1985, JODA's budget was 1,381 billion yen ($5,8 billion), of which 52 per cent (716 billion yen or $3,0 billion) was allocated to the OECF loans.[217] Table 5.9 reflects the distribution of the OECF loans (on a pledge base) to Africa between FY 1966 and FY 1985.

## TABLE 5.9
### OECF LOAN DISTRIBUTION TO AFRICA (pledge base)

| Year Region/ Country | FY 66  FY 82 Amount    % | FY 1983 Amount    % | FY 1984 Amount    % | FY 1995 Amount    % | Total Amount    % |
|---|---|---|---|---|---|
| Africa | 2,151  (12,0) | 302  (11,9) | 323  (12,7) | 400  (13,5) | 3,176  (12,2) |
| North Africa | (1,236)  (6,9) | (265)  (10,4) | (265)  (10,4) | (246)  (8,3) | (2,012)  (7,7) |
| SSA | (915)  (5,1) | (37)  (1,50) | (58)  (2,3) | (154)  (5,2) | (1,164)  (4,5) |

Source:  The OECF, and as adapted from Hiroaki Suzuki (1986), Table 10.2.

From this table it is clear that the larger amount of loan goes to North Africa rather than to SSA. However, more capital cash and technical aid grant go to the latter than to the former. A breakdown of these 26 African countries and the respective yen amount commitments for the two decades period (1966-1986) is reflected in Table 5.10.

## TABLE 5.10
## OECF COMMITMENTS TO AFRICAN GOVERNMENTS

| Region | Country | FY 1982 | FY 1983 | FY 1984 | FY 1985 | FY 1986 | FY 1966-85 | ( %) |
|--------|---------|---------|---------|---------|---------|---------|------------|------|
| Africa | Algeria | 450 | | | | | 12 000 | 0,2 |
| | Botswana | | | | | 2 100 | 2 100 | 0,0 |
| | Cameroon | | | 3 588 | | | 3 588 | 0,1 |
| | Egypt | 17 500 | 45 100 | 13 077 | 22 210 | | 245 387 | 4,1 |
| | Ethiopia | | | | | | 3 700 | 0,1 |
| | Ghana | | 5 888 | | 5 912 | | 11 800 | 0,2 |
| | Guinea | | 6 150 | | | 5 000 | 11 150 | 0,2 |
| | Ivory Coast | 5 000 | | | | | 5 000 | 0,1 |
| | Kenya | 6 100 | 7 841 | | 13 361 | 5 605 | 53 882 | 0,9 |
| | Liberia | | 176 | 129 | 129 | | 4 543 | 0,1 |
| | Madagascar | 823 | 568 | | 1 211 | | 12 301 | 0,2 |
| | Mauritania | | | | | | 3 600 | 0,1 |
| | Morocco | 12 000 | 4 682 | | | 765 | 24 065 | 0,4 |
| | Malawi | | | 297 | | 9 436 | 14 677 | 0,2 |
| | Nigeria | | | | | | 16 900 | 0,3 |
| | Rwanda | | | | | | 1 587 | 0,0 |
| | Senegal | | | | | | 2 500 | 0,0 |
| | Sierra Leone | | | | 257 | | 2 257 | 0,0 |
| | Somalia | | 5 270 | | | 1 200 | 6 470 | 0,1 |
| | Sudan | 2 500 | | | | | 10 500 | 0,2 |
| | Tanzania | 3 300 | | | | | 18 611 | 0,3 |
| | Togo | | | | | 2 500 | 2 500 | 0,0 |
| | Tunisia | 10 940 | | | | | 23 550 | 0,4 |
| | Zaire | | | | | | 34 496 | 0,6 |
| | Zimbabwe | 4 100 | | 2 536 | | | 6 636 | 0,1 |
| | Zambia | | 8 029 | 6 342 | 722 | | 30 044 | 0,5 |
| | TOTAL | 62 713 | 83 703 | 25 969 | 43 803 | 26 606 | 563 844 | 9,4 |

Source:    Adapted from the OECF (1987).

Grants of aid have become more the active form of aid to Africa mainly because many of the African countries are LDDCs, and thus their ability to repay loans is low. Frequent delays or defaults in payment of interest and principal are often the case because of this economic crisis. Indeed the crisis faced by each country has rapidly increased SSA's international indebtedness.[218, 219] The special OAU Debt Summit in December 1987 appealed for ODA loans to Africa to be converted into grants and suggested that part of Africa's debt should be repaid in local currencies.

Although in general ODA disbursements have levelled off in the 1980s, JODA's African disbursements have increased, especially in 1986, and it is expected that 1987 will most likely be the same. But as Table 5.9 and 5.10 indicate, OECF loan activities are sporadic at best, reflecting a similar tendency of ODA from DAC countries which has levelled off even in the midst of the African crisis in the 1980s. Nevertheless, JODA is 0,35 % of GNP which is far below the international target of 0,7 % set by DAC, suggesting an increased need for expansion of JODA which, in the case of Africa, has already begun. Thus the situation equally lends itself to increased OECF lending activities to SSA, where potential demand for concessionary loans exists.

If SSA's share of OECF loans is increased say by 50 % (from 4,5 % to 6,75 %), and if OECF pledges to SSA between 1987 and 1992 are factored in, the amount might reach $2 223 million, which would make it nearly twice the value of all OECF loans to SSA to the end of fiscal 1985.[220] In 1992 the amount actually was 1,6 billion US dollars. Donor nations — especially the DAC countries — are still dogmatically working on the goal of giving 0,7 % of their GNP for development. It is hoped such a goal would take care of the sick man of Africa. Japan, however, through the OECF, JICA, and JOCV, is mixing quantity with quality of aid. But first on the issue of OECF loans: their aim is to help improve the structural adjustments and reforms of African economy.

Examples of these yen credits (OECF loans) in Africa are numerous. Some have financed internationally known large-scale projects. For example the construction of Zaire's Matadi Bridge was financed by a 34,5 billion yen credit, the largest single loan to a SSA country. The Matadi project, as already noted, involves the construction of a suspension bridge for both railroad and motor vehicles across the Zaire River. Japan also extended a 5,9 billion yen loan for the construction of the Nyali Bridge and the Mtwapa Bridge in Kenya in 1975 and 1977.[221] In February of 1984 Kenya received another commodity loan — 1 000 million yen whose interest rate was 3,5 per cent per annum repayable in 30 years with a 10-year grace period. The condition for procurement was LDC untied.

Kenya used the funds to procure products (steel, textile, and chemical products, spare parts for agricultural machinery, industrial machinery, vehicles, etc). Other yen credits have been extended for African communications' projects:

14,3 billion yen in 1979 and 1982 for microwaves, toll telephones, etc. in Kenya

12,5 billion yen for expansion of *Zambia's* radio and television broadcasting and microwave networks (1978 and 1982)

6,7 billion yen for the extension of *Madagascar's* microwave networks (1973 and 1978)

6,5 billion yen for construction of *Nigeria's* coaxial cable networks (1966)

5,9 billion yen for the improvement of *Ghana's* microwave network (1982)

5,7 billion yen for the establishment of *Tanzania's* satellite communications earth station and local and toll telephone exchanges, as well as the extension of its microwave networks (1978 and 1980)

5,3 billion yen for the establishment of *Somalia's* telephone and telex switching systems (1983)

1,8 billion yen for the improvement of *Liberia's* microwave networks (1975). Numerous other projects financed by yen loans dot the entire continent of Africa, such as, for example, the Anhwia Nkwanta-Yamoransa road in Ghana which in 1986 was repaired with a 12 billion yen from Japan.[222]

Not only in civil engineering and communications were yen credits advanced, but also in transportation, manufacturing, mining, electric power, commodity loans and, most important, in agriculture, food, forestry and fisheries. It is indeed a truism that every day is a new agreement with the Japanese, in the words of the Ghanaian Secretary for Foreign Affairs.

**TECHNICAL COOPERATION: JICA's ROLE**

The Japanese Government established the Japan International Cooperation Agency (JICA) on 1 August 1974, as the official Japanese agency whose main function was to extend technical cooperation to developing countries based upon prior agreements between the governments of Japan and those of other countries. Pursuant to this purpose JICA

   (i)   invites people from developing countries for technical training in Japan,

  (ii)   dispatches Japanese experts and JOCV members,

 (iii)   dispatches survey teams to help in formulating development plans and projects,

  (v)   recruits and trains Japanese experts to be dispatched abroad, and

 (vi)   supplies the equipment necessary for technical cooperation.[223]

JICA also facilitates DIF — Development Investment and Financing — to some African countries too. JICA's DIF programme is a system of financial support for economic cooperation with Japanese private businesses (including foreign corporations financed by Japanese firms) in developing countries. It is designed to build up a closer relationship between government level cooperation and private level cooperation, as well as between financial and technical cooperation. JICA's support for Japanese enterprises such as DIF is extended to activities which cannot qualify for financial assistance from the OECF or the EX-IM Bank of Japan, but require funds for improvement and expansion of facilities and for experimental projects in developing countries to promote social development, agricultural and forestry development as well as mining and manufacturing activities.

The JICA experts are active in various fields such as agriculture, forestry, fisheries, medicine and health, civil engineering, telecommunications, mining, manufacturing, transportation, etc. By the end of 1978 Japan had received a total of 1 495 technical trainees from the SSA countries. These African trainees are offered training from more than 140 courses and seminars under a group training system, as well as under an individual system.

African trainees in Japan who are under the auspices of JICA are involved in diverse training activities. In 1978, 156 trainees participated in seminars, course or specific programmes in agriculture, 80 in fisheries, 113 in construction, 34 in heavy industries, 60 in mining, 99 in light industries, 21 in the chemical industry, 31 in public works, 162 in transportation, 345 in postal services and telecommunications, 113 in health and welfare, 62 in management technology, 14 in education, 162 in administration, and 43 in other fields.[224] These trainees do not only focus on their respective courses; they mingle with Japanese people and steep themselves in Japanese culture. Visits to the village squares where they join local people in dancing are common.

Japan, on the other hand, dispatches technical experts to Africa. By the end of 1978, when 1 500 African trainees had been to Japan, JICA dispatched 2 081 technical experts to the African countries. The JICA experts endeavour to teach technology to the youth of Africa in diverse fields such as rice cultivation, irrigation, fishing, bridge construction, etc. The Matadi Bridge construction depended, for example, on a great number of Japanese experts dispatched by JICA to the *Organisation pour L'Equipment de Banana-Kinshasa*, where they supervised the project with the *Organisation* technicians.

JICA's motto is human resources development: i.e. nation-building through human resources. The acceptance of African trainees, the dispatch of Japanese experts, and the grant of equipment constitute three basic components of JICA's technical cooperation programmes. These three programmes are often combined to constitute a technical cooperation scheme called "project-type technical cooperation". Project-type cooperation falls under the following four categories:

(i)   Technical cooperation centres

(ii)  Health, medical, population, family planning cooperation

(iii) Agriculture, forestry, and fisheries development cooperation

As of 31 March 1987 Project-type technical activities were going on in Morocco (1), Senegal (1), Ghana (1), Nigeria (1), Zambia (2), Egypt (3), Kenya (4), and Tanzania (2). In contrast, in FY 1986, JICA's performance of grant aid was in 37 African countries.

The latter is a form of cash assistance extended to developing countries (including Africa) without repayment obligation. It is an assistance which includes general grant aid, aid for fisheries, food aid, and for the increase of food production and others. This is closely tied in with technical cooperation.[225] Thus JICA offers services related to the promotion of capital grant assistance and for the realisation of the aid objectives.

In 1985 Japan extended a grant of 856 million yen to the Government of Ghana for the improvement of the technical standards of the Ghana Broadcasting Corporation.[226] This was an agreement for the design, supply, installing and commissioning of colour television studio equipment as well as installation of the microwave telecommunication by Nippon Electronic Company (NEC). JICA's role was important here. The aid was in addition to the grant from Japan for materials for child malnutrition treatment development. The Hideyo Noguchi Medical Institute in Ghana is constructed and supported with the aid of Japanese grants, and is named after the Japanese medical scientist who died in Ghana in 1928 while conducting research on the prevention and cure of yellow fever. He was the Japanese Albert Schweitzer. Today Ghana is Japan's largest aid programme in Africa. The Ghanaian attitude is summed up not only by the military general who remarked that the "Japanese are very generous to us", but more importantly, by the Ghanaian Secretary of Foreign Affairs who authoritatively stated: "We never feel that Japanese aid is conditioned on us being good boys from their point of view". A similar attitude is found in Malawi, Mozambique, Kenya and Tanzania.

Virtually all of Africa that once was under European colonial rule holds this Asamoah-like view *vis-a-vis* Japan. Even those East Africans who confronted the Japanese in some of the fiercest battles on the Burma front have less antipathy towards the Japanese than the hostility they still harbour towards Europe for her colonialism. Many reasons account for this of course; but Japan, a non-European power, whose belated entry to Africa has been noted for her proportionate blend of altruism and egoism, has been greatly aided of late by her generous aid to Africa. Japan's strategy has been immensely successful in projecting a positive image, and reflecting the basic trait of a generous and reliable nation. It was such doctrine that the Foreign Minister at the time, Shintaro Abe, expressed when he noted that a succesful diplomacy should be based on reliability, as well as ability to keep promises made. (see Chapter 10).

∠As a conclusion, it would therefore not be remiss to note that Japanese aid to Africa in the 1980s has been based primarily on humanitarian considerations. The image of Japan consequently rose in Africa because of the perceived reliability of Japan by most SSA countries. A select number of countries (e.g. Kenya, Zaire, Ethiopia, Egypt, Ivory Coast, Zimbabwe and Nigeria) receive JODA on the basis of their economic or political interest to Japan, even though Japanese humanitarianism now plays a critical role. In either case, however, Japan has emerged as a major beneficiary, especially since she has proven herself to be reliable *vis-a-vis* SSA. (France and Great Britain, for example, have stopped non-project aid type to Zambia, while Japan has not. In fact, Japan has substantially increased her aid to SSA, despite the existence of some wrinkles). One of the greatest pay-offs awaiting Japan is the political influence she would wield in Africa in the near future. Ironically, Japan is finally about to win the political influence over Africa that European Imperial Powers had denied her when African colonies still belonged to these powers. Despite Africa's socioeconomic problems — or because of them — Japan continues to express interest in Africa. For instance, during October 1993 the Tokyo Government is due to host an International Conference for the Development of Africa to which 46 African countries, major donors, and international organisations will be invited. The conference will deal with strategies for African development and regional co-operation (Sezaki 1993:20).

## CHAPTER 6

# AFRICA'S GREEN REVOLUTION, JAPAN'S ROLE

*An African Green Revolution would greatly alleviate the African food crisis.*

MOFA (1985)

*Africa produces what she doesn't consume, and consumes what she doesn't produce.*

A Common African Saying

*Japan intends to continue cooperating with African nations in their efforts to increase food production, boost manpower training, improve water resources, and secure better facilities for transporting farm produce in order to achieve all-round agricultural development.*

Ministry of Foreign Affairs (Tokyo)[227]

*Africa is dying. If things continue as they are only eight or nine of the present countries will survive the next few years ... Our ancient continent ... is now on the brink of disaster.*

Edem Kodjo, former Secretary-General of the OAU[228]

Africa — especially those Sub-Saharan countries stretching from the Sudano-Sahelian region downwards — is beset with innumerable problems. There is no other region in the world in which food production has declined so steadily for the last two decades. Population growth remains the highest in the world, and consequently food production is unable to keep pace with this population growth. Thus, there are more hungry people and more people starving to death, because the ability of the continent to feed itself has been deteriorating since the late 1960s. A UN symposium on Africa held in Tokyo in 1984 painted a grim picture of the cereal food aid needs of 20 African MSACs; however, the symposium ended on a rather optimistic note.

Land degradation, periodic droughts and other environmental limitations, governmental policies and official mismanagement, inadequate incentives to farmers, a virtual absence of infrastructure, poorly developed extension and management systems, lack of appropriate research on food crops, a galloping population growth, the legacy of colonial underdevelopment, the constraints and condition of the international economy, etc., all are factors which have conspired to define and perpetuate the African problem. The result is that Africa is getting poorer by the day, despite its immense industrial potential. There is, for example, no African state with an annual turnover which equals that of Exxon Corporation. In fact according to Ieuan Griffiths[229] only South Africa, Nigeria, Egypt, Morocco and the Ivory Coast have GNPs large enough to get them on a list of the world's largest 100 corporations.

Because of its size, Africa (which is 3 ½ times the size of the US — the SSA alone is over twice the size of the entire USA) has diverse climatic, environmental, socio-economic, cultural, and political characteristics. Her agricultural systems also vary. Climatic and ecological systems range from the hot, humid rainforests of the Congo River Basin, to the highlands of Kenya and Uganda, to the short and tall grass savannas that grade into the Sahara Desert to the north, and the Kalahari and Namib Deserts to the southwest in Botswana and Namibia.

Consequently over 70 per cent of the 600 million African people live in rural areas, and they tend to be clustered around water supplies, roads, and areas with better soil. A degradation of *this* environment in turn replicates the environmental bankruptcy that has already occurred in other parts of the continent. African governments are further faced with several conflicting forces that threaten their economic, and thus political independence. The International Monetary Fund (IMF) is increasing the restrictions on foreign aid and rescheduling loans (as we noted in the case of Zambia in Chapter 4). Many governments find it difficult to fulfil these strict restrictions while they pursue their own national agendas at the same time. A special two-day OAU summit in December 1987 called for all debt to be rescheduled over 50 years, without interest. Africa now spends 40 % of its export income to make payments on its debt. The classic expression of this dilemma remains that of the then President of Tanzania, Julius K. Nyerere: "We cannot pay. You know it and all our other creditors know it ... (S)hould we really let our people starve so that we can pay our debts?"[230] A logical answer would be in the negative of course; but so would it further devalue the credit-worthiness of an already discredited conglomeration of theoretical states.

It was in recognition of the tragedy expressed by these two Africans (Kodjo and Nyerere) and also as a result of his own eye-witness observation, that Foreign Minister Abe

> felt that the calamity of drought (was) a menace to world peace and stability ... The international community at large (must) recognize the necessity and importance not only of the emergency assistance to African countries but also of positively carrying out agricultural and food-related assistance for them from medium- and long-term perspectives and supporting their self-reliant efforts.[231]

Since the soils of tropical Africa have generally the same characteristic of marginality of fertility, the bulk of the land-areas in the northern Savannah and the tropical rainforest is laterite, and

219

thus is composed of different degrees of iron and aluminium hydroxides. Because the soil is susceptible to leaching and erosion, the environmental condition ranges from delicate to precarious. Hence, availability and arability of land has deteriorated. Increased population pressure has led too increased pressure upon the land. The need for increased production has given rise to expanded use of marginal land with low and unreliable productivity.

Thus, the regeneration of Africa is a massive enterprise to which Japan has entered with an invigorating sense of mission. Yet despite Japan's imaginative (though limited) involvement in Africa's agricultural and food crisis, the crisis remains not amenable to easy solutions. The problem is rather long-term in nature, and calls for regional cooperation first before multilateralism, and Japan has been calling for a strategy for improved food productivity since the early 1980s. African governments will have to first address and confront their complex political, technical, and structural problems and provide a clear-cut long-term food strategy. The reason the green revolution has bypassed Africa is not simply due to the fact that the crash food production projects of the 1970s in the Sahel were merely of a band-aid type designed to alleviate short-term problems; there was an additional complex of other factors beyond the scope and purview of this work.[232] An obvious factor to consider is the discrepancy between current plans seeking higher agricultural growth rates and the ingrained investment bias against agriculture. If we consider that agriculture still provides 30 %-60 % of GDP, and 60 %-90 % of employment in most African countries, the problem falls into perspective. Only in Ivory Coast did planned investment in agriculture reflect these proportions, being 52 % of total investment in the plan covering the early 1980s.

Whereas food production for subsistence and local markets managed to keep pace with population in the previous decade, per caput production of major food crops in 1985 averaged 12 % lower than the comparable figure for 1974. Between late 1982 and early 1985 there were 25 MSAC countries (seriously affected by drought). Some recovery was seen in 1985 with per caput food production up by 2 % from the 1984 levels, though still below those of 1980. In 1985-1986 six countries still continued to experience food emergencies: Angola, Botswana, Cape Verde, Ethiopia, Mozambique and Sudan. In 1991-1992 severe drought also devastated many Southern African countries, especially Zimbabwe, Zambia, Namibia, Botswana, and South Africa.

## FOOD AID AND AGRICULTURAL DEVELOPMENT

The 1968-1974 Sahelian drought and famine, in the course of two years (1972-1974), left some 250 000 Africans dead. This figure was to be surpassed by the famine of the 1980s which actually began in 1978. It was in June of that year when the Ethiopian state-controlled radio broadcast an alert that some one and a half million people in its northern provinces were facing starvation. Mention has already been made that in November of that year, the leader of Ethiopia made a public pronouncement of the hunger situation in his country, and warned of the impending "frightening" situation. This was to be the first of many hunger alerts that followed the 1978 warning.

Shortly after the Mengistu alert of 1978 Ethiopia was hit with the beginning of a massive food crisis in 1979. It was in the same year that the Japanese government decided that agriculture and forestry should have a greater emphasis in Africa. This was not only because the major cash crops which had been cultivated since colonial times (e.g. peanuts) were inadequate to provide food, especially to a largely rural population that depended on subsistence economy; but also because deforestation, loss of soil fertility, and other types of land degradation were rapidly compounding the food problem in Africa.

Although Japan had provided continuous technological assistance to agriculture and forestry from the mid-1970s (espcially from 1978), and had emphasised increasing the production of food,[233] she was fully conscious of the fact that national independence in Africa (or anywhere else for that matter) could only be achieved first with self-sufficiency or possessing the means to achieve such sufficiency in food production. After a score of years of rising commercial food

221

imports and food aid, much of Africa is now facing an economic malaise. Consequently Japan has stepped up her food assistance to nearly the entire continent of Africa. At the OECD Ministerial Conference Japan announced that she would extend over $100 million in food-related assistance. But at the June 1984 World Food Council meeting in Addis Ababa (Ethiopia), when Africa requested a billion dollars' worth of food aid, Japan correctly dissuaded such fantastic nostrums, since what was needed was not just another infusion of aid without a planned strategy. The absence of a strategy would be a disincentive to those African farmers who still produced food. Japan was ready, in any event, to provide food assistance in the quantity desired, provided an ideal long-term strategy was devised beforehand.

This Japanese assistance to Africa was more visible during the tenure of the Japanese Foreign Minister, Shintaro Abe, (who inexplicably was dismissed by one Japanese scholar as "idiosyncratic")[234] than it was perhaps during the tenure of any other Foreign Minister. There is no objective evidence nonetheless, to substantiate a charge of Abe's "idiosyncrasy", even in his African activism. In Chapter 3 reference was made to Abe's visit to Zambia, Egypt, and Ethiopia in November 1984. While in Addis Ababa, Abe announced that in view of the serious food shortage in African countries, Japan would extend supplemental food and agricultural aid to Africa amounting to 11,7 billion yen (approx. $50 million) in fiscal year 1984. This was in addition to the 27,6 billion yen ($115 million) already pledged for food supplies, fertilizers, and farm equipment to boost the continent's agricultural production. Abe became the first Foreign Minister from a Western-bloc nation to observe first-hand the conditions in the drought areas of Africa (hence his "idiosyncrasy"). In December 1984 MOFA was instructed by the Japanese Cabinet to compile a comprehensive food strategy. Hence the Nakano Mission to Africa (see below).

In his appeal to the international community Abe noted that while on this tour he became

> acutely aware of the need to strengthen not only food assistance to those afflicted in African countries, but also

cooperation with them in such areas as storage and transportation of food, water supply, and agricultural development.[235]

It was a few days after he returned from his African trip that he hosted the so-called "starvation lunch", proceeds of which were sent to drought relief efforts. Twice a month the foreign ministry officials would gather in the room of a bureau director-general or in a reception room and made do with bread and milk for lunch. Each participating official donated to drought relief a sum of money equivalent to the price of an ordinary meal. The "starvation lunch" was also designed to publicize the "Africa Month" (28 September to 27 October) during which period a variety of events aimed at increasing understanding of Africa among the Japanese people would be conducted. The highlights of the "Africa Month" included an African film festival, exhibition of nature conservation campaign posters, lecture meetings, African fashion shows, African dance, exhibition of wooden masks, and performances of African musicians. Abe writes in his *Creative Diplomacy* (p. 26) that he initiated the "African Month" activities as well as sponsoring the "serial of 'Charity Lunches'" in order to raise funds for the suffering people in the famine-stricken areas of Africa". This was a dramatic illustration of the futility and morass to which Africa had sunk. No further proof of the "sick-hungry-man-of-Africa" syndrome is required than this.

The "starvation lunch" idea was proposed by a deputy of Abe's, Masamichi Hanabusa, who was then Deputy-Director of the Middle Eastern and African Affairs Bureau. (The foreign ministry service had not yet caught up to the irony of an "Africa Month" devised by a bureaucrat from the *Middle Eastern* and African Affairs Bureau! Some critics had concluded that Japan's juxaposition of African affairs with Middle East issues reflected Japan's lack of seriousness about Africa.) The "starvation lunch", in any event, was only a small part of the public awareness programmes and social mobilisation for Africa's support. After having called for charity groups, women's and religious organisers to raise money for drought victims, the MOFA African affairs service felt it imperative that they to do something themselves. President Omar Bongo of Gabon and Prime Minister Mohamed Mzali of Tunisia visited Tokyo during the activities of the "Africa Month". Bongo had come with an entourage of at least four cabinet ministers (see Appendix B).

In the summer of 1984 Japan's parliamentary Vice-Minister for Foreign Affairs had announced to the ICARA-II delegates assembled in Geneva that Japan would provide food aid of approximately $6,5 million through the World Food Program, and would attach particular importance to projects relating to water supply and health and hygiene, which have direct relevance to the welfare of both refugees and local people. (See Chapter 5 for Japan's further contribution to ICARA-II).

In April 1985 the Nakano (Agricultural Project Finding) Mission was sent to survey the agricultural situation and to confer with African governments in Senegal, Kenya, and Ethiopia. The Mission's aim was to formulate plans to increase food production on a mid- and long-term basis, as well as emergency food relief supplies. The Nakano Report further stated that food supplies and agriculture to Africa should be increased both qualitatively and quantitatively by integrating technical cooperation with capital grant assistance from Japan and other donor countries. The report was released as a *Ministry of Foreign Affairs Task Force Committee on Food and Agricultural Cooperation.* It noted, *inter alia,* that the "drought that began in some areas as early as 1981 revealed the fragility of African agriculture with a mass famine in 1983. As a result, expansion of aid to Africa has become a global issue."[236] (The real cause, of course, is the legacy of capitalist agriculture and its mechanisation which, since its inception with the European settlement and industrialisation of Africa, when combined with the weak character of the state, led to the depletion of rural male workers in urban centres. It thus led to the collapse of local food production. More about this argument later.)

In June 1985 foreign minister Shintaro Abe had proposed to the seven ministers of the OECD a comprehensive plan termed the "Green Revolution For Africa" as a follow-up to the Bonn Summit. The African Green Revolution concept combined technical cooperation loans and grant aid in order to provide long-term assistance to African agriculture, forestry and fisheries. It has now been over two decades since Dr Norman Borlaug received the Nobel Peace Prize in 1970 for his pioneering research in breeding the high-yield wheat that helped launch the green revolutions that started India and Mexico down the road to self-sufficiency in food grains. India used Borlaug's wheat crossed with local strains to raise her production from 11 to 47 million tons in 1966. China raised hers from 41 million tons in 1979 to 87 million tons in 1984. Asian countries had largely attained their "green revolution" in the late 1960s and early 1970s. The Abe proposal was based on the belief that such a green revolution could be attained in Africa. This plan was composed of five main pillars:

- Strengthening of agricultural research activities.

- Promotion of re-afforestation movements.

- Assistance for the formulation of appropriate national development plan.

- Improvement for infrastructure for rural and agricultural development.

- Support for policy reforms for rural development and increased assistance to small farms.[237]

In September of that year, the Summit member countries adopted the Abe Plan at their meeting. As a follow-up to Foreign Minister Abe's African visit, JICA sent three missions of its own to Africa. These included two surveys of small-scale rural development in East Africa. One mission went to Kenya, Tanzania, Zambia and Zimbabwe. The second returned to Tanzania and Zambia, while the third crossed the continent to West Africa: Ivory Coast, Mali, Senegal and Cameroon.

JICA had concluded that cooperation with small farmers who produce staple foods was essential. And so it became involved in small-scale rural development in semi-arid areas of Cameroon, Mali, and Senegal. The Cameroonian paddy crop productivity was expected to contribute to the political and economic stability of the neighbouring countries. A rehabilitation project in Mali to provide water to expand agriculture on dry and semi-arid land was undertaken by the JICA in order to rehabilitate these lands and revitalise farming areas around the Niger. In Senegal JICA began a new approach in which a small-scale project was undertaken on a trial basis. The full-scale project would then be revised and carried to completion. This new approach would thus cut short the lengthy bureaucratic period normally undertaken by JICA to plan and evaluate before implementing a cooperation project. The difficulties that are often confronted by the JICA experts in Francophone Africa — to wit, lack of French language expertise by the Japanese technicians and specialists — are overcome somewhat in Senegal, because at the Senegal Vocational Training Center, Senegalese counterparts who were sent to Japan for training and for their Japanese language study, often serve as contact points with Japanese experts.

JICA has carried out such projects as 2KR (2nd Kennedy Round) aid for increased food production, as well as establishing the Jomo Kenyatta College of Agriculture and Technology in Kenya, a small irrigation project in Ethiopia, a road construction project for food transportation in the Sudan, and a project to expand and improve food grain storage in Tanzania. JICA's development survey teams have helped formulate development plans and projects in the public sector such as Small Scale Rural Development Project and the Agricultural Verification Study in Senegal, Baigom Agricultural Development Project in Cameroon, updating a feasibility study for the Bagaineda Agricultural Development Project in Mali, and the Mwea Irrigation Development Project in Kenya.[238]

## MAP 6.1
## AFRICA: Food shortage countries, deserts and arid areas

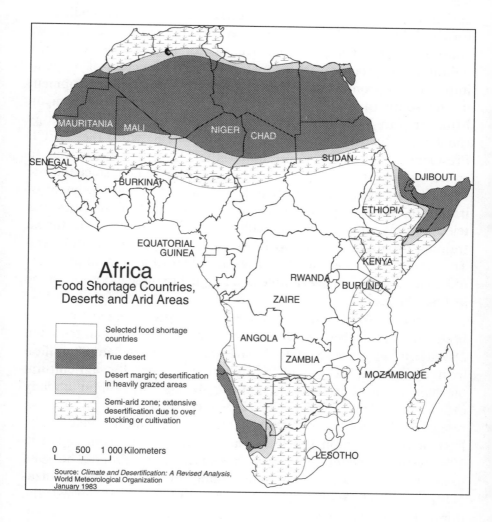

Africa
Food Shortage Countries,
Deserts and Arid Areas

Selected food shortage
countries

True desert

Desert margin; desertification
in heavily grazed areas

Semi-arid zone; extensive
desertification due to over
stocking or cultivation

0     500    1 000 Kilometers

Source: *Climate and Desertification: A Revised Analysis,*
World Meteorological Organization
January 1983

At the request of the Tanzanian government JICA carried out the highly successful Kilimanjaro Agricultural and Forestry Development Center Project. Rice planting and harvesting at the foot of Mt Kilimanjaro is one of the major agricultural activities. Dairy farming, veterinary fields, digging of wells for daily living and agricultural purposes are some main JICA activities on a small-scale for rural Africa. In East Africa, especially, many such activities are constantly introduced. In 1982 Kenya, for instance, signed a $25 million loan agreement with Japan for the construction of roads to improve and promote agricultural and agro-industrial development in the southern and coastal areas of the country. The Kenyan Minister for Regional Development, Science and Technology (Nicholas Biwott) in signing the agreement with the OECF President (Takashi Hosomi) noted that Kenya's policy was to endeavour to tap and exploit natural resources. In fact, since the late 1960s Japan has given Kenya mixed loans for the development of irrigation, water supply, road construction, medical supplies and telecommunications. The agricultural and engineering technical training programme at Jomo Kenyatta College of Agriculture and Technology — inaugurated by President Daniel arap Moi at a cost of $20 million — is one example of a major Japanese aid programme in East Africa.

Numerous food and agricultural cooperation agreements have been entered into between Japan and various African countries. On 28 August 1985, for instance, Japan and Egypt signed an $8 million loan agreement, of which $6 million was used for agricultural mechanisation. This was in addition to the $6 million already extended in April 1984 to develop a centre for rice production research,[239] as well as the establishment of agricultural machinery. Part of the 10 billion yen loan that Zaire received from Japan in 1986 went for water supply projects and for fertilizers. The 1984 grant-in-aid was also for a water supply project — the Mbanza-Ngungu project. A 400 million yen grant to Niger went towards the improvement of transport resources of the Niger Foodstuffs Board. Two earlier grants-in-aid were for nutrition improvement projects, while the November 1984 grant-in-aid was for the underground water exploitation project. In 1986 Tanzania received 29 million shillings to purchase vehicles for crop transportation. She also received 75 million shillings worth of rice from Japan. The December 1984 grant-in-aid was for the project to improve the Dar es Salaam water supply system. Madagascar received 10 868 tons of rice in food-aid and a subsidy of 150 million yen to improve agricultural transport. Ethiopia used the 6,7 million birr from Japan for agricultural projects. This was in addition to the 2,5 billion birr that Japan granted her towards famine agricultural development in May 1984. For the 1986-1987 year Mozambique received a grant of 3 billion yen to buy farming equipment, pesticides, and fertilizers. Mali spent the 150 million dollar grant she received for strengthening her agricultural transport facilities.[240]

In May 1984 Burundi and Japan signed a 300 million yen aid agreement for agricultural equipment and vehicles. Kenya received yet one more grant: a 350 million yen from Japan to purchase US grain for famine relief.[241] Agreements were ratified by Rwanda and Japan for a 150 million yen grant to increase food production, as well as for assistance in the provision of domestic water in Kigali and Kibungo areas. This was in addition to 400 million grant to purchase health equipment and vehicles. A cooperation agreement was also signed to provide 200 million yen worth of pesticides. A 60 million yen grant to buy fertilizer was earlier extended to Rwanda. In 1984 Zambia received K37 million loan for the rehabilitation of nitrogen chemicals' fertilizer plant at Kafue, bringing the total of Japanese loans since 1973 to K230 million.[242] In 1981 both the United Nations Food and Agricultural Organization (FAO) and the Japanese Government had provided trucks for the agricultural sector. In June 1984 the grant-in-aid advanced was for the establishment of the School of Veterinary Medicine of the University of Zambia. Sierra Leone received a $1 million dollar loan for rice purchases. This was in addition to the million dollar grant she received to purchase fishing boats and equipment. The foregoing are merely some of the numerous diverse examples of the green revolution that the Abe Proposal would like to see institutionalised and extended.

Regarding the first pillar of the Abe Green Revolution Plan for Africa, Japan's consultative role with African agricultural research centres is increasing. The International Livestock Centre for Africa (ILCA) in Addis Ababa considers poor animal health and nutrition during dry seasons as the main constraints to increased production. ILCA emphasizes research on mixed farming systems as its main objective, providing a forage-legume link between cropping and livestock enterprises.[243] ILCA, as well as other research centres which conduct studies in arid and semi-arid zones on the control of the tsetse fly — transmitted trypanosomiasis, (e.g. the Japanese financed Noguchi Medical Institute), dry season water management, range management for communal livestock systems, etc., participated in the attempts to bring to Africa the agricultural explosion necessary to redress the land degradation that has long been going on. The International Laboratory for Research on Animal Diseases (ILRAD) in Nairobi also enjoys an occasional infusion of expertise from Japan, similarly as the West African Rice Development Association (WARDA) in Liberia, the Jomo Kenyatta Agricultural College in Nairobi, and the Veterinary Institute in Zambia do. Japan is also a major donor to the world's umbrella organisation for tropical agriculture — the Consultative Group on International Agricultural Research (CGIAR).

The JOCV participants in Africa — (Chapter 7) — contribute in diverse ways to the production of food, such as the agricultural instructors' activities in the Kenya highlands who teach prevention of insect diseases, types of fertilizers, the timing of their application, and the pruning of fruit trees. Japan has marshalled a not inconsiderable effort to help develop irrigation and other water system infrastructures for afforestation programmes, forestry preservation, technical aid in fertilizers, pesticides, insecticides, seedlings, desalinization, etc., especially in those areas devastated by desertification and loss of arable land.

## AFFORESTATION AND DESERTIFICATION AID

Forestry is the science of managing woodlands, along with associated wastelands and waters in order to benefit humankind.

Objectively, it is generally to raise and harvest successive crops of timber, but increasingly it has come to involve related activities of conservation of soil and water, and the preservation of wildlife resources. Thriving forest forms a natural protective covering over the earth's soil and bedrock. The impact of large raindrops and hailstones of summer storms could easily damage bare soil, but the forests' leafy canopy constitutes a natural protection.

In both the developing and developed worlds forestry is being devastated at an alarming rate by a variety of causes. In the developing world tropical forests are devastated at an estimated 11 million hectares annually as a result of slash-and-burn agriculture and excessive logging for firewood and charcoal. While in advanced countries, on the other hand, forests are being devastated by air pollution.

Consequently, the 20th century has seen the steady growth of national forest laws and policies designed to protect woodlands as enduring assets. In the Communist world all forests are owned by the state. The US deems it prudent for the Federal and State governments to hold substantial portions of natural forest, while an ever larger portion is given to commercial exploitation and private individuals to own outright. In much of Asia, Western Europe and the British Commonwealth, similar patterns of ownership prevail. Village ownership is found in most African countries and thus effective forest management in impeded. In Japan the extensive forests are largely state-owned.

Japan's interest in afforestation/reforestation is based mainly on three reasons; firstly, having herself reforested 10 million hectares of land, she is certainly an advanced nation on forestry. Secondly, she depends on foreign timber for most of her domestic demand for wood and wood products. Thirdly, reforestation would help arrest desertification (a concept I shall deal with presently). Consequently, when the 86th Council of the United Nations Food and Agricultural Organization (FAO), held in Rome in November 1984, proclaimed the year 1985 as the International Year of the Forest, Japan, naturally, became an enthusiastic and active participant — worldwide — in the efforts to reverse deforestation, soil erosion

231

and the expansion of desert areas. The 9th World Forestry Congress in Mexico (which was held in commemoration of 1985 International Year of the Forest) strongly supported the Tropical Forestry Action Plan which was concerned with the annual devastation of the 11,3 million hectares of land. Japan played a critical role in both the Action Plan and the Forestry Advisors Meeting (attended by forestry experts from developed countries). Thus the JICA, Forestry Agency (FA) and the Ministry of Agriculture, Forestry and Fisheries (MAFF) join in forestry cooperation activities which include basic surveys — essentially subsidized programmes — on topics such as the promotion of appropriate development of overseas forests, afforestation promotion, and the selection of appropriate species for planting in different areas. >

Together with the Forestry Department of the FAO, the FA and MAFF have undertaken a Special Study on Forest Management Resources in the Developing Regions.[244] It was clearly in recognition of Japan's status as a highly developed nation on forestry issues that the headquarters of the International Tropical Timber Organization (ITTO) — whose objectives include the expansion and stabilisation of tropical timber trade and execution of research and development for tropical forests — is located in Japan (Yokohama). The Japanese corporations also engage in forest development projects in the developing regions, such as pilot afforestation and upgrading infrastructure to improve developing regions when essential funds are not forthcoming from ExIm Bank and the OECF.

Japan's interest in African forestry began in the early seventies. In the words of a JICA official, Katsuhiro Kotari:

> I had long been concerned about the green resources of the world, the acceleration in global deforestation, and the spread of arid desert land, particularly in Africa, when I first began to visit the West African nations around 1973.[245]

Once he realized the extent of European involvement in the afforestation and forestry industries of Africa, when JICA was formed, Kotari saw not only the necessity for Japan's participation in the forestry programme in the developing world; he articulated the belief that a successful forestry cooperation would need to involve a system in which reforestation and its conservation are coordinated and integrated with its economic and environmental functions. Hence, JICA began conducting a new project in semi-arid regions called the Afforestation Trials in semi-Arid Areas in Kadung, Nigeria.

Besides the purely food-oriented activities in some of the agricultural projects in Africa, that JICA is involved in, this organisation dispatches missions of specialists and experts not only to conduct surveys but also to promote overseas forestry cooperation. Although the FA and the MAFF are active in Africa, the scale and scope of their involvement is less when compared with their role in Southeast Asian and South American countries. For example, by the beginning of 1985, 48 experts — technical staff and researchers of the FA — were working on a long-term programme in 10 projects JICA had been implementing in the two regions named above.[246] Yet various initiatives have been undertaken by Japan to extend cooperative efforts to preserve the greenery as well as to rehabilitate the forests of Africa, especially since the desertification degradations are advancing at a rate not to be taken as lightly as African governments have done in the past.

Desertification is such an ugly word; no wonder the United Nations held a conference on it in 1977: the UN Conference on Desertification (UNCOD) in Nairobi, Kenya. Nevertheless, it is a word whose reality, as well as its definition, needs to be grasped, and Timberlake has provided a clear definition: Desertification is

> used to describe the primarily climatic phenomenon by which what is now the Sahara desert dried over many hundreds of years, although strictly speaking, the right word for this is *desertisation*. Secondly, it is also used, more accurately, to describe the conversion of productive land into wasteland by human mismanagement. Croplands are overcultivated; range lands are overgrazed; forests are cut;

irrigation projects turn good cropland into salty, barren fields. Good land becomes bad. Soil bakes into near-rock, or becomes sand or salt-crusted dirt.[247]

In short, desertification is human mismanagement, as well as lack of sufficient governmental concern.

And African governments are largely at fault, not only because desertification is not a high priority with them,[248] but also because they tend to have a lackadaisical attitude towards agriculture as reflected in budgetary allocations: in a 1983 FAO study of 17 African countries, government spending on agriculture per head of a nation's agricultural population between 1978 and 1982 fell by 0,1 % per year (whereas spending rose in Latin America, the Near East, and the Far East). In Gambia and Ghana it fell by 10 % per year.[249] This is particularly grave since nearly 7 million sq. km of SSA is under direct threat of desertification.

Since the increase in desert areas is one of the reasons for the food crisis, technical cooperation assistance was offered by Japan for afforestation, such as the Kilimanjaro Agricultural Development Centre Project, Horticultural Development Project in Kenya, Nursery Training and Technical Development Project for Social Forestry in Kenya, Jomo Kenyatta College of Agriculture and Technology and many other projects. Water projects in the Sahel regions (especially in Mali and Niger) as well as in Ethiopia, Somalia and Sudan have also been undertaken. We have also seen that small-scale rural development in other semi-arid areas of Cameroon, Mali, Senegal, etc. have also received the attention of Japan.

## FISHERIES DEVELOPMENT AID

Fishing, which involves the recovery of food and other valuable resources from bodies of water, is certainly one of the oldest of mankind's occupations. Ancient heaps of discarded mollusc shells, some from prehistoric times, have been found in coastal areas throughout the world, including those of Brazil, Denmark,

Portugal, China and Japan. Even in Africa fishing has been going on since ancient times. In East Africa and the Congo, as one Swedish museum study discovered nearly six decades ago, fish-hooks are indigenous to the area, unlike in some areas of West Africa where fish-hooks are a result of European influence. Although the study claims that no "fish-hooks have archaelogically been discovered in Africa (with the exception of Egypt, the Mediterranean coast and the Canary Islands)",[250] the reality is that in Central Africa, especially in the Congo and Zambia, fish-hooks — some made of iron, wood, or other material from the vegetable kingdom — have been found, and are indigenous to the region.

Fisheries, in any event, are classified in part by type of water: in fresh-water (lakes, rivers, and ponds), and in the ocean (inshore, midwater, and deep-sea). Fishing is like farming — it is a form of primary food production, and the Japanese play a vital role in fishing production for Africa, just as in other food production activities (already mentioned), although to a lesser extent than in the latter. What is unique about Japanese aid in African fisheries is that, just as she has extended assistance on a larger scale (macro-aid), she has also done it on a smaller scale (micro-aid). That is, neglected peasant fisheries, like neglected peasant farming, have begun to enjoy the attention of Japanese fisheries' aid. The seas around Africa are very rich in fish — from the off-shore coast of Morocco to the Guinea Coast to the Southwest coast (off Namibia and the Western Cape of South Africa). Because of the heavy fishing in these areas by European, Russian, American and Asian trawlers, the larger and more valuable fish species such as cuttlefish, octopus, hake and seabream, are subjected to a faster depletion rate than, for example, the less commercially attractive anchovy. Both the Fishery Committee for the Eastern Central Atlantic (CECAF) — a regional fishery body set up by FAO, and the International Commission for the South East Atlantic Fisheries (ICSEAF) govern the Western coast regions.

Japan has one of the largest catches of fish anywhere in the world. Hence the Japanese fishing industry commands a dominant international position. Yet her fisheries aid is not as advanced as her other aid activities. The reason may perhaps lie in that the industry faces some serious problems which are partly the outcome of structural weaknesses within the industry itself, and partly the result of restrictions placed upon it by nations that have claimed a 200-mile economic zone in their coastal waters. In any event Japanese aid to African fisheries is normally in three sectors: instruction, research and construction and equipment. The JOC Volunteers (Chapter 7) participate actively in a variety of small-scale instruction in the techniques of fish catching, cultivation, processing, preserving, etc. In the area of research the JICA experts and those from MAFF play a vital role here. In the construction and provision of fishery equipment a variety of Japanese institutions — OECF, MOFA, MAFF, etc., play an indispensable role in the grant-in-aid projects, such as those referred to below.

Reflecting the close ties that Japan and Tanzania maintain, Japan granted the latter 124 million shillings to rehabilitate her fisheries projects and power distribution lines in 1984. A part of the grant took the form of fishing equipment, including trawler and power equipment. In East Africa it is Kenya, however, which enjoys a much greater role of Japanese volunteers in the development aid projects. Lake Victoria is Africa's largest lake, which is almost as big as Taiwan. It is the world's second largest lake and it borders on Kenya, Uganda and Tanzania. A variety of fish is found here and the Japanese instructors teach fishing methods at the Fisheries Bureau at a city on the shore of the lake. In the Albion Fisheries Research Centre, Japan's role has been decisive, especially the contribution of JICA and JOCV.

Inland fisheries of Africa play key roles in feeding a large population. In fact, Africa's inland fisheries are so extensive that they surpass the non-recreational island hauls of both the Americas and Europe. Lakes such as Kariba, Kainji, Tanganyika, Victoria, Malawi, Kivu, and Chad, etc., in addition to the river swamps, drainages, basins, and other waterways produce vast quantities of fish. Japan is active in the regions named (i.e. Zambia, Nigeria, Tanzania, Uganda-Kenya-Tanzania, Malawi, Rwanda, and Chad, respectively. But the Sahel droughts have also dried the affected fisheries. The rivers of Senegal, Niger, Chad and Mali have greatly reduced even the effectiveness of Japanese fishery aid — whatever its scale.

But Japan is active in all these parts of Africa nonetheless; for example on 16 February 1984 Guinea received a grant-in-aid assistance for a small-scale fishery promotion project. The following month it was Senegal that received a grant-in-aid assistance for the project to construct a vessel for oceanographic and fishery research activities. During earlier years Japan played a key role in the fisheries development of Senegal. For instance, the economic cooperation part of the 1977 Japan-Senegal Trade Agreement (referred to in Chapter 4) included a 350 million yen grant for the Fishery Development Plan, two light round hawl-net fishing training vessels, eight FRP light fishing vessels. Senegalese eat a lot of fish and their best known dish *(chambsen)* consists partly of fish. Along the entire 500 km of coastal waters of Senegal many fishing areas are to be found, especially at Mbour which is the nation's foremost fishing area. On 3 April 1984 Japan advanced Nigeria a grant-in-aid assistance for the skipjack Pole-and-Line Fishing Research and Training Project; a grant-in-aid was also advanced to the Ivory Coast for the regional Maritime Academy a few months later.[251]

In the southern part of the continent Zambia's extensive fishing areas (like neighbouring Malawi's Lake Malawi) provide a rich source of fish. Besides the Zambezi River, the world's fourth longest river (along the Zambia-Zimbabwe border) there are other lakes and rivers for this land-locked nation's fish protein. Pisciculture is successfully pursued in such Lakes as Tanganyika, Bangweulu, Mwera, Kariba and in the basin (330 square km) of the Zambezi River. Japanese instructors at the Chilanga Cultivation Institute play a critical role of instruction in diverse fishing methods. Certain parts of Zambia have long been known to use fish as their staple food. For example, a colonial officer in what was then known as Northern Rhodesia, observed the long-held tradition of fish-eating in this region:

The Unga eat fish every day and usually more than once a day during the greater part of the year. There may be some days in the height of the seasons, January to March, when the Natives of the central swamps cannot catch or obtain fish from friends, but such occasions are rare. It is the normal relish eaten with the staple diet of cassava porridge and when cassava is plentiful a family or group of men at a fishing camp may have eight or more meals or snacks a day with fish at every one.[252]

Japanese technical contribution to the food development of Africa is primarily the product of *human* intervention of course, as I show in Chapter 7. Stress is often put on the technical element but the human one is the decisive factor, particularly when clear policy has been annunciated and implemented. But off the east coast of Africa fisheries are generally on a small scale — i.e. the fishing is done mostly by peasant fishermen, especially since Mozambican, Kenyan, Tanzanian, Ethiopian and Djiboutian fish resources are not as abundant as those of the West Coast.

**DEPENDENCY ON FOREIGN AID**

Africa's food dependency on foreign aid is a function of many problems, chief of which is the European colonial economy in Africa whose emphasis on "industrial development" (and thus agricultural underdevelopment) of the colonies permanently distorted African priorities. Migrant labour from the rural areas played a pivotal role in railroad works, mining, plantations, and consequently depleted these areas of male farm workers. Thus the "pull" effect of industrialisation led to the "pull" impact produced by the capitalisation of African agriculture (i.e. *Afrigulture*, and this is distinct from *Africulture* in Chapter 8). Africa's rich lands were taken over by capital for the production of agricultural products which were virtually all for export. Local food production became focalised on poor lands as agriculture became mechanized and capitalised. Urbanisation and pseudo-self-industrialisation became the *coup d'grace* of African self-sufficiency. African leaders became beggars for aid at every conceivable gathering of multilateral agencies, or even during bilateral conferences.

After over three decades of African independence the weak state of African agriculture can neither primarily be attributable to externally induced factors, nor be of accidental origin. Thus the action or inaction of the African state and its parastatals is largely responsible for the backwardness of African agriculture. Without a clear policy, state action cannot produce clear and positive changes. With clear coherent positive policies, for example, Libya converted the Fezzan desert into one of the greenest agricultural revolutions. African — as well as World Bank — policies are largely responsible for perpetuating a frame-of-mind of dependency, encouraging shortsighted policies.

In 1983 the President of Cape Verde, Aristides Pereira, in his capacity as chairman of the Interstate Committee to Combat Drought in the Sahel, made the plaintive plea on behalf of Mali, Mauritania, Chad and his country that international aid to overcome that year's drought was urgently needed. President Pereira correctly characterised the situation as "bad, worse than last year".[253] But it is yet one more dramatic proof that many African nations have come to depend greatly on foreign aid. In 1986 foreign aid accounted for nearly 30 % of the collective gross product of the seven SSA countries: Burkina Faso, Cape Verde, The Gambia, Mali, Mauritania, Niger and Senegal. In places like Sao Tome and Principe foreign aid accounted for 41 % of the GNP for 1986. Neither were the other island nation states better: Comoros (43 %) and Cape Verde (50 %). Even the OAU Debt Summit in December 1987 concluded its two-day deliberations on calling for more aid for the continent to help pursue economic development. The OAU further urged industrial nations to pay more for Africa's commodity exports and open their markets to its goods. In Chapter 4 we dealt with the concepts of dependency and self-reliance, as well as the diplomatic expectations of the globe-trotting African leaders: the barometer of their successful foreign missions is the commitments of foreign assistance that they bring on their return home. In

1983 when the IDA reduced its budget from $4,1 billion to $2,6 billion many African LDDCs faced economic ruin.

There is a basis to conclude that Western aid is not really geared to make African dependencies independent. Let us recall the frank statement cited elsewhere by US President Nixon: "The main purpose of American aid is not to help other nations, but ourselves." In this context consider France which had long professed *Tiers Mondiste* sympathies. She has maintained favourable international trade balances by long depending on her trade with the African region. For example the profits and salaries that she repatriated from the Ivory Coast in 1980 were greater than the total official French ODA for that year. In the case of Japan much of her aid between 1980 and 1985 came from her huge home surplus of rice. When the surplus was exhausted Japan purchased rice from both the US and Thailand to ship to African states as part of her food aid package. The latter case achieved two objectives: she mollified, somewhat, the irascible US whose temper tantrums resulting from perceived injury to her "national security" interests sometimes borders on the juvenile. Secondly, and simultaneously, she supplied food to the famished Africans. Thus Japanese aid to Africa remains to this day qualitatively different. Aid agencies have mostly played their own dubious games in places such as Burkina Faso, for example.

Burkina Faso, one of France's former colonial possessions, had the dubious distinction of being deluged with 340 external aid missions which descended on the capital of Ouagadougou in 1981! Today Burkina Faso remains a full-fledged member of the Club of the LDDCs — where poverty, aid, rhetoric and homicidal power successions are the norm. This of course is not to say that development aid has been conceived without good intentions. But there is little doubt that it has failed to live up to its original billing: that the gulf between the rich and the poor would be narrowed. Instead, as we have already seen, Africa remains in the doldrums of poverty — where the poor grow poorer, the hungry hungrier, and grow larger in number still, while the environment is further degraded, the African humanity denigrated, as *Afrigulture* continues to deteriorate, Western good intentions have not been sufficient to correct the deterioration of African agriculture and environment.

Neither does the large aid dispenser — the World Bank — offer much hope. In fact since the so-called Reagan Revolution (1981-1988), the World Bank activities in Africa have been designed to help the private sector home-in on profitable contracts and business opportunities. African economies have become the hostages of the World Bank and its sister organisation, the IMF. True, the World Bank in 1981 suggested that aid to SSA should be doubled by 1990, that is from $4,9 billion to $9,1 billion. True also that the Bank argues that increments in aid disbursements must be accompanied by reforms, especially in agriculture. In its *An Agenda For Action* the Bank argued that

> trade and exchange-rate policy is at the heart of the failure to provide adequate incentives for agricultural production and for exports in much of Africa ... A trade based on exchange-rate system that relies heavily on import restrictions biases the incentive system against agriculture in several ways. First, it forces farmers to purchase high-cost local implements. For example, in Upper Volta (now Burkina Faso) there is a 66 per cent tariff on animal-drawn plows and a 58 per cent tariff on engines used for irrigation pumps.[254]

The World Bank complaint against Burkina Faso's imposition of trade tariffs would have made more sense had the bank argued in the same breath about the EEC tariff on, for example, *manufactured African tobacco which faces an EEC tariff of 55 per cent, while raw African tobacco enters the EEC duty free*. Africa seems valuable only as a raw materials' supplier. It is for this reason that the World Bank stresses African agricultural production for export. On the other hand, the *Lagos Plan of Action* proposes industrial development for self-reliance. The *Lagos Plan* hopes to advance the collective efforts of Africa to meet her demands, rather than global ones. While this *Plan* stresses a collective African self-determination, the World Bank emphasizes African output to meet the needs of major Western economies.

Considering the failure of conventional foreign aid in the "development" of Africa, it was not surprising that a former Minister of Foreign Affairs as well as former head of OECF, and currently the President of the International University of Japan, wondered aloud whether it was not time for a Japanese Marshall Plan for Africa.[255] Indeed it was the Marshall Plan that rescued the collapse of European economies after the devastation of World War II. Okita noted that very soft loans to reconstruct the infrastructure — roads, railways, harbours, telecommunications, hydropower stations, irrigation, agriculture — could be used in conjunction with human resources development, especially the training of engineers, technicians, scientists, etc., in the regeneration of Africa. However, while Japanese production technology and technological assistance could be transferred to Africa, Okita noted that the African states must themselves abandon the blame-it-on-the-other syndrome: "In the past these countries have blamed their difficulties on the richer countries". But "they are now coming to realize that they must do something themselves". Africa must be inward-looking first before she can go out and meet the rest of the world: China did it, Japan did it. So can Africa do it, if wise and creative leadership would assume ascendancy. The fact that the Japanese Government may not have a comprehensive strategy to initiate a massive food production programme in Africa is not a critical point, even with public backing. (In the past the Japanese Government had depended largely on private business to implement, supervise, and administer the aid). The important thing is that Africa must eschew the national go-it-alone strategy of incompetence for a regional, more effective, collective strategy. Regional cooperativeness should then lead to continental collectivity. As I have noted with regard to the Fezzan Libyan Desert, the green revolution — in both its Qaddafian connotations and conventional sense — has transformed the desert into a greenery, agriculturally and otherwise. This is the result, clearly, of a corrective, constructive, creative policy, bolstered, some might add, by the immense petrodollar wealth without which the Fezzan would have remained a desert.

African leaders, nevertheless, singly or collectively, proclaim a principle of lip-service self-reliance; no sooner do they pronounce the virtues of self-reliance than they switch caps and don the "aid-me" one, and ask the West instead to pay for their "self-reliance". ECOWAS, SADCC (now called SADC), and even the OAU periodically engage in this practice of dependent self-reliance. As we have already seen, even the President of the ADB goes to Tokyo with the great expectations that more aid will devolve upon Africa. This dependence psychology would tend to inculcate insidiously an expectant attitude of normalcy in government elite corruption, even in the hallowed halls of such institutions as SADCC, OAU, ADB, ECOWAS, etc. This in any event, is due to the fact that African leaders' grasp of the fundamentals of development still eludes most of them. An African graduate student in Japanese history (at Kyoto University) was prompted to caustically write:

> Discussions about development, nation-building and so on, especially among (African) politicians, have been clouded in meaningless platitudes so much as to make concerned serious-minded citizens of poor countries despair.[256]

Needless to say, the best (and thus real) form of development aid is the one that advances visible, positive, and effective change, and retards dependency. Neither does the World Bank nor the IMF aid policy advance genuine independence.[257] In the circumstances, the infusion of Japanese human voluntarism in the African complex becomes not only a new qualitative improvement on the aid factor, it becomes the only meaningful one. Not that the US Peace Corps failed to do some good; it simply did not go far enough. The human example factor provided by the dedication of the Japanese volunteers in Africa has provided a psychic boost and cultural spur to the rural people and youth of Africa, and imparted in them the meaning of total commitment even with a minimum of material supports, and the value of a productive work-ethic, however remote the prospects of material gratification may seem.

<To recapitulate, two additional factors encourage African food dependence: as stated earlier, before independence, the colonial administrations discouraged indigenous food production. Africans were instead encouraged to cultivate cash-crops for export, and were simultaneously urged to consume imported foodstuffs. After independence, the cocoa, coffee, peanut, etc., plantations suffered because world prices dropped, and production in turn fell. Secondly, the crisis in African food production is also due to sheer human lethargy and inertia, poverty notwithstanding. A less developed work-ethic would clearly not lead to creative labour. African labour initiative is further vitiated by the dependency complex, wittingly or unwittingly encouraged by government bureaucracies and foreign aid bureaus and agencies who, naturally, have a vested interest in perpetuating this dependency. The vicious cycle becomes assured particularly when poor agricultural policies continue to be implemented. Regarding Africulture, Japan believes that priority should be given to development of agricultural infrastructure such as irrigation and drainage, experimental development of agro-industry; and organisation of farmers and improvement in marketing of agricultural products. But African food problems would likely be relieved by increasing food production initiated through African own efforts in the rural areas and agricultural development, not for any esoteric reasons but simply because self-reliance is, eventually, the final guarantor of continuity in production for one's survival.

第四部
人的交流問題

# PART IV

## THE HUMAN EXCHANGE ISSUE

## CHAPTER 7

# JAPANESE VOLUNTEERS IN AFRICA

---

*Technological assistance, while important, must also be accompanied by strong human bonds, by "heart-to-heart" communication between Japan and Africa.*

Professor Junzo Kawada[258]

*But fortunately, I read a JOCV pamphlet in which I found a request from the government of Malawi for an architect to teach at a secondary school ... and so I applied.*

Kazuo Yasumatsu, Look Japan[259]

*It may seem strange, but just as the people of Senegal are familiar with such things as Toyota cars and Sony radios and yet know very little about the Japanese, so do the Japanese know of elephants and lions but little of the Senegalese people ... I did a little to change this ...*

Hisashi Maeda
JOCV Volunteer in Senegal[260]

*The young men and women who go to Africa with the JOCV are sent on their own to farming and fishing communities, where they work and live with local people.*

Ichiro Murakawa
LDP Policy Research Council[261]

Mention has already been made that the JOCV was established in 1965 as an agency under the direction of MOFA, and integrated into JICA when the latter was established in 1974. Mention should then be made of the motto of the first 26 members of JOCV, "advancing to the frontier," eating the same food, speaking the same language, and living among the people.[262] Of the diverse governmental aid programmes world-wide there is perhaps no other institutional structure whose human activism can boast a successful and qualitative immersion into Africa's remotest corners as the JOCV. The US Peace Corps blazed the trail and initiated the value and potency of idealism; it was left to the Japanese volunteers to deepen the meaning of development aid to qualitative new heights.

JOCV's activism is particularly remarkable given the familiar Japanese refrain: "Africa has been relatively unfamiliar to the Japanese people because of its geographical and historical remoteness",[263] a refrain still exercising the minds of Japanese officials in 1992 (cf. Ambassador Masatoshi Ohta 1992:2). That being so, it is indeed exceptional that in a matter of two decades Japanese youth had changed the perception and attitudes or rural (and urban) Africans, not only regarding Japanese people and culture, but also concerning their own attitude toward and value-system regarding the work-ethic. It is the scope and objective of this chapter to present the *human* dimension of the Afro-Japanese relations as reflected in JOC Volunteerism, because quantity of goods and material services alone can never be the complete yardstick of evaluating development aid.

After Japan had been defeated in World War II her international image plummeted greatly; as a consequence the Japanese people, traditionally less egregious, tended to become even more clannish, shrinking away from non-essential contact with the rest of the world as if governed by a uniform, collective guilt complex. The idealism of the US President, John F. Kennedy led him to create the US Peace Corps in 1961. The Japanese youth who were toddlers in 1945 (at the end of World War II), were now offered an ideal opportunity to play an international role without the guilt complex of their elders. The Peace Corps youth were thus inspirational to the formation of the JOCV four years later. Thus began Japan, a technological and scientific powerhouse, an internationalisation that elevated her beyond the simple pedestal of a wheeler-dealer in money, commodities and goods; to one which is now a fulcrum of international interchange of people, cultures and information.

## JOCV AFRICAN ACTIVITIES

Between 1966 and the beginning of 1979 over 920 JOC Volunteers were sent to SSA. While the JICA experts who were sent to Africa (SSA and North Africa) endeavoured to impart technological learning to African youth in a variety of fields ranging from rice cultivation, irrigation, fishing, bridge construction, etc., the JOC Volunteers on the other hand, most of whom prefer rural parts of African states, are engaged in diverse experiences such as the dissemination of knowledge regarding farming or fishing techniques; mathematics or physics, Japanese language and other activities. Others are engaged in architectural, civil engineering or telecommunications projects.

Every year the range of activities increases to include rice cultivation, telecommunications, automobile maintenance, nursing, surveying, education, sports, etc.

### TABLE 7.1
### JOCV VOLUNTEERS IN SSA (As of June 1979)

| Country | Number | Field |
|---------|--------|-------|
| Ghana | 29 | Science and Mathematics Teachers |
| Kenya | 70 | Agriculture |
| Tanzania | 29 | Automobile Maintenance |
| Zambia | 46 | Radio Communication |
| Malawi | 89 | Agriculture, Construction, Science, and Mathematical education |
| Liberia | 3 | Vocational Training |

Source:    Japan and Africa (1979), p. 13.

Activities now cover no fewer than 120 fields. Thus JOCVism is a form of bilateralism — indeed it is more than that, a multilateralism given the extent of Japan's involvement in Africa — which is designed to help develop a viable society and an ecologically stable economy.

By the end of 1987 there were 12 JICA/JOCV field offices in Africa: 8 JICA and 4 JOCV officers distributed as follows:

| JICA offices | JOCV offices |
|---|---|
| Ethiopia | Rwanda |
| Kenya | Liberia |
| Tanzania | Niger |
| Malawi | Senegal |
| Zambia | |
| Ghana | |
| Tunisia | |
| Morocco | |

These numerous JOCV activities can be classified into four main categories:[264]

(i) Village work: The JOC Volunteer becomes a member of a village community (and some are even inducted into the chieftaincy, as I will show presently), and promotes its development through such activities as demonstrations and the dissemination of information about agricultural technologies, etc.

(ii) Educational work: The JOC Volunteer provides guidance and practical training in fields such as vocational training, science, mathematics, and Japanese language, etc.

(iii) Job site work: The JOC Volunteer provides on-the-job training for local personnel in civil engineering, housing construction, and communications projects, etc.

(iv) Head office, experiments and research, etc.

Although they are volunteers the JOCVs have very strong technical qualifications. They are more than mere volunteers: they are junior experts in their respective fields. Prior to their departure to Africa they first undergo two rigorous selection processes before further undertaking a three months' JOCV training programme. In the host country the JOC Volunteer undergoes yet another month of training before she begins a 730 days' (2 years) tenure. Many even ask for extension after their 2-year of tour of duty.

## TABLE 7.2
## JOC VOLUNTEER YEAR OF ENTRY/EXIT 1965-1987

| Country | Year entered | Year departed | Year re-entered |
|---------|--------------|---------------|-----------------|
| Kenya | 1966 | | |
| Tanzania | 1967 | | |
| Morocco | 1967 | | |
| Zambia | 1970 | | |
| Malawi | 1971 | | |
| Ethiopia | 1972 | 1977 | 1977 |
| Tunisia | 1975 | | |
| Ghana | 1976 | | |
| Liberia | 1979 | | |
| Senegal | 1980 | | |
| Niger | 1983 | | |
| Rwanda | 1987 | | |

Source:    Japan overseas cooperation volunteers.

### JOCV IN EAST AFRICA

The largest number of JOC Volunteers are found in Kenya. As of 1 June 1987 the total number serving in Kenya was 123 — of whom 21 were female — 18 served in agriculture, forestry, and fishery; 20 in maintenance and operations; 27 in civil engineering and architecture; 54 in education and information services; one in the field of sport and three other fields. Kenya welcomed the first three JOC Volunteers to serve in Africa in March 1966.

The Jomo Kenyatta College of Agriculture and Technology, built in 1980 with the assistance of a Japanese official untied loan, was in its first year staffed by 10 JICA Volunteer experts, and four were from the JOCV. These 14 were responsible for instruction in the 11 agricultural and engineering courses offered there; but not all JOC Volunteers are attached to urban prestigious institutes. Many go to the rural areas generally located far from urban centres, for example, a mathematics teacher, Midori Nakayama, who was located 300 km from Nairobi. At the Kisumu Fisheries Bureau on the shore of Lake Victoria, fisheries instructors teach fishing methods, culture, cultivation, and preservation. In the western highlands, agricultural instructors such as Tamotsu Seiji and Yoshiyasu Ito, teach prevention of insect disease, types of fertilizers, fruit pruning.[265] The Kenya highlands are particularly suitable for the cultivation of cabbage, rice, tea, and potatoes, and the many JOCV participants are active in turning the highlands into the greenlands.

One year after JOC Volunteers had landed in Kenya, the Tanzanian Government made strong representations to the Japanese Government. As a result 30 of the JOC Volunteers were dispatched to Tanzania in 1967. Six were agricultural volunteers and 24 were home economics volunteers (all female) whose objective was to teach Tanzanian women how to make Western clothing.

> The agricultural volunteers worked from morning till night, even on Sundays, to cultivate vegetables and create landscape gardening ... Top (Tanzanian) government officials praised the Japanese volunteers saying that they had 'instilled in the farmers of Tanzania the real spirit of work'.[266]

Agricultural machinery engineers (e.g. Akira Wada) in farming areas have joined others such as occupational therapists (e.g. Mariko Hara), not only to learn Swahili themselves, but also to impart their skills and knowledge to a village populace, the overwhelming majority of whom have never seen a Japanese. At the Niegeje Agricultural Institute volunteers (e.g. Sakae Inoue) offer scientific lectures on the geology of farms, and ecology of the environment.

In Ethiopia when they first arrived in 1972 the 28 JOC Volunteers were primarily involved in assisting in smallpox eradication projects begun by the World Health Organization (WHO). Smallpox eradication called for the placing of inspectors in the hinterland of the country, and thus a way was paved for volunteers to go to Ethiopia. When JOCV suddenly found themselves without responsibilities after the elimination of small-pox, the paradox that is Africa could not, however, leave them for long without responsibility; fields of opportunity opened as fast as volunteer experts could arrive. Agricultural public works and construction, vegetable growing, ceramics and pottery manufactur-ing, programming, statistics, photography, and many other fields became the new areas of JOCV activism in Ethiopia. But agriculture — food growth, irrigation and water wells, drought combat and forest management became increasingly the focus of the new regime once the revolutionary turmoil brought about after the overthrow of Emperor Selassie had ended. Perhaps because of the severity of the elements, Ethiopia since then has commanded a lot of attention, because the famine of the 1980s dramatised the nature of the problems. It is the only country where, because of violent internal political problems, JOCV was compelled to temporarily suspend its activities. Extremely low rainfall causes constant water shortages in some areas, while in others heavy rainfalls precipate soil erosion and water shortages. Hence the construction of new waterways (such as those engineered by the JOC Volunteer, Sadaaki Awaji) was finally completed 15 months later. Frequently, automobile mechanics devise ingenuous methods of instruction. For instance Masashi Kurihara did not only construct a cut-away engine model himself, he used the local language (Amharic) in his instruction lessons to impart more than simple knowledge about maintenance mechanics; he demonstrated the value of individual initiative and national discipline — a value which he hoped would be replicated in the African areas hosting the JOC Volunteers.

## JOCV IN NORTH AFRICA

In Morocco and Tunisia, the only North African countries where the JOC Volunteers currently operate in, an intimate relationship has developed between the Japanese participants and the people of these areas. Algeria had earlier hosted Japanese agricultural experts, Morocco received the first JOCV participants in September 1967, and over 250 JOCV members have been dispatched by 1987. Their efforts were concentrated in two major areas — the maintenance operation sector (which includes vocational training with a focus on civil engineering and construction), and the sports sector. In 1987 there were thirty-seven in the civil engineering and architecture sectors; fourteen in the maintenance and operations; three in education and information service; two in agriculture, forestry and fishery; four in sports; and one in the unspecified category.

Despite being confronted with the typical procrastination habit of *Bukra* in some Arab cultures — in Spanish, the *"Manyana* complex,"* i.e. "tomorrow is still another day," — Japanese volunteers (such as Kan Yamato who taught horticultural techniques at the Regional Greenery Bureau in Rabat) continue hoping that their urban greenification plans will one day take off from the drawing board to the field. But the *bukra* habit was not the only "spanner in the wheel" the JOC Volunteers encountered in Tunisia. There were the cultural differences, not only regarding attitude towards work, but also expectations of the role of the JOCVs. Although in Japan traditional culture and modernity have blended together, unlike in some Arab lands, the work-ethic and reverence for work is highly developed in the Nippon culture.

In Tunisia the JOCV program began in 1975. It was targeted at a wide range of sectors which included education and culture, health and hygiene, maintenance mechanics, sports, etc. The first Japanese nurse volunteers arrived in Tunisia imbued with the spirit of imparting to their Tunisian counterparts' Japanese nursing technology and experience. But the Tunisians had a different view of things; they expected the volunteer nurses to be actual hospital workers doing the day-to-day nursing chores. Tunisian thinking, then, was that JOC Volunteers were guest workers — rather than experts there to impart particular skills and experience. Subsequent nurse volunteers tended to avoid hospitals in large cities, and opted for the rural villages or smaller cities whose hospitals and clinics would have benefited more from the mission and objective of JOC Volunteer nurses: teach local nurses efficient and modern nursing techniques. As of June 1987 there were 17 JOC Volunteers; some instructors (such as Kenji Miyaji) taught volleyball to both the local youth and the women's national team. Miyaji's compulsory training camps, and the habit of bivouacking his players as part of his coaching methods, played no small part in the Tunisian women's national team's winning of the 1985 Arab Volleyball championship. Other sports instructors (such as Hiroshi Enomoto at the Sfax school on the Gulf of Gabes) taught the popular judo course.

## JOCV IN WEST AFRICA

Ghana was the first West African nation to host a total of nine JOC Volunteers in August 1977. In the 1970s Ghana was host to about 300 US Peace Corps volunteers, and the Japanese numbered a mere 15, and whose maximum number totalled no more than 30 by 1979. By the middle of 1987, however, there were 77 Peace Corps volunteers and 78 JOC Volunteers. This was in keeping with the systematic manner with which the Japanese had quietly surpassed the Western aid donors in Ghana, as I have already indicated elsewhere in this book. In both Anglophone and Francophone Africa, Japanese volunteers have systematically made inroads, and built roads, in a subtle and successful manner, and thus increased Japanese influence in Africa, if not with the governments, certainly with the African general populace.

Ghanaian representatives were first dispatched to Tokyo to negotiate the dispatch of volunteers, the first nine of whom were involved in the field of science and mathematics education. They were placed under the Ghanaian Ministry of Education. Since then Japanese agricultural volunteers, in the fields of rice cultivation and vegetable gardening, have expanded the area of activities to include irrigation projects under the host country's Ministry of Agriculture.

Others were placed in diverse institutions such as the Tema Development Corporation, National Construction Corporation, and the National Vocational Training Institute.

Perhaps the total dedication with which the Japanese volunteers undertake their responsibilities may be illustrated by one graduate of the agricultural department of Hokkaido University (Naoki Okada), who was stationed at a village hundred kilometres from the Ghana capital. He was more than a mere instructor in village development; he joined the villagers in a variety of manual labour chores. He carried water from a nearby river and carted baskets of coal to the local town market to sell. He so blended in the village community that he was incorporated into the advisory council to the village headman. But it is another volunteer, Kiyoshi Takei, who became the first Japanese to become a chieftain of a small village in Ghana.[267] But the exchange of learning was sometimes mutual, since some of the volunteers (although teaching such subjects as physics and mathematics) became proficient in local languages. Hisatoshi Ohkubo was one example of a JOCV participant who became fluent in Fanti, one of the Ghanaian languages. It is the success of such cultural diffusion that has catapulted the Japanese to such an influential and successful role in Ghana. This JOCV success has been extended to other areas.

In Senegal the JOC Volunteers arrived in October 1980. Their objective was to help Senegal break away from the traditional industrial structure characterised by dependence on peanut production, (peanuts are the nation's largest export) and to work towards the achievement of food self-sufficiency and small-scale industrial development in regional cities.[268] As we have already seen, Senegal's dependency on foreign aid is very high, hence the introduction of agricultural technical guidance. With $400 million a year in foreign aid, Senegal has now become a favourite of international aid donors, more than any other country in the Sahel. JOC Volunteers have contributed significantly enough for Senegal to enjoy a most favoured status among the Sahelian countries, as far as Western aid donors are concerned.

JOC Volunteers to Senegal actually came fortuitously, because Mauritania requested Japan for the dispatch of volunteers to work for the country's fishery expansion project. The Japanese embassy in Senegal, which also doubled as the embassy for Mauritania, had approached the Senegalese Government on the problem of dispatching Japanese volunteers to Senegal. Under the Senegalese Government policy of diversification in agricultural development there had been moves to promote the cultivation of cotton, tomatoes, cabbages, and onions. At a UN refugee farm project, a Japanese volunteer instructor in market gardening (Yoshio Hori) carried out the daily physical chores as well as those of instructing the local farmers on the most effective means of vegetable farming. On the other hand in the same village as Yoshio, Kazunori Yoshida, an instructor in fisheries processing, taught the fish farmers not only the techniques of producing fish cakes and dumplings, but also, because of poor refrigeration technology in Mbour, fish preservation by smoking.

There are JOC Volunteers in other West African nations such as Liberia and Niger. The 1977 Liberian economic cooperation team that visited Japan also began talks about the dispatch of JOCVs to Liberia. The following year the Liberian Ministry of Foreign Affairs requested the dispatch of JOCVs to teach at the soon-to-be established vocational training centre. In Liberia (a country nearly one third the size of Japan, but with only 2 million people) the vegetable cultivation that the volunteers became engaged in may ultimately provide more than mere self-sufficiency: Liberia could become an exporter of food! Although Liberia has the largest deposits of iron ore in Africa, there is a great need for the nation to improve the one essential life activity that may bring self-sufficiency: food cultivation. Civil war has however disrupted much of the foreign aid activities in the 1990s. But the JOC Volunteers are also engaged in other activities such as judo instruction, maintenance and telephone exchanges repair, instructions in physics and mathematics, teaching, etc.

In Niger, similarly, a diversity of volunteer activities also goes on. But because Niger — more than five times the size of Japan — is

257

taken up largely by the Sahara yellow sand, desertification and drought problems confront the Japanese volunteers and severely reduce their efficiency in demonstrating the ideal methods and techniques of agro-forestry. At the Niamey Experimental Farm, however, some of the problems confronting the JOCVs were overcome, not without herculean efforts, with a minimum of means. Some instructors were engaged in noxious insect damage (e.g. Yoshifumi Kozu) while others were involved in soil fertilisation (e.g. Motohiko Kondoh) in a combined effort of stemming the expansion of arid areas, increasing food cultivation, and digging water wells. Rice crop estimation and automobile repair and maintenance instruction, nonetheless, generally go hand-in-hand with these activities, given the inhospitability of the region and the scarcity of technical material and climatological bounty.

## ZAMBIA AND MALAWI

The first volunteers to Zambia arrived in March 1970, and they were six in number: six men in the areas of wireless communications and judo! As European technicians continued their emigration from Zambia on account of Africanisation, the skilled responsibilities of maintenance and operation of communication facilities increasingly fell upon Japanese volunteers, without whom the operation of these facilities would have collapsed. This accounts for the large number of wireless communications volunteer specialists to arrive in Zambia between 1970 and June 1979. Naturally, the Japanese became uneasy and thus questioned the real motivations behind their invitation to Zambia.[269] They ill-considered the role of being mere replacements for white technicians. Perhaps as a result the number dispatched declined sharply in 1978 (5) from the previous year's number of 22.

In any event the situation has changed since then. As of 31 October 1987 there were 90 JOC Volunteers serving in Zambia, 25 of whom were female. Agriculture, forestry and fishery constituted the largest number (23). In the already mentioned Chilanga Cultivation Institute, JOCVs (such as Nakatoshi Kyoizumi) had been instructors to Zambians in fresh water pisciculture, artificial breeding, and insemination techniques, as well as in other areas. Although Zambia is a land-locked nation there are a number of lakes — such as the previously mentioned Kariba, Tanganyika, Mweru, Bangweulu — and the Zambezi River basin which provide fish protein. The JOC Volunteers play a critical role in fisheries, just as they do in forestry, agriculture and communications. Education and information services command nearly as large a contingent of JOCVs as the food, fisheries and forestry sectors. By June 1987 this sector had 21 JOCVs. At the Masaite Farm, under the auspices of the Ministry of Agricultural Agency and Fisheries Resource Development, an instructor (such as Tadao Miyagawa) had taught the techniques and methods of raising broiler chicken. Others worked as clinical veterinarians in institutions such as the Livestock Tsetse Elimination Bureau in the capital city. Thus the activities varied from anti-rabies vaccinations to wireless communications. Automobile maintenance instructions took place even at such an institution as the Fisheries Bureau of the Land and Natural Resources Ministery.

Malawi had the highest number of female JOCVs: 30 %. Of the 108 JOC Volunteers serving in Malawi as of 1 June 1987 36 were female, followed by Zambia with 25 of 90 JOCVs. Actually, Malawi is currently second only to Kenya in the number of JOCVs serving all over the world. Malawi is one of the most successful examples of Japanese volunteer activities in Africa. Because of the need for nurses, midwives, dieticians, pharmaceutists, home-economists, physical therapists, and teachers, this makes for this utilisation of a large number of female JOCVs in Malawi. The country has a high infantile mortality rate owing to the prevalence of malaria, kwashiokor, dysentery, tetanus, and malnutrition.

Since the first 22 JOCVs arrived in 1971 the fields of volunteer activities have increased greatly. The rate of assimilation of JOCVs by Malawi was so high that between 1971 and 1981 when Yasumatsu arrived almost 500 JOCVs had each done their two-year stints. Volunteers in the health sector in the early 1970s were under the finance ministry's Overseas Assistance Department. They also were:

assigned to the fields of agricultural public works, repairing of radio sets and maintenance (of) the operation of construction machinery. Still others are assigned to work at surveying, refrigerating plants and automobile repair and maintenance plants ...[270]

One of the senior JOCV officials, who was my source of information on the JOCV, Takashi Nagakura, had spent three and a half years as a JOC Volunteer in Malawi. His reminiscences about Malawi remain nostalgic to this day. He also spent some time in Tanzania. His colleague, Ichiro Toyoshima, also a senior JOCV executive, had also spent a number of years (four) in Africa. The two officials informed the author that JOC Volunteer interest in Africa remained high, despite the harsh regime of the African environment.

## RATIONALE FOR JOCV SUCCESS

Sufficient details have been proffered to suggest that Japanese volunteerism in Africa is not only grounded on firm philosophical basis or political convictions, but that it is also designed to be more than a mere successful bureaucratic undertaking to balance the North-South problems. JOCVism (more than Peace Corpism) in Africa is an embodiment of cultural education, political give-and-take, economic efficiency, technical skills and technology transfer, and, above all, humanity. The Japanese live in a homogenous society and their discovery of the value of cultural and human exchanges has become central to their understanding of mutual international relations.

The severe human conditions that JOCV participants were confronted with[271], constituted a test not of the technical skills of the participants, but rather of their spirit of endurance and humility. In many rural areas where these volunteers chose to go, there is neither electricity, refrigeration, transportation, nor telephones. Tropical diseases and insects increase the scope and magnitude of adversity. The elements compound the severity by disproportionately abusing the nearly limitless capacity for patience and endurance of the participants: hot humid days, cold wet nights;

torrential rains and storms and floods when added to the material poverty of these rural areas make even more dramatic the successes of these JOCVs.

The JOCV participants have been successful precisely because they understood only too well the nature of their responsibility: theirs was not merely to pass technical skills to the "natives", it was an inward journey in search of the roots of one's universal spirit of humanity. It was, that is, a quest after humanity. But the JOCVs are not those pathetic Weberian dispirited denizens of the "iron cage" of rationality who are oppressed by the metaphysical weight of the meaninglessness of a bureaucratic social condition. These were not the "specialists without spirit" that Max Weber warned of with the coming "mechanical petrification". They were the technocultural revolutionaries out to transform not only a backward social condition and thus tame a harsh environment, but also to transform themselves. Yet their enthusiastic dedication to their tasks was full of frustration. That the overwhelming majority of them completed the 730 days' sojourn in their various posts is further testimony of the depth of commitment as well as the successful training methods of JOCV. These JOCVs were not prompted by a quixotic spirit of adventure to seek the exotic, nor did they go to Africa to do research. Rather, they went to extend the benefits of research findings to farmers, children, the sick, the poor, the rural communities at large, as well as to help expand the urban infrastructure.

Beyond extending the benefits of research, they also were motivated by a desire to extend the hand of humanity. The Japanese youth have thus rendered obsolete a common expression of Japanese government officials and academic scholars and journalists: the "Far Continent" theory and the notion of the "remoteness" of African peoples *vis-a-vis* the Japanese, which theory and notion have been employed to rationalise the "absence" of historical and cultural ties between Japanese and Africans. It is primarily on the human exchange factor, rather than on the material and financial contribution issue to Africa, that the success of the JOCV is unique. Human exchange is the most complex form of

261

exchanges. On the other hand, it is the most permanent and effective form of Afro-Japanese international relations. As of 31 October 1987 the largest number of JOC Volunteers were in Africa (614 in SSA), whereas Asia had 515. Japanism and Africulture found in JOCVism the apotheosis of human exchange. The Malawi experience of the architect, Kazuo Yasumatsu, is illustrative:

> For the first year I went to the office and back by bicycle. But partly because the slope was so steep and it was hard going during the rainy seasons, I started commuting by bus just like ordinary Malawi residents ... I could absorb the vitality of Malawians' daily life ... I was interested in Malawi's traditional clay-wall houses, which couldn't be found in the city, that I wanted to try living in one for a while. Since every man in Malawi learns to build a house by himself, I decided to follow suit, with the guidance and help of my Malawian friends ... I was able to see and learn about the construction process.

(See note 259.) Although in Japan Yasumatsu lived in a society characterised by the symbiosis of traditional culture and modernisation, in Africa he was confronted by the daunting enormity of a foreign traditional culture that seemed frozen in time and space. His successful adjustment to this society thus was testimony to part of the success of the JOCV. But JOCV successes are only a microcosm of the larger, spectacular, but quieter successes of Japan *vis-a-vis* the rest of world. In Africa the JOCV is further laying the foundation for future Japanese successes, for it demonstrates the real *and* symbolic meaning of human bonds and human exchange. The Japanese having long mastered the material and financial forms of international interchanges to the omission of the human, have now embarked, at least in Africa, upon this most complex of human enterprises. Evidence, nonetheless, suggests that Japanese culture, of all cultures that are foreign to Africa, is the ideal, the one most likely to succeed: not European, not American, not even Chinese or Russian.

## CHAPTER 8

# AFRICANS AND AFRICULTURE IN JAPAN

---

*As an African who studied in the UK and US, furthering my studies here (in Japan) was only a logical outcome of my prior exposure. It was impossible not to have been attracted by the genius of the stylish architectural technology and cultural universality of Japan.*

Prisca Molotsi[272]
African Graduate Student of Architecture (Nagoya)

*In Africa, reason seems to dictate that we unite on a continental level. This is the only way ... In Japan, the concept of a nation is too close to the outdated European ideal; one language, one national dress, one tradition ... We couldn't adopt such a method in Africa even if we wanted ...*

Gordon Cyrus Mwangi[273]
African Graduate Student of Japanese Politics (Kyoto)

*Japan and Africa have much in common in the art of making masks ... Japanese and African masks are considered to be in a class by themselves and are highly valued objects of museums and collectors all over the world.*

Ryo Yanagi[274]
Japanese Scholar and Writer (Tokyo)

263

*"Africulture"* is a word I have coined to reflect and mean the cultural attributes of African peoples. Included in this concept are such aspects of African civilisations as sculptures, handicrafts, folk-dance, music, masks, fashion, film, education, customs, and so forth. *Africulture,* in short, means the culture of Africa. It is distinct from the earlier term *Afrigulture* (Chapter 6). In the context of this Chapter, *Africulture* signifies the cultural dynamics of Africans (students, visiting performers, etc.) in Japan as well as the museum exhibitions and theatre performances relating to African life and civilisation. That is, African national folk dance troupes, film festivals, masks, music, and skits of African students or artists or sportsmen in Japan reflect what is here termed Africulture. Some Japanese artists and artisans have since taken to *Africultural* artifacts and activities especially in the Tokyo area.

As a historical cultural antecedent Africa has neither been valued, recognised, nor understood. Much of this has to do with a set of factors:

The inherent factor of skin tone (the colour black in Euro-American historiography connotes much that is low in the scales of human appreciation).[275]

Slavery and colonial legacy (no more savage a slavery has there been than that visited upon the Africans by the transatlantic traders).

Technological backwardness, all loom large in this scale of human depreciation and cultural denigration. As already demonstrated in this study, Japan has had a sparse but unique cultural intercourse with Africa, but in the last decade Japan had confounded the world with the speed with which she has moved from the Edo Period (1603-1867) view of Africans,[276] through Meiji Japan's view of Africans,[277] to the more culturally advanced view now held.

The recent *re-arrival* of Africans in Japan since the 16th century (Chapter 1) made it possible for Africans to greatly augment their knowledge of Japanese culture as well as understanding the people of Japan. Naturally, this Afro-Japanese human encounter improved the image of Africans in Japanese eyes from that of the earlier Meiji-Taisho eras. It facilitated the international ties between the governments of Africa and Japan and encouraged more daring explorations of human interactions. Japanese perceptions of Africans qualitatively changed from those which were imparted by the European colonial experience in Africa. It is no longer unusual today to find Africans married to and residing with Japanese citizens. Nor is it an unusual sight to see many Japanese families residing in Africa. A few Africans with Japanese spouses have even become citizens of Japan. The situation is thus different from the early 1960s when Japanese grants to Africa were confined to the costs of training Africans in Japan and dispatching Japanese technicians to Africa. Human contact between Africans and Japanese, in the view of a Japan Foundation director, Junpei Kato, is essential, especially because of the difficulties between Japanese and Africans that have been introduced by the distortions of Western history. These distortions are, in fact, artificial, considering the natural affinity between African and Japanese cultural world-view systems, as I shall show momentarily.

I have of course dealt at some length with some of these distorting difficulties in previous chapters. Junpei Kato, like some MOFA officials, holds the view that these distortions could be successfully eliminated if more African scholars are invited to Japan, especially since many Japanese Africanists are beginning to proliferate, and broaden Japanese awareness of Africa. Thus *kokusaika* (internationalisation) will make it easier for Japan to share her cultural values and feature with African countries, and *vice versa*, since, in fact, Africa and Japan are not that culturally remote, despite popular belief.

The Japan-Africa *Kokusaika*, moreover, could easily be renderable to practical utility, given elements of cultural congruity that exist between yellow Japan and black Africa. Consider for example Japanese *haiku*, the world's shortest verse form; it has found cultural response in Senegal where it has been accepted as a new form of nature-oriented poetry, as the *Kokusai Koryu* reported. *Haiku* is easily acceptable in Senegal — and would be in Africa as a

265

whole — not because of any idiosyncrasy, but because of the cultural congruities between Japanese and Senegalese modes of thought. Because animism still imbues much of Africa — where nature is still regarded as possessing spiritual force, and thus natural phenomena is worshipped as the norm of some guardian spirit — *haiku* thus shows characteristics similar to Senegalese culture. As nature-oriented, *haiku* has animistic foundation too, like much of *Africulture*.

## AFRICAN TRAINEES AND STUDENTS

In the human exchange between Japan and Africa it is, needless to say, Japan that has played the critical and creative role in facilitating and expanding the interchange. By the beginning of 1979 Japan had received approximately 1 500 technical trainees from Africa, especially from the SSA, even though in 1970 there were only 113 African students (as opposed to trainees) studying in Japan. Every year over 6 000 foreigners come to Japan for training. As Chapter 6 has already outlined JICA is responsible for bringing these foreign trainees to Japan, since the latter is an agency that is responsible for administering the technical cooperation aspects between Japan and Africa. With the cooperation of various Japanese institutions (such as ministries, universities, local municipalities, private and public corporations, etc.), JICA arranges for these students to undertake various courses — ranging from rice cultivation, Japanese language, to nuclear energy. Most of these trainees come from developing countries — Africa included of course.

Several hundred African trainees enrol in over 200 group training courses each year. The courses are offered at a variety of institutions which range from universities to special training centres. Examples of the latter are: Kanagawa International Fisheries Training Center, Okinawa International, Tokyo International, (2) Hyogo International, Osaka International, Nagoya International, Hachiosi International, Tsukuba International, Tsukuba International Agricultural, etc. The latter, for example, has a number of experimental paddy fields, as well as greenhouses, practice buildings, experiment upland fields and so forth. The courses offered at the Tsukuba International Agricultural Training Center include rice cultivation, rice production mechanisation, irrigation and drainage, vegetable crops, facilities for making fishing tackle, coastal fishing, and fishery management, etc.[278] These, indeed, are institutions specifically designed to absorb foreign trainees. The thoroughness with which Japan prepares to facilitate foreign trainees' study is merely a small item in Japan's internationalisation programmes, but it reflects the extent of Japan's desire to enter the global stream of intercultural diffusion.

It is to institutions such as the abovenamed, among others, that the African trainees come to Japan every year. In the beginning of 1979 over a hundred Africans were under training in the following courses, programmes, and seminars:

Agriculture — 156
Fisheries — 80
Construction — 113
Heavy industries — 34
Mining — 60
Chemical industry — 21
Postal services and telecommunication — 345
Other fields — 43
Management technology — 62
Education — 14
Health and welfare — 113
Light industries — 99
Administration — 162
Transportation — 162
Public works — 31

Because of the brief periods that the trainees remain in Japan (6-12 months) — traditional students could and do remain for longer periods — many of the trainees often use their leisure times to explore the culture of Japan, and thereby spread theirs in turn. That means that the trainees often take advantage of the many other cultural festivities and leisure activities in order to augment their repertoire of expertise and understanding of things Japanese. For example, during weekends or evenings, some trainees often take lessons in Japanese language or tea ceremony *(chanoyu)*, flower arrangement *(ikebana)*, etc. Others, on the other hand, often join festivities, especially in the summer, such as "Bon" or Lantern festival — which is based on the belief that the souls of one's ancestors would visit one in summer, so they had to be consoled.[279] Soul consolation of one's ancestors is of course very much as African a tradition as it is Japanese.[280]

Through the activities described above, as Africans come to understand the lifestyle and values of the Japanese, they simultaneously come to impart their own cultural stamp and values to the Japanese. For instance in Japan one often meets African students who, in addition to savouring and enjoying *sento* (Japanese public bath) with their Japanese acquaintances, spend some of their free time teaching African languages (such as Swahili) to the Japanese. Others are often invited to schools, women's or religious organisations to speak about their countries and cultures. Probably the most famous African graduate is the Kenyan marathon runner whose victory at the 1987 World Marathon in Rome highlighted not only Japanese training methods, but also the influence of Japan in African sports. The Kenyan runner, Douglas Waikihuru, like many other African students such as those from Swaziland, Senegal, Kenya, Tanzania, Tunisia, Mauritania, Egypt, Ghana, South Africa, Nigeria, Sudan, Ethiopia, Burkina Faso and Uganda, is fluent in the Japanese language. As we saw in the last chapter these students often become useful on their return home, when they are called upon to work alongside Japanese experts whose ability in local languages may be poor. These African Japanists often facilitate communication between the Japanese and Africans. African students in Japan, like Japanese volunteers in Africa, clearly exchange more than mere material acquisitions — i.e. linguistic instruments and spiritual values as well. Some of these students perform even better than expected and thus end winning prestigious merit prizes. The Nigerian student who was studying marine resources at Tokai University is a classic example. The student, Oloketuyi D. Olukayaode, received the Matsumae Prize in 1979 for his academic achievement. Shigeyoshi Matsumae, an engineer by training, was president of the prestigious Tokai University at the time the Nigerian was cited for his excellence, and the Matsumae International Foundation is named after him.

## AFRICA MONTH ACTIVITIES

The most dramatic manifestations of Africulture were in the late 70s and mid-80s. A number of Japanese institutions organised the Africa Month activities during September and October 1984; the Africa Society of Japan, APIC, MOFA, Japan Foundation, NHK, NAB, International Cultural Association, Japan Graphic Designers' Association, Fuji Television, National Museum of Ethnology, etc., all supported or organised the Africa-related cultural activities that took place during 28 September to 28 October.[281] Other activities overflowed into the next month. For instance "The Last Nomadic Tribe on Earth" — a documentary feature of the photographic life and customs of the Wodaabe ethnic people of Niger took place in November 1984.

These activities included the Tokyo exhibition of African folk art entitled "Nurturing Love (of Africa)", which in turn included exhibits of the Makonde ebony sculpture, African dyed goods, African products, African photography, contemporary art, and stamps. It featured a mini-concert with African folk music instruments.[282] One of the most popular African singers, King Sunny Ade, performed at Festival Hall in Osaka and the Yoyogi National Stadium in Tokyo. The National Folk Dance Troupe of Tunisia as well as the Mobutu Sese Seko National Theater Troupe of Zaire (sic) performed their national ballet dance in Tokyo, Nagoya, and Osaka. The then exiled South African pianist, Dollar Brand, performed to large crowds in Tokyo during December 1987. African music is rapidly becoming popular in Japan thanks to some Japanese musicians who have since taken to playing African music exclusively, such as drummer Ishikama whose interest in and knowledge of Africa extends beyond the Kenyan *pika-pika*, to a variety of African traditional music and dance.

269

The "Africa, Africa, Africa!" show introduced African fashions and folk dances "which had become popular among the Japanese in recent years".[283] A presentation of African national costume by ladies and children of members of African diplomatic corps was one of the central features of the show. Not only African dance teams performed; African students in Japan provided the Japanese audiences with the African youth perspective of Japanese culture, and were thus offered the opportunity to reflect, simultaneously, on Afro-Japanese interchanges, and so brought a comparative under-standing of Japanese and African cultures. Hence the shows and exhibitions ranged from costumes, to cookery, to college life. A film festival was sponsored by the Japan Foundation; films from 10 African nations were shown, after which festival a symposium of the films was conducted. African film directors from Egypt, Tunisia, Nigeria, Morocco, Algeria, Senegal, Ivory Coast, Burkina Faso, and Ethiopia also participated in the symposium. These films reflected modern Africulture. Another symposium — "Poor Africa, Rich Africa — In Search of an Accurate Image" was held at the Asahi Hall (Tokyo) to probe the multidimensional character of Africa. Thus the poverty and richness of Africa were viewed within not only the cultures of Africa, but also within her international relations with the rest of the world. Spiritual affluence and the rich natural resources of Africa were viewed and contrasted with the material poverty of the continent. Thus the "Poor Africa, Rich Africa" search for an accurate image was not only contrastive, but corrective, constructive and creative. We have already seen in Chapter 2 (see note 79) another Japanese perspective of Africans which did not mesh with the Japanese view through JOCV eyes, or that of many other Japanese.

## NATIONAL MUSEUM OF ETHNOLOGY AND AFRICULTURE EXHIBITS

In contrast to modern Africulture of the African Film Festival, the traditional dance and music shows at the theatres and stadia, as well as cooking exhibits, were displayed by the Ethnological Museum. For instance, the exhibition of about 300 African folk handicrafts by the National Museum contrasted modern Africa with traditional African arts and crafts. But even before the Africa Month activities began in 1984, the Ethnological Museum had already installed a permanent Africa Display at Senri, near Osaka, where Africa through an ethnological window was made familiar to the Japanese.

The Africa Display — which is second only to the Southeast Asian display in size — consists of at least 1 000 specimens which describe *Africulture* from numerous dimensions. The themes of the display are broad: "History of African Civilization", "African Peoples and Life-Styles", "The World of Ritual and Plastic Arts", "Life-Style and Culture of the Coastal Swahili", "Ethiopian Culture."[284] In discussions with the Museum's general affairs director, Imori Takeshi, during the 10th anniversary celebrations of the inauguration of the Museum, he observed to the author that for the celebrations the "Mask-and-Heart" African display was one of the greatest interest to the 1 200 daily Japanese visitors. During a poll conducted by the museum researchers and university professors, a question was posed to 1 500 museum visitors: "What do you think was the most interesting display you saw in the museum?" The answer was unequivocal: "The majority of the visitors said it was the African display. This is an eloquent indication that a great number of Japanese people are strongly attracted and interested in African culture".[285] Given the large number of visitors to the museum many Japanese continue to show interest in Africa. In a 10-year period, 4,4 million visitors have come to the museum. Thus an average of 1 205 visitors per day come across some aspects of African culture and civilisation. This has continued to inspire Japanese interest in African culture and Africa.

At the corner for "The World of Ceremonies and Formative Arts", which is one of the most interesting of the African displays, are exhibited numerous masks and carvings of various gods and goddesses of African ethnic groups. The many cultural artifacts from the Congo Basin, Cameroons, Sahelian, Coastal Swahili, and Ethiopian areas continue to generate interest among the Japanese, whose formidable repertoire of masks naturally constitutes a basis for comparison with other cultures. Especially regarding this aspect,

Japanese culture shares features with African culture, and the likelihood is much greater for African incorporation of Japanese cultural values than even for European cultures. African museums, particularly those in Senegal, Mali, Nigeria, Cameroon, Zaire, Central Africa, Uganda, Tanzania, Kenya, Ethiopia, and Malagasy, have, in the past, cooperated with the National Museum in Osaka.[286] Inarguably, there is a growing interest of things African among the Japanese today, just as there has been growing interest of things Japanese among Africans in the last two or more decades. Internationalisation is increasingly reflected in cultural contacts as well as in the human bonds that have qualitatively and quantitatively grown in recent years between Africa and Japan.

Because African students and trainees seem to have access to any field of study or training for which they are qualified, it would seem that Japan is ready to initiate a genuine transfer of knowledge and technology even to those regions of the world whose "absorptive capacity" of such knowledge and technology would seem to be rudimentary.[287] In the process, African students and trainees seem equally ready to reciprocate in kind and are thus willing to learn the thought and social structure of a new culture, which, in any event, has readily accepted them at a critical juncture in their scientific and technological learning. The process is a two-way issue of course. Africans also do impart to the Japanese what one Japanese JOCV youth has called "spiritual affluence".[288] The Africa Society of Japan — an organisation formed by Japanese corporations doing business in Africa — has also given African students in Japan an occasional forum from which they could express not only their views of Africa, but also their understanding of Japanese culture — an understanding which has been facilitated by their learning of the Japanese language. In the African-Japanese cultural exchanges, once again, Japan demonstrates more than mere thoroughness in undertaking her engagements. She displays the power and meaning of the art of national discipline turned to good use. Africa would thus be better served, were she to attempt to emulate the Japanese model. Learning the Japanese language by Africans facilitates not only their preparation for understanding specific learning materials and teaching methods, it advances Japan's cultural influence world-wide, and Africans have probably been the most successful peoples in propagating the cultures, languages, and value systems of others — European, American, Arabic, Chinese, Indian, and so forth.

Yet Africans abroad have not often enjoyed a pacific, productive, and prosperous experience: from the US to China, from Sweden to the UK, from France to Australia, etc., Africans have experienced the sting of the negative "Other". They have often gravitated towards embracing their host's cultures, yet they have been rejected in various fashions, sometimes bordering on the openly hostile, at others subtly so. However, bias against foreigners is not specifically confined to Africans; it is only more pronounced and visibly crude when directed against Africans. Often it has been said that if you want to hate a foreign society, study there. My observations world-wide are replete with examples of the curses of former students in the UK, US, China, India, France, etc. and whose reminiscences about their former home away from home are far from flattering. Bitter tirades have been unleashed against these societies for one ill or another, especially for a myriad of discriminatory practices; but not once have I recorded an anti-Japanese tirade by present or former African students in Japan. In the People's Republic of China, the USA, France, and Spain, for example, Africans have regularly been called "monkeys", an unflattering epithet in the age of AIDS. In Sweden, Belgium, India, USA, etc., they have recently been labelled, especially by some lunatic right-wing elements, "AIDS carriers", and caricatured as the companion of the so-called African "Green Monkey" which was alleged to carry the AIDS virus.

There are numerous instances of which, even this late in the 20th century, Africans have been subjected to an on-going process of denigration. Yet in my research in Japan I found only one or two neglible race-baiting incidents; systematic discrimination against or stereotypical treatment of African students and residents in Japan is virtually unheard of, even in some sections of Tokyo that have come to be known of late for their xenophobic tendencies. Not even in Arab countries in Africa (with the possible exception of Libya,

273

Morocco, and Egypt) does one find the tolerant, even friendly feelings and attitudes towards Africans, as one finds in Japan, the racist ultra-rightwing excepted. In prerevolutionary Russia Africans have co-existed with Russians for over a thousand years, especially in Colchis, particularly around the Caucasus Mountains, hence the "Caucasus Blacks". Blacks were called Colchians. Russia is perhaps the only major culture where Africans became successfully integrated in its society — truly melting-pot reality. Of course, as I have already indicated by citing a number of Japanese scholars (e.g. Shinoda, Morikawa, etc.), there is a powerful school which holds that not all is well in the attitude of the children of the Rising Sun towards those of the "burnt-sun" of the Black Continent.*
Current personal exchanges between Africans and Japanese, as well as in the intimate writings and personal observations of many Japanese who had sojourned in Africa for a couple of years, and of course including African students who have resided in Japan for several years, indicate an unofficial consensus: rancour and racism are now almost alien in the meeting between *Africulture* and *Japanism*. After all, Japanese and African traditional cultures have some profound basic things in common. Afro-Americans married to Japanese seem to encounter no unusual discriminatory racial practices in Japan, although some Black American radio/television correspondents who are based in Tokyo often complain of racist discriminatory practice by Japanese citizens. Racist comments by Japanese leaders or the myopic marketing strategies adopted by

---

\* In certain sections of Tokyo some Japanese commercial houses have begun to peddle black caricatures — long considered racist in the West — such as black Sambo and his sister Hanna, as well as black mannequins with exaggerated and grotesque facial features (cf. Marco Polo in China, Chapter 1, especially pp. 12-13). The Sanrio Company, Yamato Mannequin Company and the Sogo Department stores in Tokyo have introduced, although in the spirit of *kokusaika*, and exploited black exotica in the form of black mannequins, and characters such as the unmistakenly africanized Bibinda. Many Japanese still have a poor image of blacks; however their *attitudes* to blacks may appear to appproximate those of racist Westerners, Japanese have yet to show overtly racist or discriminatory *behaviour* towards blacks, Yasuhiro Nakasone and Michio Watanabe notwithstanding.

some Japanese corporations only reinforce perceptions of the latent xenophobic proclivities among the Japanese — particularly in regard to Black Americans. The Japanese have been excellent copiers of course — during SCAP occupation of Japan they saw US military personnel housed in segregated barracks. American culture through movies, television, books, personal associations invariably transmitted its racism toward blacks, and some Japanese became excellent copiers: hence the Little Black Sambo syndrome, etc. If the pupil learns too well then the teacher must take some credit. Japanese automakers' practice of hiring fewer blacks at their American plants than US car producers do is proof not only of the fact that the US is struggling to divest itself of its centuries' old heritage of racial bias and discrimination against blacks, but that having escaped the yellow-black trauma in Japanese history, Japanese tend to ignore this latter lesson from the master. Having been race-conscious for millenia, Japanese mimesis of racist nuances and practices from the US and Europe, especially between 1902 and 1952, subtly but insidiously took form and shape in the Japanese mind, particularly as it concerned black Americans. The Japanese, however, never flaunted nor overtly displayed their racist chauvinism against blacks *per se*; only recently has there been public display by some prominent political leaders and business concerns regarding racial contempt towards blacks, especially, for some strange reason, of black Americans.

# 第五部
## 通商・貿易規則

# PART V
## THE COMMERCIAL/ TRADE IMPERATIVE

## CHAPTER 9

# ECONOMIC AND TRADE RELATIONS, 1961-1987

*Japan is attracted to Africa because of its resources and potential as a consumer market. Africa, which has a population of more than 500 million, is seen by Japan as an indispensable trading partner. Africa is becoming more and more essential to Japan ... (which) imports 45 percent of its copper, 80 percent of its cobalt, 46 per cent of its manganese and 40 percent of its cotton from Africa.*

Lu Miaogeng
(Beijing, 1985)[289]

*As for Japanese relations with Africa, as long as there is only trade there will be a big deficit in Japan's favour. Black Africa wants Japanese products but Japan is only interested in coffee, cocoa, some ore, a few other natural resources and little else. It's not enough to adjust the balance of trade.*

Hiroyuki Tasaka[290]
JETRO Executive

*Unfortunately, Japan's interest in Africa is mainly as a place to exploit for raw materials.*

Professor Iwao Kobori,[291]
Tokyo University; Secretary-General,
Japanese Association of Africanists (1970)

*Japan's interest in Africa is twofold: to promote human and social development, and to increase industrial development in order to expand a two way trade. Japan has a consensus on this.*

Makito Takahashi[292], MOFA Official (1987)

Japan depends on developing countries for a number of important commodities, and Africa holds a considerable portion of these: bauxite, manganese, cobalt, iron ore, gold, and diamonds. Africa also possesses, and Japan needs, mineral fuels — such as oil, gas — and foodstuffs: coffee, cocoa, etc. Africa's poverty and backwardness, and Japan's affluence and modernity, make for close trading partnership, South Africa's erstwhile complicating factor notwithstanding.

In Chapter 2 I dealt extensively with the commercial links between Japan and the African continent (except South Africa) from the Meiji Japan's times to the "African Year" (i.e. 1960). Chapter 9 is somewhat of a continuation of Chapter 2; i.e. the 1961 to 1990 Japan-Africa trade is an extension of the earlier 1885-1960 commercial ties between the Sunny Island and the Black Continent. It should be recalled that Chapter 2 was devoted not solely to the interwar period, but also to the postwar period, 1945-1960, during which time African colonies became independent. Hence this chapter will focus on the enormous trade linkages between the "Far Continent" and the "Far East" Empire. Chapter 10 will be devoted to Japan-South Africa ties as they evolved, diplomatic-wise, to commercial linkages.

## TRADE DURING THE "AFRICAN SIXTIES"

Following the independence of the majority of African states in 1960[293], Africa, in a sense, became for Japan what America had become for Europe after World War II; a large consumer of her surplus production. Indeed, between 1960 and 1964, Africa imported more from Japan than did either the European Common Market or the European Free Trade Association.[294] In fact, with the exception of ship exports to Liberia, Japan's trade with Africa had increased markedly since 1955. During the eight-year period between 1954 and 1962, exports had increased by 2,4 times, and imports by 4,3 times; although from 1961 onwards Africa began to import more from Japan than she exported to the latter. In 1961 Japan exported to Africa goods worth 137 460 million yen, and imported from the latter goods to the value of 68 513 million yen, but in 1962 Japan's export trade with Africa totalled $335 million, which was a 12 per cent decrease compared with that of the preceding year, while her imports amounted to $218 million, which was a 15 per cent increase.[295] (See Tables 9.1 and 9.2.)

TABLE 9.1

EXPORTS TO AFRICAN COUNTRIES *(Unit: $1 000)*

| Export goods | 1960 | 1961 | 1962 | Ratio to total (%) | Ratio to total excl. ships to Liberia (%) | Amount of increase or decrease compared with 1961 | Rate of increase or decrease compared with 1961 (%) |
|---|---|---|---|---|---|---|---|
| Total | 351,771 | 381,834 | 335,165 | 100,0 | - | -46,669 | 87,8 |
| (Total excl. ships to Liberia) | (276,516) | (285,827) | (286,747) | - | (100,0) | (+920) | (100,3) |
| Foods and beverages | 8,994 | 6,824 | 8,855 | 2,6 | 3,1 | +2,031 | 129,8 |
| Tea | 3,847 | 2,872 | 3,598 | 1,1 | 1,3 | +726 | 129,8 |
| Textiles | 185,334 | 188,583 | 183,741 | 54,8 | 64,1 | -4,842 | 97,4 |
| Cotton fabrics | 61,635 | 70,332 | 68,343 | 20,4 | 23,8 | -1,989 | 97,2 |
| Rayon fabrics | 8,397 | 7,618 | 5,119 | 1,6 | 1,9 | -2,199 | 71,1 |
| Spun rayon fabrics | 46,071 | 44,224 | 34,916 | 10,4 | 12,2 | -9,308 | 79,0 |
| Synthetic fibre fabrics | 4,570 | 4,189 | 4,984 | 1,5 | 1,7 | +795 | 119,0 |
| Woolen fabrics | 3,084 | 2,191 | 2,230 | 0,7 | 9,8 | +39 | 101,8 |
| Clothing | 30,247 | 32,968 | 28,327 | 8,5 | 9,9 | -4,633 | 85,9 |
| Metals and metal products | 19,129 | 24,439 | 27,184 | 8,1 | 9,5 | +2,745 | 111,2 |
| Iron and steel | 14,660 | 20,730 | 22,608 | 6,7 | 7,9 | +1,898 | 109,2 |
| Metal products | 4,290 | 3,504 | *3,920 | 1,2 | 1,4 | +416 | 111,9 |
| Machinery and instruments | 110,631 | 133,759 | 86,719 | 25,9 | 30,2 | -47,040 | 64,8 |
| (Machinery) | 107,148 | 130,818 | 82,429 | 24,6 | 28,7 | -48,389 | 61,6 |
| General machinery | 8,536 | 10,488 | *5,515 | 1,6 | 1,9 | -4,973 | 52,6 |
| Textile machinery | 1,166 | 3,540 | 971 | 8,3 | 0,3 | -2,569 | 27,4 |

\*  Approximations only.

## TABLE 9.1 *(continued)*

| Export goods | 1960 | 1961 | 1962 | Ratio to total (%) | Ratio to total excl. ships to Liberia (%) | Amount of increase or decrease compared with 1961 | Rate of increase or decrease compared with 1961 (%) |
|---|---|---|---|---|---|---|---|
| Sewing machines | 2,123 | 2,810 | 1,835 | 0,5 | 0,6 | -175 | 91,3 |
| Electric machinery | 11,762 | 9,660 | *13,916 | 4,1 | 4,3 | +4,256 | 118,3 |
| Radios | 8,736 | 6,610 | 8,216 | 2,5 | 2,9 | +1,556 | 124,3 |
| Transportation equipment | 86,225 | 118,239 | *62,984 | 18,8 | 22,0 | -47,255 | 57,1 |
| Rolling stock | 6,461 | 6,741 | 5,066 | 1,5 | 1,8 | -1,675 | 75,2 |
| Automobiles | 2,266 | 4,070 | 7,197 | 2,1 | 2,5 | +3,127 | 176,8 |
| Bicycles and parts | 2,111 | 2,142 | 2,294 | 0,7 | 0,8 | +152 | 107,1 |
| Ships and boats | 75,258 | 97,196 | 48,418 | 14,4 | 16,9 | -48,778 | 49,8 |
| Precision instruments | 3,483 | 3,372 | *4,286 | 1,3 | 1,3 | +914 | 127,1 |
| Cameras | 691 | 764 | 1,056 | 0,3 | 0,4 | +292 | 138,2 |
| Nonmetallic mineral products | 3,641 | 1,652 | 3,668 | 1,1 | 1,3 | +16 | 100,4 |
| Pottery | 2,101 | 2,287 | 2,488 | 0,7 | 0,9 | +201 | 100,8 |
| Glassware | 607 | 529 | 498 | 0,1 | 0,2 | -31 | 94,1 |
| Chemical and pharmaceutical products | 3,337 | 2,493 | 3,885 | 1,2 | 1,2 | +1,392 | 155,8 |
| Others | | | | | | | |
| Toys | 2,217 | 2,131 | 1,716 | 0,5 | 0,6 | -415 | 80,5 |
| Footwear | 4,511 | 4,580 | 4,354 | 1,3 | 1,5 | -226 | 95,1 |
| Buttons | 433 | 513 | 562 | 0,2 | 0,2 | +49 | 109,6 |
| Paper | 2,993 | 3,731 | 1,511 | 0,5 | 0,5 | -2,220 | 40,5 |
| Rubber tires and tubes | 2,057 | 2,083 | 3,501 | 1,0 | 1,2 | +1,418 | 168,1 |

\*    Approximations only.

Source:    JETRO (1963).

## TABLE 9.2

## IMPORTS FROM AFRICAN COUNTRIES *(Unit: $1 000)*

| Import goods | 1960 | 1961 | 1962 | Ratio to total (%) | Amount of increase or decrease compared with 1961 | Rate of increase or decrease compared with 1961 (%) |
|---|---|---|---|---|---|---|
| Total | 163,895 | 190,315 | 218,117 | 100,0 | + 27,802 | 144,6 |
| Foods and beverages | 24,112 | 41,716 | 78,929 | 36,2 | + 37,212 | 189,2 |
| Maize | 16,834 | 27,599 | 53,630 | 24,6 | + 26,931 | 194,3 |
| Coffee beans | 1,810 | 2,297 | 2,239 | 1,0 | -58 | 91,5 |
| Cocoa beans | 3,741 | 5,479 | 8,221 | 3,8 | + 2,742 | 150,0 |
| Wheat bran | 500 | 1,795 | 2,085 | 1,0 | + 290 | 116,8 |
| Textiles | 43,310 | 43,846 | 37,459 | 17,2 | -5,587 | 87,0 |
| Wool | 8,907 | 10,665 | 14,294 | 6,6 | + 3,629 | 134,7 |
| Raw cotton | 27,338 | 23,491 | 16,044 | 7,3 | -7,187 | 68,1 |
| Hard and bast fibres | 4,992 | 6,191 | 4,985 | 2,3 | -1,206 | 80,5 |
| Metallic materials | 58,399 | 61,988 | 41,972 | 19,2 | -20,016 | 67,7 |
| Iron ore | 5,233 | 8,043 | 13,042 | 6,0 | + 3,999 | 144,2 |
| Iron and steel scrap | 10,618 | 10,027 | 12,801 | 5,9 | + 2,774 | 127,7 |
| Copper ore | 9,483 | 8,257 | 7,048 | 3,2 | -2,215 | 78,1 |
| Non-ferrous metal scrap | 1,523 | 1,883 | 2,002 | 0,9 | + 19 | 101,0 |
| Non-metallic minerals | 15,949 | 19,689 | 19,281 | 8,8 | -408 | 97,9 |
| Phosphate ore | 5,747 | 6,599 | 7,294 | 3,3 | + 695 | 110,5 |
| Salt | 3,058 | 3,342 | 3,872 | 1,8 | + 530 | 115,9 |
| Asbestos | 2,926 | 4,295 | 3,328 | 1,5 | -967 | 77,5 |
| Chemical and pharmaceutical products | 3,038 | 3,718 | 3,306 | 1,5 | -412 | 88,9 |
| Tannin extracts | 3,515 | 2,989 | 2,888 | 1,3 | -101 | 96,5 |
| Metal and metal products | 29,226 | 27,594 | 28,683 | 13,2 | + 1,089 | 103,9 |
| Pig iron | 13,837 | 15,069 | 17,489 | 8,0 | + 8,420 | 116,1 |
| Copper and copper alloy | 12,102 | 6,766 | 7,929 | 3,2 | + 263 | 103,9 |
| Machinery | 8,207 | 8,302 | 2,065 | 1,2 | + 363 | 115,8 |
| Ships for scrapping | 1,454 | 1,185 | 785 | 0,4 | -380 | 47,1 |
| Others | 8,815 | 3,564 | 3,065 | 1,4 | -499 | 36,0 |
| Cotton seeds | | | | | | |

## TABLE 9.2 *(continued)*

| Import goods | 1960 | 1961 | 1962 | Ratio to total (%) | Amount of increase or decrease compared with 1961 | Rate of increase or decrease compared with 1961 (%) |
|---|---|---|---|---|---|---|
| Miscellaneous | | | | | | |
| All seeds | 8,431 | 4,809 | 0,001 | 0,5 | +1,358 | 138,1 |
| Sawlugs and lumbers | 533 | 1,185 | 718 | 0,3 | -447 | 60,1 |
| Hides and skins | 301 | 359 | 354 | 0,8 | -5 | 98,8 |

Source:     JETRO (1963).

On the whole, however, Africa's consumption of Japanese production continued to climb. The result of Africa's heavy importation of Japanese commodities without a commensurate reciprocity in Japanese consumption of African raw materials invariably led to huge trade imbalances to the disfavour of Africa. The resultant African discontent created, in turn, trade frictions between the superpower island and the developing continent. For instance, only a few weeks after she established diplomatic relations with Japan, Uganda stopped issuing import licences for Japanese goods. (Ironically, in 1987, it was Uganda which, because of *endaka/* high yen, became the first African country to close her embassy in Tokyo). In 1965 Tanzania expressed her displeasure by placing restrictions on import of goods from Japan. The Nyerere Government further turned down a Japanese Government offer of a long-term credit to Tanzania. Kenya also placed restrictions on textile imports. Similarly, Nigeria prevented her banks from issuing further letters of credit for Japanese imports.[296] The basic problem was that the trade imbalances heavily favoured Japan, especially since African countries were covetous of the blossoming two-way trade traffic between Japan and the African nemesis — South Africa (Chapter 10).

Of course part of the African resentment was manufactured by European powers, which had encouraged African nations to apply the restrictive measures of Article 35 of GATT, especially after Japan became an Article VIII nation in the IMF in 1964, and also joined the OECD. There were at least 18 African states which were associated with the European Common Market in the mid-1960s. In certain instances — e.g. Tanzania — the Japanese Government blamed the influence of Communist China regarding African hardline stance towards the Japanese trading role. But by and large Japan correctly diagnosed the problem to be one of European instigation in origin and causation.[297] Understandably, the Japanese Government and corporations were displeased by the then growing tendency of African and other developing countries to discriminate against Japanese products. Her sense of being discriminated against increased when she saw France, for example, taking more out of some African countries than she was bringing into these states (e.g. Ivory Coast) and yet was not denounced by Africans, nor by Westerners for "unfair" trading practices. Especially annoying to Japan was Francophone Africa's tendency to echo her master's voice — Francophone Africa placed stiffer tariffs on Japanese than on European Common Market goods.

In order to diffuse these tensions and effect better trade relations, Japan began to alter her strategy. She began to increase her investments in Africa (see below), as well as initiating a couple of new strategies: in 1965 she granted the most-favoured-nation trading status to several Francophone states: Cameroon, Central African Republic, Chad, Dahomey (now Benin), Guinea, Madagascar, Mali, and Togo. Subsequently, similar pacts were signed with yet more of these Francophone states: Congo, Gabon, Ivory Coast, Mauritania, Senegal, and Upper Volta (now Burkina Faso). Yet in 1984 a MITI official could still detect the strong influence of France on Africa (as we saw in Chapter 4), when he observed that "western African nations still have strong relations with their former suzerains in Europe and are unfamiliar with yen credits".[298]

The other strategy to diffuse the Afro-Japanese trade tensions was the initiation of development aid to Africa (Chapter 5). Like everything else that Japan has done in Africa, her aid commitments began in East Africa, the latter being the closest African region to Japan. Moreover Japan has a much longer history of contact with East Africa than with any other parts of Africa.

Between 1961 and 1970 Japanese exports rose from $400 million to $1 400 million, an increase of 250 %. On the other hand, imports from Africa during the same period, jumped from $300 million to slightly above $850 million, an increase of 183 %. (See Charts 9.1 and 9.2.) Most of the exports went to a few African countries, including South Africa. Similarly with imports: they were largely confined to the same countries plus South Africa — i.e. Egypt, Ghana, Nigeria, Liberia, Zambia, Kenya, and Sudan.

## CHART 9.1
### Japan's trade with African countries *(in million dollars)*

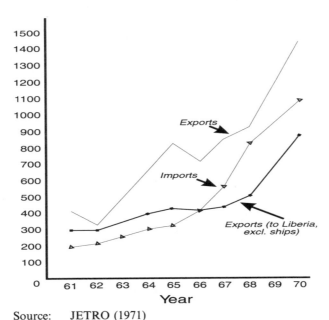

Source:    JETRO (1971)

## CHART 9.2
## Japan's exports to major African countries *(in million dollars)*

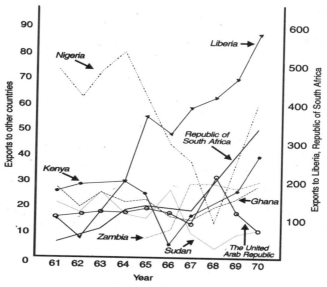

Source:  JETRO (1971)

While the 1960s were "African" in the sense that most African states became independent, it was also a decade of rapid economic growth in Japan — a decade during which Japan simultaneously sought to open her economy to foreign competition by liberalising trade and the flow of international capital. The resultant imbalance in Afro-Japanese trade was due largely to the fact that while Japan was providing industrial machinery and consumer goods — for which most of Africa was hungry — the latter, on the other hand, provided fewer attractive commodities to Japanese customers, besides the customary raw and primary products. Consequently by the close of the 1960s Japan was importing from Africa mainly raw materials, mineral fuels, foodstuffs and fishes as well as pig iron, copper and copper alloys, cobalt and cobalt alloys, and other precious metals. Throughout the mid- to late 60s Africa's share in Japan's total trade never exceeded 10 % in terms of exports, nor 7 % in terms of imports. (See Table 9.3.)

287

The lion's share of African consumption of Japanese goods for the three years (1966, 1967 and 1968) could be apportioned to Nigeria, Egypt, Libya, Zambia, Ghana, Tanzania, Sudan and Mozambique. In turn Japan consumed sizeable amounts of Zambian, Mozambican, Ghanaian, Sudanese, Egyptian, Tanzanian, Nigerian, and Angolan products (Table 9.3). In 1969 the same growth tendency reflected in the previous three years was registered: Japanese exports reached $1 152 953 million and imports from Africa reached $982 435 million. The 70s followed more or less a similar pattern as the 60s. Consider for example the Japan-Liberia trade: this dominated the Japan-Africa trade in the 1960s and early 1970s. In the decade 1961-1971 trade jumped from a puny $44 million to over $1 billion. It reached the apex in 1976 when it amounted to $2,87 billion. In the same year however the trade imbalance also reached a pinnacle of $2,8 billion.

## TABLE 9.3
## JAPAN'S AFRICAN TRADE *(Unit: $1 000 U.S.)*

| | Exports | | | Imports | | |
|---|---|---|---|---|---|---|
| | 1966 | 1967 | 1968 | 1966 | 1967 | 1968 |
| World trade | 9 776 399 | 10 441 576 | 12 971 662 | 9 522 709 | 11 663 087 | 12 987 243 |
| Africa (total) | 728 678 | 850 387 | 939 992 | 119 920 | 661 233 | 839 082 |
| Africa's share in Japan's total trade (%) | 7,45 | 8,14 | 7,25 | 4,41 | 5,93 | 6,46 |
| Africa (excluding ships to Liberia) | 252 980 | 258 077 | 286 564 | - | - | - |
| Black Africa* | 494 366 | 584 607 | 641 714 | 217 738 | 297 866 | 377 226 |
| Africa's share in Japan's total trade (%) | 5,06 | 5,6 | 4,95 | 2,29 | 2,55 | 2,90 |

\*   Excluding North Africa, South Africa and all non-independent areas.

## TABLE 9.3A
## MAIN AFRICAN TRADING PARTNER *(Unit: $1 000 U.S.)*

|  | Exports | | | Imports | | |
|---|---|---|---|---|---|---|
|  | 1966 | 1967 | 1968 | 1966 | 1967 | 1968 |
| South Africa | 126 983 | 156 317 | 169 312 | 133 354 | 267 390 | 334 587 |
| Zambia | 14 366 | 29 359 | 29 380 | 81 832 | 138 138 | 168 419 |
| Ghana | 17 749 | 15 510 | 10 070 | 16 681 | 19 274 | 33 540 |
| Sudan | 16 422 | 12 774 |  | 13 137 | 17 255 | 23 196 |
| Mozambique | 11 115 | 15 466 | 21 788 | 7 155 | 16 515 | 17 676 |
| Uganda | 6 390 | 5 835 | 12 025 | 7 818 | 14 968 | 25 269 |
| Congo (Kinshasa) | 8 012 | 5 291 | 19 988 | 3 887 | 8 978 | 14 161 |
| U.A.R. | 24 739 | 10 740 | 4 813 | 17 787 | 19 116 | 27 081 |
| Tanzania | 12 667 | 9 074 | 16 320 | 14 248 | 11 289 | 15 880 |
| Kenya | 7 370 | 17 068 | 5 550 | 5 561 | 6 694 | 22 513 |
| Nigeria | 39 573 | 38 335 | 13 094 | 13 671 | 16 163 | 14 502 |
| Angola | 4 567 | 9 036 | 9 938 | 4 819 | 10 854 | 18 220 |
| Libya | 12 597 | 21 406 | 24 391 | 272 | 82 | 500 |
| Liberia* | 322 889 | 393 314 | 439 029 | 16 968 | 12 262 | 17 280 |

\*   Mostly ships registered in Liberia but owned elsewhere.

Source:   Africa Report (1970).

A similar pattern emerges if we take Nigeria, or Zaire, or Kenya, etc., but no useful purpose would be served. All that I can say here, for the benefit of researchers and college students, is that the Nigeria-Japan trade, for example, rose from $81 million in 1961 to $122 million in 1971. This figure jumped 20-fold to $2,5 billion 10 years later. The trade imbalance widened from 1975 till it reached $1,8 billion in 1981.

### TRADE IN THE 1980s

Continuing on that quiet but by now familiar drive to excellence that has characterised much of the doings of Japan domestically and globally, she raised her total exports from the 1979 figure of $5,231 billion to the 1980 figure of $8,231 billion. Her imports from Africa

289

followed a similar pattern. They increased from $3,201 billion in 1979 to $4,465 billion in 1980. The growth was even phenomenal in 1981, a watershed year in Afro-Japanese trade ties. For it was in 1981 that Japanese exports to and imports from Africa broke all barriers and reached their peak. The Japanese finally did in Africa what no other non-colonial power (*vis-a-vis* Africa) had previously done — topped the $14 billion mark in trade volume.

Her 1981 imports from Africa totalled $4,8 billion while her exports reached $10 billion for a total of $14,8 billion. This implies that Japan's exports grew by 25,2 per cent between 1980 and 1981, her imports from Africa rose by 7 %, while total Japanese imports rose by only 2 per cent.[299] Since then however, the volume of trade between the island economic superpower and the developing continent has declined as is reflected in Tables 9.4 and 9.5.

## TABLE 9.4
## JAPAN'S EXPORTS TO AFRICA BY COMMODITY 1981-1984*
### *(in millions of dollars)*

| Exports | 1981 | 1982 | 1983 | 1984 |
|---|---|---|---|---|
| **Total** | **$10 038,5** | **$6 930,4** | **$6 006,1** | **$6 358,1** |
| Food | 227,3 | 200,0 | 166,8 | 78,0 |
| Industrial raw materials and fuels | 35,5 | 31,7 | 19,6 | 19,0 |
| Light industrial products | 967,5 | 657,9 | 638,4 | 608,6 |
| Heavy industrial products | 8 782,8 | 6 031,7 | 5 170,3 | 5 644,2 |
| Metals | 1 163,9 | 968,9 | 623,1 | 638,1 |
| Steel | 855,0 | 683,6 | 394,7 | 412,2 |
| Machinery | 7 441,0 | 4 928,6 | 4 427,1 | 4 882,0 |
| Motor vehicles | 2 154,6 | 1 245,7 | 1 041,1 | 1 253,2 |
| Vessels | 1 793,7 | 1 066,7 | 708,0 | 951,8 |

\*   Figures include North African countries, which in 1984 accounted for 35,3 per cent of total Japanese exports to Africa.

Source:   JETRO, White paper on international trade.

Thus, the 1982 imports declined by a billion dollars from the 1981 figures and continued declining by another $468 million in 1983. Similarly, her 1982 exports to Africa declined but, even more dramatically, by the huge figure of $3,108 billion, which declined further by nearly a billion dollars in 1983. In 1982 however only the West African countries of Mauritania, Ghana, Burkina Faso, C.A.R. and Zaire showed a surplus on their trade with Japan. The other states in the region all reflected deficits, some very large, on bilateral trade.

TABLE 9.5

JAPAN'S IMPORTS FROM AFRICA BY COMMODITY

1981-1984* *(in millions of dollars)*

| Imports | 1981 | 1982 | 1983 | 1984 |
|---|---|---|---|---|
| **Total** | **$4 779,2** | **$3 740,2** | **$3 272,0** | **$3 112,4** |
| Food | 779,7 | 826,0 | 628,2 | 483,4 |
| Industrial raw materials | 903,8 | 822,4 | 811,9 | 888,3 |
| Textile raw materials | 222,3 | 173,1 | 201,0 | 220,7 |
| Metallic raw materials | 403,7 | 389,0 | 356,6 | 368,3 |
| Other raw materials | 277,9 | 260,3 | 254,2 | 299,2 |
| Mineral fuels | 1 727,3 | 1 039,5 | 864,6 | 638,4 |
| Manufactured goods | 1 045,0 | 826,8 | 868,8 | 1 003,5 |

*  Figures include North Africa countries, which in 1984 accounted for 18,5 per cent of total Japanese imports from Africa.

Source:  JETRO, White paper on international trade.

As Table 9.4 reflects industrial products, especially machinery, constituted the bulk — almost 90 % — of Japan's exports to Africa in 1984. While, on the other hand, her imports from the region were largely (i.e. nearly 70 %) based on foodstuffs, mineral fuels and raw materials. Manufactured goods made up the remainder. Such manufactured goods as vanadium pentoxide, wood chips, ferroalloys (ferrosilicon, ferromanganese, ferrochromium), non-ferrous

291

metals (platinum, copper and copper alloys, unwrought aluminium, unwrought nickel, cobalt and cobalt alloys, uranium) diamonds, and gold, constituted the bulk of manufactured goods Africa exported to Japan in the mid-eighties. Because of the drop in Japanese steel production, Africa's contribution to the Japanese industrial might, has led to the drop of iron ore sales.

Foodstuffs that Japan imported from the continent in 1984-1985 were mainly fish and shell-fish (shrimps, prawns, lobsters, cuttle fish, squid, octopus), maize (often to be transshipped to another African area as part of her ODA aid to Africa), fruits and vegetables, sugar, coffee beans and cocoa. Thus Japan is a heavily dependent country — in virtually all raw materials.

Yet the trade imbalance continued to the aggravating extent where the Kenyan President, Daniel arap Moi, threatened, at one stage, to impose import restrictions against Japanese products.[300] In 1985 trade with African countries was reflected in the traditional African supplies to Japan. Outside South Africa, the 10 major suppliers to Japan were Egypt, Zambia, Morocco, Algeria, Mauritania, Ghana, Liberia, Zimbabwe, Zaire, and Sudan. The first 10 major consumers of Japanese products for the same year — again with the exception of South Africa — were (in that order) Swaziland, Egypt, Liberia, Algeria, Nigeria, Libya, Kenya, Canaries Is., Tanzania, and Ivory Coast.[301] Table 9.6 gives the detailed values.

The declines in Afro-Japanese trade which first registered on a massive scale in 1982, continued in 1986, till the early 1990s. The total value of Japan's exports to African countries decreased during the year by 4,2 per cent from the 1985 figures. In 1985 Japanese exports to Africa were valued at $4,650 billion compared with $4,46 billion. This was basically a result of the depletion of the foreign currency reserves, particularly of the oil-producing countries of Angola, Algeria, Egypt, Libya, and Nigeria. With the drop in oil prices there was a reduction in the value of oil exports. Secondly, because of the low level purchasing power of African countries, the latter countries reduced their imports. Hence the large declination of Japanese exports in 1986 to the abovenamed countries especially:

## TABLE 9.6
## TRADE WITH AFRICAN COUNTRIES IN 1985
### *(Unit: $1 000)*

| Region and country | Exports | | | Imports | | |
|---|---|---|---|---|---|---|
| | Export value | Compared with previous year (%) | Share (%) | Import value | Compared with previous year (%) | Share (%) |
| **Total** | **4 650 242** | **73,1** | **100,0** | **3 538 582** | **113,7** | **100,0** |
| Morocco | 50 478 | 36,6 | 1,1 | 138 672 | 112,3 | 0,0 |
| Ceuta and Mehtla (Spain) | 37 362 | 120,0 | 0,8 | 0 | 0,0 | 0,0 |
| Algeria | 430 413 | 76,3 | 9,3 | 112 907 | 133,1 | 3,2 |
| Tunisia | 24 861 | 20,7 | 0,5 | 3 921 | 209,3 | 0,1 |
| Libya | 253 385 | 61,1 | 5,4 | 7 253 | 15,0 fold | 0,2 |
| Egypt | 730 882 | 74,9 | 15,7 | 544 468 | 214,8 | 15,4 |
| Sudan | 39 865 | 75,2 | 0,9 | 48 911 | 100,4 | 1,4 |
| Spanish Sahara | 21 | 21,0 fold | 0,0 | 0 | 0,0 | 0,0 |
| Mauritania | 3 287 | 71,9 | 0,1 | 89 682 | 143,7 | 2,5 |
| Senegal | 16 733 | 119,5 | 0,4 | 22 263 | 229,5 | 0,6 |
| Gambia | 5 201 | 120,4 | 0,1 | 1 193 | 23,9 fold | 0,0 |
| Republic of Guinea-Bissau | 494 | 457,3 | 0,0 | 0 | 0,0 | 0,0 |
| Guinea | 3 828 | 90,2 | 0,1 | 858 | 289,9 | 0,0 |
| Sierra Leone | 8 316 | 111,4 | 0,2 | 1 261 | 631 fold | 0,0 |
| Liberia | 647 141 | 75,7 | 13,9 | 57 991 | 58,8 | 1,6 |
| Republic of Ivory Coast | 70 839 | 173,7 | 1,5 | 33 416 | 51,4 | 0,9 |
| Ghana | 41 580 | 137,5 | 0,9 | 67 494 | 95,0 | 1,9 |
| Togo | 22 988 | 145,9 | 0,5 | 632 | 57,9 | 0,0 |
| Benin | 25 620 | 189,1 | 0,6 | 974 | 33,6 | 0,0 |
| Mali | 5 028 | 155,5 | 0,1 | 12 | 0,4 | 0,0 |
| Upper Volta | 7 550 | 125,7 | 0,2 | 2 498 | 19,4 | 0,1 |
| Republic of Cape Verde | 859 | 88,5 | 0,0 | 0 | 0,0 | 0,0 |

## TABLE 9.6 *(continued)*

| Region and country | Exports | | | Imports | | |
|---|---|---|---|---|---|---|
| | Export value | Compared with previous year (%) | Share (%) | Import value | Compared with previous year (%) | Share (%) |
| Canarias ls. (Spain) | 106 791 | 125,9 | 2,3 | 54 | 16,7 | 0,0 |
| Nigeria | 342 029 | 76,8 | 7,4 | 5 832 | 83,2 | 0,2 |
| Niger | 9 374 | 118,3 | 0,2 | 3 374 | 90,6 | 0,1 |
| Rwanda | 22 936 | 124,2 | 0,5 | 1 778 | 94,6 | 0,0 |
| Cameroun | 69 720 | 121,0 | 1,5 | 16 889 | 76,3 | 0,5 |
| Chad | 687 | 347,0 | 0,0 | 133 | 3,5 | 0,0 |
| Central Africa | 4 887 | 102,3 | 0,1 | 7 149 | 74,3 | 0,2 |
| Equatorial Guinea Republic | 368 | 142,6 | 0,0 | 0 | - | 0,0 |
| Gabon | 44 660 | 119,2 | 1,0 | 15 546 | 49,0 | 0,4 |
| Congo | 14 720 | 84,1 | 0,3 | 8 271 | 94,8 | 0,2 |
| Zaire | 43 542 | 106,7 | 0,9 | 52 364 | 62,0 | 1,5 |
| Burundi | 7 055 | 74,3 | 0,2 | 1 290 | 14,9 | 0,0 |
| Angola | 45 838 | 216,2 | 1,0 | 1 301 | 154,5 | 0,0 |
| Democratic Republic of Sao Tome and Principle | 175 | 48,9 | 0,0 | 0 | - | 0,0 |
| St Helena and Attached Islands (U.K.) | 24 | 342,9 | 0,0 | 1 359 | 392,8 | 0,0 |
| Ethiopia | 56 791 | 114,5 | 1,2 | 41 402 | 125,2 | 1,2 |
| Republic of Djibouti | 20 012 | 90,6 | 0,4 | 0 | - | 0,0 |
| Somalia | 10 692 | 194,0 | 0,2 | 408 | 87,6 | 0,0 |
| Kenya | 140 052 | 93,1 | 3,0 | 11 030 | 64,9 | 0,3 |
| Uganda | 19 516 | 113,4 | 0,4 | 11 071 | 37,6 | 0,3 |
| Tanzania | 75 695 | 96,7 | 1,6 | 16 680 | 97,7 | 0,5 |
| Seychelles | 4 107 | 79,2 | 0,0 | 676 | 94,2 | 0,0 |
| Mozambique | 11 996 | 103,8 | 0,3 | 14 818 | 104,7 | 0,4 |
| Madagascar | 10 762 | 116,3 | 0,2 | 30 863 | 76,1 | 0,9 |

## TABLE 9.6 *(continued)*

| Region and country | Exports | | | Imports | | |
|---|---|---|---|---|---|---|
| | Export value | Compared with previous year (%) | Share (%) | Import value | Compared with previous year (%) | Share (%) |
| Mauritius | 20 710 | 104,8 | 0,4 | 229 | 23,8 | 0,0 |
| Reunion ls. (Franch) | 15 787 | 103,4 | 0,3 | 41 | 89,1 | 0,0 |
| Zimbabwe | 24 676 | 69,5 | 0,5 | 55 883 | 78,5 | 1,6 |
| Namibia | 543 | 37,7 | 0,0 | 17 926 | 63,7 | 0,5 |
| South Africa | 1 019 915 | 55,4 | 21,9 | 1 843 883 | 114,5 | 52,1 |
| Lesotho | 211 | 6,1 | 0,0 | 33 | 366,7 | 0,0 |
| Malawi | 16 788 | 127,6 | 0,4 | 11 727 | 98,5 | 0,3 |
| Zambia | 60 134 | 173,7 | 1,3 | 222 552 | 110,0 | 6,3 |
| Botswana | 607 | 25,7 | 0,0 | 338 | 268,0 | 0,0 |
| Swaziland | 1 267 | 39,1 | 0,0 | 9 167 | 95,8 | 0,3 |
| British Indian Ocean Territory | 26 | 433,3 | 0,0 | 3 | 2,6 | 0,0 |
| Comores ls. | 415 | 33,8 | 0,0 | 104 | 157,6 | 0,0 |

Source: JETRO. White paper on international trade — Africa (Tokyo: JETRO, 1986), pp. 364-365 — Table III.

| | | | |
|---|---|---|---|
| Angola | ↓ | 59,9 | per cent |
| Algeria | ↓ | 45,9 | per cent |
| Nigeria | ↓ | 43,1 | per cent |
| Egypt | ↓ | 23,1 | per cent |
| Libya | ↓ | 22,9 | per cent[302] |

When these reductions are combined with those of the non-oil-producing countries which also experienced a foreign currency squeeze, because of the reduction in the value of exports of primary products (such as copper, iron ore, cocoa, tea, lumber, sisal hemp, and tobacco), the significant decline in Japanese exports becomes evident. The world slump in demands for these products and the latter's reduced prices accounted for African countries' depreciation of their foreign currency reserves. Zambia, Ghana and Uganda, traditional consumers of Japanese goods, reduced their imports of Japanese goods by 35 per cent, 19,3 per cent, and 20,8 per cent respectively over the 1985 figures.

But, on the other hand, Japan increased her exports to the agricultural countries such as Kenya (22,2 % increase), Tanzania (31,5 % increase), Ethiopia (16,4 % increase), Zimbabwe (28,3 % increase), and Sudan (37,1 %).[303] These countries were able to benefit from the lower oil prices and thus they could increase their purchase of Japanese goods because of their lowered oil energy prices. Additionally, other African countries such as Cameroon, Ivory Coast, Morocco, and Canary Islands increased their imports of Japanese goods (respectively 47,3 %, 36,1 %, 10,9 % and 39 %). Both Morocco and the Canaries had enjoyed a hefty fish export to Japan, thus easing their foreign currency situation, but it is also correct to suggest that not all the increases were real price increases owing to the rise in the value of the goods themselves; because most of these increases were actually as a result of increases in dollar-denominated prices as a result of *endaka* − high yen relative to the dollar. Japanese exports to Africa even in 1986 remained rather misleading, nevertheless, because the large burden of African consumption of Japanese goods generally fell to six countries as Table 9.7 clearly shows.

Table 9.6 shows that South Africa (see Chapter 10) was the leading importer of Japanese goods, followed (in that order) by Egypt (12,6 % share), Liberia (10,4 % share), Algeria (5,3 % share), and Libya and Nigeria (4,4 % share each). The value of Africa's 1986 imports of Japanese goods ($4,56 billion) was only a small fraction (2,1 %) of Japan's world-wide exports which amounted to $209,15 billion in 1986. Actually, the 1986 decline was a continuation of that trend referred to earlier which began in 1982:

## TABLE 9.6A
## AFRICA'S RATIO TO JAPAN'S WORLD-WIDE EXPORTS

| | Year | | | | | |
|---|---|---|---|---|---|---|
| | 1981 | 1982 | 1983 | 1984 | 1985 | 1986 |
| Ratio % | 6,6 | 5,0 | 4,1 | 3,7 | 2,6 | 2,1 |

The $4,46 billion African imports of Japan's products in 1986 was even less than half the $10,04 billion figure reached in 1981. Most of these Japanese exports with items greater than 10 per cent were transportation equipment (25,8 %), vessels (15,4 %), electric equipment (14,9 %), metal products (14 %), and machinery (13,3 %). These figures were for 1982. In 1986 the figures were essentially the same except that there was a noticeable decline in vessels (10,3 %) and metal products (8,8 %). On the import side, the ratio of Japan's African imports to Japan's world-wide imports decreased from 1981 until 1984, but in 1985 the share began to increase, and continued also in 1986 as reflected below (Table 9.6B).

## TABLE 9.6B
## AFRICA'S RATIO TO JAPAN'S WORLD-WIDE IMPORTS

| | Year | | | | | |
|---|---|---|---|---|---|---|
| | 1981 | 1982 | 1983 | 1984 | 1985 | 1986 |
| Ratio % | 3,3 | 2,8 | 2,6 | 2,3 | 2,7 | 3,1 |
| Value of imports in dollars | 4,78 bill. | 3,74 | 3,27 | 3,11 | 3,54 | 3,93 |

Item-wise, Japan's African imports in 1986 saw an 81,6 % per cent increase in import of sea-food — squid, octopus and shrimp. Crude oil, on the other hand, declined significantly (by 70 per cent).

## TABLE 9.7
## EXPORTS AND IMPORTS BETWEEN JAPAN AND
## AFRICAN COUNTRIES 1986 *(Unit: $1 000)*

| Countries | Exports | | | Imports | | |
|---|---|---|---|---|---|---|
| | Value | Annual rate (%) | Share (%) | Value | Annual rate (%) | Share (%) |
| Total | 4 456 520 | 95,8 | 100,0 | 3 934 201 | 111,2 | 100,0 |
| Morocco | 56 002 | 110,9 | 1,3 | 177 167 | 127,8 | 4,5 |
| Ceuta and Melilla | 45 499 | 121,8 | 1,0 | 122 | - | 0,0 |
| Algeria | 235 830 | 54,8 | 5,3 | 128 152 | 113,5 | 3,3 |
| Tunisia | 23 685 | 95,3 | 0,5 | 2 370 | 60,4 | 0,1 |
| Libya | 195 298 | 77,1 | 4,4 | 7 878 | 108,6 | 0,2 |
| Egypt | 561 888 | 76,9 | 12,6 | 255 112 | 46,9 | 6,5 |
| Sudan | 54 657 | 137,1 | 1,2 | 42 924 | 87,8 | 1,1 |
| West Sahara | 0 | - | 0,0 | 666 | - | 0,0 |
| Mauritania | 7 027 | 213,8 | 0,2 | 138 013 | 153,9 | 3,5 |
| Senegal | 19 189 | 114,7 | 0,4 | 27 356 | 122,9 | 0,7 |
| Gambia | 4 317 | 83,0 | 0,1 | 8 906 | 746,5 | 0,2 |
| Guinea-Bissau | 549 | 110,0 | 0,0 | 350 | - | 0,0 |
| Guinea | 1 530 | 40,0 | 0,0 | 1 087 | 126,7 | 0,0 |
| Sierra Leone | 8 923 | 107,3 | 0,2 | 62 | 4,9 | 0,0 |
| Liberia | 461 403 | 71,3 | 10,4 | 96 571 | 166,5 | 2,5 |
| Ivory Coast | 96 436 | 136,1 | 2,2 | 43 219 | 129,3 | 1,1 |
| Ghana | 33 549 | 80,7 | 0,8 | 74 050 | 109,7 | 1,9 |
| Togo | 33 817 | 147,1 | 0,8 | 5 174 | 818,7 | 0,1 |
| Benin | 24 081 | 94,0 | 0,5 | 1 251 | 128,4 | 0,0 |
| Mali | 8 523 | 169,5 | 0,2 | 2 659 | 222 | 0,1 |
| Burkina Faso | 14 643 | 193,9 | 0,3 | 2 475 | 99,1 | 0,1 |
| Cape Verde | 931 | 108,4 | 0,0 | 0 | - | 0,0 |
| Canaries I. | 148 701 | 139,2 | 3,3 | 84 353 | - | 2,1 |
| Nigeria | 194 767 | 56,9 | 4,4 | 5 175 | 88,7 | 0,1 |
| Niger | 8 216 | 87,6 | 0,2 | 13 | 0,4 | 0,0 |
| Rwanda | 24 974 | 108,9 | 0,6 | 1 796 | 101,0 | 0,0 |
| Cameroun | 102 674 | 147,3 | 2,3 | 40 878 | 242,0 | 1,0 |
| Chad | 815 | 118,6 | 0,0 | 1 367 | 10,2 (times) | 0,0 |
| Central Africa | 4 883 | 99,9 | 0,1 | 5 425 | 75,9 | 0,1 |
| Equatorial Guinea | 63 | 17,1 | 0,0 | 0 | - | 0,0 |

## TABLE 9.7 *(continued)*

| Countries | Exports | | | Imports | | |
|---|---|---|---|---|---|---|
| | Value | Annual rate (%) | Share (%) | Value | Annual rate (%) | Share (%) |
| Gabon | 40 537 | 90,8 | 0,9 | 16 877 | 102,1 | 0,4 |
| Congo | 18 337 | 124,6 | 0,4 | 5 473 | 66,2 | 0,1 |
| Zaire | 47 324 | 109,8 | 1,1 | 56 126 | 107,2 | 1,4 |
| Burundi | 9 585 | 137,3 | 0,2 | 1 785 | 138,4 | 0,0 |
| Angola | 18 365 | 40,1 | 0,4 | 617 | 47,4 | 0,0 |
| Sao Tome and Principe | 2 532 | 14,5 | 0,1 | 0 | - | 0,0 |
| St. Helena | 25 | 104,2 | 0,0 | 2 390 | 175,9 | 0,1 |
| Ethiopia | 66 099 | 116,4 | 1,5 | 43 567 | 105,2 | 1,1 |
| Djibouti | 20 646 | 103,2 | 0,5 | 49 | - | 0,0 |
| Somalia | 24 757 | 231,5 | 0,6 | 28 | 6,9 | 0,0 |
| Kenya | 171 087 | 122,2 | 3,8 | 13 175 | 119,4 | 0,3 |
| Uganda | 15 464 | 79,2 | 0,3 | 18 426 | 166,4 | 0,5 |
| Tanzania | 99 556 | 131,5 | 2,2 | 22 953 | 137,6 | 0,6 |
| Seychelles | 6 645 | 161,8 | 0,1 | 134 | 19,8 | 0,0 |
| Mozambique | 18 495 | 154,2 | 0,4 | 17 542 | 118,4 | 0,4 |
| Madagascar | 22 209 | 206,4 | 0,5 | 44 490 | 144,2 | 1,1 |
| Mauritius | 34 613 | 167,1 | 0,8 | 1 380 | 602,6 | 0,0 |
| Reunion | 22 875 | 144,9 | 0,5 | 523 | 12,8 | 0,0 |
| Zimbabwe | 31 664 | 128,3 | 0,7 | 61 707 | 110,4 | 1,6 |
| Namibia | 1 870 | 344,4 | 0,0 | 19 626 | 109,5 | 0,5 |
| Lesotho | 317 | 150,2 | 0,0 | 30 | 90,9 | 0,0 |
| Malawi | 11 659 | 69,4 | 0,3 | 15 060 | 128,4 | 0,4 |
| Zambia | 39 117 | 65,0 | 0,9 | 200 662 | 90,2 | 5,1 |
| Botswana | 616 | 101,5 | 0,0 | 157 | 46,4 | 0,0 |
| Swaziland | 1 804 | 142,4 | 0,0 | 8 983 | 98,0 | 0,2 |
| British Territory Indian Sea Region | 1 233 | 47,4 | 0,0 | 0 | 0,0 | 0,0 |
| Comoro | 430 | 103,6 | 0,0 | 164 | 157,7 | 0,0 |

Source:    DJIT No. 234 (1987), pp. 13-14.

In the first six months of 1987 the *value* of Japan's exports to Africa increased by over 40 per cent over the previous year to $2,88 billion, while imports also increased, though only by a slight 1,6 per cent to $2,01 billion. This in turn generated a trade surplus of $0,87 bill. One of the reasons for the Japanese export to Africa rebound in the first six months of 1987 may lie in the economies of the oil-producing countries such as Algeria, Nigeria and Libya creeping back up from the 1986 summer doldrums of $9 per barrel. In 1986, owing to decreasing revenues from oil sales, the oil-producing countries severly restricted imports. The other reason was the large foreign debts of these countries which clearly curtailed further expenditure.

As for the non-oil-producing countries, especially those which produce and export primary products in the agricultural and minerals sectors, the decline in falling prices under the influence of falling oil prices was expected to fall for the 1987 calendar year.[304] But even with an improved African purchasing power, Japanese companies will continue to face difficulties in selling to Africa because of the rapidly growing pressures from the fast industrialising countries — Korea, Taiwan, Singapore, and Hong Kong — in addition to the yen appreciation. But the versatility and ingenuity of Japanese companies should not be underestimated. For example, the huge Marubeni Corporation was itself able to extend credit to Ethiopia and Ghana according to discussions I had with two Marubeni executives.[305] Other companies that deal with Africa (and there are probably over 70) will remain guaranteed of the African contracts as long as Japan continues to provide ODA to African countries.[306] Others, such as NEC, are so heavily wedded to the future — precisely because of the nature of the communications and computer revolution that the NEC is engaged in — that their involvement in Africa can only but grow: "NEC is the only company in the world whose sales rank in the top 10 in each field".[307] Compared with others, Japanese companies in Africa are doing so well that their ingenuity may eventually induce them to scale down competition among themselves in Africa, and intensify it *vis-a-vis* other foreign firms. That is to say they may divide territories among themselves rather than wage suicidal competition against one another.

On the other hand, for Africa to survive, African economies will have to undergo structural reforms, facilitate export expansion by developing new export-intensive industry, and simultaneously reduce their heavy reliance on the exports of primary products. These three adjustment issues are more significant than the African states' continued reliance on foreign aid (see Chapters 5 and 6). African states should thus convert the aid assistance from Japan and the rest of the world, and seek to create new products such as, for example, macadamia nuts (while production was aided by a Japanese joint venture) and papyrus mats from Kenya which are now being exported to Japan.

African economy lacks diversity, and the absence of added value to African commodity production will clearly retard African competitiveness outside of primary products in the international area.

## JAPANESE INVESTMENTS IN AFRICA

By "investments" I refer to "direct investments", by which, to use one analyst's definition, is meant direct buying into the stock ownerships of foreign business enterprises, existing or prospective, or direct monetary loans to them, both for participation in their operations, managerially, technologically or otherwise.[308] Most Japanese corporations in the sixties and early seventies preferred joint ventures with government, or other partners. And because Africa has remained the least favoured of the regions in the geographical distribution of Japan's foreign direct investment,[309] Japanese business firms preferred small investment ventures. In the late 1960s and 1970s Japanese firms preferred joint ventures with African governments or other partners. For instance, because of their preference for small ventures, the seven enterprises the Japanese engaged in Tanzania — which ranged from cashew nut processing to blankets manufactures to off-shore fishing — were no more than $20 million by the middle of 1970. This accounts not only for the small growth rate but also for the fact that Japan's foreign direct investment (FDI) in SSA has been concentrated in a limited number of countries; even then, mining occupies a large share. Although, as Table 9.8 reflects, Japanese investment in Africa, in 1981 for example, had grown by 24,4 % over the previous year, Africa, by then had, attracted only about 2,5 per cent of Japan's overseas investment. By the end of Japan's 1982 tax year, Japan's FDI in Africa had reached $2,5 billion, representing over 920 separate investments since Japan began to invest abroad since 1951, and making up about 4,72 % of Japan's total FDI of some $53 billion.

Even these investments were rather characterised by their uniformity and the limited regions in which they were invested, if Terutomo Ozawa's analysis could be relied upon:

> Japan's investments in Africa are concentrated in resource-rich, relatively underpopulated countries such as *Nigeria* (sic!) and Zaire or in countries developing with relative rapidity such as Kenya and Tanzania — countries that can be used as production bases to serve neighbouring African countries, in light manufactures ...[310]

In the 1980s Japanese firms showed great interest — as they had since the 1970s — in mining investments. After all, in 1982 from the open-cast mining at Mt Nimba in Liberia, Japan took 360 000 tonnes of iron ore.

Between 1951 and 1970 Japan invested the small sum of $92,4 million in Africa. This figure reached $252 million by 1973, $1 399 million by 1980. For the past 25 years, Japanese concerns have been investing in a variety of fields, such as in West Africa. For instance, one year after Nigeria became independent, Afprint was set up with Japanese participation to make textiles. But nearly 30 years later Japanese firms play a leading role in Nigeria's electronic industry. Japan's second largest storage battery maker, Uyasa, beginning in 1985, is making nearly half-a-million batteries annually. The steady cumulative rise of Japan's FDI in Africa then did not reflect the weak commitment of Japanese resolve to invest in Africa, because the mid-70s saw a slight retreat despite the fact that in 1976

Japanese investment reached the record figure of $271,9 million. But this figure was almost halved by 1980, $139 million. The record of

Japan's investment in Africa appears no less bleak in Japan's total overseas investment. In cumulative figure terms, Africa's share stagnated through the past decade (2,5 percent between 1951 and 1971, 3,1 percent up to 1975 and 4,0 percent to 1980)[311]

TABLE 9.8

1951-1981: JAPAN'S TOTAL FDI

| FY | FDI (Millions $) | Cumulative value (Millions $) | Growth rate (%) |
|---|---|---|---|
| 1951-1961 | 447 | 447 | |
| 1962 | 98 | 545 | 21,8 |
| 1963 | 126 | 671 | 23,1 |
| 1964 | 119 | 790 | 17,7 |
| 1965 | 159 | 949 | 20,1 |
| 1966 | 227 | 1 176 | 23,9 |
| 1967 | 275 | 1 451 | 23,4 |
| 1968 | 557 | 2 008 | 38,4 |
| 1969 | 665 | 2 673 | 33,1 |
| 1970 | 904 | 3 577 | 33,8 |
| 1971 | 858 | 4 435 | 24,0 |
| 1972 | 2 338 | 6 773 | 52,7 |
| 1973 | 3 494 | 10 267 | 51,6 |
| 1974 | 2 396 | 12 663 | 23,3 |
| 1975 | 3 280 | 15 943 | 25,9 |
| 1976 | 3 462 | 19 405 | 21,7 |
| 1977 | 2 806 | 22 211 | 14,5 |
| 1978 | 4 598 | 26 809 | 20,7 |
| 1979 | 4 995 | 31 804 | 18,6 |
| 1980 | 4 693 | 36 497 | 14,8 |
| 1981 | 8 906 | 45 403 | 24,4 |

Source:   Terutomo Ozawa, *Multinationalism, Japanese Style* p. 12 (1951-1977); MITI, DOI (annual).

In the industrial sectors Japan had invested more in mineral extraction. In the two decades between 1951 and 1971 Japan placed 63,4 per cent of her African capital investments into this sector. But this figure fell, leading to the cumulative capital in this sector to just about half of Japan's total investment in Africa. The manufacturing similarly declined. Only the service-commerce sector attracted more attention from Japanese investors. By the number of cases of Japan's FDI in Africa in 1979, mining had 82, fishery 57, textiles 44, food stuffs 28, iron, steel, non-ferrous metals 19, real estate 15, and others 283. The grand total of cases was 592, amounting to $1,1 billion, (see Table 9.8A: "Direct Investments to the End of March 1979").

Some analysts hold that Japanese investments in Africa will not rise because

> Africa is viewed in Japan as a bad risk. Another is that Japan has had no long-standing relationship with Africa, as it has had with Asia, Europe, or the US. Japanese firms know little about Africa and the Japanese do not like to invest in a place they know little about. In fact Japanese firms just do not like to invest abroad.[312]

Although the figures do agree with this analysis — total Japanese FDI in 1983 in Africa stood at $2,57 billion, accounting for a mere 4,7 % of Japan's total world foreign investment,[313] — sectorially, however, Africa occupied, comparatively, a large share of Japanese foreign investment services, transportation, and mining, and a small share in manufacturing. In any event, were African industrialization to reach the take-off stage, Japanese investments in Africa would soar to new heights. In fact Japan today has invested more in Africa than Europe had in Japan in 1913, at a time when Japan needed capital desperately to prepare her world-wide activities that began with the Anglo-Japanese Treaty (1902), Russo-Japanese War (1904-1905), and culminated in World War II. In fact 85 per cent of foreign borrowing was done by the Japanese Government and was not related to industrial development, but it financed the Russo-Japanese War.[314]

## TABLE 9.8A
## DIRECT INVESTMENTS TO THE END OF MARCH 1979
*(Unit: $ million)*

| Category | Cases | Total amount invested | Constituent ratio |
|---|---|---|---|
| **Manufacturing industries** | | | |
| Textiles | 44 | 34 | 3,0 % |
| Foodstuffs | 28 | 8 | 0,7 % |
| Iron, nonferrous metals | 19 | 17 | 1,5 % |
| Electrical equipment | 5 | 4 | 0,4 % |
| Chemicals | 5 | 13 | 1,1 % |
| Others | 10 | 4 | 0,4 % |
| Subtotal | 111 | 80 | 7,0 % |
| **Other industries** | | | |
| Mining | 82 | 442 | 38,8 % |
| Fisheries | 57 | 38 | 3,3 % |
| Commerce | 15 | 1 | 0,1 % |
| Financing, insurance | 10 | 2 | 0,2 % |
| Agriculture, forestry | 9 | 6 | 0,5 % |
| Others | 283 | 566 | 49,7 % |
| **Real estate** | 15 | 2 | 0,2 % |
| **Branch offices** | 10 | 1 | 0,1 % |
| **Total** | 592 | 1 138 | - |

In Africa, Japanese investments are simply awaiting a favourable climate to take off. Zaire, Nigeria, Zambia, and Niger, rich in copper and uranium, and Liberia, enjoy the largest share of Japanese investment. (See Table 9.9.) Much of the investment in Liberia, with shipping pre-eminent, in which, by 1982, $1,7 billion went into 483 ventures clearly led Japanese FDI in Africa. Nigeria's 83 ventures which absorbed $156 million (1982 dollar-value) was next. But it is Zaire which, in cash terms, came second to Liberia in 1982 dollar figures ($267 million). The specialised unique trading companies, such as Mitsui, provide commercial and industrial development assistance to African states. Moreover, Africa is still

305

ahead of the Middle East in terms of Japanese FDI, and the situation (in that region) is not likely to improve, especially with the "bath" that the Japanese firms took with the coming of the Islamic Revolution in Iran.

The fact is, however, that the number of Japanese joint ventures — and Japanese corporations prefer joint venturing in Africa more than in any other form of investment — have not been increasing greatly in recent years. This does not mitigate the fact that those ventures already on the continent are performing as well as can be expected (e.g. Sanyo Electric, Toyota Motor Co., Marubeni, Suzuki, Taisei Corporation, Ishika-wajima-Harima Heavy Industries, etc.). In fact the Japanese companies already in Africa are doing so well that in other regions they have almost eliminated non-Japanese competition, as the remarks of a Toyota Motor Company executive in Africa suggested.[315]

In 1980 Mitsubishi Petroleum Development Company began commercial production of crude oil in Gabon, nearly 15 years after

TABLE 9.9

JAPAN'S FOREIGN DIRECT INVESTMENT IN AFRICA

FY 1981-FY1985* *(in millions of dollars)*

|  | FY 1981 | FY 1982 | FY 1983 | FY 1984 | FY 1985 | Cumulative 31 March 1986 |
|---|---|---|---|---|---|---|
| Total | 573 | 489 | 364 | 326 | 172 | 3 369 |
| Liberia | 466 | 434 | 323 | 281 | 159 | 2 455 |
| Zaire | 12 | 11 | 15 | 15 | - | 282 |
| Nigeria | 1 | 2 | 1 | 0 | - | 157 |
| Zambia | 55 | 20 | - | 22 | - | 142 |
| Others | 39 | 22 | 24 | 23 | 13 | 333 |

\*   Countries not listed by name have less than $100 million in cumulative investments.

Source:   Ministry of Finance.

Japan's 10 major spinning companies had constructed spinning mills at Kaduna in Northern Nigeria in a joint operation with the Northern Nigerian Development and North Nigerian Investment Companies (both agencies of the Nigerian government).[316] Mitsui (like the many Japanese companies that have Africa operations)[317] has been active in Africa since the early sixties in countries ranging from Rhodesia to South Africa and Cameroon.

Total accumulated figures invested in Africa by Japan are puny, of course, when compared with the entire accumulated total of Japanese direct investments abroad during 35 years — from FY 1951 when Japan's post-war economic recovery expansion began through FY 1986 — which is approximately $106 billion. Japan's FDI increased so dramatically in FY 1985 and FY 1986 that the combined total of $34,5 billion was nearly equal to the past 30 years (fiscal 1951-1980) total of $36,5 billion.

Having said that Japan preferred small investment ventures does not mean that she now eschews all large-scale investment projects. Trading companies, however, have begun to play a crucial role. These companies have now introduced off-shore trading in their portfolios. Mitsui, Nichimen, Marubeni, Nisho-Iwai, Kanematsu-Gosho, Tomen, Mitsubishi, Sumitomo, etc. have since acquired capabilities of arranging transactions to the extent that they have become global business organisers. Japanese FDI has helped in the exploitation of minerals such as oil and uranium. The International Resources Corporation (IRC) of Japan resumed prospecting for uranium ore in Niger. The IRC has carried over 60 drill holes in the Air district of south-western Niger, and continued prospecting until the end of 1988.[318] It is perhaps necessary to illustrate Japanese investments in Africa by looking at a "typically big" investment.

One of the classic "big" Japanese investments in Africa is the Suzuki Motor Company's joint small truck and wagon production venture with an Egyptian company in Egypt. This venture was launched jointly with Modern Motors Ltd. of Egypt to start production of small trucks and wagons during 1988. A joint corporation was set up in Egypt at a starting capital of one billion yen (in Japanese currency terms) with Suziki Motor putting up

20 % and Modern Motor 80 % of that capital.[319] Suzuki Motor's venture is a second Japanese industrial attempt of the kind in Egypt, where General Motors and Isuzu Motors, Suzuki Motors' close allies, are already jointly manufacturing small trucks. In a rather shameless manner Suzuki hoped that its venture with Modern Motors would be developed into "a springboard for our future advances into many South African markets". In any event, on-site production in Egypt is essential for any foreign motor industry wishing to develop markets in and around Egypt because Cairo, since January 1985, has been banning imports of completed automobiles for a variety of reasons, including foreign exchange shortage.

**CONCLUSION**

That Japan has become not only a quantity factor in African perceptions but also a quality factor may be expressed by the words of a prominent African Japanophile:

> When you compare a Japanese car with one from the US and one from Britain, the Japanese car is so much cheaper and performs so much better ... The Japanese obviously see Africa as a good opportunity — as a good market.[320]

Especially coming from a cabinet official this is a clear testimony that Japan's image in African eyes had finally been transformed from that European-propagated image which, in the 1950s, equated anything "made-in-Japan" with "poor quality". Growing up in Africa in the late 50s "made in Japan" was a sound equated with just about the most inferior quality one can imagine.

Japanese economic development, however, had defied conventional wisdom since the Meiji Era. Indeed, Meiji Japan is a classic case of a system having rebutted Marxist historical materialism and confirmed Ghana's founding president, Kwame Nkrumah's dictum: "Seek ye first the political kingdom and all other kingdoms shall be added unto you". As we saw in Chapter 2 the *samurai*, when feudalism began to decay, and when the *black ships* of US Commodore Perry and company began to menace Fukabori, Edo,

Kyoto, Nagasaki, Kobe, etc., the *samurai* and *daimyos* launched a *political* response which triggered *economic* changes. Since Japanese capitalism in the 1800s was at an incipient stage, this is yet further proof that the African economy, if it is to follow the Japanese model, needs a strong political leadership, first and foremost, and with a clear vision, policy and commitment. In the decade of the 1890s a turning point was reached in the evolution of the Japanese economy. With the state leading the way in terms of policy and leadership, the assimilation of machine technology, the accumulation of banking and industrial capital, the expansive influences of world prosperity and rising prices — all conspired to catapult the rapid rise of industrial output in *Dai Nippon*.

The above therefore leads to the question of not what but *how* can Africa learn the Japanese model as fast as possible? Probably this is merely one of the "secrets" that Professor William D. Perdue suggests in his correspondence, although he believes "that one secret to the Japanese economic revolution ... is that *many do not believe there are contradictions! In other words, opposing conceptions are simply synthesized".[321] It is this belief of the absence of contradictions that had propelled Japan to simultaneously wade deep in the mire of the *apartheid* economy on the one hand, and the African economy on the other. But there is of course that other persuasive but dated reason advanced by then Secretary-General of Japanese Association of Africanists, Professor Iwao Kobori of Tokyo University: "Unfortunately, Japan's interest in Africa is mainly as a place to exploit for raw materials."[322] But if this is Japan's interest, what then is *Africa's?* Japan is the only economic power known to this writer which has risen to eminence without having been an innovator, but rather by catching up. Conscious of her dependency for natural resources and primary products, Japan became an international state by recognising one ineluctable law of a developed world: that is, in such an environment one pursues a multinational strategy.[323] It is for this reason that the transition from the post-traditional to the post-industrial had been so rapid in Japan as to seem to have virtually been non-existent. Japan simply

309

borrowed technology — not finance capital, not cultural values, not the work-ethic, not labour, but simply technology without strings. Hence her independence, despite the massive military defeat she suffered in 1945.

## CHAPTER 10

# THE JAPAN-SOUTH AFRICA CONNECTION

---

*Japan is a major source of advanced technology for South Africa, both from production under licence from Japanese corporations and direct sale ...*
John Ravenhill, "Japan and Africa"[324]

*But the Japanese have recently been promoted to the special status of honorary whites! Ponder that ... the Japanese (are) too strong to be conquered, plundered and despised, and who therefore must be wooed if South Africa is to profit from dealing with them ...*
Chinweizu, The West and The Rest of US[325]

*Japan recognises South Africa "diplomatically", but does not maintain an embassy, but uses a consulate general instead ...*
Edward Olsen, "Japan/Africa"[326]

*Japan finds the racial discrimination in the RSA intolerable and takes the firm position that it must be abolished totally and without delay ... Japan deplores the present situation in South Africa ... (Therefore) ... Japan believes that there is an urgent need for the government of the RSA to clearly state in no uncertain terms that it intends to disband apartheid and to enter unconditionally into discussions with the leaders of the Black community on specific steps toward ending apartheid.*
Foreign Minister Shintaro Abe,
40th Session, UN Gen. Assembly, (1985)

*What can one make of a situation in which Japanese businessmen play golf at white clubs in South Africa ... and at the same time are courted by black socialist leaders elsewhere in the continent ...?*
Don Shannon, "Japan in Africa ..."[327]

*... the issue of a balanced and better relationship between South Africa and Japan has become of prime importance.*
Japanese Ambassador to South Africa, Masatoshi Ohta (1992)

## INTRODUCTION

In 1988 and 1989 Japan was South Africa's largest trading partner; and South Africa Japan's largest African trading partner, and their two-way annual trade was in billions of dollars. But under the "guidance" of MOFA and MITI, trading companies had begun to scale down their trade with South Africa, and it began to fall in 1988. In 1990 and 1991 it fell to 3,3 billion dollars, which was a decrease of some 20 per cent. Although in 1991 South Africa's share in Japan's total trade was only 0,6 per cent, and only 0,5 per cent as far as Japan's total export was concerned, this total trade in 1992 — export and import — was a whopping 41,2 billion dollars. In Japanese terms this was miniscule, but in South Africa's terms it was huge. How did this situation arise? And why did this not detract from Japan's relations with the rest of Black Africa? Moreover, did African states have a legitimate basis to criticise Japan's economic ties with the erstwhile *apartheid* economy, regardless of her sanctions against the RSA? What of African states' trade with South Africa? But first, how did Japan begin to get herself in this mess of being the number one trading partner of apartheid South Africa?

Japan is now a core, a world economy, and having largely supplanted the US in major sections of international trade, her trade with South Africa was bound to increase and elevate the tensions attendant on trading with the apartheid economy, had the De Klerk Government *not* changed course in 1990. Regarding trade with the RSA, Japan is of course one of the major world players — the others include such nations at the US, UK, West Germany, Taiwan, Turkey, Italy, Spain, and Switzerland. When the nearly 50 African states were included, this conclave of conniving hypocrites was certainly large enough to diffuse the impact of sanctions against the then apartheid regime. Thus, prior to 1990, it was impossible to view Japan *vis-a-vis* South Africa in isolation, either in trade or in her attitudes towards blacks. For both have largely been influenced by colonial and/or conservative Western (Euro-American) views of and behaviour towards blacks. Still, as we have already seen, Japan's view of Africans is relatively innocuous compared with that of most

312

major Western nations. Her ties to the RSA, nevertheless, remained problematic and this continued to detract from her image as an international state, despite the number of sanctions she imposed on South Africa. These sanctions were as follows:

1969:   Ban on direct investment

1974:   Ban on loans with a maturity of six months or more

1985:   Ban on exports of computers and 4-wheel drive vehicles to apartheid-enforcement agencies (e.g. South African police)

1986:   Ban on imports of pig iron

Ban on issuance of tourist visas for South Africans

Ban on sports and cultural exchanges

It did, in fact, increase the perception of some nations of Japan as a rapacious, racist, chauvinist state. Japan's major contributions to the African world in consequence became distorted, and she suffered from an image of a xenophobic "economic animal" governed by that pathological egoism once characterized by a German scholar as "backward orientalism".

"Economic animals" in both Japan and South Africa had long contrived to tie the knot of trade tighter, despite the Japanese Government's skittishness about it. Indeed, in Japan, members of the Japan-South Africa Parliamentarians' Friendship League (JSAPF League), fully committed to strengthening bonds with South Africa, continued calling for the need to protect Japanese industries by restoring full diplomatic and economic ties, since these were severed on account of the apartheid regime's then intransigence. Members of the JSAPF League did in fact give South Africa's foreign minister, Roelof "Pik" Botha, a warm welcome when he visited Japan in 1986. The JSAPF League is composed of businessmen as well as more than 40 members of the ruling LDP, including the then Prime Minister, Noboru Takeshita. Japan-South Africa ties were growing, regardless of the noble sentiments expressed (above) by then Foreign Minister Shintaro Abe. So in view of the Abe sentiments, why in the late 1980s was Japan the leading trading partner of South Africa? Of course, until 1986 the Japanese Government did not intervene in trade affairs because the United Nations resolutions calling for sanctions were adopted only by the General Assembly, meaning that they were not mandatory. Still there is a lot of history between Japan and South Africa, some of it not so salubrious.

As the South African Boers (white Afrikaners) and the British imperialists were battling each other (during the Anglo-Boer War of 1899-1902) as to who had the right to exercise suzerainty over the black man in South Africa and expropriate his land, the Japanese Meiji Government began to initiate its interest in South Africa. During the Japanese Imperial Army's preparations for the Russian Czarist Army in 1904-1905, Tokyo became interested in Boer military tactics that were demonstrated in the course of the Anglo-Boer War. Consequently, Japan sent its captain, Hachiro Hiraoka, to South Africa on a study tour. This was only one of several reasons for the beginning of Japanese interest in South Africa, which has continued to date, albeit made more complex by the dynamism of the trade factor which ultimately gave rise to the two strange bed-fellows.

The other reason, similar to that of the Dutch East India Company's interest in the 17th century, was Japan's interest in Cape Town as a half-way station for refuelling and supplies for Japanese ships ferrying immigrants to Brazil. Actually, the Dutch East India Company made it possible for the first contacts between Japan and South Africa (what was then known as the Cape of Good Hope). That is, before coming to South Africa in April 1652, Jan van Riebeeck was stationed in Nagasaki in Western Japan in 1647 and 1648, after which he sailed for Table Bay (Cape Town). The importance of Cape Town has been established since then for Japanese to take advantage of it. Cape Town had become important because after Japanese emigrants' movement from the Hawaii islands to the US had become significantly large, the so-called

Gentleman's Agreement led Japan to restrict Japanese emigration to the US. It thus became necessary for alternative sites to be sought.

Moreover, in 1922 the US Supreme Court eventually decided that Japanese were ineligible for citizenship, and two years later, the Quota Immigration Act was passed, containing a clause denying the right of entry into the US for permanent residence of any person not eligible for citizenship. In any event, Japan had discovered the Brazilian solution. In 1908 Japanese ships began to sail between Japan and Brazil via Cape Town. Consequently, on 5 April 1910, the Meiji Government in Tokyo appointed Ieppe Julius, a white resident of Cape Town, as its honorary consul. Nearly two months later, what came to be known as the Union of South Africa (1910-1961) was formed on 31 May 1910. A year after the Union of South Africa was accorded the status of a dominion (1 July 1910), Japan formally entered the world arena of politics with the revision of unequal treaties with Western powers — as we have already seen in Chapter 2. That is, in 1911 Japan recovered her tariff autonomy. Having now tamed Formosa (1895), pacified Russia (1904-1905), subdued Korea (1911), and placed Euro-American imperialists in East Asia on notice, Japan began to increase her long-distance contacts with Africa, as I have extensively detailed already.

In the year of transition (i.e. 1912, from the Meiji to the Taisho Period) Japanese trade with South Africa was middling, and continued hovering on piddling levels till boosted by World War I, and finally busted by World War II, (Table 10.1). (South Africa had declared war on Japan on 8 December 1941, one day after the latter almost levelled Pearl Harbor). As World War I was raging on, Japan and South Africa were not only becoming leading economic powers in their respective regions, they were inching ever more towards each other. For instance, Japan's first economic mission to Africa in 1916 included the Union of South Africa, during which tour two Japanese businessmen who accompanied the Fact-Finding Mission were denied entry to Cape Town, because they were classified under the "prohibited immigrant" category, since the Immigration Act of 1913 not only excluded Asian immigrants from South Africa, it prevented Japanese also from expanding commerce

315

and trade. It was only after the Japanese Consul (i.e. the white South African, Acting Honorary Consul Johnson) had "guaranteed" them, and after they had paid a 10 pound sterling deposit, that they finally were permitted a 10-day visa, subsequently extended for six months, though only after further haggling.

## TABLE 10.1
## TRADE WITH SOUTH AFRICA 1912-1942
### *(Unit = 1 000 yen)*

| Year | Exports | Imports | Year | Exports | Imports |
|------|---------|---------|------|---------|---------|
| 1912 | 454 | 0 | 1928 | 11 695 | 1 341 |
| 1913 | 475 | 46 | 1929 | 13 179 | 1 448 |
| 1914 | 493 | 0 | 1930 | 14 196 | 1 618 |
| 1915 | 1 000 | 0 | 1931 | 19 283 | 1 333 |
| 1916 | 4 276 | 7 | 1932 | 16 418 | 2 636 |
| 1917 | 6 788 | 18 852 | 1933 | 26 741 | 4 313 |
| 1918 | 18 343 | 29 449 | 1934 | 29 540 | 8 234 |
| 1919 | 8 195 | 37 164 | 1935 | 32 769 | 4 762 |
| 1920 | 8 206 | 73 895 | 1936 | 41 534 | 22 561 |
| 1921 | 3 851 | 2 865 | 1937 | 53 749 | 88 852 |
| 1922 | 4 820 | 3 778 | 1938 | 35 291 | 1 810 |
| 1923 | 4 749 | 665 | 1939 | 16 802 | 9 486 |
| 1924 | 4 764 | 991 | 1940 | 61 366 | 25 197 |
| 1925 | 9 539 | 1 325 | 1941 | 24 545 | 13 915 |
| 1926 | 10 741 | 917 | 1942 | 0 | 0 |
| 1927 | 11 640 | 1 082 | | | |

Source:     Adapted from Morikawa (1985), p. 41.

One year after this Mission's visit, two-way trade between Japan and South Africa topped 35 000 000 yen for the first time.[328] Two years after the mission's visit, Japan opened her first consulate in Africa, and it was established at Cape Town on 14 August 1918. Eight years later the OSK Line linked Kobe (Japan), Mombasa (East Africa) and Durban (South Africa).

During World War I Germany was expelled from the South African market, and was immediately supplanted by Japan, according to Japanese government documents of the World War I period. But at the end of the War, Britain, France, and Germany resumed their economic activities, and this led to a decline in Japan-South Africa trade, with the trade imbalance in Japan's favour (Table 10.1). By 1930 Japan was importing a lot of wool from South Africa, and thus the Empire of the Rising Sun had come to economically "bail out" the whitest part of the Black Continent.

South Africa needed to acquire new markets for her various products, wool being the chief of these. This led to the agreement between the acting Japanese Consul in Cape Town and the acting South African Vice-Minister for Foreign Affairs to exclude Japanese from the prohibited immigrant category. Japanese merchants, clerks, and tourists were thus given the freedom to enter South Africa without restriction, to receive the same treatment in housing as whites, and to carry out economic activities without the political, administrative, and social hindrances faced by other Asians. This was the origin of the "honorary white" status which was held for over half a century (not just since 1961, as most Japanese generally assume)[329]. It was in 1961, however, that the RSA government conferred the status of "honorary whites" upon all Japanese who came to the RSA. But South Africa, like the US, Australia, New Zealand and Canada nevertheless provided, by various devices and stratagems, for the exclusion of Japanese. The situation regarding anti-Japanese sentiment in the 1930s was such that a Japanese nationalist passionately and bitterly complained:

We are like a great crowd of people packed into a small and narrow room, and there are only three doors through which we might escape, namely emigration, advance into world markets, and expansion of territory. The first door, emigration, has been barred to us by the anti-Japanese immigration policies of other countries ... (W)e are looking for some place overseas where Japanese capital, Japanese

317

skills and Japanese labor can have free play, free from the oppression of the white race.[330]

Kingoro went on to condemn the whites in India, Australia and South Africa. Between 1924 and 1932, nevertheless, Japanese emigration to South Africa showed a net gain of only two, compared with Chinese net gain of 345, both of which were far less than the Indian net gain of 12 868.[331]

Indeed, between 1931 and 1936, Japanese in other parts of South Africa, such as the Transvaal, were encountering, like other Asians (let alone Africans), discriminatory practices to the extent that the Tokyo-based Foreign Association observed:

> The authorities of the Transvaal in South Africa having prohibited the residence of Coloured races in the gold producing district including Johannesburg, the capital of the Transvaal (sic), and having refused to permit Coloured races to engage in wholesale business which is closely related to the export and import trade, Mr Ohta, Japanese Consul at Cape Town, endeavoured to have the unjustified regulation revised and the Japanese claims were accepted by the authorities in their entirety on 15 June 1936, the Parliament of South Africa passing a bill dividing the said regulations, and settling the question.[332]

The question was, of course, not settled. At this time Japan was exporting to South Africa textile goods such as knitted materials, silk tissues, silk handkerchiefs, cotton tissues, etc. The flourishing commerce between the two created a paradox: as Japanese were being accorded the "honorary white" status and simultaneously discriminated against in the gold and diamond complexes (i.e. the Transvaal and the Orange Free State provinces respectively), a new development was taking place nevertheless. Japan's dispute with Australia over wool merely increased South Africa's importance as a wool supplier. This in turn led to the opening of the Japanese legation in Pretoria in October 1937. Four years later, however, South Africa declared war against Japan. In 1948, the year the *apartheid* regime came to power in South Africa, Japan resumed her trade relations with South Africa. At the Canberra Conference after the war, South Africa had played a significant role in restoring Japan to the international arena. On 8 September 1951 South Africa was one of the 49 San Francisco Peace Treaty signatories. In November 1952 the Japanese opened their consulate-general in Pretoria, the year of South Africa's people's greatest defiance campaign against *apartheid*, courtesy of the African National Congress and the allied Congress Movement.

Japan has highly sophisticated diplomacy (Chapter 3), yet she has historically lacked sensitivity when dealing with *apartheid* South Africa. One analyst was constrained to make the pungent observation that

> Japan was not particularly responsive to black appeals for support against racism. The Japanese were 'yellow' people following gray policies in a gray area between sharply defined black-white alternatives. Japanese attitudes toward racism are schizophrenic.[333]

Such criticism has fuelled charges, sometimes unfairly so, that Japan was not concerned with the plight of blacks, though such a view is no longer credible today despite some occasionally inconsiderate and myopic statements by Japanese political leaders*, and commercial activities by one or two business companies in Japan. Consequently, the Japanese anti-*apartheid* movement became one of the harshest critics of official Japanese attitude towards South Africa, as well as towards black Africans. (I shall deal with this charge in a moment.)

Twenty days before the first anniversary of the "Sharpeville Massacre" in South Africa, Japan and the latter announced their intention to establish diplomatic relations as soon as the necessary procedural issues by each country were completed.[334] During the

---

* During March 1993, for example, a Japanese local legislator, Masao Kokubo, told fellow legislators: "When you shake hands with someone who is completely Black, you feel your hands getting black." (See also Chapter 3.)

same year (1961) her exports to South Africa, although less than those of 1960, amounted (f.o.b.) to $79 million.[335] But before dealing with this Japan-South Africa issue in detail, African states' past complicity in the South Africa *apartheid* trade traffic is no less imperative, particularly as we have already seen that African states were rather vocal about Japan's and the West's ties to South Africa. Japan's trade, like *all* Western trade, with South Africa had serious implications, *yet what about the African states themselves?* Why did they demand of Japan what they themselves were unwilling to conform to; eager to contravene with impunity? Were the Japan-South Africa trade links *qualitatively* different from the African-South Africa commercial traffic? Japan's aggressive commercial linkages with the *apartheid* economy notwithstanding, Africa's clandestine trade and commercial dealings with the same *apartheid* economy was certainly more regrettable, given that Africans should themselves have retained the moral high ground re RSA, for whatever it was worth. A perspective on the Japan-South Africa ties is provided by the obtuse angle in the triangle Japan-Africa-RSA. Thus, in no way was it a diminution of the seriousness of Japan's relationship with the *apartheid* economy. It was merely one of the complex spokes in the evil wheel of the past *apartheid* dimension.

## AFRICAN TRADE WITH APARTHEID

There is an invisible but definite Black Africa movement on the continent from North to South to the once citadel of one of the most pernicious forms of racism. It was not only labourers — such as mineworkers and farmhands from Mozambique, Lesotho, Zimbabwe, Malawi, etc. — who flocked to South Africa; it was also academic figures, intellectuals, from as far afield as Ghana, Zaire, Nigeria, Uganda, Kenya, Sierra Leone, etc., who flocked to seek employment in and were in turn accepted by South Africa's *apartheid* universities.[336]

A more significant involvement, however, was that of African *states* themselves (or their parastatals) which not only sought trade with South Africa, but were reportedly involved in various aspects of science, technology and business information. These institutions were involved with their counterparts in the RSA, in obvious contravention not only of UN resolutions, but of their own OAU declaration, as well as their much touted national rhetoric against *apartheid.* Naturally, such activities tended to detract from the seriousness with which the Japan-RSA links were looked at. On the other hand, however, Africa, through the OAU, and in certain cases through individual states, had continued to provide material and moral support to the "Liberation Movement" in the RSA and Namibia.

There was, nonetheless, the brutal embrace of *apartheid* in the form of regional economic "cooperation" in Southern Africa, especially with hapless states like Botswana, Lesotho and Swaziland. These BLS countries seemed to have had no choice, but to wriggle inside the belly of the *apartheid* beast. Despite the fact that the South African Government kept a tight lid on figures and items of trade with African states (just like MITI, South Africa hid the *true* trade figures and items between her and Japan for a long time), my analysis on this issue, nevertheless, was based on reliable sources and research in African states, Europe, Asia and the US. There was the well-known trade linkage that South Africa had with the SADCC countries. It should be recalled that the purpose for SADCC's existence was to reduce economic dependency on South Africa because of her *apartheid* policies and practice, and increase African interdependence. Yet South Africa maintained trade missions with *five* of the nine SADCC countries. Her investments in *seven* of the nine played a significant role in the economies of these states. Ironically, between 1985 and 1987, SADCC countries received tens of millions of dollars from Japan as part of a programme of securing the SADCC nine a self-reliance strategy of economic survival against the *apartheid* juggernaut. This figure was in addition to the traditional ODA aid detailed in Chapter 5. In 1987 Zambia was pledged $20 million, Tanzania $15 million, Zimbabwe and Malawi (two other SADCC countries) were also provided in 1987 with additional grant aid type, according to government documents in MOFA. All these merely suggests that while African states were receiving Japanese aid, they correctly but hypocritically complained against the Japan-South Africa trade ties, while they themselves had their own economic pipeline to the RSA. (The charge by Shannon, above, that African socialist regimes were wooing Japan while the latter was going to bed with the *apartheid* Caesar is less a *non sequitur* than the African states' erstwhile trading with the *apartheid* Republic. All African states should ideally have upgraded much of their economies so as to be able to trade with Japan in order to help pry her loose from South Africa. But they were unwilling or unable to do this. More about this later.)

South Africa's trade mission in Mozambique was one of the most active, since Mozambique had close economic ties with South Africa, even outside the area of the mineworkers in the Vaal-Reef complex. South Africa exported a wide range of goods to Mozambique, and because of the credit-worthiness of Mozambique with South African trading and financial houses, her importers enjoyed hefty open credit lines from South African banks and traders. South Africa also sold Mozambique electricity, even as South Africa was busy rebuilding power lines (which she herself had helped destroy) in Mozambique so that she could import electricity from the huge Cabora Bassa hydroelectric facility on the Zambezi River. Similarly, the giant state-owned power utility company, Eskom/Escom, was, during February 1988, engaged in negotiations for power projects in several of the SADCC countries — such as Botswana, Malawi, and Swaziland. More importantly however, even as Mozambique had accused South Africa of having "sabotaged" her aeroplane which crashed, killing Mozambique's founding president, Samora Machel, it was South Africa which maintained the Maputo Government's fleet of commercial airlines! Service and maintenance of these airlines was provided in South Africa, at the Jan Smuts International Airport. In the meantime however, African rhetoric against the apartheid regime was at full blast, including that against the Japan-South Africa ties.

Many other African countries — such as Zimbabwe, Zambia, Tanzania, Guinea, Zaire, Gabon, Uganda, Botswana, Sao Tome and Principe, Ivory Coast, Malawi, Nigeria, Morocco, Swaziland,

322

Lesotho, Kenya, Somali, etc. — had increasing and incontrovertible trade links with South Africa, long before February 1990. In fact, trade between the SSA and the RSA was growing to the extent that only two African countries, Guinea Bissau, and Libya, should be exempted from the list of African countries which traded with South Africa. Other neighbouring states — Lesotho, Botswana, Swaziland and Zimbabwe — may have of course argued the "no-choice" logic, the "belly-in-the-beast" argument, as I have just indicated. Regardless, South Africa had a trade mission in Zimbabwe, even as President Robert Mugabe correctly thundered on the need for more sanctions against South Africa. The problem with this RSA-Zimbabwe trade, however, was that it was not confined to the "essential" items that Zimbabwe was constrained to buy, but, rather, it included also non-essentials, such as alcoholic beverages: e.g. the popular South African Lion Lager beer which is consumed in large quantities in Zimbabwe from Bulawayo to Harare. If there ever was a good cause to distance a nation from the intoxicating effect of *apartheid*, Lion Lager beer should have been the first to be removed from the Zimbabwe beer stalls and stores.

In fact, if we exclude trade figures with the BLS countries — i.e. Botswana, Lesotho and Swaziland — with which South Africa had an official customs arrangement, her 1986 two-way trade with the OAU member states amounted to more than $1,5 billion. A feature of these growing economic ties between South Africa and the African countries was the factor of West Africa.

States such as Senegal, Sierra Leone, Sao Tome and Principe, Liberia, Nigeria, Ghana, Guinea, Gabon and Ivory Coast played a critical emerging role — the latter three were, in the late 1980s, engaged in arrangements to host industrial and agricultural development projects by South Africa. Agricultural trade, especially, was growing between the *apartheid* economy and the SSA during the 1980s. Apart from maize (which is the staple food throughout the SADCC as well as many other countries to the north) and wheat, smaller quantities of barley, oats, millet, buckwheat and sorghum were also exported by the RSA to the SSA. Other foodstuffs also played a role. For instance in 1983/1984,

545 679 (15 kg units) of table potatoes and 45 647 bags of seed potatoes were exported to African states, while 179 tons of factory-made cheese and 682 tons of factory-made butter were purchased by African countries in the same year. South Africa also shipped fresh fruit to West Africa and rice or fruits canned as well as fresh fruit to Central Africa.[337] By 1983 the RSA was supplying 18 per cent of Africa's wheat imports and as much as 36 per cent of its maize imports. In 1979/1980 South Africa shipped 250 000 tons of maize to Zambia, 150 000 tons to Mozambique, and 128 000 tons to Kenya — for a total of 528 000 tons. Other equally large amounts were shipped to Malawi, Mauritius, Ivory Coast, Zaire and Zimbabwe. Official figures on much of trade between the RSA and Africa as well as between the RSA and Japan are not available.

In order to disguise the origin of these shipments, many African states engaged in elaborate subterfuges. Zambia, however, simply transferred her maize shipments from South African Railway trains to Zambian railway trucks at the Victoria Falls bridge. During the same year, Kenya imported its maize via Mozambique, claiming that it was grown in Mozambique, which, incidentally, had a shortfall of 50 000 tons that season. In the 1980/1981 season Africa imported 783 000 tons of maize. Kenya took 27 800 tons and Uganda imported 18 000 tons.

A country such as Malawi evokes no surprise when it is noted that she maintained ties with South Africa — since she was the only African country to have maintained diplomatic ties with the *apartheid* regime. Nor should it surprise to discover that Zaire was actively involved in trade activities with South Africa, since Zaire, like Malawi, had been unpredictable in her "foreign policy" for over 20 years. To a certain extent, then, even Zambia (which was the headquarters of the African National Congress of South Africa — ANC, the nemesis of *apartheid*) no longer surprised the Africa watcher on learning of the Zambia-South Africa business ties: given the legendary hot-cold blowings of the Zambian President, Kenneth Kaunda. It is, however, Tanzania (the headquarters of the then equally outlawed Pan African Congress of Azania), whose active trade with South Africa should have raised eyebrows. For Tanzania

— whose former President, Julius K. Nyerere, was not only the world-renowned, elder stateman, but was, for many years, chairman of the "Frontline" states which were constantly menaced by the violent aggressions of the *apartheid* regime — had no legitimate and sufficient cause to have been involved with South Africa on trade.

Indeed, both Zambia and Tanzania did more than trade, they dispatched their citizens to South Africa for specialised training in the fields of industry, technology, medicine, health and science. Additionally, one often saw sewage pipelines in Tanzania with the unmistakable markings of ISCOR — the giant iron and steel conglomerate of South Africa. Similarly, Malawi had long played the role of repacking South African goods for export with the "made in Malawi" labels before reshipping them to other African states and abroad. Malawi, however, was the honest one in terms of trade with South Africa. Swaziland had also joined this backdoor transshipment and repacking of South African-made goods.

African elites, in government, business, education, academia, etc. from the Ivory Coast, Nigeria, Uganda, Kenya, Burkina, Zaire, the BLS countries, Zimbabwe, Zambia, Tanzania, Gabon, Somalia, Senegal, Mauritius, Malagasy, Mozambique, and Morocco, regularly trooped to South Africa. Between March and May 1988 several delegations from African states converged in South Africa. At this juncture neither had President F.W. de Klerk assumed power, nor were the ANC-PAC unbanned. South African airplanes were frequently seen in African capitals during daylight, unlike in previous years when they landed and took off at night. Many arrived in African capitals to load and unload goods, especially during their nocturnal clandestine missions. South African business-men and business consultants were frequently seen in African trade fairs and these people did not hide their South African citizenship or origin. In fact, a few did flaunt it, since there were enough independent African "trading" hands which eagerly awaited to snap them up.

Trade between Black Africa and White South Africa was rapidly mounting, to the extent that, in the case of Botswana for instance, her purchase of South African goods had topped the half-a-billion dollar mark. But Botswana is a special case, or is it not? What was even more puzzling however is that it was the African states themselves which were doing the soliciting for economic and technological ties with South Africa. In no way could the South African regime be blamed for African hypocrisy. A RSA government-orientated scholar observed that "the intemperate anti-South Africa rhetoric of African countries is in marked contrast to their commercial dealings with this country".[338] At least they seemed to need little encouragement from South Africa as their nocturnal tip-toeing to and from the RSA showed. What were the territorial, political, or commercial imperatives between Ivory Coast and South Africa trading together, for instance? Nor was it only Black Africa that was the culprit; North Africa and other Arab and Muslim states — rhetoric to the contrary notwithstanding — were also cutting economic deals with the *apartheid* regime.[339]

In 1988 the Persian Gulf nations, for instance, broke their own self-imposed embargo against the RSA and delivered no fewer than 15 oil cargoes to the regime. These deliveries were in excess of 30 million barrels of crude, which was 45 per cent of the country's needs.

It is this context that has to be borne in mind when we analyse the 1980s trends in the Japan-South Africa ties — particularly where we remember how African envoys lamented the Japanese business ties and dealings with South Africa (see Chapter 4). The Africa-South Africa ties were in fact the result of the poverty of leadership in Africa.[340] To return to our original question: What then could we make of a situation in which African states condemned not only the economic ties between Japan and South Africa, but were themselves engaged in some trade with South Africa? Japan's commercial and some would say racial, blindspot regarding *apartheid* was one of her biggest weaknesses, reflective of an impecunious strategy of *business first* before anything else. Japan's argument however does have strong moral arguments in favour of her commercial ties with South Africa before 1990, as I shall show presently.

The African states had partly adopted this position nonetheless, although on a smaller scale. Hence the African pot should not have called the Japanese kettle black on the issue of white South Africa's repression of black South Africa. For SSA, charity should have first begun at home, just as morality should first have been *practiced* internally before it was *preached* externally. This, of course, is not to minimize past Japanese commercial affinity for racist linkages with the *apartheid* economy. Nor should it be construed as denying the reality of African contribution and support for the Liberation Movement in Namibia and RSA. Africa should simply have stopped balancing the scales; it should have arrested any linkages with South Africa, or else it should have just shut up against the Japanese-South Africa ties and continued to pursue its own interest.

## THE RISING SUN AND THE WHITE CLOUDS OF APARTHEID

Japan chalked up yet another first in the 1980s — this time it was the dubious distinction of being South Africa's leading trade partner after having supplanted the US in that role in 1987. Indeed, an observer has noted the irony that for Japan, South African trade was a "diplomatic embarrassment of riches"[341]. In fact when the South African foreign minister, Roelof "Pik" Botha, visited Japan in September 1986, he received a cool reception from the Japanese Government, but a very warm one from the trade and business sector as well as from the quasi-official JSAP League. Foreign minister Botha met with his Japanese counterpart, Tadashi Kuranari, making this the first high-level diplomatic visit between the two countries before either Nelson Mandela's 1990 and 1991 visits and President De Klerk's 1992 visit. Botha requested Japan's "understanding" in South Africa's gradual dismantling of *apartheid*. Botha had argued that trade with Japan also "benefits" South Africa's black majority. Therefore sanctions would "hurt" that group if they were increased. Kuranari protested RSA *apartheid* policies and called for an end to South Africa's military aggressions against her neighbouring states. The Japan Socialist Party and other anti-apartheid activists displayed signs reading: "Botha go Home", "Pik Botha, We Aren't Honorary Whites. We are Asians Against Apartheid".

This incident clearly illustrated Japan's best-of-both-worlds' dilemma; since 1985, a frontrunner in sanctions against the South

African regime, Japan can claim moral leadership in the anti-apartheid crusade, even while raking in billions of dollars from a sizable foreign market which also supplied her with natural resources. That is, she condemned *apartheid* even while her firms were heavily engaged in business dealings with the very same *apartheid* economy. Japan's schizophrenia was bound to complicate her relations not only with Africans and Black Americans but also with those Western nations that had scaled down their trade with South Africa, as well as those prone to Japan-bashing.

Japan buys platinum, asbestos, manganese, chrome, vanadium, coal and corn from the RSA. In turn South Africa buys from Japan primarily cars, trucks, electronic equipment, textiles, steel and industrial machinery. There were over 75 Japanese companies in the 1980s located in South Africa,[342] which in 1985 sold goods to South Africa worth $1,02 billion, and bought about $1,844 billion in the same year from the same source. In dollar terms Japanese exports to South Africa fell in 1985, but rebounded in 1986. In 1984 Japan had ordered her banks to stop making loans to South Africa-related operations. This came nine years after Japan, in solidarity with the Afro-Asian nations, banned direct investments in South Africa and barred Japanese firms from setting up subsidiaries, even though the latter remained free to date to own up to 10 per cent of individual South African companies. In 1985 Japan joined the West in stopping purchases of Krugerrand gold coins and sales of computers to military and police agencies in South Africa. In autumn 1986 Japan, in conjunction with her allies, enacted yet another sanctions package, prohibiting purchase of iron and steel products and tourist trips by Japanese to South Africa or by South Africans to Japan.[343] But Japan stopped short of imposing sanctions on coal, by this act alone suggesting that the rare materials that Japan buys from South Africa were the life-blood of her economy. In 1985 for example, South Africa provided about 45 per cent of Japan's chromium ore, 35 per cent of her manganese ore, and 45 per cent of her anthracite coal.

The 1985 two-way trade traffic between Tokyo and Johannesburg was $2,86 billion, in 1986 it rose to $3,66 billion, and in 1987 it reached $4,3 billion.[344, 345, 346] Japan's South African trade was moving so rapidly that in 1986 she increased her exports in particular to South Africa, a 32,9 % increase. On the other hand, a feature of Japan's imports from Africa was the high dependence on South Africa. Indeed, imports from South Africa were 56,6 per cent of the total imports from the entire continent during 1986.[347] The reason was not only that South Africa produces coal and rare metals that Japan needs, but also because South Africa is Japan's largest supplier of anthracite coal, platinum-alloys, manganese ore, ferro-alloys, chromium ore and pig iron. South Africa is, moreover, the second largest supplier of steam coal and palladium, the fourth largest of coking coal and iron ores, and the sixth-largest of non-monetary gold lumps.

The attraction of *apartheid* for Japan was that the SSA is undependable, unstable and inefficient, while resource-starved Japan seeks reliable, dependable and stable sources of raw materials.

Despite these Japan-RSA ties, the MOFA officials were categorical in rejecting *apartheid* policies, even while labouring to explain Japan's policies towards South Africa. Horie and Ukita[348] — one of whom had just returned from South Africa when I discussed this with them — stated that:

1. Japan strongly opposed *apartheid.*

2. Japan was constantly exploring views and ways of encouraging *peaceful* change in South Africa.

3. The Japanese Government would cooperate with other international organisations and countries in looking for solutions to put political pressure on the RSA Government.

These officials conceded that trade with South Africa in 1986 had increased by 25 % to nearly $4 billion. They also argued the *"Endaka factor"* — i.e. the high yen-low dollar distortions were largely responsible for these increases. In yen terms, Japanese trade continued to *decrease* — there was a 12 % decrease in 1985/1986,

329

and the 1986 figure in yen terms was the lowest since 1980.[349] On the other hand, US exports to RSA increased while imports decreased in 1986, and her 1987 purchases of the RSA goods declined by over a billion dollars. Still, Japan's 1987 purchases of RSA goods (mainly coal, corn, wool, platinum and other metals) increased by 44 per cent — i.e. by nearly $750 million. Argued the Horie-Ukita team nevertheless, Japan prohibits any direct investment or financing loans to the RSA regime. She issues (i.e. before 1990) no visas to South African tourists in Japan. She has banned Krugerrand coins in 1985, as well as banned iron and steel imports from RSA. Japan had banned use of the SAA by Japanese officials; she had no diplomatic relations with the RSA, and there was only a small Japanese official presence in Pretoria, etc.[350] Japan-South Africa diplomatic relations were broken in 1941 when South Africa declared war on Japan.

But when challenged to show what the point was in refusing RSA tourist visas to Japan while *business* visas were allowed for the same citizens, the MOFA executives conceded the symbolism of these "anti-tourist" measures. That is, anti-tourism is certainly not to be equated with anti-terrorism. Moreover, before it could be pointed out to them that, similarly, prohibiting Japanese officials from flying SAA when the rest of Japan had the latitude to do so ... a SAA passenger jet, with 38 Japanese fishermen on board on their way to Cape Town, disappeared to the bottom of the Indian Ocean. Incidentally, when this happened, the Pretoria regime cabled Tokyo, and the cable, true to what the MOFA officials had just asserted a few days earlier regarding the Pretoria-Tokyo diplomatic channels, was handled by mid-level MOFA officials.[351] But MOFA — unlike the more rigid and secretive MITI[352] — was willing to discuss the morality (or otherwise) of the South African-Japan ties.

For instance several MOFA officials interviewed, readily saw the "necessity" of Japan extending moral and material support to the black people of South Africa — within, of course, the context of Japanese policy of pacifism and peaceful resolutions of conflicts.[353] The MITI officials interviewed were uncooperative regarding any aspects of Japan-South Africa ties, while the MOFA were less defensive.

The latter pointed out that private companies in Japan were providing scholarships to blacks in South Africa. (More about this momentarily). There was not much irony to these officials regarding the quality of segregationist education or the smallness of the group granted scholarships *vis-a-vis* the multi-billion dollar trade of Japanese firms in South Africa. What was important in official thinking at MOFA was the Japanese opposition to *apartheid*, even if it was largely moral for the time being. After all, continued the MOFA policy executives, Japan was cooperating with a United Nations agency programme, UNEPTSA, in providing annually $300 000 to educate black South African students abroad. Indeed, these officials could have pointed out that in 1987, the Japanese government provided $400 000 to a South African black charity, Kagiso Trust, for humanitarian purposes. They could, in fact, also have wondered aloud, what major material contribution had the anti-apartheid movement in Japan, USA, etc., provided for black people? Japan's overtures to blacks were nonetheless miniscule palliatives mostly designed to calm down anti-Japanese rhetoric. The MOFA realized the explosive potential of such rhetoric regarding Japan's trade ties with a pariah state that behaved like a vampire hungry for blood. It was in fact the same MOFA which had invited the President of the ANC, Oliver Tambo, to visit Tokyo in April 1987, as well as the South African black anti-apartheid activist, Rev. Alan Boesak, who told the Japanese about the imperative need to scale down the Japan-South Africa economic ties. Moreover, argued the MOFA officials, hadn't the anti-apartheid movement in the US shunned the ANC until only "recently" (especially 1984) — that is, after the US State Department had indicated willingness in talking to Oliver Tambo? Regardless, the Tambo-Boesak visit to Japan was part of a strategy of MOFA (unlike such institutions as MITI, MOF, JETRO, etc.,) to strengthen contacts with anti-apartheid blacks. Internally, as well as externally with other ministers, the MOFA Africa Desk argued that Japan should focus, properly, on South Africa's future — i.e.

with blacks,[354] nor should Japan, a vulnerable, dependent nation in terms of natural resources, be expected to sever ties completely with South Africa when there was no guarantee that Africa, or any other nation for that matter, would provide stable supplies for resource-poor Japan.

Nevertheless, as if in rebuke of this moral stance, the Japanese economic links continued to grow in the 1980s. In order to cast a broad perspective of the development of these ties, a quick review of the decades 1960-1992 would suffice.

From the following presentation it becomes evident that the Japanese-South Africa connection has almost reached a point of no return. Something substantial would have to give before it could be reversed, severed or even increased. Such reversal, in 1993, is no longer necessary though.

## THE STUBBORN GROWTH: 1960-1992

Business ties between Japan and South Africa took a new qualitative and quantitative dimension in the early 1960s, in the aftermath of the Sharpeville Massacre and South Africa's unilateral withdrawal from the (British) Commonwealth of Nations and her establishment of the Republic of South Africa. Trade grew as rapid economic expansion in Japan and her trade liberalisation was now in full swing.[355] During this period, Japan's economic ties with South Africa remained mostly in the realm of trade, as was typically the case with the rest of Africa, i.e. Japan was importing raw materials from, and exporting manufactured industrial goods to, South Africa. Trade between the two increased by 500 per cent from the 1960 import-export figures of $45 million and $61,5 million, to the 1970 figures of $271,5 million and $338,5 million respectively. As African states mounted condemnation of South Africa in the UN (in 1963) Japan was selling 28 million pounds sterling goods to the RSA and buying *35 million pounds sterling worth of wool, ore, and other items.*

The 1960s actually saw the rapid introduction and expansion of Japanese cars in South Africa. In 1966, 99 per cent of Japanese car sales in South Africa consisted of three models, the Datsun Bluebird

130 sedan, its station-wagon variant and the Toyota Corona 1.5. But Japanese cars represented only 2 per cent of the South African market. But in the same year Japanese car sales in the RSA increased threefold in comparison with the 1965 figures, and by the first six months of 1967 these cars represented more than four per cent of the South African market.[356] (In 1987 Japanese cars accounted for more than 55 per cent of the South African market, and by the end of 1988 they even went up to 60 per cent. This figure was more than that of any other foreign car maker in the South African auto market. Between January and October 1986 Toyota Motor Corporation sold more than 76 000 cars in South Africa. Cars and parts were all sold through Japanese-owned companies).

In February 1970 Fumihiko Kono, board chairman of Mitsubishi Heavy Industries, led an economic mission of 26 businessmen and government officials to several SSA countries. In November of the same year, Japan dispatched a 10-man economic mission to the RSA. A cynic could claim that the Kono Mission to the SSA was a stratagem, a subterfuge, to hide the real intentions of *Keidanren* and Japanese industry: to send a mission to the RSA to strengthen ties. The mission to the RSA was composed of representatives of six major iron and steel corporations and four major shipping companies. Two years earlier — i.e. in 1968 — imports from South Africa, which amounted to $334 million, were more than one third iron. The Japanese mission was interested in the prospects of Japan's participation in South Africa's large-scale development plan.

Four months earlier — i.e. July 1970 — the huge state-financed South African Iron and Steel Corporation (ISCOR) had sent a mission to Japan headed by its chairman, T.F. Muller, in order to promote its Sishen-Saldanha Bay Project.[357] Muller's interest that Japan's iron and steel industry provide massive long-term loans for this project and that the RSA would provide a long-term supply of iron ore and coking coal for export to Japan, of course, could not pass up such an opportunity. Moral scruples, inconvenient, were thus conveniently shelved.

In Chapter 2 I have argued that Japan was not complicit in the colonisation of Africans in East and West Africa, as she joined other European imperial powers in the economic harvesting of African resources and labour. The same argument cannot be made, however, with regard to her involvement in South Africa, especially during a period which could be regarded as one of the darkest days in South African history: the Verwoerd-Vorster-Botha eras, 1961-1985 especially.[358] In 1971 Japan exported goods — automobiles, electronic equipment, textiles, steel and industrial machinery — to the value of $412 million, and imported goods — raw materials, rare metals, agricultural products and coal — to the value of $319,1 million. In 1972 her exports to the RSA totalled $364,1 million while her imports from same amounted to $398,9 million.

The Japan Atomic Energy Industry Council's interest is in uranium. Japanese purchase of uranium and chromium ores from the RSA, compounded the controversy of her involvement in South Africa. Uranium, vital in nuclear energy/weapons' development, is extracted from Namibia — which was illegally hostaged by a South African Government that retained not a scintilla of reason to be there in the first place. Regardless, however, the oil crisis following the Arab-Israeli October War in 1973 had panicked Japan into scrambling to enter into long-term contract agreements with South Africa on alternative energy resources such as uranium. In December of that year Japan signed a contract with South Africa covering an estimated 80 per cent of her import needs for a 10-year period. Moreover, the Mitsubishi Corporation and Kansai Electric Power Company — both of Japan — the Rossing mining group of South Africa, as well as the Japanese and South African governments, became parties to the agreement that provided for selling Japan 8 200 short tons of uranium from the Rossing mine of Namibia.[359] Indeed, contravening UN resolutions prohibiting trade with the South Africa-occupied territory of Namibia, Mitsubishi Corporation allied with the Japanese government to exchange nuclear technology for a guaranteed supply of uranium.[360] The Japanese Government was constrained to protect its flanks in SSA as trade with RSA was mounting: Japan increased her trade links with Black Africa and invested more in these states. She began to systematically make strong political attacks on the *apartheid* system. These attacks, of course, did not hide her complicit doings with the RSA economy. Japan, in any event, had correctly argued that the UN sanctions were not mandatory since they were imposed by the General Assembly.

As trade between Japan and RSA continued to expand in the 1970s, Japanese businessmen became more and more confident in their dealings with South Africa, while the Japanese Government was growing more and more uneasy. As one analyst noted: "Until their mid-1970s policy conversion, the Japanese were not particularly reluctant to accept the 'honorary white' status granted them by South Africa." Though this clearly was an act of condescension toward Japanese by Pretoria and an implied slap in the face of Asians not accorded that status, many Japanese businessmen willingly accepted the South African designation. They used it to gain entry into South Africa's commercial inner circle, ignoring the suffering around them.

Though Japanese officials long have formally respected black African sensibilities, many Japanese businessmen — enjoying the clubs, golf courses, and other perquisites of their dishonourable "honorary white" status — seemed confident they deserved such special treatment because of "Japan's remarkable economic achievements".[361] When in the late 1960s a Japanese businessman was struck dead by lightning while playing golf outside Johannesburg, the writer recalls a chorus of approval and murmurs of "poetic justice" among the Soweto citizens. We have already seen in any event a prominent African writer (see title page of this chapter) heartily endorsing this "economic animalism" issue of "honorary whites" status in the RSA — i.e. not because white South Africans love Japanese more than any other Asians, but rather because they respect and fear the economic might of Japan.[362] Yet Japan's might was a double-edged sword with the potential of cutting both ways, thus inflicting irreparable harm on Japan herself. It diminished her moral claims of an international state firmly committed to human rights and pacifism.

But while the South Africa-Japan trade had grown tremendously, until 1988 South Africa accounted for only about one per cent of Japan's world trade in the 1980s although it accounts for half its trade with Africa. In fact Japanese imports from South Africa fell 7,4 per cent in yen terms in 1987.[363] The 17 per cent increase in exports to South Africa, moreover, was due to the rand-rebound and the overall improvement of the South African economy following the flight of capital during the 1984-1986 *apartheid* violence.[364] In yen terms, *trade* increased only slightly by 2,1 per cent — i.e. from 607 billion to 620 billion, which was, in turn, lower than the 1985 figure of 687 billion yen or even the higher figure in 1984 of 816 billion yen.

In 1983 South Africa had bought 28,9 % of Japan's total exports to Africa (compared to Egypt — 14,2 %, and Liberia — 10,4 %). On the other hand, South Africa shipped 48 % of total Japanese imports (compared to Algeria — 10,5 % and Egypt — 7,9 %). Japanese business successes in South Africa were, however, not always attributed to honest and fair means, as noted for example by a South African expert, Professor Duncan Innes, on ABC Television news programme, that Japan was moving to "fill in" when other countries were moving out as a result of sanctions.[365]

Other critics had also cited Hitachi's computer sales to the RSA which flowed to a West German company, BASF, which sold them to a South African company called Persetel Ltd. The latter in turn sold them to consumers.[366] In January 1988 a 16-member trade delegation visited the RSA to find out how local corporations would try to circumvent a cutback in Japanese technology trade.

Japan's kind of success was of course embarrassing to both the Japanese Government and Japan's corporations, because one of Japan's greatest strengths was her moral stance as being the pacifist nation on the side of justice and peace. Japan had argued that, buying 20 per cent of South Africa's coal exports in 1986 worth $1,57 billion, for instance, was not proof of her complicity with *apartheid*, but that it was the result of the dictatorship of need. Nowhere in Africa, in any event, would she have had a "stable" supply of coal for instance; even during moments of crisis, resource-insecure Japan felt secure that South Africa would keep the energy pipeline open, thanks also to the *migrant labourers from other African states* who could be relied upon to replenish whatever mine labour was depleted by the strikes. Indeed, Swaziland alone had over 16 000 workers in South Africa. This is a fickle stability of course since the existence of *apartheid* meant a permanent state of war or conflict and tension. That is, RSA could never be stable till *apartheid* was dismantled. Stabilisation of *apartheid* was always an internal contradiction, and no amount of opportunistic rationalisation could wipe away this impossibility.

## SUMMARY OF JAPANESE TRADE WITH SOUTH AFRICA 1991-1992*

Japanese trade figures for 1991

| | |
|---|---|
| Export: | $320 billion |
| Import: | $237 billion |
| Trade surplus: | $84 billion |

Japanese trade figures for 1992 (estimated):

| | |
|---|---|
| Export: | $340 billion |
| Import: | $230 billion |
| Trade surplus: | $110 billion |

The trade surplus is rapidly on the increase. An important priority of the Japanese Government is to increase the amount of imports to Japan. The abovementioned trade surplus amounts to approximately 3 % of the GDP. Throughout the ages, no single country has faced the same situation that Japan has had to face today.

---

* The Japanese Embassy (Pretoria) provided the information on trade that follows.

## MAIN JAPANESE EXPORTS

| | |
|---|---|
| Transportation vehicles and components | $70 billion |
| Audio-visual equipment | $50 billion |
| Chemicals | $20 billion |
| Steel | $20 billion |
| Manufacturing machinery | $20 billion |

More than 95 % of the exports are final products.

## MAIN JAPANESE IMPORTS

| | |
|---|---|
| Machinery | $43 billion |
| Foodstuffs | $34 billion |
| Oil | $27 billion |
| Energy resources (excluding oil) | $23 billion |
| Chemicals | $17 billion |
| Mineral Resources | $ 9 billion |

More than 50 % of imports are resources such as food and energy.

### TRADE RELATIONS BETWEEN JAPAN AND THE RSA

Exports from Japan to South Africa in 1991 were $1 635 billion. Imports from South Africa to Japan were $1 819 billion, the total being $3 454 billion. The estimated amount of exports from Japan to South Africa is $1,7 billion and imports were $2 billion in 1991.

The above trade figures only represent 0,7 % of Japan's total foreign trade. In South Africa this represents 10 % of the total foreign trade.

During 1991 Japan was South Africa's fourth largest trade partner. Japan was importing gold and platinum through Switzerland and the UK, but recently Japan has been importing directly from South Africa, thus the import figure will increase.

Japan is at present importing more than 90 % of the raw materials used in production. Japan exports $700 million in transport goods to South Africa. Japan imports many raw materials from South Africa. These raw materials include metal, coal, steel, iron ore, platinum and maize. This trade takes place

## TABLE 10.2
## JAPAN'S AID PROGRAMMES FOR SOUTH AFRICAN
## BLACK COMMUNITIES

| Type of programme | Accu-mulated up to March 1991 | April 1990-March 1991 | April 1991-March 1992 | April 1992-March 1993 |
|---|---|---|---|---|
| **CONTRIBUTION TO UN FUNDS** **UN Trust Fund for SA** (Financial support for legal trials of South African political prisoners/financial support for the families of political prisoners | $380 000 | $ 20 000 | $ 20 000 | $ 20 000 |
| **Trust Fund for Publicity against Apartheid** (For the financial support of anti-apartheid public relations activities by UN Anti-Apartheid Special Committee) | $150 000 | $ 10 000 | $ 10 000 | $ 10 000 |
| **United Nations educational and training programme for Southern Africa** (Support for SA and partially Namibian University of graduate students to study abroad) | S3,92 m | $400 000 (5th largest international contribution) | $560 000 | $660 000 |
| **Unhor's cooperation for the Return to SA of South African Expatriates** | | | $3,2 m | |
| **Contribution through the Kagiso Trust** | $2,45 m | $1 m | $1,5 m | $2,5 m |
| **Small Scale Grant Assistance Programme** | $110 000 | $110 000 | $240 000 | $270 000 |
| **Japan International Cooperation Agency (JICA)** (Training programme for South African black people) | 6 people | 6 people | 21 people $430 000 | 44 people $800 000 |
| TOTAL | approx. $7 080 000 | approx. $1 600 000 | approx. $6 000 000 | approx. $4 260 000 |

Source:     Japanese Embassy (Pretoria).

almost entirely through the Japanese trading houses in South Africa.

Other potential goods which may be imported by Japan from South Africa are specialised items such as leather goods, ostrich goods, South African wines, special wooden furniture and on a smaller scale, African craft. Many of these items could be displayed at the JETRO fair and thus contact could be established between potential buyers and sellers of these products.

Clearly, then, Japan's relations with South Africa, were confined not only to the trade and commercial world, but to the *white* part of South Africa. It is only in the 1980s that Japan diverted some of her interest and resources into the *black* part of South Africa. Japan increased, beginning in the 1980s, her financial support for educational, humanitarian and "community" programmes among black South Africans. These aid programmes fell, broadly, into seven categories: UN Trust Fund for South Africans, Trust Fund for Publicity Against Apartheid, United Nations Education and Training Programme for Southern Africa, UNHCR Return programme, Kagiso Trust Contribution, Small Scale Grant Programme and the JICA training programme. (See Table 10.2.)

## DE KLERK AND JAPAN

As already noted, Japan re-established diplomatic relations with the RSA on 13 January 1992 — reasons being the "positive developments in South Africa towards establishing democratic institutions, and particularly the start of the Convention for a Democratic South Africa in December (of 1991), according to the Foreign Minister of Japan, Michio Watanabe. These positive developments led to the President of South Africa, F.W. de Klerk, to be the first South African head to visit Japan during June 1992. (The ANC president, Nelson Mandela, had previously visited Japan, but only for the purpose of boosting the fortunes of his organisation.)

In meeting with the Japanese Prime Minister, Kiichi Miyazawa, on 3 June, De Klerk won agreement to open talks on air links. President De Klerk secured a pledge from Miyazawa to encourage

Japanese companies to expand links with South Africa. De Klerk envisioned South Africa as the future Japan of Africa. But MITI Minister, Kozo Watanabe, expressed a note of caution, while De Klerk argued that Southern Africa's development depended on the RSA's economic success, which would be based on a healthy dose of foreign capital and investment. While Watanabe was encouraged by efforts to dismantle apartheid, he agreed to encourage investment on condition that the Pretoria Government maintained liberal trade policies and did nothing to arouse fears among Japanese business leaders about public order.

In his meeting with the powerful business lobby, *Keidanren* (Federation of Economic Organizations), De Klerk repeated his message expressed the previous day that South Africa attached great significance to the SA-Japan ties.

Top management of such huge conglomerates as Nissan Motor Co. Ltd, Sumitomo Corporation, Nisho Iwai Corp., Toshiba Corp. and Sumitomo Metal Mining Company Ltd attended De Klerk's meeting. He told the Keidanren that he came to explore "the miracle of your sustained economic growth". This growth was the engine to "normalise and promote sound international relations". It was necessary for Japan and South Africa to strengthen economic ties because SA had "proven itself to be a reliable and cost-effective supplier of major minerals and other raw materials important to the Japanese economy". De Klerk was of course mindful that South Africa's trade with Japan amounted to less than 1 % of Japan's total foreign trade while Japan's buying from South Africa generated as much as 6,29 % of the latter's total export trade.

De Klerk used his meeting with the Secretary General of the ruling Liberal Democratic Party, Tamisuke Watanuki, to urge Japan to buy more goods from South Africa to help stabilise its economy. Thus economic stabilisation would lead to political stabilisation, the precondition of which is economic prosperity which would greatly be enhanced by Japanese investment. During his discussions with the Transport Minister, Keiwa Okuda, De Klerk won approval to start charter flights between the two countries. Both governments had also agreed to start talks on regular air services, using the new international airport in Osaka on account of traffic congestion at the Tokyo International Airport.

A number of economic delegations from Japan had visited South Africa during 1991, visits which were reciprocated by SA businesses. Indeed, a Japan/South African Chamber of Commerce in Johannesburg was established. Thus, it was important for Japanese business houses to either upgrade their trade and increase their exports to SA or alternatively, the Japanese private sector should become fully involved through investment, joint ventures and technological involvement within SA, argued De Klerk before the Federation.

President De Klerk also met with the Japanese Emperor, Akihito, as well as with the head of the Export-Import Bank of Japan.

De Klerk was certainly correct in courting Japan because the Island nation is a veritable giant. After all her GNP in real terms expanded by 22,2 times, and in nominal terms more than 100 times between 1945 and 1990. In effect this meant an average real annual growth of 7,38 % over these 45 years. Japanese per capita GNP (in US dollars) surpassed that of Italy in 1970, the UK in 1980, West Germany in 1985, and the US in 1990 (Ambassador Sezaki 1993:3). Because of this, "world-wide competition to attract Japanese investment is extremely intense" (Ambassador Ohta 1992:8). Consequently, De Klerk saw the need to explore beyond mere economic ties: he ventured into a broader cultural sphere of sportive, educational, scientific and technological ties. His swan song, however, remained that of economic investment and trade. South Africa was presented as a veritable and reliable gateway to all of Southern Africa and beyond.

## CONCLUSION: AFRICA-JAPAN-SA TRIANGLE

The Japan-South Africa trade raises a number of questions, more particularly about the African states than about the Japanese since the Japanese had less of a moral imperative to fight against *apartheid* than did African states: after all, no Japanese have been killed in Africa as a result of South Africa's past aggression in the surrounding areas. It is the Angolans, Namibians, Mozambicans, Botswana, Basotho, Zimbabweans, Zambians, Swazis, besides the black South Africans of course, who have died because of South African military aggression.

The question then (before 1990) was: what should Africans do, and not what should Japanese do? The wandering Japanese have long settled their military scores during the Imperial period (1875-1945). Since Japan has abdicated militarism and opted for pacifism, she asked then, not too be judged in militarist but in pacifist terms in all her diplomatic and economic activities. She was like a rehabilitated felon who was now strictly playing by the book. What then about Africa?

The Black Continent (except perhaps for Angola) has never proven herself militarily against South Africa — even though thousands of Africans had, in the past, gone to do battle against the Japanese in South-East Asia on a futile and misguided mission. Since then, Africa has taken no arms against anybody but her own citizenry. (Egypt of course had done battle with Israel, Namibia, Guinea-Bissau, Mozambique, Algeria, Libya, Sudan, had of course fought valiant veritable anticolonial wars). Since SSA spends so many billions of dollars on arms, and yet remains congenitally incapable of facing her erstwhile archnemesis, it would seem her resources would have been profitably used had she simply gone the pacifist way — like Japan — rather than the militarist way — like Vietnam — because the latter was morally and psychologically prepared for militarism, as the former was psychologically prepared for pacifism. SSA was always prepared neither for pacifism not militarism, but for posturing.

The military options have, in any event, never been used anywhere to rescue black humanity if the struggle was between Black and White. In the Congo, the US and her NATO allies intervened militarily to rescue white humanity; so was it the case in Grenada, (if we accept the claims of the Reagan Administration), just as was the case in the abortive rescue mission in Iran. That is, no white government has ever gone to war on behalf of blacks (the reverse has often been the case). Once again, then, logic pointed to the pacifist direction as the feasible way, since even if she was willing, Japan was constitutionally incapable of waging war on behalf of anybody — not even of herself — unless in self-defence.

But to suggest the pacifist way was to draw attention to sanctions. Sanctions, however, had their own dynamics, as we have already shown. Sanctions, in any event, have brought down no evil regime in recent memory. No nation has ever collapsed as a result. Even land-locked Rhodesia (1965-1980) was brought down not by sanctions, but rather by the military option adopted by the ZANU-ZAPU guerilla movement. I have already shown why Japanese "sanctions" could not have succeeded. Other analysts put in this way:

Japan is the only other industrialized nation with sizeable investment in, and trade with, South Africa. The Japanese government complies with all the major international sanctions such as the arms and nuclear technology embargoes, but would suffer significant economic hardship if trading relations ceased.[367]

Without having demonstrated that they would suffer significant economic hardship if they were prohibited from trading with the RSA, SSA countries from as far as Somali (whose jets were sometimes piloted by South African whites), and Ivory Coast (whose president has often in the past made rapprochement noises regarding South Africa) — had gone down to traffic with South Africa before 1990. (This criticism exempts, of course, such South African dependencies as Lesotho, Botswana and Swaziland. The latter was seen, in fact, as the "back door" for South African exports to other SSA countries).[368]

This is obvious testimony that sanctions would not have worked because there were always enough nations who did not go by the book — even those most vocal about such sanctions.

To some, sanctions did not work in Rhodesia because the latter had South Africa as her backbone and outlet. These critics erroneously argue: whom does South Africa have besides

Antarctica? The RSA had more than enough; the wide oceans and the world's hypocrites.

The only option left then was to continue the charade and hypocrisy of moral outrage against *apartheid* , even as business as usual continued going on. Clearly this could not have led to the liberation of South Africa. Having failed to be influential with Western powers, Africans should have opted for the Japanese model. But to have done so meant that African states should have befriended Japan, developed strong rapport with her. They should have devised a strategy of wooing Japan, in order to attempt to pry her loose from the clutches of *apartheid* dependency. But for Africans to have succeeded meant that they should have begun to be *reliable* producers and suppliers of Japan's basic needs. If the SSA, and not the RSA, had the iron ore, coal, chromium, uranium, platinum, asbestos, and manganese in abundance, could Japan have depended on the SSA to provide the same without interruption?

This is the question Japan implicitly and subtly wanted the SSA to answer satisfactorily. It would also be appropriate that Africans not emulate the OPEC cartel games. Cartelisation of the SSA's resources would only have driven Japan deeper and deeper into a complex embrace with South Africa. Or even sought alternative sources of supply outside Africa. Such is the capacity for technological innovation at the disposal of Japan.

Simply put, Africa should instead have eschewed the brutal- isation of her subjects, attained some semblance of a free political climate, sustained peaceable political order and entered into a rational discourse with her potential allies (and *not* with her then foe — i.e. RSA). Africa has for too long looked to the Occident for moral guidance and pragmatic leadership. Africa had the opportunity to look the other way — the Oriental way, with the hope of learning something that a history of slavery, colonisation, and imperialism have not taught her: that is, the conflict between black and white, the white rhetoric about equity and justice would remain as long as the sand pebbles of the Sahara Desert are numberless. Such rhetoric could not have liberated South Africa.

Befriending Japan in a realistic, meaningful way might have eventually raised alarm bells in the Occident, perhaps as strong as if it was the (now defunct) USSR that was befriended. But developing good rapport with Japan would not, of course, necessarily have meant that Japan would have changed suppliers from the RSA to the SSA overnight. After all, Japan had continued to import high-grade Rhodesian chrome through the RSA's backdoor even as she was feverishly endorsing UN embargo resolutions after the 1965 UDI by Ian Smith.

But the truth is that the SSA needs Japan more than Japan needs her. The SSA cannot afford to go it alone; she needs a strong partner, especially one who in the last forty years has demonstrated impeccable credentials of non-militarism.

Only then may the continent of Africa stand a chance of consolidating her economic, industrial and agricultural infrastructure and entering the international arena not as a beggar for alms — but rather as a producer of both primary products and value-added commodities. Only then would Africa become persuasive internationally; only then would South Africa have realised that it is only the African people who could have economically driven *apartheid* into the Indian and Atlantic Oceans.

Africa should have attempted to achieve a paradox: gain the moral capital she never really possessed but which was always within reach: that of prying concessions from Japan with regard to the RSA. Africa's two primary "don'ts" were not to play the confrontational rhetoric, and, of course, not to play the Japan-South Africa *seikei bunri*. The SSA could not separate economics from politics re RSA. Africa's only hope then was, to repeat, reliability as supplier to Japan of the essential primary products that Japan was heavily dependent on. As I have shown Japan is a vulnerable, dependent *island* easily susceptible to isolation. Thus Japan's survival depends on reliable suppliers. *Of what use would an unreliable partner be in your hour of greatest need?* Why would anybody depend on such a fickle fair-weather partner? But a strategy of winning good relations and good rapport with the

Japanese would have eventually paid dividends, if only Africans would have remembered that in Japan, government and business cooperate on virtually every aspect of national economic policy. That is, Africa should, even now, seek to win the other half of the government-business partnership. That means 50 % of the battle won. With this leverage secured, with Africa's reliability assured, with Japanist pacifism embraced, and confrontationalism eschewed, Africa's rapid rise to higher development (industrially, agriculturally, etc.) while simultaneously imitating the Japanese model, at the same time as African states are moving closer to achieve some sort of Afro-Japanese integration, would all but have been guaranteed.[369]

# 第六部

## 付表・注・参考文献

# PART VI

## APPENDICES, NOTES, BIBLIOGRAPHY

# APPENDIX A
# JAPANESE DIPLOMATIC RECOGNITION OF AFRICA STATES

| Country | Recognition of state | | | Japanese embassy (since) | | |
|---|---|---|---|---|---|---|
| Algeria | 1962 | 7 | 4 | 1964 | 2 | 14 |
| Angola | 1976 | 2 | 20 | (in Zambia) | | |
| Benin | 1960 | 8 | 1 | (in Ivory Coast) | | |
| Botswana | 1966 | 9 | 30 | (in Zambia) | | |
| Burkina Faso | 1960 | 8 | 5 | (in Ivory Coast) | | |
| Burundi | 1962 | 7 | 1 | (in Zaire) | | |
| Cameroon | 1960 | 1 | 1 | (in Gabon) | | |
| Cape Verde | 1975 | 7 | 11 | (in Senegal) | | |
| Central Africa | 1960 | 8 | 13 | 1974 | 1 | 25 |
| Chad | 1960 | 8 | 11 | (in Gabon) | | |
| Comoros | 1977 | 11 | 14 | (in Madagascar) | | |
| Congo | 1960 | 8 | 15 | (in Zaire) | | |
| Djibouti | 1977 | 6 | 27 | (in France) | | |
| Egypt | 1922 | 4 | 2 | 1954 | 4 | 1 |
| Equatorial Guinea | 1968 | 11 | 12 | (in Gabon) | | |
| Ethiopia | 1955 | | | 1958 | 4 | |
| Gabon | 1960 | 8 | 17 | 1972 | 1 | 21 |
| Gambia | 1965 | 2 | 18 | (in Senegal) | | |
| Ghana | 1957 | 3 | | 1959 | 3 | 12 |
| Guinea | 1958 | 11 | 14 | 1976 | 1 | 20 |
| Guinea-Bissau | 1974 | 8 | 1 | (in Senegal) | | |
| Ivory Coast | 1960 | 8 | 7 | 1964 | 2 | 22 |
| Kenya | 1963 | 12 | 12 | 1964 | 2 | 22 |
| Lesotho | 1966 | 10 | 4 | (in Zambia) | | |
| Liberia | 1952 | 12 | 29 | 1973 | 1 | |
| Libya | 1957 | 2 | 12 | 1973 | 1 | |
| Madagascar | 1960 | 7 | 5 | 1968 | 2 | |
| Malawi | 1964 | 7 | 6 | (in Kenya) | | |
| Mali | 1960 | 10 | 4 | (in Senegal) | | |
| Mauritania | 1960 | 11 | 29 | (in Senegal) | | |
| Mauritius | 1968 | 3 | 12 | (in Madagascar) | | |
| Morocco | 1956 | 6 | 19 | 1961 | 10 | 1 |
| Mozambique | 1975 | 6 | 25 | (in Zimbabwe) | | |
| Niger | 1960 | 8 | 3 | (in Ivory Coast) | | |
| Nigeria | 1960 | 10 | 1 | 1960 | 12 | 26 |
| Rwanda | 1962 | 7 | 1 | (in Zaire) | | |

## APPENDIX A *(continued)*

| Country | Recognition of state | | | Japanese embassy (since) | | |
|---|---|---|---|---|---|---|
| Sao Tome and Principe | 1975 | 7 | 22 | (in Gabon) | | |
| Senegal | 1960 | 10 | 4 | 1962 | 1 | 6 |
| Seychelles | 1976 | 10 | 4 | (in Kenya) | | |
| Sierra Leone | 1961 | 4 | 27 | 1962 | 10 | |
| Somalia | 1960 | 7 | 1 | (in Kenya) | | |
| | | | | (strictly not yet an "African | | |
| South Africa | 1918 | 8 | 14 | State") | | |
| Sudan | 1956 | 1 | 6 | 1961 | 4 | 14 |
| Swaziland | 1968 | 9 | 6 | (in Zambia) | | |
| Tanzania | 1961 | 12 | 9 | 1966 | 2 | 18 |
| Togo | 1960 | 4 | 27 | (in Ivory Coast) | | |
| Tunisia | 1956 | 6 | 26 | 1969 | 2 | 5 |
| Uganda | 1962 | 10 | 9 | (in Kenya) | | |
| Zaire | 1960 | 6 | 30 | 1960 | 6 | 30 |
| Zambia | 1964 | 10 | 24 | 1970 | 1 | 15 |
| Zimbabwe | 1980 | 4 | 18 | 1981 | 5 | 2 |

Source:    Internal document provided by MOFA (1987).

## APPENDIX B

## VISITORS (VIPs) FROM AFRICAN COUNTRIES TO JAPAN[1]
### *(between 1984 and July 1987)*

| Country (Number of visitors) | 18 August 1987        Africa First Section | | |
|---|---|---|---|
| | Name and title | Mo./Yr | Type of visit[2] |
| Angola (1) | Figalado, Permanent Representative to UN | 6/87 | J |
| Uganda (6) | Roda Kaisho, Chief of Aid Arrangement Section, Ministry of Foreign Affairs | 2/84 | C |
| | Engora, chief of Educational Broadcasting Bureau, Ministry of Information and Broadcasting | 10/84 | |
| | | 10/84 | F |
| | Mukiibi, Minister of Foreign Affairs (with three attendants) | 5/87 and 6/87 | A |

352

| Country (Number of visitors) | Name and title | Mo./Yr | Type of visit[2] |
|---|---|---|---|
| Ethiopia (7) | Nega Beienne, Assistant Director of Asia Australia Bureau, Ministry of Foreign Affairs | 10/84 | C |
| | Goshu, Minister of Foreign Affairs (with three attendants) | | |
| | Chief Editor of *Kifrom Adugoi Ethiopia Herald* | 8/85 | A |
| | Yusuf, Minister of Transport and Communication | 10/86 1/87 | F B |
| Ghana (13) | Akurashie, Assistant Director of Economic Affairs Bureau, Ministry of Foreign Affairs | 5/84 | C |
| | Anser, Publisher and Chief Editor of *Ghananian Voice* | 9/85 | F |
| | Wilmot, Director of Africa OAU Bureau, Ministry of Foreign Affairs | 12/85 | C |
| | Anan, Chief of Budget Section, UN Executive Office | 6/86 | C |
| | Shidic, Official of Public Relations Section, Ministry of Information | 9/86 | F |
| | Ferikus Ajemang | 10/86 | I |
| | Oben, Director of General Affairs | 2/87 | A |
| | Attendants: | | |
| | Pepula, Director of Transport, Trade and Industry | | |
| | Bentam Williamgana, Director of Investment Centre | | |
| | Ranputy, Director of Economic bureau, | | |
| | Ministry of Foreign Affairs | | |
| | Kene, Vice Minister of National Resources | 3/87 | D |
| | Kenes Dodge, Director of UNCTAD (with one attendant) | 5/87 | A |
| Gabon (8) | Mabang, Deputy Minister of Information | 1/84 | C |

| Country (Number of visitors) | Name and title | Mo./Yr | Type of visit[2] |
|---|---|---|---|
| | President Bongo | 9/84 | State guest |
| | Attendants: | | |
| | Bongo, Minister of Foreign Affairs Cooperation | | |
| | Mushirue, Minister of Industry | | |
| | Emanta, Minister of Trade | | |
| | Rengunba, Minister of Economy and Finance | | |
| | Emane, Assistant Chief of *Union* Editorial Section | 9/84 | F |
| | Ango M. Joseph | 3/87 | I |
| Cameroon (3) | Assistant Secretary of Tankoo Project National Land Development Department | 10/84 | C |
| | Mpuma, Ministry of Posts and Electric Communication | 12/86 | J |
| | Assistant Secretary of Tankoo Project. National Land Development Department | 5/87 | J |
| Gambia (16) | Nja, Assistant Secretary of Economic Planning | 4/84 | C |
| | Industrial Development Department President Jawara (with 14 attendants) | 9/84 | B |
| Guinea (3) | Sow, Director of State Affairs, Ministry of Foreign Affairs and Cooperation | 3/85 | C |
| | Bangoora, Director of Ceremony, Ministry of Foreign Affairs | 5/86 | C |
| | Assistant Secretary of International Cooperation Bureau, Fafana Project Ministry of International Cooperation | 7/87 | C |
| Kenya (4) | Donald Musengi, Assistant Secretary of President's Office | 12/84 | C |
| | Nyakiamo, Minister of Health | 10/86 | J |

| Country (Number of visitors) | Name and title | Mo./Yr | Type of visit[2] |
|---|---|---|---|
| | Muendowa, Minister of Animal Industry Development | 11/86 | J |
| | Gache, Chief of Kenya Times Foreign News Section | 5/87 and 6/87 | F |
| Comoro (10) | Shahey, Vice Minister of Foreign Affairs | 8/86 | C |
| | President Abudara (with eight attendants) | 4/87 | B |
| Zaire (5) | Ramazani, President of "National News Service AZAP" | 9/84 | F |
| | Okitongo, President of Public Debt Admin. Bureau | 12/84 | C |
| | Rikonji, Mobunji | 10/85 | I |
| | Binbi, Director of "Zaire press Union" | 11/86 | F |
| | Kabongo, Assistant Director of America, Asia and Oceania Bureau | 12/86 | G |
| Zambia (10) | Mueruwa Kosta Tembo, Director of International Trade Administrative Bureau, Ministry of Commerce and Industry | 10/84 | C |
| | Chinkuri, Minister of Agriculture and Fishery | 8/85 | H |
| | Shirangua, Chairman of National Science Research Council | 10/85 | I |
| | Obias, Soresore | 10/85 | I |
| | Zulu, Secretary General (with three attendants) | 11/85 | A |
| | Piri, President Aide | 12/85 | E |
| | Chibuno, President of Central Bank | 4/87 | J |
| Zimbabwe (10) | Mugomba, Assistant of Vice Minister of Foreign Affairs | 3/84 | C |
| | Reginald Tonderai Muguwara, Director Financial Aid Bureau, Ministry of Finance | 10/84 | C |

| Country (Number of visitors) | Name and title | Mo./Yr | Type of visit[2] |
|---|---|---|---|
| | Masaruruwa, Chief Editor of *Sunday Mail* | 10/84 | F |
| | Nudondo, Assistant Secretary of Foreign Affairs | 5/85 | C |
| | Nunguen, Minister of Foreign Affairs | 11/86 | J |
| | Droy, Minister of Industrial Technology | 12/86 | B |
| Zimbabwe (10) | Chidzero, Minister of Finance | 2/87 | J |
| | Mashanyare, Superior official of Finance, Economy Planning and Development Department | 3/87 | I |
| | Kangai, Minister of Energy and Water Resources | 3/87 | I |
| | Muranga, President of Agriculture and Agricultural | 3/87 | C |
| | Village Development Public Corporation | | |
| Seychelles (5) | Gi Morele, Minister of Finance | 8/85 | H |
| | Belmon, Minister of Labour and Social Service | 4/86 | J |
| | Delpecke, member of IWC Committee (High Commission Accredited to Great Britain) | | |
| | San Jole, Vice Minister of Foreign Affairs | 10/86 | D |
| | Adam, Minister of Tourism and Transport | 4/87 | C |
| Senegal (7) | Nudau, Director of *le Soleil* | 5/87 | J |
| | Gaiyu, Chief Editor of *le Soleil* | 2/84 | C |
| | Daffe, Minister of Scinece and Technology | 9/84 | F |
| | Diob, Staff of Business Promotion and Protection Bureau, Trade Centre | 4/85 | H |
| | | 9/85 | C |
| | Dieng, President of "APS" | 1/86 | F |
| | Munomy Diuf, Director of Animal Resources | 7/86 | J |
| | Ariunne Dianne | 10/86 | I |

| Country (Number of visitors) | Name and title | Mo./Yr | Type of visit[2] |
|---|---|---|---|
| Ivory Coast (5) | Kwame, Politics and Diplomacy Desk of *Furaterunite Matan* | 9/84 | F |
| | Anguba, Minister of Commerce | 8/85 | H |
| | Bareto, Assistant Director of Textile Export, Trade Centre | 9/85 | C |
| | Kindo, Director of Cultural Activity Bureau, Ministry of Culture | 10/85 | C |
| | Kuanne Franciska Aka | 10/85 | C |
| Somalia (6) | Osman, Minister of Finance | 10/85 | B |
| | Jawari, Vice Minister of Transport | 12/85 | B |
| | Berle, Vice Minister of Agriculture | 9/86 | B |
| | Habib Jukba, Minister of Ravine | 11/86 | B |
| | Adan, Minister of Foreign Affairs | 12/86 | C |
| | Tara, UN Special Commissioner for Displaced persons | 4/87 | C |
| Tanzania (5) | George Nigura, Director of Asia Oceania Bureau, Ministry of Foreign Affairs | 10/84 | C |
| | Hamado Zanjibar, Head Minister of Government | 9/86 | B |
| | Bantoo, Director of Asia Oceania Bureau, Ministry of Foreign Affairs | 11/86 | C |
| | Tesha, Assistant Secretary of President's Office | 5/87 | C |
| | Kaigaroora, Member of Editorial Committee of *Daily News* | 7/87 | F |
| Central African Rep. (1) | Moosarabe, Vice Minister of Welfare and Social Problems | 8/86 | C |
| Nigeria (11) | Orusanya, Chief of Nigeria International Problem Research Institute | 3/86 | E |
| | Nonori, Science Editor of *Daily Times* | 9/86 | F |
| | Thompson, Editorial Director of *Guardian* | 9/86 | F |

357

## APPENDIX B *(continued)*

| Country (Number of visitors) | Name and title | Mo./Yr | Type of visit[2] |
|---|---|---|---|
| | Aryu, Vice Minister of Mine and Electricity and Steel | 11/86 | C |
| | Idio, Manager of NY Branch, *News Agency of Nigeria* | 1/87 | F |
| | James Nuwoso, Official of Ministry of Foreign Affairs | 3/87 | I |
| | Ahmed, President of Central Bank Attendants: | 3/87 | J |
| | Animashawn, Assistant Director of Overseas Investment Bureau Central Bank | | |
| | Ayanrou, Assistant Director of Overseas Investment Bureau, Central Bank | | |
| | Ayanrou, Assistant Director of Ministry of Finance | | |
| | Rukuman, Chairman of OPEC | 7/87 | D |
| | Abacha, Chief of Military Staff | 7/87 | J |
| Niger (18) | Gany, Director of International Co-operation Bureau, Ministry of Foreign Affairs Cooperation | 9/85 | G |
| | Kunche, Chairman of Supreme Military Council (Sovereign of the Nation) (with 16 attendants) | 9/86 | State guest |
| Burkina Faso (1) | Shiso, Deputy Director of State Affairs, Ministry of Foreign Affairs | 3/84 | C |
| Brundi (2) | Janku, Director of Asia Latin America and Oceania Bureau | 5/85 | C |
| | Abu League, Ministry of Foreign Affairs Cooperation | | |
| | Ngeso, Minister of Finance | 10/85 | B |
| Benan (1) | Randolf, Director of Asia Bureau, Ministry of Foreign Affairs | 6/85 | C |

## APPENDIX B *(continued)*

| Country (Number of visitors) | Name and title | Mo./Yr | Type of visit[2] |
|---|---|---|---|
| Madagascar (4) | Ratoshimandiri, Chief Editor of *Afaka* | 9/84 | F |
| | Ranurozaka, Vice Minister of Foreign Affairs | 10/86 | C |
| | Herizo Ratenbomahey | 10/86 | I |
| | Randorianosoro, Minister of Animal Industry, Fishery and Forestry | 7/87 | J |
| Malawi (1) | Muwafingo Mwila, Chief Official of Agricultural Affairs, Ministry of Agriculture | 12/84 | C |
| Mali (3) | Beie, Minister of Foreign Affairs and International Cooperation | 5/85 | A |
| | Dialo, Minister of Resources | 10/85 | J |
| | Ongoiba, Minister of Agriculture | 4/87 | J |
| Republic of South Africa (11) | Mupaka M. Manara | 3/86 | I |
| | Matyome E. Maponya | 3/86 | I |
| | Motsuenyani, President of Chamber of Commerce and Industry for Blacks | 9/86 | E |
| | Elizabeth Mokotong | 10/86 | I |
| | Tom Sengani, Lecturer at Univ. of South Africa | 10/86 | I |
| | Morris Regoabe | 11/86 | I |
| | Tema, Journalist of *South Africa Business Day* | 11/86 | F |
| | Oliver Tambo, Chairman of ANC (with three attendants) | 4/87 | Invi. AA |
| Mozambique (5) | Chisano, Minister of Foreign Affairs | 3/84 | A |
| | Sunbana, Director of International Cooperation Agency | 12/85 | C |
| | President Machely | 5/86 | B |
| | Zandamera, Director of Asia Oceania Bureau, Ministry of Foreign Affairs | 10/86 | C |
| | Verozo, Minister of International Cooperation | 5/87 | J |

| Country (Number of visitors) | Name and title | Mo./Yr | Type of visit[2] |
|---|---|---|---|
| Mauri-tius (4) | Nicholas, Vice Minister of Foreign Affairs | 7/85 | C |
| | Beedashie, Minister of Public Works | 5/86 | B |
| | Dubal, Vice Prime Minister and Minister of Employment and Tourism | 8/86 | B |
| | Dalue, Minister of Agriculture, Fishery and Natural Resources | 1/87 | B |
| Liberia (3) | Tearge, Chief Editor of *New Liberian* | 10/84 | F |
| | Davis, Coordinating Official of Asia, Africa and Asia | 8/85 | C |
| | Bureau, Ministry of Foreign Affairs James, Deputy Chief Editor of *New Liberian* | 10/86 | F |
| Rwanda (1) | Rukashaza, Vice Minister of Foreign Affairs Cooperation | 3/85 | C |
| Lesotho (2) | Polo, Director of Treaty Bureau, Ministry of Foreign Affairs | 6/85 | C |
| | Pololo, Minister of Agricultural Affairs | 6/87 | J |
| Togo (6) | Wara K. Kofi, Minister of Local Development / Kofi Jondo, Minister of National Enterprise | 5/85 | J |
| | Aribyui, Minister of Financial Affairs / Minister of Adodo Project Industry | 10/85 | J |
| | Minister of Adodo Project Industry | 8/86 | J |
| | Minister of Baruke Project Mining | 8/87 | J |
| Djibouti (1) | Fara, Minister of Foreign Affairs Cooperation | 3/86 | B |

# Note

<sup>1</sup> Countries within jurisdiction of Africa First and Second Sections.

<sup>2</sup> Types of visit.

A: Official Guest of Foreign Ministry

B: Unofficial visit of minister-level officials (invited by Japan Foreign Ministry)

C: Invitation of backbone officials

D: Invitation of higher executives

E: Opinion leaders

F: Invitation of foreign press

G: Invitation of receptive organization of the aided country

H: Official guest of Expo '85

I: Invitation of young people

J: Visiting Japan at their own expense

## APPENDIX C
## RECORDS OF PERFORMANCE OF "PAL 2000" PROJECT
### *(as of 31 October 1987)*

| Country | 2 November 1987 | Africa First Section |
| --- | --- | --- |
| | Period of stay | Name and title |
| Somalia | 4/6 - 4/13 | Tara, UN Special Commissioner for Displaced Persons |
| Comoro | 4/9 - 4/12 | President Abudara (with eight attendants) |
| Republic of South Africa | 4/19 - 4/25 | Oliver Tambo, Chairman of ANC (with three attendants) |
| Seychelles | 4/20 - 4/30 | San Jole, Vice Minister of Foreign Affairs |

## APPENDIX C *(continued)*

| Country | Period of stay | Name and title |
|---|---|---|
| Ghana | 5/5 - 5/9 | Kenes Dodge, Director of UNCTAD |
| Tanzania | 5/20 - 5/29 | Tesha, Assistant Secretary of President's Office |
| Kenya | 5/24 - 6/4 | Gache, Chief of *Kenya Times* Foreign News Section |
| Uganda | 5/28 - 6/2 | Mukiibi, Minister of Foreign Affairs (with three attendants) |
| Tanzania | 7/12 - 7/23 | Kaigarura, Journalist of *Daily News* |
| Guinea | 7/22 - 8/1 | Assistant Secretary of Fafana Project, International Cooperation Bureau, Ministry of International Cooperation |
| Nigeria | 7/26 - 7/31 | Rukuman, Chairman of OPEC |
| Tanzania | 9/7 - 9/12 | Mukapa, Minister of Foreign Affairs (with three attendants) |
| Zambia | 9/10 - 9/14 | Prime Minister Musokotowane (with three attendants) |
| Guinea | 10/1 - 10/13 | Kamara, Oficial of Middle and Near East Asia Section, Bureau of State Affairs, Ministry of Foreign Affaits |
| Central African Republic | 10/1 - 10/13 | Chibinda, Editorial Member of TV Bangi News |
| Cameroon | 10/1 - 10/13 | Chief of Personnel Section, Bono. Bere Project, National Land Development Department |
| Uganda | 10/5 - 10/17 | Oringe, Staff of Europe and Asia Section, Political Bureau, Ministry of Foreign Affairs |

362

| Country | Period of stay | Name and title |
|---|---|---|
| Mozambique | 10/7 - 10/17 | Koeryo, Translator for Asia Oceania Bureau, Ministry of Foreign Affairs |
| Ghana | 10/5 - 10/17 | Baba, Executive Official of Olympic Committee |
| Madagascar | 10/7 - 10/18 | Mireyu Rakotomarara (pianist) |
| Central African Republic | 10/5 - 10/15 | Jamani, Vice Minister of Information Communication, Art and Culture |
| Madagascar | 10/7 - 10/17 | Razon Daku, Director of Science Technology Research Support Bureau, Ministry of Science and Technology Research |
| Djibouti | 10/11 - 10/21 | Jiburiru, Director of Africa Asia Oceania Bureau, Ministry of Foreign Affairs Cooperation |
| Republic of South Africa | 10/11 - 10/22 | Ratagomo, Chief Editor of *Sowetan* |
| Sudan | 10/12 - 10/17 | Prime Minister Mahdi (with three attendants) |

Source:   MOFA (Internal Document translated from Japanese) Miss Miwa Irie.

# ENDNOTES

## CHAPTER 1

### East Asia and Africa — First Contacts

1. Publications of such institutions as Kyoto University's Center for African Area Studies (*African Study Monographs*), Japan Association for African Studies. African Society of Japan (*Africa-Japan*), Tokyo University of Foreign Studies Institute for the Study of Languages and Cultures of Asia and Africa, MOFA, (*Japan-Africa*), Tokyo University (*Memoirs of the Institute for Oriental Studies*) etc. have contributed much in opening up Japan's interest in Africa, and provided African readers with the perspective on Africa of Japanese scholars, government officials, and policy analysts, in addition to providing the Japanese with a vital understanding of African culture. ILCAA's Studies such as Morimichi Tomikawa, ed., *Sudan Sahel Studies* (1984, 1986); *African Languages and Ethnography, Vols 1-XIX*, etc., have gone a long way to provide Japanese scholars with insight into a variety of African societies and ethnic groups.

2. See Fujita, M. "Japanese Vies on Africa in the Edo Period," (Japanese) *Annals of Japan Association for Middle East Studies* No. 2 (1987); see also her "Early History of Afro-Japanese Relations — People called 'Kurobo' in the 16th century" (Japanese), *Hikaku Bungaku Kenkyu* (Studies of Comparative Literature) No. 51 (April 1987, Tokyo.)

3. Scholars and writers such as Jun Morikawa, Yoko Kitazawa, Nagato Yagi, Kenji Shiraishi, Masao Yoshida, Nishino Tertuaro, Yutaka Shinoda, Midori Fujita, are only a few of the growing number of Japanese Africanists, many of whom are increasingly becoming highly critical of Japanese policy in Africa. Some of these Africanists have adopted a Marxist analytical approach.

4. Edward W. Blyden, *Christianity, Islam & the Negro Race*, (London: W.B. Whittingham, 1887, 1967 reprint) p. 120 emphasis added.

5. See Shanti Pandit, *Asians in East and Central Africa*, (Nairobi, Kenya: Panco Publications, 1963) for some accounts of Asian families that settled in East Africa in the last couple of centuries. See also N.P. Naicker, *Indians Abroad: Asia and Africa* (New Delhi, 1971).

6. H.A.R. Gibb, trans., *Ibn Battuta: Travels in Asia and Africa*, (London: Routledge & Kegan Paul, 1929) p. 20.

7.  Graham W. Irwin, *Africans Abroad: A Documentary History of the Black Diaspora in Asia, Latin America and the Caribbean during the Age of Slavery*. (New York: Columbia University Press, 1977) pp. 138, 141. I am indebted to Irwin's work for a couple of sections that follow here.

8.  R.C. Majumdar *et al. An Advanced History of India,* (London: MacMillan, 1960, 2nd ed.), p. 287 cited in Irwin, *Africans Abroad*, p. 2.

9.  *Cambridge History of India*, 6 Vols. (Cambridge University Press, 1922-1927), Vol. 3: pp. 268-269.

10. See V.T. Rajeshekar, *Apartheid in India: An International Problem*, (Bangalore, India: Dalit Sahitya Academy, 1978, 1983 reprint), p. 37. In lengthy discussions in 1986 with me, Mr. Rajshekar, with tears freely-flowing down his black face, elaborated on the "unspeakable" conditions in which these black untouchables of India live. He called for a world-wide indictment of the Indian Government and the power behind it: the Hindu Brahmin ruling caste.

11. See Joseph E. Harris, *The African Presence in Asia: Consequences of the East African Slave Trade*, (Evanston: Northwestern University Press, 1971); Vasant D. Rao, "The Habshis: India's Unknown Africans," *Africa Report,* (September - October 1973), 18 (5); D. R. Seth, "The Life and Times of Malik Ambar", *Islamic Culture*, (1957), p. 31.

12. The phrase is adapted from the title of Harris' book, *The African Presence in Africa* (see note 11).

13. See especially C.R. Boxer, *The Great Ship from Amacon: Annals of Macao and the Old Japanese Trade* (Lisbon: Centro de Estudes Historicos Ultramarinos, 1959); — *The Portuguese Seaborne Empire,* 1415-1825 (New York: A.A. Knopf, 1969).

14. Boxer, *The Portuguese Seaborne*, pp. 13-14, 56-57, 63-64, 205-206, 211-216; C.R. Boxer, *The Christian Century in Japan* 1549-1650, (Berkely and Los Angeles: University of California Press; London: Cambridge University Press, 1951), pp. 105-110.

15. G.R. Potter, ed., *The New Cambridge Modern History:* Vol. 1: *The Rennaissance 1493-1520* (Cambridge University Press, 1964), p. 243.

16. For example, the first known record of a black African in Britain dates back to the Roman times when the Emperor Septimius Severus is recorded in the *Scriptores Historae Auguste* as having met outside the walls of Carlisle a "certain Ethiopian soldier famous among buffoons and always a notable jester". See Paul Edwards and James Walvin,

"Africans in Britain 1500-1800", in Martin L. Kilson and Robert I. Rotberg, eds, *The African Diaspora: Interpretive Essays*, (Cambridge, Mass. and London, England: Harvard University Press, 1976) p. 172.

17. Potter, *The Renaissance 1493-1520,* p. 422.

18. C.R. Boxer, "The Old Kingdom of Congo", in Ronald Oliver, ed., *The Dawn of African History,* (New York and London: Oxford University Press, 1968) pp. 77-78.

19. C.R. Boxer, *Fidalogos in the Far East 1550-1770.* (London, Hong Kong & New York: Oxford University Press, 1968) pp. 72-86.

20. This is the first known instance of a black force in history to ever defeat a European force. The Hatian force under Jean-Jacques Dessalines and Henry Christopher that defeated Napoleon's army in 1802 is usually given this accolade, perhaps because the latter had no European officer commanding it, unlike in the Canton-Macao fracas. C.R. Boxer, *The Christian Century in Japan,* p. 279.

21. Irwin, *Africans Abroad,* p. 170.

22. CFC Martin Wilbur, *Slavery in China during the Former Han Dynasty* (Chicago: Field Museum of Natural History, 1943): Teobaldo Filesi, *China and Africa in the Middle Ages* (London: Frank Cass, 1972) (see also note 24).

23. Irwin, *Africans Abroad*, p. 168 citing Ta Ming t'aitsu *Shih-lu, 14/4,* trans L. Carrington Goodrich.

24. Chang Hsing-lang, "The Importation of Negro Slaves to China Under The T'ang Dynasty (A.D. 618-907)", *Catholic University of Peking Bulletin* No. 7 (December, 1970) pp. 37-59. In Chinese, black slaves were called *K'un-lun-nu,* i.e. *K'un-lun* slaves. The term also refers to "devil slaves", "wild-men", "black servants", "barbarian servants", and the preferred Chinese epithet, *K'un-lun,* could also have referred as well to the hordes of other slaves — Turkic, Tibetan, and Iranian — who were imported into China from inner Asia at the time.

25. Quoted in Chang Hsing-lang, "The Importation of Negro Slaves to China", p. 41. Emphasis added. The Ainu natives of the mysterious Japanese island of Ezo (Modern Hokkaido) have been described in *The History of Travayle* as "savage men, clothed in beastes skynnes, rough bodyed with huge beardes, and monstrous machaches, the which they hold with little forkes as they drynke".

26. Marco Polo, *The Travels of Marco Polo, The Venetian*, trans. by Marsden, rev. ed., Thomas Wright, ed., (New York: AMS Press, 1968). Polo writes: "They are all black, and go stark naked, with only a little covering for decency. Their hair is black as pepper, and so frizzly that even with water you can scarcely straighten it. And their mouths are so large, their noses so turned, their lips so thick, their eyes so big and blood-shot that they look like very devils; they are in fact so hideously ugly that the world has nothing to show more horrid". Book III, Chapter 34.

27. Chang Hsing-lang, "The Importation of Negro Slaves to China", p. 41. Emphasis added.

28. Chang, "The Importation ..." For further studies concerning China and Africa, the following works are invaluable. J.J.L. Duyvendak, *China's Discovery of Africa* (London: Probstain, 1949); C. Martin Wilbur, *Slavery in China During the Former Han Dynasty;* Bruce D. Larkin, *China and Africa 1949-1970: The Foreign Policy of the People's Republic of China* (Berkeley, Los Angeles, London: University of California Press, 1971).

29. There were variously referred to as Zinj, Zenj, Zanzi, Zanghi, or Zanghibar (i.e. Zanzibar island, which is today part of Tanzania). Marco Polo's zinj or zenj, etc. was, in actuality, that coastal strip which, in the words of one scholar, stretched from southern Somalia to Tanzania and came to be called Zingis or Zinzion by Greek geographers, and the Land of Zanj by the Arabs. See Gervase Mathew, "The Land of Zanj", in Ronald Oliver, ed., *The Dawn of African History*, p. 45.

30. For a fuller acount of this description see Frederick Hirth and W.W. Rockwill, eds., *Chau Ju-Kua*, (St. Petersburg: Imperial Academy of Sciences, 1911). The Chinese *seng-chi* means negroes. In Malaysia blacks today are still called Zanggi or Janggi.

31. See G. Ferrand, "Le K'ouen-louen et les anciennes navigations interoceaniques dans les mers du sud", *Journal Asiatique* (March-April 1991) pp. 330-333.

32. Perhaps what this now calls for is further research on the history of migrations or movement of Africans into various parts of Oceania/South Pacific — Fiji, Solomon, Tonga, Kiribati, Tuvalu, Vanuata, Kanakland / New Caledonia, New Zealand, New Papua Guinea, etc. So much of the African diaspora still lies buried in the sand of indifferent scholarship.

33. Kitsuzo Kuwabara, "On P'u Shou-keng ...", *Memoirs of the Research Department of the Tokyo Bunko* (1928) No. 2 pp. 62-63.

34. Boxer, *The Christian Century in Japan*, p. 299.

35. Boxer, *Fidalgos In the East*, p. 235.

36. Basil Davidson, *Africa in History: Themes and Outlines*, (New York: Collier Books, 1968, 1974), pp. 184-185.

37. Davidson, *Africa In History*, pp. 226-227.

38. Perhaps it should be noted, in passing, that at about this time when the Japanese were encountering Africans, in the Americas (in that region which later turned out to be the United States) the first known revolt by African slaves was taking place when a group of 100 slaves brought by Lucas Vasquez de Ayllon in 1526 rebelled. See Daniel P. Mannix and Malcolm Cowley, *Black Cargoes: A History of the Atlantic Slave Trade, 1518-1865*, (New York: Viking Press, 1962) p. 54.

39. Fujita, "Early History of Afro-Japanese Relations ..." (Japanese) p. 2. In works such as Yauhiko Takiguchis, *Saga Rekishi Sanpo* (A Walk of the History of Saga) published by Sogenshia Company, and Akira Sugitani Sugiya's, *Saga-ken no Hyakunen* (A Hundred Years of the Saga Prefecture) published by Yamagawa Shyuppan Shya is addressed the issue of Africans in Kyushu. Translation courtesy of Kazuhiro Iwasawa (Tokyo) and Ms Chiyono Sata (Washington, D.C.). I am especially grateful to Kohei Muraoka of Africa Division, NEC, for drawing my attention to these two works.

40. Boxer, *Fidalgos in the Far East*, p. 230. See his *The Great Ship from Amacon*, pp. 41-42.

41. Arnold Rubin, *Black Nanban: Africans in Japan During the Sixteenth Century* (Bloomington: African Studies Program, Indiana University Press, 1974), p. 7. citing C.R. Boxer. This is the first study outside Japan devoted to African and Japanese interactions from the earliest period conceivable, if we discount Boxer's occasional references in his works, such as in *The Great Ship from Amacon*, pp. 41-42, 75, 82-83; see also Yosoburo Takekoshi, *The Economic Aspects of the History of the Civilisation of Japan*, 3 vols. (London: George Allen & Unwin, 1930), vol. 1, p. 449, wherein the author refers to Visitor Valignaro's meeting with Shogun Hideyoshi as cited in Boxer's work, *Ibid.*

42. Boxer, the *Christian Century in Japan*, p. 153.

43. Midori Fujita, "Japanese Views on Africa in the Edo Period," p. 240. See note 2. My discussions with Ms Fujita in Tokyo (December 1987) actually affirmed the essentiality and complementarity of this pioneering effort. Moreover, our independent but coincidental research projects certainly suggest the timeliness of this review of historical contacts between Africans and Japanese, particularly given the current significant role of Japan in Africa. Fujita's doctoral work will undoubtedly be of great value to Afro-Japanese studies.

44. Fujita, *Ibid.*

45. Boxer, *The Christian Century in Japan*, p. 35.

46. Boxer, Fidalgos in the Far East, p. 231.

47. C.R. Boxer, *Four Centuries of Portuguese Expansion 1415-1825: A Succint Survey* (Berkeley & Los Angeles: University of California Press; Johannesburg: University of Witwatersrand, 1969), p. 60. For an interesting study of liaisons of modern Western adventures — military personnel, literary figures, businessmen, etc. and Oriental women, and how, in the process, these sexual dalliances have contributed to the debasement of Asian societies, see "Sex in Asia: Sexual Revolution", *Far Eastern Economic Review*, (9 January 1976), pp. 21-33. In giving a sketch of Japanese women, Mary R. Beard, *The Force of Women in Japanese History* (Washington, D.C.: Public Affairs Press, 1953) shows how Japanese women have been caught up in a veritable dilemma in their attempts to balance Western socialisation with Oriental (Japanese) traditionalism and culture. This is part of the dilemma facing Japan today: how to be modern without becoming western, and thus losing essential Japanism. See *Ibid.*, pp. 141-142.

48. See for example Kobayashi Kazuyoshi, "Japan's Sex Industry as Number One", *Japan Quarterly* 313 (3) July-September, 1984, pp. 278-279.

49. Boxer, *Fidalgos in the Far East*, p. 233.

50. Protests by the Jesuit Mission in Japan to the King of Portugal and Spain should, of course, not be regarded lightly. See, for example, Boxer, *The Great Ship from Amacon*, pp. 8, 36; Boxer, *The Portuguese Seaborne Empire*, pp. 76, 253-254.

51. David Bergamini, *Japan's Imperial Conspiracy* (New York: William Morrow & Co., 1971, p. 208.

52. Cited in James Murdock, *History of Japan* (3 Vols.) : Vol. 2: *During the Century of Early Foreign Intercourse* 1542-1651 (New York: Frederick Ungar Publishing Co., 1964), p. 243.

53. Bargamini, *Japan's Imperial Conspiracy*, p. 212.

54. Museums in the Kansai area (Kyoto, Kobe, Hyogo, Osaka, etc.) and Tokyo abound in these fine artistic works. In this regard the following studies are helpful: Okamoto, *The Namban Art of Japan;* Tokihide Nagayama, *An Album of Historical Materials Connected With Foreign Intercourse* (Nagasaki, Japan: K. Fugimoti, 1918); Shin'ichi Tani & Tadashi Sugase, *Namban Art: A Loan Exhitibion From Japanese Collections*, (New York & Kyoto : International Exhibition Foundation, 1973).

55. Hiroshima Ishiyama, "Promotion of Science and Technology in the Meiji Period (1868-1912)", *Look Japan* (Tokyo) 10 October 1986. For a detailed analysis of the impact of The Netherlands on Japan, Grant K. Goodman, *The Dutch Impact on Japan* (1640-1853) (Leiden, The Netherlands: E.J. Brill, 1967), is instructive.

56. Herbert H. Gowen, *Outline History of Japan* (New York & London: D. Appleton & Co., 1927), p. 300. This treaty, with its galling implications of Japanese inferiority, rankled the Japanese sense of national pride for many years, and was contributory to the military rapacities subsequently launched by Japan.

57. Francis L. Hawkes, *Narrative of the Expedition of an American Squadron to the China Seas and Japan: Performed in the Years 1852, 1853, and 1854*. Under the Command of Commodore M.C. Perry, United States Navy. (New York: Appleton & Co., 1856), p. 295.

58. M. Paske-Smith, *Western Barbarians in Japan and Formosa in Tokugawa Days: 1603-1868*, (New York: Paragon Book Reprint Corporation, 1968), pp. 188-189.

59. Thanks are due to Ms Midori Fujita whose knowledge of Japanese sources was very helpful to my research.

60. Captain F. Brinkley, *Japan: Its History, Arts and Literature*, 8 Vols, (Boston and Tokyo: J.B. Millet Company, 1901-1902), Vol. 4: p. 217.

61. Ishiyama, "Promotion of Science ...".

62. For details see Japanese National Commission for UNESCO, *Japan: Its Land, People and Culture*. (Tokyo: Ministry of Finance, 1958), pp. 74-79, 182-186.

63. W.G. Beasly, "Tradition and Modernity in Post-War Japan", *Asian Affairs: Journal of the Royal Society for Asian Affairs* Vol. XI: Part 1 (February 1980), p. 5. Notions of unimaginative Japanese copying of things Western are of course wrong. A visit to both the Kobe-Hyogo and Tokyo area museums show that both the Kobe-Hyogo and Tokyo area museums show that both the Momoyama and Edo periods were fecund with original Japanese glassware manufacturing, amongst others.

64. For the state and status of US science in the third quarter of the 19th century, see Robert V. Bruce, *The Launching of Modern American Science 1846-1876* (New York: Alfred A. Knopf, 1987). For example only 3,000 Americans used scientific training in their work, and only about a tenth of this figure did it with some distinction, according to a reviewer. On the other hand, of the numerous European scientific societies, any one of them spent more on publications than all the American societies combined.

65. The late Foreign Minister, Toshio Kimura, "On the 16th Anniversary of the Inauguration of the OAU, " *Africa-Japan* No. 16 (Tokyo) p. 5.

66. Terutaro Nishino, "Japanese Views of Africa during the Meiji Era", (Japanese), *The Memoirs of the Institute for Oriental Culture* No. 32 (March, 1964), p. 3.

## CHAPTER 2

### Japan and Colonial Africa: 1885-1960

67. "Private correspondence". In a letter of October 16, 1987 to the author Professor William D. Perdue of Eastern Washington University spelled out some of his concerns regarding the Japanese role in Africa (see also Chapter 10).

68. Jun Morikawa, "The Myth and Reality of Japan's Relations with Colonial Africa — 1885-1960", *Journal of African Studies* Vol. 12: No. 1 (Spring 1985), pp. 40, 44.

69. Shigenori Doi, "A Consideration on the History of the Relation between Japan and East Africa" (Japanese) *Africa-Kenkyu* (Journal of African Studies) No. 21 (March, 1982), pp. 90-96. Acknowledgement is due to Ms Chiyono Sata of Catholic University of America (Wash. D.C.) for translating Doi's work for my purposes.

70. Cited by Nishino, "Japanese Views ..." p. 4 (see note 66).

71. *Look Japan*, 10 February 1986: "Interview with Noboru Nakahira Director-General of the Ministry of Foreign Affairs U.N. Bureau". Various editions of MOFA's *Yearbook* repeatedly make this claim without, unfortunately, any helpful elaboration.

72. See for example Hideo Oda and Kazuyoshi Aoki, "Japan and Africa: Beyond this Fragile Partnership", in Robert S. Ozaki and Walter Arnold, *Japan's Foreign Relations: A Global Search for Economic Security*, (Boulder and London: Westview Press, 1985), p. 153.

73. During my earlier (1981) discussions in Tokyo with the Deputy Director of Africa Division II, Mr Ryuichi Ishii (November 17, 1981), he often peppered his facts with this reference of "wide distance separating the two cultures". Although in my November-December 1987 discussions with a number of the directors of the Africa Divisions (see Chapter 3) there was none of this simplistic reference of the great nautical mile distance between Africa and Japan, although the Foreign Ministry's yearbooks repeat it often. In *Look Japan*, 10 October 1985, it constitutes a heading: "Japanese and The Far Continent".

74. At this point in time Japan had clearly demonstrated that it has the capabilities and technological innovativeness to engage in industrial expansion. For an analysis of some industries in Japan during the Meiji Period see Yasuzo Horie, "Government Industries in the Early Years of Meiji Era", *Kyoto University Economic Review XIV:* 1 (January 1939), pp. 67-87.

75. See *The Berlin Act, 1885* in Raymond Leslie Buell, *The Native Problem in Africa* (New York: Macmillan Co., 1928) II, pp. 891-907.

76. See for example S. Daniel Neumark, *Foreign Trade and Economic Development in Africa: A Historical Perspective*, (Standford, Cal.: Stanford University Press, 1964), pp. 194, 195.

77. See Basil Davidson, *The African Genius: An introduction To African Social and Cultural History*, (Boston and Toronto: Little Brown & Co., 1969) p. 270, see also by the same author for the machinations of German imperialism in the same area, *Africa in History: Themes and Outlines* (New York: Collier Books, 1968), pp. 251-252.

78. Davidson, *The African Genius*, p. 270.

79. Yutaka Shinoda, "Still a long way to go" (i.e. in Japan-African relations), *West Africa*, 28 November 1983, p. 2743. Shinoda's columns

on Japan- Africa have often been critical of Japanese policies towards Africans and her role in Africa. See Chapter 4 and 10.

80. Edward A. Olsen, "Japan/Africa: Building Bridges to Africa," *Africa Report*, March-April 1980, pp. 52-53 — makes a stinging rebuke of Japanese "racism". Don Shannon, "Japan in Africa: commercial payoff", *Africa Report*, May 1970, pp. 24-27 is similarly critical. The already cited works by Japanese scholars and writers — e.g. Nishino, Morikawa, Shinoda, Kitazawa, etc. — assume an equally critical stance towards Japan's view and understanding of Africa. There are many other works by Japanese writers who have stayed and worked in Africa for several years, and which show none of the alleged Japanese racial prejudice towards blacks as cited by the above-mentioned scholars, e.g. Masayuki Nishie, *African Diary: Bio of Macha Ine* (Japanese) (Tokyo: Shinchosha 1987). — translation courtesy of Ms. Yumiko Ito. (Tokyo) Nishie's work, which shows not a trace of race prejudice, recounts the length and breadth of his African experiences (see also the views expressed in Chapter 7).

81. See for example, in addition to Nishie, *ibid.*, the numerous reports of the JICA-JOCV Africa participants, as well as African comments (e.g. Nobel Laureatte Wole Soyinka) and scholars such as Chinweizu, (see note 82). These insist of course, that Japanese are neither *that* prejudiced towards Africans, as claimed by most accidental scholars, nor have they exhibited an historical accumulation of yellow supremacist ideology towards blacks.

82. Chinweizu, *The West and the Rest of US: White Predators, Black Slavers and the African Elite*, (New York: Vintage Books, 1975), p. 102. Prof. Tsuneo Morino of Tokyo University of Foreign Area Studies recounted to me similar perceptions of East Africans he met in Tanzania who fought against the Japanese in World War II. See below.

83. J. Forbes Munro, *Africa and The International Economy 1800-1960*, (London: J. M. Dent & Sons; Totowea, N.J.: Nicholson Publishers, 1976), p. 90.

84. The Japanese Government. *White Papers of Japan 1984-1985: annual abstracts of official reports and statistics of the Japanese Government* (Tokyo: Japanese Institute of International Affairs, 1985), p. 34. See also notes 71 and 73.

85. See William W. Lockwood, *The Economic Development of Japan: Growth and Structural Change 1868-1938*, (Princeton: Princeton University Press, 1954), p. 18. See also *Ibid.*, p. 508 for discussion of the Iron Works.

86. Neumark, *Foreign Trade and Economic Development*, p. 194.

87. Lockwood, *The Economic Development of Japan*, p. 94.

88. Morikawa, "The Myth and Reality of Japan's Relations..." p. 42.

89. Mahmood Mamdani, *Politics and Class Formation in Uganda*, (London and New York: Monthly Review Press, 1976), p. 93.

90. Cited by Mamdani, *Politics and Class Formation*, p. 94.

91. Cited in *Ibid.* note 109.

92. E.A. Brett, *Colonialism and Underdevelopment in East Africa: The Politics of Economic Change 1919-1939*, (New York, London & Lagos: Nok Publishers, 1973), p. 152.

93. Brett, *Colonialism and Underdevelopment*, p. 155.

94. Lockwood, *The Economic Development of Japan*, p. 348.

95. Brett, *Colonialism and Underdevelopment*, p. 156.

96. Lu Miagong, "Tokyo Draws Closer to Africa", *Beijing Review*, 3 June 1985, p. 12.

97. Sir Humphrey Leggett cited in Brett, *Colonialism and Underdevelopment in East Africa*, p. 269.

98. Tsuneto Yano Memorial Society. Nippon 1958: *A Chartered Survey of Japan*, (Tokyo: Kokusei-sha, 1958), p. 52.

99. Hla Myint, "An Interpretation of Economic Backwardness," in A.N. Agarwala and S.P. Singh, eds., *Economics of Underdevelopment*. (London, Oxford & New York: Oxford University Press, 1958, 1963, 1971 reprint), p. 122.

100. A review of the public pronouncements of postwar Japanese prime ministers will confirm this obsessive concern of the Japanese leadership with pacifism: Shigeru Yoshida; 1946-1955; Hatoyama Ichiro, 1955-1956; Ishibashi Tanzan, 1956-1957; Kishi Nobusuke 1957-1960; Ikeda Hayato, 1960-1964; Eisaku Sato, 1964-1972; Kakue Tanaka, 1972-1974; Takeo Miki, 1974-1976; Takeo Fukuda, 1976-1978; Masayoshi Ohira, 1978-1980; Zenko Suzuki 1980-1982; Yasuhiro Nakasone, 1982-1987;

Noboru Takeshita 1987-1991; Kiichi Miyazawa, 1991-1993 Nakasone was the most bellicose of these pacifists.

101. See Chapter 3.

102. In certain quarters of Japan there are some who now vigorously denounce this pacifism as idealistic and unprincipled. Most of these critics echo criticism of some Western scholars such as Wolfern (see note 141). (See also Chapter 3.)

103. The prolific scholarship of Hiroharu Seki as well as the publications of the Institute for Peace Science, Hiroshima University, and some of those of the Institute of Oriental Culture, Tokyo University, etc., outline the breadth of the peace movement. For some of these outlines see Seki, *The Asia-Pacific in the Global Transformation*, (Tokyo: University of Tokyo Institute of Oriental Culture, 1986), especially Chapters 9 and 10, pp. 139-146, for issues on peace studies and the peace movement.

104. *The Japan Year Book* 1936. (Tokyo: Foreign Affairs Association of Japan, 1936). p. 386.

105. Council on Foreign Relations. *Japan Between East and West*, (New York: Harper & Brothers; London: Oxford University Press, 1957), p. 12.

106. Ken Post, *The New States of West Africa* (Baltimore, Maryland: Penguin Books, 1964), p. 111.

107. Disingenuous Japanese officials claim what otherwise their own documentary data disprove. We know it to be incorrect when the Japanese Government claims that "Japan's economic cooperation with the countries of Africa had been relatively minor because of geographical and historical reasons," *White Papers 1984-1985,* p. 34. Japan did, in fact, have wide economic ties with the African colonies, though historically (rather than geographically), Japan was prevented by European colonial overlords from a full economic integration and interaction with the African colonies. Yet Japan could have initiated human/social contacts (as she has now successfully done) with African peoples, had these trading companies and government economic missions not been obsessed with the commercial angle of their presence in Africa.

## CHAPTER 3

### Japan's Diplomacy Towards Africa

108. See for example Japanese Institute of International Affairs. *White Papers of Japan 1976-1977: annual abstract of official reports and statistics of the Japanese Government.* (Tokyo: Japanese Institute of International Affairs, 1977), p. 76. The *White Papers of Japan* citations will henceforth be shortened as in note 109.

109. *White Papers of Japan 1974-1975,* (Tokyo, 1976), p. 79. See also *White Papers of Japan 1976-1977*: "... The basis of Japan's diplomatic policy toward Africa is the promotion of friendship and mutually beneficial cooperation" (p. 75).

110. The Tokyo-based Lotus Press publicatons (e.g. Jack Seward and Howard van Zandt, *Japan: The Hungry Guest: Japanese Business Ethics vs Those of the US.,* Tokyo: Lotus Press, 1985) frequently employ this strident tone of Japan's role in world commerce. Their shrill denunciations of Japan often sound too discordant and unbalanced to be taken seriously.

111. Some would even say South Africa was the fourth. Japan had certainly felt so at one time, for she initiated some "quasi-diplomatic" ties with South Africa as early as 1910 and subsequently opened a consular office in Cape Town in 1918. Only in 1992 did Japan elevate her diplomatic relations with South Africa (see Chapter 10).

112. Kingoro, "The Need for Emigration and Expansion", in Ivan Morris, ed., *Japan 1931-1945: Militarism, Fascism, Japanism*, (Boston: D.C. Heath & Co., 1963). See also Ryusaku Tsunada, Wm. Theodore de Bary, and Donald Keen, compilers, *Sources of the Japanese Tradition,* (New York: Columbia University Press), p. 798.

113. Morikawa, "Japan and Colonial Africa". *The Journal of Modern African Studies* (22) (1) 1984. p. 44.

114. Shigenori Doi (see note 69) has dealt in detail with the East Africa Division and the Imperial Japanese Army.

115. For the conscription of thousands of Africans during World War II and the pressures brought to bear upon many Africans to produce for the war effort, see Davis Killingray and Richard Rathbone, eds., *Africa and the Second World War* (London: Macmillan Press, 1986).

116. Ministry of Justice. *Summary of Statistics on Aliens in Japan in 1984* (Tokyo: Foreign Press Centre/Japan, December 1985, February 1986), p. 1.

117. For details of the resolutions and recommendations of the Asian-African Conference held at Bandung, Indonesia, on 18-24 April 1955, see *The Asian-African Conference: Final Communique*, (Bandung, Indonesia: May 1955). For a "non-aligned" interpretation of the Bandung spirit see Haroub Othman, "The Afro-Asian Political Map and the Bandung Spirit", *Indian Review of African Affairs* 2(3) June 1985, pp. 3-18.

118. *MOFA, Japan and Africa: South of the Sahara: Extending and Deepening Relations,* (Tokyo: Ministry of Foreign Affairs, n.d. (1979), p. 13.

119. Shigeru Yoshida, *The Yoshida Memoirs: The Story of Japan Crisis*, trans. Kenichi Yoshida, (Boston: Houghton Mifflin Co., 1962), pp. 110-111.

120. Koji Tairo, "Japan After the 'Oil shock': An International Resource Pauper", *Current History*, 68 (404), March 1975, p. 180.

121. See note 100.

122. Masashi Nishihara, *The Japanese and Sukarno's Indonesia: Tokyo-Jakarta Relations, 1951-1966*, (Honolulu, Hawaii: The University Press of Hawaii, 1976), p. 163.

123. Toshio Kimura, "On the 16th Anniversary of the Inauguration of the O.A.U.", p. 7. (See note 65).

124. Ministry of Foreign Affairs. *Diplomatic Bluebook 1986 Edition*, (Tokyo: Foreign Press Centre/Japan, 1986), p. 89.

125. Shoji Takase, "The Policies of Participating," *Japan Quarterly,* (Tokyo) 33 (3) July-September 1986, pp. 244-251.

126. *White Papers of Japan 1984-1985*, (Tokyo, 1985), p. 34.

127. *Diplomatic Bluebook* 1986, p. 88.

128. See for example Lawrence Olson, *Dimensions of Japan* (New York: American University Field Staff, 1963), p. 291 in the case of India but applicable to all the developing world; however this is no longer applicable to much of Africa today.

129. Oda and Oaki, "Japan and Africa", p. 157. (See note 72.)

130. See *Asian Recorder*, 1-7 January 1985, p. 1811.

131. John Ravenhill, "Japan and Africa: Improving on a Dismal Aid Record", *Africa Contemporary Record*, Vol. 15 1981/1982, p. A210.

132. Oda and Aoki, "Japan and Africa", p. 166. (See note 129.)

133. The Japan Institute of International Affairs. *White Papers of Japan 1982-1983*, (Tokyo: Ministry of Foreign Affairs, 1984), p. 34.

134. During this interview (26 November 1987: Tokyo) Shimizu noted that when the Ethiopian marathon runner during the 1964 Tokyo Olympics won the race "it became an emotional high for Japan". He also noted that the "Emperor-to-Emperor factor" has played an emotional (i.e. sentimental) role in the Ethiopia-Japan ties. He could, of course, also have cited (but did not) that Emperor Haile Selassie once suggested to Emperor Hirohito that Japan and Ethiopia could strengthen their imperial ties with the bonds of matrimony between the younger members of their imperial households: similarly did they feel when their African protege and Japanese speaking, Douglas Waikihuru ... won the World Marathon in Rome in 1987.

135. Prime Minister's Office. *Public Opinion Survey on Diplomacy*, (Tokyo: Foreign Press Centre/Japan, July 1987), p. 3.

136. Shimizu, "Interview", *Ibid*. The JICA/JOCV participants in Africa (see Part III) have shown remarkable ability to adapt, work, and live in Africa. Japanese diplomats are of course not JOCV participants, nor should they be expected to be willing to be exposed to the rigorous regime that the JOCV volunteers undergo. See also Shimizu's article. "The Flow of Economic Aid to Developing Countries in 1984", *Look Japan*, 10 August 1985, p. 44.

137. See Shintaro Abe, *Creative Diplomacy: Japan's Initiative for Peace and Prosperity,* (Tokyo: Ministry of Foreign Affairs, 1985) p. 26. Abe's satisfaction with the direction of the Japan-Africa ties may be expressed by the title of his article "A Gratifying Relationship", *West Africa*, 28 November 1983, p. 2 739.

138. Cited in C.L. Sulzberger, "Japan's Sun Also Rises", *The New York Times,* 10 March 1972, p. 37.

139. Ronald A. Morse, "Japan's Drive to Pre-Eminence", *Foreign Policy,* 69, (Winter 1987/1988), p. 6.

140. Abe, *Creative Diplomacy,* p. 7.

141. See for example the harsh criticism of Karel G. van Wolferen, "The Japan Problem", *Foreign Affairs*, (Winter 1986/1987), p. 289.

142. *Asahi Evening News,* (Tokyo), 24 March 1981.

143. Numerous works expounding on the respective diplomacies of these regions vis-a-vis Africa are easily available to merit further citation here.

144. For an elaboration on the firm grip that France maintains on Africa, see Martin Staniland, "Francophone Africa: the enduring French Connection", *Annals of the American Academy of Political and Social Science.* 489, (January 1987) pp. 51-62.

## CHAPTER 4
### African Diplomacy Towards Japan

145. Private Discussions, Tokyo, 27 November 1987.

146. Private Discussions, Tokyo, 3 December 1987.

147. See *Asahi Evening News* (Tokyo), 24 March 1981.

148. Only the Zimbabwe and Zambia ambassadors responded fully to the questionnaires I requested them to complete. Senegal made a partial response. One questionnaire sent to the Libyan People's Bureau was returned undelivered by the postal office. African ambassadors I discussed with in Tokyo were more enthusiastic in words but unresponsive in deeds. In any event the standard works on African diplomacy and international relations are:

    (i)    Ali A. Mazrui, *Africa's International Relations: The Diplomacy of Dependency and Change,* (London and Boulder, Col.: Heinemann and Westview Press, 1977),

    (ii)    Vernon McKay, (ed) *African Diplomacy: Studies in the Determinants of Foreign Policy,* (New York/Washington, D.C./London: Frederick A. Praeger, 1966).

149. Ali A. Mazrui, "The Monarchical Tendency in African Political Culture" in Marion E. Doro and Newell M. Stultz, (eds), *Governing in Black Africa: Perspectives on New States*, (Englewood Cliffs, N.J.: Prentice-Hall, 1970) pp. 18-33.

150. A classic analysis of the potential of great power interventionism in Africa is Timothy M. Shaw, "The Future of the Great Powers in Africa: Towards a Political Economy of Intervention", *Journal of Modern African Studies*, 21 (4), December 1983, pp. 555-586. Shaw sees the

"present post neo-colonial period in Africa in which intervention is increasingly strategic rather than structural". *Ibid.,* 556-566. For a somewhat different view see I. William Zartman, "The Future of Europe and Africa: Decolonization or Dependency?" in Timothy M. Shaw, (ed.), *Alternative Futures for Africa,* (Boulder, Col.: Westview Press, 1982).

151. See Obasanjo's article in *Foreign Policy,* 57, (Winter 1984/1985), pp. 80-91.

152. Edmund J. Kellex, "The Politics of State Survival: Continuity and Change in Ethiopian Foreign Policy", *Annals of the American Academy of Political and Social Science,* 489, (January 1987), pp. 76-77, makes an in-depth analysis of this issue.

153. "In November 1987, Mengistu himself publicly called the hunger situation in Ethiopia 'frightening', and the Ethiopian Relief and Rehabilitation Commission (RCC) claimed that some two million peasants were at risk in Wollo alone". Jack Sheperd, "Ethiopia: The Use of Food as an Instrument of U.S. Foreign Policy", *Issue,* Vol. XIV (1985), p. 5.

154. See for example *Africa Research Bulletin,* 23 (8), 15 September 1986, p. 8176.

155. For the perennial problems of ideology in political behaviour or sociological theory a number of studies are instructive especially the classic works by William D. Perdue, *Sociological Theory: Explanation, Paradigm and Ideology,* (Palto, Cal.: Mayfield Publishing Co., 1986) cf. pp. 388-400, and Mark N. Hagopian, *Regimes, Movements, and Ideologies,* (New York and London: Longman, 1978).

156. See Timothy M. Shaw and M.J. Grieve, "Dependence as an Approach to Understanding Continuing Inequalities in Africa", *Journal of Developing Studies,* 13 (1979) pp. 229-246.

157. Ali A. Mazrui, *The African Condition,* (Cambridge University Press: Cambridge, etc. 1980), p. 80.

158. Olajide Aluko, "Ideology and Foreign Policies of African States", *Jerusalem Journal of International Relations,* 9 (1) March 1987, pp. 121-134. But this classification seems to me to have been overtaken by the march of events as I shall indicate presently.

159. I. William Zartman, "Issues of African Diplomacy in the 1980s", *Orbis* 25 (4) Winter 1982, p. 1028.

381

160. Cf. Edourd Bustin, "The Foreign Policy of the Republic of Zaire", *Annals of the American Academy of Political*, pp. 63-75. See note 152.

161. Staniland, "Francophone Africa: The Enduring French Connection", *Annals*, p. 51. See *Ibid*. The former Assistant Secretary of State, G. Mennen Williams, in his book, *Africa for Africans* (Grand Rapids, Mi.: Willima B. Eerdmans Publishers, 1969) writes that "in French speaking African countries the civil service code provided for a periodic 'home leave' to France for black civil servants just as it did for Frenchmen". p. 14.

162. Quoted in John D. Battasby, "Land of Apartheid Befriends an Indian Ocean isle", *The New York Times*, 28 December 1987.

163. See Timothy M. Shaw, "Nigeria Restrained: Foreign Policy Under Changing Political and Petroleum Regimes", *Annals*. pp. 40-50. (See note 161.)

164. Zartman, "The Future of Europe and Africa", *Alternative*, pp. 275-277. (See note 150.)

165. Zartman, "Issues of African Diplomacy", p. 1028. (See note 159.)

166. I. William Zartman, *International Relations in The New Africa*, (Lanham,New York and London: University Press of America 1987, originally published by Prentice-Hall in 1966), p. 56. Zartman distinguishes as major foreign-policy ideologies "African Socialism, Pan-Africanism, and comprehensive anticolonialism". *(Ibid.* p. 57). In my work I restrict ideology in foreign policy to the latter, particularly *vis-a-vis* Japan's involvement in South Africa.

167. See for example Zartman, "Issues of African Diplomacy in the 1980s". (See note 165.)

168. See Olsen, "Japan/Africa". (See note 80.)

169. See *Africa* (London) No. 171 (November 1985), pp. 59-67.

170. Richard J. Payne, "Japan's South Africa Policy", *African Affairs,* Vol. 86 No. 343 (April 1987).

171. Guy Arnold, *Aid in Africa*, (London: Kogan Page; New York: Nicholes, 1979), pp. 89-92, et cetera.

172. Denis Martin, "Par de la le boubou et la cravate: pour une sociologie de l'innovation politique en Afrique noire". *Canadian Journal of African Studies*, 20 (1) 1986: 4-35. The subtitle translates: "for a sociology of political innovation in Black Africa".

173. John Hatch, *Africa Emergent,* (London: Secker and Warburg, 1974), p. 188.

174. Arnold Rivkin, *The African Presence in World Affairs: National Development and Its Role in Foreign Policy,* (London: The Free Press of Glencoe, 1963) pp. 234-235. Clearly then the appearance at the UN General Assembly in 1960 of a large number of newly independent states from tropical Africa introduced a new type of diplomacy into the conduct of international affairs. It is for this reason that we constantly read in Japanese government documents such phrases as: "... we note the remarkably increased role being taken by African countries in international society. Their activities at various international conferences and over resources and other problems in recent years have been spectacular, and the Japanese interest in Africa has greatly increased as a result". *White Papers of Japan,* 1974-1975, p. 78.

175. John Ravenhill, "Japan and Africa", p. A210. (See note 131.)

176. McKay "International Conflict Patterns", in McKay, (ed) *African Diplomacy,* p. 3. (See note 148.)

177. See *the Liberal Star,* (LDP monthly) Vol. 15: No. 174 (10 July 1986), p. 13.

178. *Asahi Evening News* (Tokyo), 24 March 1981.

179. *Africa Diary* (New Delhi), 21 (4) June 11-17, 1981, p. 10553.

180. *Africa Research Bulletin,* 15 May 1981, p. 6059.

181. Yutaka Shinoda, "Japan-Zimbabwe 'Love Affair'," *Mainichi Daily News* (Tokyo), 22 March 1981.

182. *Facts on File,* 19 June 1981, p. 429.

183. *Africa Research Bulletin,* 15 July 1981, p. 6126.

184. Cited in John Mukela, "The IMF Fallout", *Africa Report,* (January-February 1987), p. 65.

185. See note 145.

186. *The Japan Times* (Tokyo), 5 May 1987.

187. *Africa Diary,* 23 (27) July 2-8, 1983, p. 11512.

188. The Government of Japan. *Relations Between Japan and the Republic of Senegal,* (Tokyo: MOFA Africa Division, April 1979), trans. by Foreign Press Centre/Japan.

189. The 1987 Japanese Ministry of Justice statistics state that 112 Japanese reside in Dakar while the Senegalese Embassy in Tokyo in a response to my inquiries state that approximately 50 Japanese reside in Senegal, and 30 Senegalese reside in Japan. It is the Japanese figures that are clearly reliable however. Nonetheless the Ministry of Justice (Tokyo) errs slightly when it says they all reside in the capital. In Chapter 7 I show some of them residing outside Dakar.

190. See *the Liberal Star,* 10 August 1987, p. 14.

191. Ministry of Foreign Affairs. *Information Bulletin 1983,* (Tokyo 1983). pp. 150-151.

## CHAPTER 5

### Japan's Aid To Africa

192. Suzuki, "Cooperation Between the Overseas Economic Cooperation Fund and the World Bank in Sub-Saharan Africa", (Mimeo), March 1986/The OECF. Hiroaki Suzuki is a World Bank official in Washington, D.C. He remains on the staff of the OECF.

193. Oda and Aoki, "Japan and Africa", pp. 154-155. (See note 129.)

194. White, *Japanese Aid* (London: Overseas Development Institute, 1964), p. 1.

195. Cited in James Brooke, "Japanese Make Roads, and Inroads, in Africa", *The New York Times,* 17 May 1987. (See also note 320.)

196. MITI, *White Paper On the International Trade 1987,* (Foreign Press Center, Japan (November 1987), pp. 42-44.

197. For a detailed analysis of Japanese private economic diplomacy and the role that private business plays in Japan's economic cooperation with other countries, see William E. Bryant, *Japanese Private Economic Diplomacy: An Analysis of Business-Government Linkages,* (New York, Washington, D.C., and London: Praeger Publishers, 1975).

198. See John Ravenhill, "Japan and Africa" p. A210, 213. (See note 131.)

199. White, *Japanese Aid,* p. 68. See note 194. F.C. Langdon, *Japan's Foreign Policy* (Vancouver: University of British Columbia, 1973), argued that Japan had not been particularly generous in her aid, and thus he endorsed White's views. See p. 193.

200. Cited in Joanna Moss and John Ravenhill, *Emerging Japanese Economic Influence in Africa*, (Berkeley: University of California Press, 1985), p. 66.

201. Eileen Marie Doherty, "Japan's Foreign Aid Policy: 1986 Update", *JEI Report* No. 39A (Washington, D.C., 24 October 1986) p. 11.

202. Jossleyn Hennessy, "Tied Aid", *Eastern Economist,* Vol. 56: No. 17 (23 April 1971) p. 724.

203. Ministry of Foreign Affairs. *Japan's ODA 1984 Annual Report,* (Tokyo: Goverment of Japan, 1984) p. 6.

204. In addition to the works cited in Chapter 1 (e.g. see note 55) see especially Noboru Umetani, *The Role of Foreign Employees in the Meiji Era in Japan,* (University of Tokyo Press, 1971): Ardath W. Burks, *The Modernizers: Overseas Students, Foreign Employees and Meiji Japan,* (Boulder, Col.: Westview Press, 1985).

205. Alan Rix, *Japan's Economic Aid,* (New York: St Martins Press, 1980), p. 25.

206. Kwame Nkrumah, *Neocolonialism: The Last Stage of Imperialism,* (New York: International Publishers, 1966).

207. Rix, *Japan's Economic Aid,* p. 226. (See note 205.) But even Rix's view could be challenged by the simple device of invoking Prime Minister Shigeru Yoshida's statement in the 1950s: "It is our duty to aid the peoples of ... Africa in their economic development and thus foster an awareness in the countries concerned that the political institutions and way of life of the free nations of the earth are best suited to bring prosperity to their nations and happiness to the peoples therein." Yoshida, *The Yoshida Memoirs,* p. 13. (See note 119.)

208. Cited in *Liberal Star,* 10 May 1986, p. 4.

209. These diplomats, academics, and corporate executives are too numerous to cite here. See Acknowledgements page for a select few. In Japan's Official Development Assistance 1986 Annual Report Japan's aid policy is, inter alia, stated as follows: "Japan recognizes that the political, economic and social stability of developing countries indispensable for the maintenance of global peace, since economic disorder in developing countries may give rise to political and social instability, eventually leading to international tension or triggering of regional conflicts". Published by the Association for the Promotion of International Cooperation (APIC), Tokyo, 1987, p. 2.

210. Miyazawa, "The International Mission of Japan", *Liberal Star*, 10 May 1985, p. 15.

211. MITI, *White Paper 1987*, pp. 43-44 (see note 196.)

212. Doherty, "Japan's Foreign Aid Policy," p. 1. (See note 201.)

213. See their work, "Japan's Foreign Economic Assistance", *Asian Survey*, 25 (3) March 1985, p. 323.

214. Rix, *Japan's Economic Aid*, p. 223 (See note 207.)

215. For a detailed analysis of these sectors see Yoshitaka Koshino, "Development Aid for Sub-Saharan Africa", *Look Japan*, 10 October 1984, pp. 17-19.

216. A more complete account of the OECF is found in Kazumi Goto, "OECF in Japan's Aid Administration", (Mimeo). The OECF/Tokyo 8 November 1982.

217. Suzuki, "Cooperation Between The Overseas Economic Cooperation ..." p. 3. (See note 192.)

218. See Trevor Parfitt and Stephen Riley, "The International Politics of African Debt", *Political Studies*, 35 (1) March 1987, pp. 1-17.

219. See also Jeff Haynes, Trevor W. Parfitt and Stephen Riley, "Debt in Sub-Sahara Africa. The Local Politics of Stabilisation", *African Affairs*, 86 (344) July 1987. African indebtedness in 1984 ranged from the World Bank's $78,4 billion estimate to the OAU's estimate of $158 billion.

220. With German aid to Africa, which is increasingly becoming generous, a similar tendency as OECF Africa loans is detectable (though the two donoring institutions are not comparable). For German aid on Africa see Rolf Hofmeier, "Aid From the Federal Republic of Germany to Africa", *Journal of Modern African Studies*, 24 (4), December 1986: pp. 577-601.

221. See Koshino, "Development Aid for SSA ..." p. 18. (See note 215.)

222. *Africa Research Bulletin*, 31 July 1986, p. 8299.

223. Information provided by JICA executives: Haruo Suzuki and Ichiro Toyoshima during my discussions with them at JICA Offices/Tokyo, 3 December 1987.

224. See *Japan and Africa: South of the Sahara*, p. 13. (See note 118.)

225. *JICA* (n.d.) p. 21.

226. See *Ghana News* (Embassy of Ghana, Washington, D.C.) Vol. 14: No. 10 (October 1985), p. 9; see also *African Recorder*, 29 January-11 February 1985, p. 6663 for other details regarding this "Colour Television Agreement". During the same year OBed Asamoa, Ghana's Secretary for Foreign Affairs, noted to the 40th session ofthe UN General Assembly on October 3rd: "... developed countries, in view of their economic development and predominance in international trade, bear a special responsibility to complement the adjustment efforts already made by African and other developing countries through measures to facilitate a restoration of financial flows, alleviation of debt burden and improvement of commodity prices". *Ghana News*, p. 5.

## CHAPTER 6
### Africa's Green Revolution and Japan's Role

227. Ministry of Foreign Affairs. *Information Bulletin*, (Tokyo) No. 10 (4 September 1984) p. 98.

228. Cf. David Lamb, *The Africans*, (London: The Bodley Head, 1982).

229. Cf. his an *Atlas of African Affairs*, (London and New York: Methuen, 1984).

230. Cited in Lloyd Timberlake, *Africa in Crisis: the causes, the curses of environmental bankruptcy*, (Philadelphia: New Society Publishers, 1986), p. 32. President Nyerere's planning minister, Kighoma Malima, defined the IMF/World Bank's conditionalities laconically but accurately: "As a condition for assistance, a developing country is often required to scrap public enterprises and hand them over to the private sector; to abandon price controls, agricultural subsidies, free medical and other social services; to take these things away from a population which everyone agrees is already too deprived. The political and ideological slant of such conditionality is beyond doubt". *South*, No. 46 (August 1984), p. 15.

231. Quoted in MOFA. *Information Bulletin*, (see note 227), No. 54 (7 December 1984), pp. 174-175.

232. Uma Lele, "Rural Africa: Modernization, Equity, and Long-Term Development", *Science*, 6 February 1981, pp. 547-53.

233. Yuro Sakashita, "Increasing Food Production", *Look Japan*, 10 September 1986.

234. Toru Kotani, "Africa and Japan: Rising Sun Over Africa?", *Africa Report,* November-December 1985, p. 68: "The current emphasis seems

to owe much to his ideosyncratic activism". As noted below perhaps the fact that Abe visited Ethiopia's drought areas, sponsored the so-called "starvation lunches", and initiated the "Africa Month" activities, may have contributed to this image. See his *Creative Diplomacy*, p. 26.

235. MOFA. *Information Bulletin*, p. 174 (see note 231.)

236. Kunio Nishimura, "Increasing Need — More Aid", *Look Japan*. (See note 233.), p. 26.

237. MOFA. *Japan's ODA 1985*, p. 8.

238. Sakashita, "Increasing Food ..." (See note 233.)

239. *Africa Contemporary Record*, 1984/1985, Vol. 17 p. B.40. (See note 198).

240. *Africa Research Bulletin*, 31 May 1986.

241. *Africa Contemporary Record*, p. B. 334. (See note 239.)

242. *Ibid.*

243. See *International Lifestock Centre for Africa (ILCA)*, ILCA: Objectives and Achievements (Addis Ababa, Ethiopia: ILCA, 1984).

244. Takushi Fujiwara, "First Aid for the Forests", *Look Japan*, (Tokyo), 10 July 1985, p. 18.

245. Kunio Nishimura and Yuko Sakashita, "Saving The Earth and Its People", *Look Japan*, January 1987, p. 16.

246. Fujiwara, "First Aid", p. 18. (See note 244.)

247. Timberlake,*Africa in Crisis*, p. 59 (See note 230.)

248. See Harold E. Dregne, *Evaluation of the Implementation of the Plan of Action to Combat Desertification,* (Nairobi: UN Environment Programme, 1983).

249. Cited in Timberlake, *Africa in Crisis*, p. 61. (See note 247.)

250. See S. Lagercrantz, *Fish-Hooks in Africa and Their Distribution*, (Stockholm: Riksmuseum Ethnographical Section, 1934), p. 31. In page 30 he writes: "From the Hausa I have no material available, and am therefore unable to determine where they have obtained their hooks. It may however well be supposed that they are of European origin". That is, if no evidence available, assume European origin! For there can be nothing that is technologically sophisticated and at the same time be indigenous to Africa! This is merely an extension of the Hegelian, Jungian, Humean, etc. racism against Africans.

251. Facts cited in Foreign Press of Japan, January 1985.

252. W.V. Brelsford, *Fishermen of the Bangweulu Swamps: A Study of the Fishing Activities of the Ungu Tribe*, (Livingstone, Northern Rhodesia: Rhodes-Livingstone Institute, 1946), p. 37.

253. Cited in *Africa Diary*, 19-25 March 1982, p. 11373. Dharam Ghai and Samir Radwan (eds.), *Agrarian Policies and Rural Poverty in Africa*, (I.L.D., 1983) and Keith Hart, *The Political Economy of West African Agriculture* (Cambridge University Press, 1982) detail some of the chief weaknesses of African agriculture.

254. World Bank. *Accelerated Development in Sub-Saharan Africa: An Agenda for Action,* (Washington, D.C.: World Bank, 1981) pp. 24, 25.

255. See Dr Saburo Okita's comments in "Time for a Japan Marshall Plan?", *Look Japan,* 10 January 1986.

256. Gordon Cyrus Mwangi, "Is Japan an Appropriate Model for Nation-Building in Africa", *Africa-Japan*, No. 17 (1981), p. 23.

257. For a detailed and unusual analysis of the IMF, the World Bank and Africa, see Michael Hodd, "Africa, The IMF and Wolrd Bank", *African Affairs*, 86 (344) July 1987, pp. 331-353. See Cheryl Payer, *The Debt Trap: The IMF and The Third World* (Aarmondsworth: Penguin, 1974), Ch. 2, and "The IMF in the 1980s ..." in Third World Foundation, *Third World Affairs 1985*, for a thorough explication of the essentially capitalist and non-egalitarian mode of development that the IMF promulgates.

## CHAPTER 7

### Japanese Volunteers in Africa

258. "Overcoming The Paradoxes", *Look Japan,* 10 February 1986, p. 4. Professor Kawada of ILCAA (Tokyo Gaiko Kugo Baigaku) is author of such books as *Textes Historiques Oraux Des Mosi Meridionaux (Burkina-Faso) — 1985; Geneseet Evolution du Systeme Politique des Mosi Meridionaux (Haute Volta) — 1979*; both published by ILCAA, Tokyo University of Foreign Area Studies.

259. "Japanese Volunteer Spirit in Malawi", *Look Japan*, 10 September 1984, p. 22.

260. JOCV. *Together: Meeting Needs, Making Friends*, (Tokyo: JICA/JOCV, 1985), p. 61.

261. "Japanese Volunteers in Africa", *Liberal Star*, (LDP/Tokyo), 10 June 1987, p. 14.

262. See *Look Japan*, 10 October 1985. Today the motto seems to be meeting needs, making friends, together moving ahead. (See note 260.)

263. See "Japanese and the Far Continent", *Look Japan*, 10 October 1984, p. 4. Japanese officials are fond of saying that Africa is the Far Continent perhaps as an unconscious defensive attempt to counter the notion of Japan (and East Asia) as the *Far East* — a notion clearly propounded by the Westerners. East Africa is by sea nearer to Japan than say the Netherlands or Sweden. In any event as we have seen in Chapters 1 and 2 Japan had to go via Africa (either Suez Canal or Cape of Good Hope) before she could reach Europe. But Japan, nevertheless, is the only *humane* culture to consider Africa the *Far* Continent rather than the *Dark* Continent.

264. Acknowledgement is hereby accorded to *Japan Overseas Cooperaton Volunteers*, (Tokyo: JOCV/JICA, 1987) for the descriptive analysis of the four JOCV categories herein.

265. *Together*, p. 81 (see note 260). Most of the personal references regarding these volunteers are either from this source or from the JOCV film I reviewed at the JOCV Headquarters on 3 December 1987, courtesy of Ichiro Toyoshima and Takashi Nagakura.

266. Quoted in *Africa-Japan*, No. 16 (1979), pp. 26, 35.

267. See *Look Japan,* 10 August 1983.

268. *Together*, p. 89. (See note 265.)

269. *Africa-Japan*, p. 35. (See note 266.)

270. *Ibid.* p. 40.

271. Nagakura and Toyoshi noted to the author that JOC Volunteers "prefer rural rather than urban areas despite the harsh conditions in Africa; and they are very satisfied". Discussions held 3 December 1987 in the JOCV offices in Tokyo.

## CHAPTER 8

### Africans and Agriculture in Japan

272. Prisca Molotsi: In a conversation with me in Tokyo, 4 December 1987.

273. Mwangi, "Is Japan an Appropriate Model ...?" p. 31. (See note 256.)

274. Ryo Yanagi "Japanese and African Masks", p. 39. (See note 273.)

275. See the excellent work of Winthrop D. Jordan, *White Over Black: American Attitudes Toward the Negro 1550-1812,* (Baltimore: Penguin Books, 1965). Prominent European philosophers, psychoanalysts, and historians, such as George F. Hegel, David Hume, Carl G. Jung, Hugh Trevor-Roper, etc. have bruited loudly about the alleged subhumanity and cultural irrelevance of Africans. See the *Collected Works* of Carl Jung, for example. This is a subject for another book.

276. As we saw in Fujita's "Japanese Views on Africa in Edo Period" (see note 2), Africans — called *kurobo*, (Black Africans) in the 16th century — came to arouse much curiosity among the Japanese during this period. They were part of the exotica of the Namban presence in Japan. The African culture now fascinates the Japanese and the latter have in fact begun to define common cultural elements between Japan and Africa such as in religion, masks, etc.

277. In Nishino's study, "Japanese Views of Africa During the Meiji Period", (see note 16) we see "that the Japanese of Meiji Era were much interested in Africa without taking the Africans into consideration". p. 4. In the Edo Period they were fascinated by blacks, but in the Meiji Period they ignored them since they preferred rather African raw goods more in line with the Meiji industrial and technological revolution. (See Chapters 1 and 2.)

278. See *Japan International Cooperation Agency* (1987), p. 6.

279. See Mitsusada Fukasaku, "Festivals of Japan", *Africa-Japan*, pp. 15-20. (See note 65 for more details about these and other festivals of Japan.)

280. See for example in John S. Mbiti, *African Religions and Philosophy*, (New York: Doubleday and Co. 1970), pp. 208-216, especially p. 213 about appeasement of African ancestral souls. In his *Ancestor Worship in Contemporary Japan*, (Stanford University Press, 1974), Robert J. Smith writes in detail about the nature of the deities, the various kinds of spirits, and the character of memorialism and veneration.

281. For the details of the activities see "Africa Month Outline", (Mimeo), MOFA/Africa Society of Japan: Tokyo, September 1984, pp. 1-7.

282. "Japanese and The Far Continent" *Look Japan*, p. 18. (See note 215.)

283. *Ibid.*

284. See *Kokurito Minzokugaku Hakubutukan* (Osaka, Senri Expo Park, Japan: 1985), p. 14.

285. Nobuyuki Hata, "The Opening of the National Museum of Ethnology and the African Display", p. 13. (See note 279.)

286. Hata, "The Opening", p. 13.

287. There are some Japanese scholars who are not yet satisfied with the pace and scope of Japan's international exchange. See for example Yasusuke Murakami and Yutaka Kosai, (eds). *Japan In The Global Community*, (Tokyo: University of Tokyo Press, 1986), especially pp. 83-85. And since Japan is a "condition that is neither completely oriental nor occidental but a precarious mixture of the two", according to one Japanese scholar (Chitoshi Yanaga, *Big Business in Japanese Politics*, (New Haven and London: Yale University Press, 1968), p. 268), one could postulate that a more real close relationship and affinity between the Japanese and African peoples could develop even much more deeper than that between Africans and their former imperial European suzerains.

288. See "Open Hearts and Helping Hands" *Look Japan,* 10 October 1984, p. 22: Keiko Kurashige says: "It was we Japanese rather than developing countries who benefit most from international cooperation. There are a number of things we can learn from them, such as spiritual richness". Africans, on the other hand, are primarily in search of material richness. In Japan I met Africans who expressed sentiments regarding the Japanese similar to those expressed by a Japanese JOCV in Africa: "I've never been treated as kindly by other non-black people. I doubt I'll ever again have such a good friend who is not African". See *Look Japan,* (note 259.)

## CHAPTER 9
### Trade Relations, 1961-1987

289. Lu Miaogeng, "Tokyo Draws Closer ..." *Beijing Review.* (See note 96.)

290. "Japan and Africa", *Africa Economic Digest* 3:49 (10-16 December 1982), p. 11.

291. Cited in Don Shannon, "Japan in Africa: Commercial Payoff". p. 27. (See note 80.)

292. "Interview" with the author. 3 December 1987, (Tokyo).

293. For the dates of African independence and Japanese diplomatic recognition of each state see Appendix A.

294. *The Economist,* No. 216 (1 May 1965), p. 544: "Japan's Hard Sell in Africa".

295. See *Foreign Trade of Japan,* (Tokyo: JETRO, June 1963), p. 217.

296. *The Economist,* No. 216 (18 September 1965), p. 1126: "Japan in Africa: Blacker Than it Looks?".

297. After the Rhodesian white colonists had declared UDI in 1965 and the colony of Rhodesia was slammed with UN sanctions, the US, Japan and many other industrialised countries circumvented the sanctions. The British Government correctly accused Japan of cheating — even though British firms were doing likewise and the British Government did nothing about it. Japan was incensed at this (? racist) selective criticism. (See Chapter 10 for more details.)

298. Koshino, "Development Aid for SSA", p. 19. (See note 221.)

299. "Japan and Africa", *Africa Economic Digest,* Vol. 3: No. 49, (10 December 1982), p. 11.

300. Cited by Eileen Marie Doherty, "Japan and Sub-Sahara Africa", p. 4. (See note 212.)

301. See JETRO, *White Paper on International Trade,* (Tokyo: JETRO, 1986), Table III — pp. 364-365.

302. Katsuhide Sato, "More Economic and Technical Cooperation from Japan is Needed: Japan's Trade Relations with African Countries", *DJIT,* No. 234 (1987), p. 11.

303. *Ibid.*

304. *Ibid.*

305. On 2 December 1987 Marubeni Corporation executives, H. Ogawa (who spent 44 years in Libya) and S. Jibiki (another African executive specialist) informed the author about the diverse activities of Marubeni in 48 African countries. In September 1986 Marubeni helped to form the Ghana - Japan Friendship Association. See also Marubeni Corporation, *1987 Annual Report,* p. 29.

306. The Nippon Koei Company is one such example. Three executives (M. Furudate, Yusaku Toya and Akikazu Tokumasu) informed me that since their clients are one hundred per cent government — Japanese or

African — the fate of their operation rests with government policy. Nippon Koei Co has been extensively involved in Africa (current projects are in Mali, Nigeria, Tanzania, Kenya and Sudan). Interview date 1 December 1987, Tokyo.

307. Interview with NEC executives (Yokohama Plant): Tadao Furukawa, Mikio Yamada, and Kohei Muraoka, 1 December 1987. The NEC is a world-wide conglomorate (since 1899) that deals in satellite and micro-wave communications, radios and radars, electronic devices, home appliances, computers, communications devices, etc. NEC's involvement in Africa is equally extensive.

308. See *The Japan Economic Review*, 15 July 1987, p. 9.

309. Moss and Ravenhill, *Emerging Japanese Economic Influence in Africa*, p. 43. Table 3-2. (See note 200.). See also Ravenhill, "Japan and Africa", p. A211. (See note 131.)

310. Terutomo Ozawa, *Multinationalism, Japanese Style: The Political Economy of Outward Dependency*, (Princeton: Princeton University Press, 1979), p. 158. Italics mine. Ozawa has clearly made an error: Nigeria is *not* a "relatively underpopulated" African country; it has the *largest* population (about 100 million citizens) of all the African countries. It may not have as high a population density — ratio-wise — as, say, Rwanda, but it is certainly highly populated, contrary to Ozawa's thesis. The Francophone state, *Niger,* is the one that is underpopulated, rather than Nigeria.

311. Kochiro Horie, "How Japan Has Grown in Africa", *West Africa*, 28 November 1983, p. 2755. (See note 74.)

312. *AED*, p. 13. (See note 290.)

313. See "Economic Ties", *Look Japan*, 10 October 1984, p. 5.

314. See Yoshihara Kunio, *"Japanese Economic Development: A Short Introduction*, (Tokyo, Oxford, New York and Melbourne: Oxford University Press, 1979), p. 39.

315. "In English-speaking Africa our main rivals are now other Japanese firms ... We are very aggressive about training (our African) people. And we look to the long-term, so we continue with these policies during a slump". Masayoshi Kanazawa, quoted in *AED* (note 290), p. 10, Kanazawa is Manager of Toyota Motor Co Africa Department.

316. For a more detailed account of the Japan-Nigeria trade relations, see Gabriel O. Ogunremi, *Nigeria-Japan Trade Relations 1914-1979*, (Tokyo: Institute of Developing Economies, 1982).

317. For some of the 70 plus Japanese companies that operate in Africa, see Chapter 10.

318. *Africa Research Bulletin*, 15 June 1986, p. 8256.

319. *The Japan Economic Review*, 30 June 1986, p. 5. Japanese automakers' moves to start production ventures in developing countries were prompted by the steadily squeezing impact of the current exchange rate changes (vis-a-vis the US dollar) on the export of Japan's auto industry, (especially Suzuki Motor Co., Fuji Heavy Industries, and Toyota Motor Co.). Since finding fault with Japan and Japan-bashing have recently been elevated to art form in the US, this is yet another reason for Japanese auto industry's diversification programme.

320. Obed Asamoah, Ghana's Secretary for Foreign Affairs. (See note 195.)

321. Perdue, "Private Correspondence", p. 2. (See note 67.) Italics in the original.

322. Cited in Shannon, "Japan in Africa", p. 27. (See note 291.)

323. Perdue (see note 321) is suggesting a similar view when he writes that Japanese "corporations are structurally embedded in the international economic order and they define their worth in terms of 'triad position'," but he errs, I think, when he concludes that "their management consultants appear to ignore 'backward economies' as not important as a source of raw materials". The role played by these corporations in nudging the Japanese Government to increase her ODA to "backward economies" is an attempt to resurrect these economies by raising the infrastructure so as to make the economies of these nations marketable. (See page 152 of my work.)

## CHAPTER 10
### Japan-South Africa Connection

324. See *Africa Contemporary Record*. (See note 198.)

325. See Chinweizu, *The West and The Rest*, p. 404. (See note 82.)

326. Olsen, *"Japan Africa"*, p. 54. (See note 168.)

327. Shannon, "Japan in Africa", pp. 24-25. (See note 322.)

328. For many of the details of Japan-South Africa trade during this, earlier, and later, periods see *The Japan Year Book*, (1936-1937), (1939-1940), (1946-1948). (See note 104.)

329. Jun Morikawa, "The Anatomy of Japan's South African Policy", *The Journal of Modern African Studies* 22:1 (1984), p. 140 cites Dr Ujiro Uyama's 1930 work on South Africa's racial bias and the Japanese entry issue to South Africa. Uyama was the leader of the 1927-1928 Japanese Government Economic and Diplomatic Mission to Africa",4 > referred to in Chapter 2. A foreign ministry official in Tokyo, Ryochi Horie, angrily told me that he categorically rejects the "honorary white" appellation, arguing that "We are Asians period; We are nobody's honorary negative".

330. Hashimoto Kingoro, "The Need for Emigration ...", p. 64. (See note 112.)

331. Yamato Ichibashi, "International Migration of the Japanese," *International Migration,* Vol. 1 (1931), p. 621.

332. *The Japan Year Book* 1939-1940, p. 186. (See note 328.)

333. Olsen, "Japan/Africa", p. 52. (See note 326.)

334. Japan, incidentally, has yet to sign the UN General Assembly International Convention on the Elimination of All Forms of Racial Discrimination of 21 December 1965. It is of course true that at the Versailles Treaty Japan vigorously sought to enter into the Treaty a clause on the declaration of racial equality, but was solidly stymied by the racist Ango-Saxons. This, however, should not be equated with a formal anti-racist, pro-African stance of Japan at the 1919 Paris Peace Conference.

335. Ministry of Foreign Affairs. *Statistical Survey of Economy of Japan 1963*, (Tokyo: MOFA, 1963).

336. Cf. my unpublished work, *Intellectual Hypocrisy of Free Africa: Academics and Apartheid Education*, (1988).

337. RSA. *South Africa 1986 Official Yearbook,* (12th ed.) (1986).

338. Eric Leistner, "South Africa's agricultural interaction with Africa", *Africa Insight* 17 (2), 1987, p. 98.

339. Regarding the Arab and Iranian economic collaboration with South Africa, see Robert Whitehill, "The Sanctions that never were: Arab and

Iranian Oil Sales to South Africa", *Middle East Review*, 19 (1), Fall 1986, pp. 38-46.

340. See my "Theoretical and Empirical Limitations of Representative Democracy: The Case of Africa", in Hans Koechler, (ed.) *The Crisis of Representative Democracy*, (Berne Frankfurt. New York: Peter Lang, 1987, pp. 189-203, for a critique of the poverty of African leadership, political theory and system.

341. See John Burgess, "Japan: South African Trade Is Diplomatic Embarrassment of Riches", *The Washington Post*, 8 January 1987.

342. For a comprehensive list of Japanese companies in South Africa and for a detailed account of the Japan-South Africa account, see Yoko Kitazawa, *From Tokyo To Johannesburg: A Study of Japan's Growing Economic Links with the Republic of South Africa*, (New York: Interfaith Centre for Corporate Responsibility, 1975), pp. 42-43.

343. Burgess, "Japan: South African Trade ..." (See note 339.)

344. *Ibid.*

345. Stuart Auerback, "Japan Outstrips United States as S. African Trade Partner", *The Washington Post,* 22 October 1987.

346. Fred Hiatt, "Japan Has Become South Africa's Leading Trade Partner", *The Washington Post,* 26 January 1988.

347. Katsuhide Sato (of JETRO), DJIT No. 234, pp. 11, 15. (See note 302.)

348. That is Ryochi Horie, deputy-director, 2nd Africa Division, MOFA and his deputy Hidetoshi Ukita — see page 78. (27 November 1987, Tokyo.)

349. *Ibid.*

350. In 1986 Japanese residents in South Africa numbered 771, and South African residents in Japan numbered 124. The latter were all on "business" visas, except the handful on diplomatic visas. Close to 70 Japanese government officials resided in South Africa during the same period.

351. The South African Consul-General in Tokyo during the crisis of the doomed SAA jet seems to have played a rather minor role — outside those of issuing visas and arranging flights to the grieving relatives of the dead Japanese fishermen — if the Japanese newspapers reflected accurately.

352. The rigidity and illogicality of MITI was, for instance, amply demonstrated when I kept a previously arranged appointment, on 3 December 1987, with the Director of Africa Office in MITI, Yoshiaki Umemura and his assistants. Umemura bureaucratically and arrogantly stymied my research on the Japan-Africa trade; this despite an advance warning regarding the nature of my research. In fairness to Umemura, however, he pleaded "miscommunication", between ministries, even if he still failed to live up to his promise to later provide some data concerning my research.

353. Besides the few specific cases of sanctions (such as those mentioned above), the Japanese Government is often vague when addressing the issue of solving the South African problem. For example: "Japan makes it a basic policy to lend as much positive cooperation as possible so that the problems will be solved in a just and peaceful manner". *White Papers of Japan 1982-1983*, p. 27. (See note 133). However, in certain instances, such as the issue of South Africa's then continued illegal occupation of Namibia, the Japanese Government consistently called for the implementation of UN Security Council Resolutions 385 and 435. In certain cases of course she has been more specific than any Western country vis-a-vis sanctions against South Africa.

354. But such strategies are not necessarily successful with the vocal and active *anti-apartheid* movement in Japan. For example, during my stay in Japan, one of the pro-African MOFA officials was shouted at and chased away by *anti-apartheid* activists when he attempted to enter a cinema to watch the *anti-apartheid* movie, *Cry Freedom*. He was harangued as an *apartheid* collaborator by a group that had, for its own purposes and interests, appropriated to itself the mantle of being the legitimate opponent of the RSA regime, as if it alone had the monopoly to that legitimacy; and while the Right was hell-bent on fascism, the Left kept wallowing in vacuous and fatuous moralism totally devoid of an effective strategy to alter the turn of events. The Left in Japan, like the Left in the US, UK, France, etc., is nevertheless, not *the* problem regarding *apartheid*; but it tended to exhibit this phony air of selfrighteousness, as if it alone was the true and sole representative of the conscience of the oppressed in South Africa. In any event, for more about the *anti-apartheid* movement in Japan, see Japan Anti-Apartheid Committee, *Africa: news and reports*, (Tokyo), 22 November 1979. Or care of: Professor Jun Morikawa, Dept. of International Relations, Tokai University.

355. See Alfred Kuo-liang Ho, *Japan's Trade Liberalization in the 1960s*, (White Plains, New York: International Arts and Sciences Press, 1973) for details on Japanese trade liberalization.

356. I.L. Griffiths, "Japanese Cars in Southern Africa", *Geography* 53 (January 1968), p. 90. What was particularly amoying, as Griffiths shows, is that the Japanese firms located themselves in the proclaimed "border" areas on the margin of the Bantustans, thus complicit with *apartheid*.

357. Kitazawa, *From Tokyo to Johannesburg*, p. 22.

358. As Japanese trading firms were establishing their branches in South Africa in 1971 the writer, in remarks to a student audience at the tribal University of the North, noted that the South African struggle for justice would be better served were the West, Japan and Malawi's Hastings Banda just to fade away whence they came. South Africa's repression of blacks between 1960 and 1970 had been such that all black political opposition groups had been effectively muzzled, till the formation of the black consciusness organisation, SASO, which the writer headed in 1971. From 1971 to 1987 Japanese-South Africa business ties grew by leaps and bounds. On hindsight, this view of the author was of course wrong.

359. Payne, "Japan's South Africa Policy", p. 169. (See note 170.)

360. Moss and Ravenhill, *Emerging Japanese*, p. 64. (See note 309.)

361. Olsen, "Japan/Africa", p. 53. (See note 333). The South African Consul General in Tokyo in 1970 (David de Villiers du Buisson) denied, of course, that there was any status as "honorary whites" in existence in the RSA. Such protestations however are meaningless.

362. Chinweizu's view, however, was intended as a strong challenge to African states to industrially, agriculturally, and technologically bring themselves up to date, to approximate the level of a Japan: — and only then could they begin to deal with the "West" (the White World) as equals.

363. Hiatt, "Japan Has Become South Africa's", (See note 344.)

364. "... It is important to note that the current economic plight of South Africa was triggered by the refusal in 1985 of two US banks to roll over a small amount of loans or to further extend lines of credit. In so doing, these two banks did more to harm South Africa than all the governmental sanctions of the past 20 years", writes Kent Hughes Butts and Paul R. Thomas, *Geopolitics of Southern Africa: South Africa*

*As a Regional Superpower*, (Boulder and London: Westview Press, 1986), p. 146.

365. See ABC *World News Tonight*, 2 October 1987: "South Africa, Sanctions Busters". The strategy was to use 3rd countries through SAA passenger and freight jets, which ferried all sorts of goods — especially computer goods to the RSA.

366. Burgess, "Japan: South African Trade", (See note 341.) Burgess, however, cites a Hitachi offical on 17 June 1986 displaying a memo between Hitachi, its trading company and BASF in which the three confirmed that no Hitachi computers have been sold in violation of the sanction.

367. Butts and Thomas, *Geopolitics*, p. 147. (See note 362.)

368. See for example Alister Sparks, "Swaziland Seen as 'Back Door' for South African Trade", *The Washington Post*, 9 July 1986.

369. See also note 287, and its related subjects.

# A GLOSSARY OF ACRONYMS

| | | |
|---|---|---|
| ADB | — | African Development Bank |
| ADF | — | African Development Fund |
| ANC | — | African National Congress of South Africa |
| ASEAN | — | Association of South East Asian nations |
| BCC | — | British Cotton Corporation |
| CGIAR | — | Consultative Group on International Agricultural Research |
| DAC | — | Development Assistance Committee |
| ECOWAS | — | Economic Commission of West African States (Lome) |
| EEC | — | European Economic Community (Brussels) |
| EPA | — | Economic Planning Agency (Tokyo) |
| FA | — | Forestry Agency (Tokyo) |
| FAO | — | Food and Agricultural Organization of the UN. |
| FDI | — | Foreign Direct Investments |
| FIDES | — | Fonds d'Investissement pour le Development Economique et Social |
| GATT | — | General Agreement on Trade and Tariffs |
| GNP | — | Gross National Product |
| IMF | — | International Monetary Fund |
| IRC | — | International Resources Corporation |
| ISCOR | — | Iron and Steel Corporation (RSA) |
| JES | — | Japan Emigration Service |
| JESA | — | Japanese Expert Service Abroad (Programme) |
| JETRO | — | Japan Export Trade Organization |
| JICA | — | Japan International Cooperation Agency |
| JOCV | — | Japan Overseas Cooperation Volunteers |
| JODA | — | Japanese Official Development Assistance |
| JODC | — | Japan Overseas Development Corporation |
| JSAPF | — | Japan South Africa Parliamentary Friendship League |
| ICARA | — | International Conference on Assistance to Refugees in Africa |
| ICSEAF | — | International Commission for the South East Atlantic Fisheries |
| IDA | — | International Development Association |
| IFC | — | International Finance Corporation |
| ILCA | — | International Livestock Center for Africa (Addis Ababa) |
| ILCAA | — | Institute for the Study of Languages and Cultures of Asia and Africa |
| ILRAD | — | International Laboratory for Research on Animal Diseases (Nairobi) |

| | | |
|---|---|---|
| ITTO | — | International Tropical Timber Organization (Yokohama, Japan) |
| KEIDAREN | — | Federation of Economic Organizations |
| LDDCs/ | — | Least Developed among Developing Countries |
| LDP | — | Liberal Democratic Party (Japan) |
| MAFF | — | Ministry of Agriculture, Forestry and Fisheries (Tokyo) |
| MITI | — | Ministry of International Trade and Industry (Tokyo) |
| MOF | — | Ministry of Finance (Tokyo) |
| MOFA | — | Ministry of Foreign Affairs (Tokyo) |
| MSAC | — | Most Seriously Affected Countries |
| OAU | — | Organization of African Unity (Addis Ababa) |
| ODA | — | Official Development Assistance |
| OECD | — | Organization for Economic Cooperation and Development (Paris) |
| OECF | — | Overseas Economic Cooperation Fund |
| OPEC | — | Organization of Petroleum Exporting Countries |
| OSK | — | Osaka Shosen Kaisha |
| OTCA | — | Overseas Technical Cooperation Agency (Tokyo) |
| NEC | — | Nippon Electric Company (Tokyo) |
| UDI | — | Unilateral Declaration of Independence (in Rhodesia, 1965-1980) |
| UNCOD | — | United Nations Conference on Desertification |
| UNCTAD | — | United Nations Conference on Trade and Development |
| UNDP | — | United Nations Development Programme |
| UNHCR | — | United Nations High Commissioner for Refugees |
| UNIP | — | United National Independence Party (Lusaka) |
| UNEPTA | — | United Nations Expanded Programme of Technical Assistance |
| UNTAG | — | United Nations Transition Assistance Group |
| RSA | — | Republic of South Africa |
| SAA | — | South African Airways |
| SADCC | — | Southern African Development Coordinating Conference |
| SCAP | — | Supreme Command, Allied Powers |
| SDR | — | Special Drawing Rights |
| SSA | — | Sub-Sahara Africa |
| WARDA | — | West African Rice Development Association, (Monrovia, Liberia) |

402

# SELECT BIBLIOGRAPHY

Abe, Shintaro, 1985. *Creative Diplomacy: Japan's Initiative for Peace and Prosperity.* (Tokyo).

— in 1985 *West Africa*, 28 November.

*Africa*, 1971-1978 (Periodical).

*Africa Contemporary Record*, 1971-1986.

*Africa Diary.* 1975-1986 (Periodical).

*Africa Economic Digest.* 1981-1987 (Periodical).

*Africa-Japan.* 1970-1987 (Periodical).

*Africa Report.* 1970-1990 (Periodical).

*Africa Research Bulletin.* 1973-1989 (Periodical).

Africa Society of Japan. 1984. *Africa Month Outline.* (Mimeo) Tokyo.

*African Affairs.* 1980-1988 (Periodical).

*African Recorder.* 1982-1986 (Periodical).

Agarwala, A.N. and S.P. Singh, (eds) 1958. *Economics of Underdevelopment.* (London, Oxford and New York).

Agbi, Sunday O. 1982. *Japan's Attitudes and Policies Towards African Issues Since 1945: A Historical Perspective.* (Tokyo).

Aluko, Olajide, 1989 in *Jerusalem Journal of International Relations.* 9 (1), March.

American Broadcast Corporation. 1987. *ABC World News Tonight.* (2 October).

*Annals of the American Academy of Political and Social Science.* 1987. 489, (January).

Arnold, Guy. *Aid in Africa.* 1979 (London and New York).

*Asahi Evening News.* 1987. Tokyo (Daily).

*Asian Affairs*, 1970-1987 (Periodical).

Asian-African Conference. 1955. *The Asian-African Conference: Final Communique.* (Bandung).

*Asian Recorder.* 1972-1986 (Periodical).

*Asian Survey.* 1980-1986 (Periodical).

Association for the Promotion of International Cooperation. 1987. *Annual Report.* (Tokyo).

Auerbach, Stuart. 1987 in *The Washington Post* (22 October).

Battasby, John D. 1987 in *The New York Times* (28 December).

Battuta, Ibn. 1929. *Ibn Battuta: Travels in Asia and Africa*, trans. H.A.R. Gibb. (London).

Beard, Mary R. 1953. *The Force of Women in Japanese History*. (Washington, D.C.).

Beasly, W.G. 1980 in *Asian Affairs XI: Part I* (February). (Periodical).

*Beijing Review*. 1982-1987 (Periodical).

Bergamini, David. 1971. *Japan's Imperial Conspiracy*. (New York).

Blyden, Edward W. 1967 (1887). *Christianity, Islam and the Negro Race*. (London).

Boxer, C.R. 1968. *Fidalgos in the Far East 1550-1770*. (London, Hong Kong, New York).

—    1969. *Four Centuries of Portuguese Expansion 1415-1825: A Succinct Survey*. (Berkeley, Los Angeles, Johannesburg).

—    1951. *The Christian Century in Japan 1549-1650* (Berkeley & Los Angeles London).

—    1959. *The Great Ship From Amacon: Annals of Macao and the Old Japanese Trade*. (Lisbon).

—    1968. "The Old Kingdom of Congo" in Ronald Oliver, (ed.), *The Dawn of African History*. (New York & London).

Brelsford, W.V. 1946. *Fishermen of the Bangweulu Swamps: A Study of the Fishing Activities of the Ungu Tribe*. (Livingstone).

Brett, E.A. 1973. *Colonialism and Underdevelopment in East Africa: The Politics of Economic Change 1919-1939*. (New York, London & Lagos).

Brinkley, Captain F. 1901-1902. *Japan: Its History, Arts and Literature*. 8 Vols. (Boston & Tokyo).

Brooke, James. 1987 in *The New York Times*, 17 May.

Brookes, William L.F. & Robert M. Orr. 1985 *in Asian Survey*, 25 (3).

Bruce, Robert V. 1987. *The Launching of Modern American Science 1846-1876*. (New York).

Bryant, William E. 1975. *Japanese Private Economic Diplomacy: An Analysis of Business-Government Linkages*. (New York, Washington and London).

Buell, Raymond Leslie. 1928. *The Native Problem in Africa*. (New York).

Burgess, John. 1987. in *The Washington Post*, 8 January.

Burks, Ardath W. 1985. *The Modernizers: Overseas Students, Foreign Employees and Meiji Japan.* (Boulder).

Bustin, Edourd. 1987 in *Annals of the American Academy of Political and Social Science.* (January).

Butts, Kent Hughes & Paul R. Thomas. 1986. *Geopolitics of Southern Africa: South Africa As a Regional Superpower.* (Boulder & London).

Cambridge University Press. 1922-1927. *Cambridge History of India,* 6 Vols.

*Canadian Journal of African Studies* (1986) (Periodical).

*Catholic University of Peking Bulletin.* (Nos. 1-8). (Periodical).

Chang, Hsing-Lang. 1970 in *Catholic University of Peking Bulletin* (No. 7) December.

Chinweizu. 1975. *The West and the Rest of US: White Predators, Black Slavers and the African Elite.* (New York).

Council on Foreign Relations. 1957. *Japan Between East and West.* (New York & London).

*Current History.* 1975-1991 (Periodical).

Davidson, Basil.1974, (1968). *Africa in History: Themes and Outlines.* (New York).

—      1969. *The African Genius: An Introduction To Africa and Cultural History.* (Boston and Toronto).

DJIT. *No. 234.* (Tokyo, 1987).

Doherty, Eileen Marie. 1986 in *JEI Report.* (Washington, D.C. 24 October).

Doi, Shigenori. 1982 in *Africa-Kenkyu* (Japanese). No. 21 (March).

Doro, Marion E. & Newell M. Stultz, (eds) 1970. *Governing in Black Africa: Perspectives on New States.* (Englewood Cliffs).

Dregne, Harold E. 1983. *Evaluation of the Implementation of the Plan of Action to Combat Desertification.* (Nairobi).

Duyvendak, J.J.L. 1949. *China's Discovery of Africa.* (London).

Embassy of Ghana (Washington, D.C.). 1985-1988. *Ghana News.* (Periodical).

*Facts on File.* 1958-1987 (Periodical).

Ferrand, G. 1919 in *Journal Asiatique.* (March-April).

Filesi, Teobaldo. 1972. *China and Africa in the Middle Ages.* (London).

*Foreign Affairs.* 1975-1987 (Periodical).

Foreign Affairs Association of Japan. 1936-1948. *The Japan Year Book.*

*Foreign Policy.* 1980-1987 (Periodical).

405

Foreign Press Center of Japan. 1985-1987. *Occasional Releases.*

Fujita, Midori. 1987 in *Annals of Japan Association for Middle East Studies* (Japanese). No 2. 1987.

— 1987 in *Hikaku Bungaku Kenkyu* (Japanese). No. 51, April.

Fujiwara, Takushi. 1985 in *Look Japan.* (10 July).

Fukanaga, Eiji. 1975. *Japan's Position Toward Africa: Documentary Compilation on Recent Moves.* (Tokyo).

Fukasaku, Mitsusada. 1979. in *Africa-Japan* (Periodical). No. 16.

Furudate, M. 1987. "Interview with the Author" (Tokyo).

Furukawa, Tadao 1987. "Interview with the Author" (Tokyo).

Ghai, Dharam & Samir Radwan, (eds) 1983. *Agrarian Policies and Rural Poverty in Africa.* (ILO, 1983).

Gibb, H.A.R. trans. 1929. *Ibn Battuta: Travels in Asia and Africa.* (London).

Goodman, Grant K. 1967. *The Dutch Impact on Japan* (1640-1853). (Leiden).

Government of Japan. 1980-1986. *Diplomatic Blue Book.* (Year Book) (Tokyo: MOFA).

— 1975-1984. *Information Bulletin.* (Tokyo: MOFA).

— N.d. *Japan and Africa: South of the Sahara: Extending and Deepening Relations.* (Tokyo: MOFA).

— N.d. *JICA. (Tokyo: JICA).*

— 1987. *Japan International Cooperation Agency.* (Tokyo: JICA).

— 1983-1990. *Japan's ODA: Annual Report.* (Tokyo: MOFA, 1983-1986).

— 1987. *Japan Overseas Cooperation Volunteers.* (Tokyo: JOCV/ JICA).

— 1984-1987. *Organization of Economic Cooperation Fund Annual Reports.* (Tokyo: OECF).

— 1981-1987. *Public Opinion Survey on Diplomacy.* (Tokyo: Prime Ministers' Office).

— 1979. *Relations Between Japan and the Republic of Senegal.* (Tokyo: MOFA).

— 1963. *Statistical Survey of Economy of Japan.* (Tokyo: MOFA).

—  1984. *Summary of Statistics on Aliens in Japan in 1984.* (Tokyo: Ministry of Justice).

—  1985. *Together: Meeting Needs, Making Friends.* (Tokyo: JICA/ JOCV).

—  1983-1987. *White paper on the International Trade.* (Tokyo: MITI).

Gowen, Herbert H. 1927. *Outline History of Japan.* (New York and London).

Griffiths, Ieuan. 1984. *Atlas of African Affairs.* (London and New York).

Griffiths I.L. 1968 in *Geography*, 53 (January).

Hagopian, Mark N. 1978. *Regimes, Movements, and Ideologies.* (New York & London).

Halloran, Fumiko Mori. 1986 in *Look Japan* 10 July.

Harris, Joseph E. 1971. *The African Presence in Asia: Consequences of the East African Slave Trade.* (Evanston).

Hart, Keith. 1982. *The Political Economy of West African Agriculture.* (Cambridge).

Hatch, John. 1974. *Africa Emergent.* (London).

Hata, Nobuyuki. n.d. in *Africa-Japan*, No. 16 (Tokyo).

Hawkes, Francis L. 1856. *Narrative of the Expedition of an American Squadron to the China Seas and Japan: Performed in the Years 1852, 1853 and 1854.* (New York).

Hennessy, Jossleyn. 1971 in *Eastern Economist*, 56 (17), 23 April.

Haitt, Fred. 1988 in *The Washington Post,* 26 January.

Hirth, Frederick and W.W. Rockwill, (eds). *1911. Chau Ju-Kua* (St Petersburg).

Ho Alfred Kuo-liang. 1973. *Japan's Trade Liberalization in the 1960s.* (New York).

Hodd, Michael in *African Affairs.* 1987 86 (344), July.

Hofmeier, Rolf. 1986 in *Journal of Modern African Studies* 24 (4), December.

Horie, Kochiro. 1983 in *West Africa,* 28 November.

Horie, Yasuzo. 1939 in *Kyoto University Economic Review XIV: 1* (January).

Ichibashi, Yamato. 1931 in *International Migration*, 1 (Periodical).

*International Migration* 1931-1937 (periodical).

ILCA. *International Lifestock Centre for Africa.* 1984 (Addis Ababa).

407

Irwin, Graham W. 1977. *Africans Abroad: A Documentary History of the Black Diaspora in Asia, Latin Caribbean During the Age of Slavery.* (New York).

Ishiyama, Hiroshima. 1986 in *Look Japan* (Tokyo), 10 October.

Ishii, Ryuichi. 1981. "Interview with the Author". Tokyo.

Japan Anti-Apartheid Committee. 1979-1985. *Africa: news and reports.* (Tokyo).

Japan Export Trade Organization. 1963. *Foreign Trade of Japan.* (Tokyo).

— 1986. *White Paper on International Trade.* (Tokyo).

*Japan Quarterly.* 1970-1987 (Periodical).

Japanese Institute of International Affairs. 1972-1986. *White Papers of Japan: annual abstract of official reports and statistics of the Japanese Government.* (Tokyo).

Japanese National Commission for UNESCO. 1985. *Japan: Its Land, People and Culture.* (Tokyo: Ministry of Finance).

Jibiki, S. 1987. "Interview With The Author" (Tokyo).

Jordan, Winthrop D. 1965. *White Over Black: American Attitudes Toward the Negro 1550-1812.* (Baltimore).

*Journal of Developing Studies.* 1979-1984 (Periodical).

*Journal of Modern African Studies* 1975-1987 (Periodical).

Jung, Carl G. 1953. *Collected Works,* 19 Vols. (New York).

Kanazawa, Masayoshi. 1982. in *Africa Economic Digest* 3 (49) (10-16 December).

Kawada, Jun. 1979. *Geneseet Evolution du Systeme Politique des Mosi Meridionaux (Haute Volta).* (Tokyo).

— 1986. In *Look Japan.* (Tokyo, 10 February).

— 1985. *Textes Historiques Oraux Des Mosi Meridonaux* (Burkina Faso). (Tokyo).

Kazuyoshi, Kobayashi. 1984. in *Japan Quarterly* 313 (3).

Kellex, Edmund J. 1987. in *Annals of the American Academy of Political and Social Science* (489) (January).

Killingray, Davis and Richard Rathbone, (eds) 1986. *Africa and the Second World War.* (London).

Kilson, Martin L. and Robert I. Rotberg, (eds) 1976. *The African Diaspora: Interpretive Essays.* (Cambridge and London).

Kingoro, Hashimoto. 1963 in Ivan Morris, (ed). *Japan 1931-1945: Militarism, Fascism, Japanism.* (Boston).

Kimura, Toshio. 1979. in *Africa-Japan* No. 16 (Tokyo).

Kitazawa, Yoko. 1975. *From Tokyo To Johannesburg: A Study of Japan's Growing Economic Links with the Republic of South Africa.* (New York).

Koechler, Hans, (ed) 1987. *The Crisis of Representative Democracy.* (Berne, Frankfurt, & New York).

Koshino, Yoshitaka. 1984. in *Look Japan.* (Tokyo, 10 October).

Kotani, Toru. 1985. in *Africa Report.* (November-December).

Kunio, Yoshihara. 1979 *Japanese Economic Development: A Short Introducton.* (Tokyo, New York & Melbourne).

Kuwabara, Kitzuzo. 1928. in *Memoirs of the Research Department of the Tokyo Bunko.* (Tokyo).

Lagercrantz, S. 1934. *Fish-Hooks in Africa and Their Distribution.* (Stockholm).

Lamb, David. 1982. *The Africans.* (London).

Langdon, F.C. 1973. *Japan's Foreign Policy* (Vancouver).

Leistner, Eric. 1987 in *Africa Insight.* 17 (2).

*Liberal Star*, 1984-1987. (LDP, Tokyo).

Lockwood, William W. 1954. *The Economic Development of Japan: Growth and Structural Change 1868-1938.* (Princeton).

*Look Japan*, 1980-1987. (Tokyo).

Majumdar, R.C. *et al.* 1960. *An Advanced History of India.* (London).

Mamdani,Mahmood. 1976. *Politics and Class Formation in Uganda.* (London and New York).

Mannix, Daniel P. and Malcolm Cowley. 1962. *Black Cargoes: A History of the Atlantic Slave Trade 1518-1865.* (New York).

Maquet, Jacques. 1972. *Africanity: The Cultural Unity of Black Africa.* (Oxford, etc.).

Martin, Denis.1986 in *Canadian Journal of African Studies.* 20 (1).

Marubeni Corporation. 1987. *Annual Report.* (Tokyo, 1986).

Mazrui, Ali. 1977. *Africa's International Relations: The Diplomacy of Dependency and Change.* (London and Boulder).

—   1980. *The African Condition.* (Cambridge).

—   1970 in Doro & Stultz, (eds). *Governing in Black Africa.* (Eaglewood Cliffs).

409

Mbiti, John S. 1970. *African Religions and Philosophy.* (New York).

McKay, Vermon, (ed.). 1966. *African Diplomacy: Studies in the Determinants of Foreign Policy.* (New York, Washington, D.C. & London).

Miagong, Lu. 1985. in *Beijing Review.* 3 June.

Miyazawa, Hiroshi. 1985. in *Liberal Star.* 10 May.

Morikawa, Jun. 1985. in *Journal of African Studies.* 12 (1).

— 1984. in *The Journal of Modern African Studies.* 22 (1).

Morris, Ivan (ed.) 1963. *Japan 1931-1945: Militarism, Fascism, Japanism.* (Boston).

Morse, Ronald A. 1987-1988 in *Foreign Policy.* 69.

Moss, Joanne and John Ravenhill. 1985. *Emerging Japanese Economic Influence in Africa.* (Berkeley).

Mukela, John in 1987. in *Africa Report.* (January-February).

Munro, J. Forbes. 1976. *Africa and The International Economy 1800-1960.* (London).

Murakami, Yasusuke and Yutaka Kosai (eds) 1986. *Japan in the Global Community.* (Tokyo).

Muraoko, Kohei. 1987. "Interview with the Author" (Tokyo).

Murdock, James. 1964. *History of Japan.* 3 Vols. (New York).

Mwangi Gordon Cyrus. 1981. in *Africa-Japan.* No. 17.

Myinti, Hla. in A.N. Agarwala and S.P. Singh, (eds.), 1971. *Economics of Underdevelopment.* (London, Oxford and New York, reprint).

Nagayama, Tokihide. 1918. *An album of Historical Materials Connected With Foreign Intercourse.* (Nagasaki).

Naicker, N.P. 1971. *Indians Abroad: Asia and Africa.* (New Delhi).

Nakahira, Noboru. 1986. in *Look Japan.* 10 February.

National Museum of Ethnology. 1985. *Kokurito Minzokugaku Hakubutakan.* (Japanese). Osaka.

NEC. *Annual Report.* (Tokyo, 1986, 1987).

Neumark, S. Daniel. 1964. *Foreign Trade and Economic Development in Africa: A Historical Perspective.* (Stanford).

Nippon Koei Corporation. *Annual Report.* (Tokyo, 1986, 1987).

Nishie, Masayuki. 1987. *African Diary: Bio of Macha Ine* (Japanese). Tokyo, 1987.

Nishihara, Masahi. 1976. *The Japanese and Indonesia: Tokyo-Jakarta Relations 1951-1966*. (Honolulu).

Nishimura, Kunio. 1986. in *Look Japan*. 10 September.

Nishino, Terutaro. 1964. in *The Memoirs of the Institute for Oriental Culture*. (Japanese). 32 (March).

Nkrumah, Kwame. 1966. *Neocolonialism: The Last Stage of Imperialism*. (New York).

Obasanjo, Olugusen. 1984/1985. in *Foreign Policy* 57 (Winter).

Oda, Hideo and Kazuyoshi Aoki. in R.S. Ozaki and W. Arnold. 1985. *Japan's Foreign Relations: A Global Search for Economic Security*. (Boulder).

Ogawa, H. 1987. "Interview With the Author" (Tokyo).

Ogunremi, Gabriel O. 1982. *Nigeria-Japan Trade Relations 1914-1979*. (Tokyo).

Ohta, Masatoshi. 1992. *The Importance of Japan/South Africa Relations: Address Before the SAIIA*. (Pretoria: Japanese Embassy).

Okamoto, Yoshitomo. 1972. *The Namban Art of Japan*. (New York).

Okita Saburo. 1986. in *Look Japan*. 10 January.

Oliver, Roland (ed.). 1986. *The Dawn of African History*. (New York).

Olsen, Edward A. 1980. in *Africa Report*. March-April.

Olson, Lawrence. 1963. *Dimensions of Japan*. (New York).

Othman, Haroub. 1985. in *Indian Review of African Affairs*. 2 (3) June.

Ozaki, Robert and Walter Arnold (eds). 1985. *Japan's Foreign Relations: A Global Search for Economic Security*. (Boulder and London).

Ozawa, Terutomo. 1979. *Multinationalism, Japanese Style: The Political Economy of Outward Dependency*. (Princeton).

Panti, Shanti. 1963. *Asians in East and Central Africa*. (Nairobi).

Parfitt, Trevor and Stephen Riley. 1987. in *Political Studies* 35 (1), March.

Paske-Smith, M. 1968. *Western Barbarians in Japan and Formosa in Tokugawa Days: 1603-1868*. (New York).

Payer, Cheryl. 1974. *The Debt Trap: The IMF and The Third Wolrd*. (Aarmondsworth).

Payne, Richard. 1987. *African Affairs*. 86 (343), April.

Perdue, William D. 1986. *Sociological Theory: Explanation, Paradigm and Ideology*. (Plato).

*Political Studies*. 1982-1987 (Periodical).

411

Polo, Marco. 1968. *The Travels of Marco Polo, The Venetian*. trans. by Marsden. (New York).

Post, Ken. 1964. *The New States of West Africa*. (Baltimore).

Potter, G.R. (ed.) 1964. *The New Cambridge Modern History: Vol. 1: The Rennaissance 1493-1520*. (Cambridge).

Rajshekar, V.T. 1978. *Apartheid in India: An International Problem* (Bangalore).

Rao, Vasant D. 1973 in *Africa Report* 18 (5) September-October.

Ravenhill, John. 1981/1982. in *Africa Contemporary Record*. 15.

Rivkin, Arnold. 1963. *The African Presence in World Affairs: National Development and Its Role in Foreign Policy*. (London).

Rix, Alan. 1980. *Japan's Economic Aid*. (New York).

Rubin, Arnold. 1974. *Black Nanban: Africans in Japan During the Sixteenth Century*. (Bloomington).

Sakashita, Yuro. 1986. *Look Japan*. 10 September.

Sato, Katsuhide. 1987. in *DJIT (Tokyo) 234*.

Seki, Hiroharu. 1986. *The Asia-Pacific in the Global Transformation*. (Tokyo).

Seth, D.R. 1957. in *Islamic Culture* (London).

Seward, Jack and Howard van Zandt. 1985. *Japan: The Hungry Guest: Japanese Business Ethics vs. Those of the U.S.* (Tokyo).

Sezaki, Katsumi. 1993. *Japanese and South Africa: Address Before the South African Institute of International Affairs*. (Pretoria: Japan Embassy).

Shannon, Don. 1980. in *Africa Report*. (March-April).

Shaw, Timothy M. (ed.). 1982. *Alternative Futures for Africa*. (Bouler).

—— & M.J. Grieve. 1979. in *Journal of Development Studies* 13.

—— 1983. in *Journal of Modern African Studies* 21 (4) December.

Shepherd, Jack. 1985. in *Issue* 15.

Shimizu, Kunio. 1985. in *Look Japan*. 10 August.

Shinoda, Yutaka. 1981. in *Mainichi Daily News*, 22 March.

—— 1983. in *West Africa*, 28 November.

Sono, Themba. 1987. in Hans Koechler (ed.) *Crisis of Representative Democracy*. (Berne, Frankfurt and New York).

Smith, Robert J. 1974. *Ancestor Worship in Contemporary Japan*. (Standford).

Sparks, Alister. 1986. "Swaziland Seen as 'Back Door' for South African Trade". *The Washington Post*. 9 July.

Staniland, Martin. 1987. "Francophone Africa: the enduring French Connection". *Annals of the American Academy of Political and Social Science*. 489 (January).

Sugiya, Akira Sugitano. n.d. *Saga-Ken no Hyakunen* (A 100 years of the History of Saga). Tokyo.

Suzuki, Haruo 1987. "Interview With the Author". (Tokyo).

Suzuki, Hiroaki. 1986. "Cooperation Between the Overseas Economic Cooperation Fund and the World in Sub-Sahara Africa". (Washington D.C.).

Tairo, Kosi. 1975. "Japan After the Oil Shock: An International Resource Pauper". *Current History*. 68 (404).

Takase, Shoji. 1986. "The Politics of Participating". *Japan Quarterly*. (Tokyo) 33 (3).

Takekoshi, Yosoburo. 1930. *The Economic Aspects of the History of the Civilization of Japan*. 3 Vols. (London).

Takiguchis, Yauhiko. n.d. *Saga Rekishi Sanpo* (A Walk of the History of Saga) Yokohama.

Tani, Shin'chi and Sugase, Tadashi. 1973. *Namban Art: A Loan Exhibition From Japanese Collection*. (New York & Kyoto).

Timberlake, Lloyd. 1986. *Africa in Crisis: the causes, the curses of environmental bankcruptcy*. (Philadelphia).

Tokumasu, Akikazu. 1987. "Interview With the Author". (Tokyo).

Toto, Kazumi. 1982. "OECF in Japan's Aid Adminstration". (Mimeo) Tokyo.

Toya, Yusaku. 1987. "Interview With the Author". (Tokyo).

Ukita, Hidetoshi. 1987. "Interview With the Author" (Tokyo).

Umetani, Nobon. 1971. *The Role of Foreign Employees in the Meiji Era in Japan*. Tokyo.

Wilbur, C. Martin. 1943. Slavery in China During the *Former Han Dynasty*. (Chicago).

Williams, G. Mennen. 1969. *Africa for Africans*. (Grand Rapids).

World Bank. 1981. *Accelerated Development in Sub-Sahara Africa: An Agenda for Action*. (Washington, D.C.).

Yamada, Mikio. 1987. "Interview With the Author". (Tokyo).

Yanaga, Chitoshi. 1968. *Big Business in Japanese Politics*. (New Haven & London).

413

Yanagi, Ryo. 1981. In *Africa-Japan* 17.

Yoshida, Shigeru. 1962. *The Yoshida Memoirs: The Story of Japan Crisis.* trans. Kenichi. Yoshida. (Boston).

Zartman, I. William. 1982. In Timoth Shaw (ed.). *Alternative Futures for Africa.* (Boulder).

— 1987. *International Relations in the New Africa.* (Lanham, New York & London, reprint).

— 1982. in *Orbis* 25 (4) Winter.

# INDEX

425

442

This book examines the nature of African-Japanese contacts and ties from the mid-16th century to the present. Although its major focus is the 20th century economic, political, cultural and commercial links between Japan and the countries of Africa, the study begins by probing the 16th century origins of Afro-Japanese ties, and the sporadic 19th century contacts between the two nations. The growing diplomatic, trade and human ties between the Empire of the Rising Sun and the continent of the "Burnt Face" actually have their roots and origins going back further than those between Africans and North Anglo-Americans. This book covers a broad area of the role played by Japan in Africa. It essentially answers the fundamental question: what are the historical, political, economic, diplomatic, cultural and commercial factors involved in the process of Afro-Japanese relations? It therefore owes its existence to the profound gaps in historical research, political analysis and cultural economic exposition, re Africa-Japan ties. While the study deals with the origins of and the continuing ties between Japan and Africa, it also looks at the future of Afro-Japanese relations.

RAAD VIR
GEESTES-
WETENSKAPLIKE
NAVORSING
RGN
HSRC
HUMAN
SCIENCES
RESEARCH
COUNCIL

ISBN 0 7969 1525

9 780796 915252